# The Doyayo Language

## Selected Studies

Summer Institute of Linguistics and
The University of Texas at Arlington
Publications in Linguistics

Publication 121

Editor

Donald A. Burquest
University of Texas at Arlington

Assistant Editor

Rhonda L. Hartell

Consulting Editors

Doris A. Bartholomew
Pamela M. Bendor-Samuel
Desmond C. Derbyshire
Robert A. Dooley
Jerold A. Edmondson

Austin Hale
Robert E. Longacre
Eugene E. Loos
Kenneth L. Pike
Viola G. Waterhouse

# The Doyayo Language

## Selected Studies

Elisabeth Wiering and Marinus Wiering

A Publication of
The Summer Institute of Linguistics
and
The University of Texas at Arlington
1994

© 1994 by the Summer Institute of Linguistics, Inc.
Library of Congress Catalog No: 94–60051
ISBN: 0–88312–620–6
ISSN: 1040–0850

Printed in the United States of America
All Rights Reserved

No part of this publication may be reproduced, stored in a retrieval system, or transmitted in any form or by any means—electronic, mechanical, photocopy, recording, or otherwise—without the express permission of the Summer Institute of Linguistics, with the exception of brief excerpts in journal articles or reviews.

Cover sketch and design by Hazel Shorey

Copies of this and other publications of the Summer Institute of Linguistics may be obtained from
    International Academic Bookstore
    7500 W. Camp Wisdom Road
    Dallas, TX 75236

# Contents

Abbreviations . . . . . . . . . . . . . . . . . vii

Preface . . . . . . . . . . . . . . . . . . . . ix

Phonological Description of Doyayo (Poli dialect) . . . . . . . . 1
   *Marinus and Elisabeth Wiering*

The Indicative Verb in Doyayo . . . . . . . . . . . . . . 53
   *Elisabeth Wiering*

Tone Patterns of Nominals in Doyayo . . . . . . . . . . . 85
   *Marinus Wiering*

Some Major Structures of Doyayo Syntax . . . . . . . . . 117
   *Elisabeth Wiering*

Features of Doyayo Folk Tales . . . . . . . . . . . . . 267
   *Elisabeth Wiering*

# Abbreviations[1]

| | | | |
|---|---|---|---|
| V | vowel | AUX | auxiliary |
| V: VV | long vowel | BEN | benefactive |
| Ṽ | nasalized vowel | C | consonant |
| Ṽ: | long nasalized vowel | CAUS | causative |
| C | consonant | CIND | circumstantial indicator |
| C: | lengthened consonant | CIT | citational particle/pronoun |
| [ ] | phonetic data | CJ | conjunction |
| / / | phonemic data | CMKR | circumstantial marker |
| { } | mutually exclusive variants | CMPD | compound, compounder |
| # | zero morpheme | CMPL | completive aspect |
| 1 | high tone | CNV | converter |
| 2 | mid-high tone | CO | coordinate |
| 3 | mid tone | CONTR | contrastive |
| 4 | low tone | COP | coordinate possessor |
| 3p | third person | CP | circumstantial phrase[2] |
| A | adverb | CUM | cumulative |
| ACC | accessory | DEF | definite/definer |
| AJ | adjective | DEIC | deictic |
| ANA | anaphoric | DEM | demonstrative |
| ANT | anterior | DEP | dependative mood |
| AOR | aorist | DIM | diminutive |
| APP | appositional | DIR QUOT | direct quotative |
| ART | article | DIST | distributive |
| ASS | associative | DLM | delimiter |
| ASSC | assimilation of consonant | DPL | duplicative |
| ATT MKR | attention marker | DRV | derivational |
| AUG | augmentative | EJAC | ejaculation |

[1] Abbreviations will generally be given in SMALL CAPS but in the formula of the third article they will remain in lower caps according to tagmemic convention.

[2] A summary of the various types of circumstantial phrases is given in §4.3 of the fourth article.

# Abbreviations

| | | | |
|---|---|---|---|
| EM | emphatic, emphasizer | OF | optative future |
| EM QUOT | emphatic quotative | O | object |
| EP | epenthesis, epenthetic | OPT | optative |
| EXCL | exclusive | PART | particle |
| FIN | finalizer | PL | plural/pluralizer |
| FOC | focal | POL | polarizer |
| FS | front-shifted | POS MKR | position marker |
| FUNC | functional/functionalizer | POSS | possessive |
| FUT | future | POT | potential |
| GEN | genitive | PR | pronoun |
| GH | genitive head | PRED | predicative |
| HAB | habitual | PREF | prefix |
| HD | head | PREPC | prepunctive |
| HI | high tone | PRES | present |
| HRT | hortatory | PRF | perfective |
| IA | indicative aorist | PROG | progressive |
| I1 | intermediate (verbal) form 1 | PROP | proper |
| I2 | intermediate (verbal) form 2 | PROX - | proximate |
| I3 | intermediate (verbal) form 3 | PURP | purposive |
| ID | ideophone | Q | question |
| IMM | immediate | QLF | qualified/qualifier |
| IMP | imperative | QNT | quantity/quantifier |
| INC | incompletive aspect | QUOT | quotative |
| INCL | inclusive | RDP | reduplicated/reduplication |
| IND | indicator | REF | referent |
| INDC | indicative | REINF | reinforcer |
| INDF | indefinite | REL | relative conjunction |
| INDP | independent (=final) form of verb | REM | remote(ness) |
| | | RES | resultative |
| INDR | indirect | RIT | reiterative |
| INF | infinitive | RLN | relational |
| INFL | inflexional ending | RT | root |
| INTDC | interdictory | S | subject |
| INJ | injunctive | SF | suffix |
| INTM | intermediate | SFOC | semifocal |
| INTRR | interrogative | SG | singular |
| INTS | intensive | SHT | short, shortening |
| INTV | intentive | SMEM | semi-emphatic |
| ITER | iterative | SPEC | specifier |
| ITR | intransitive | ST | standard |
| LGTH | length | STM | stem |
| LOC | locative slot/particle | SUBCJ | subordinating conjunction |
| LOSSC | loss of consonant | TEMP | temporal |
| M | modified | TERM | terminal slot |
| MAR | margin | TN | tone |
| MID | mid tone | TNS | tense |
| MOD | modifier | TR | transitive |
| N | noun | V | verb |
| NEG | negative | VOC | vocative |
| NM | number | VP | verb phrase[4] |
| NP | noun phrase[3] | WD | word |

[3]A summary of the various types of noun phrases is given in the fourth article.
[4]For a summary of various types of verb phrases see §4.4 in the fourth article.

# Preface

The present volume contains five articles reflecting research on the Doyayo language done from a descriptive linguistic point of view.

*Doo²waa²³yąą¹yɔ¹*, also referred to by its speakers as *Doo²³yąą¹yɔ¹* and *Doo²waat²yąą¹yɔ¹*, is a member of the Adamawa-Eastern language family, spoken by 15,000 Doowaayo people living in an area of 1,400 square kilometers around Poli, at a distance of 140 kilometers southwest of Garoua in northwest Cameroun. There are two main dialects, the Markɛ of the plains and the Tɛɛrɛ of the plateau. Tɛɛrɛ, in turn, may be subdivided into a Poli and a mountain dialect.

The purpose of this publication is to make our collected data available to the academic community, as well as to educated Dowayos, in the hope that it may be a contribution to the ongoing study of their language.

The effective amount of time spent on personal research within the framework of an agreement between the Summer Institute of Linguistics (Société Internationale de Linguistique) and the Federal University of Cameroun was limited to about seven years between 1971 and 1981. We were thankful to keep in close contact with Mr. Pascal Djataou by means of correspondence and occasional visits, which made possible the continuation of the work at a distance for a number of years.

A special word of gratitude is due to Ewald den Blaauwen, who not only keyboarded the whole manuscript of this volume (including extensive revisions of some articles), but also took care of the intricate software adjustments needed to arrive at a readable printout.

Finally, we want to express our sincere thanks to our many Doyayo friends who shared their language with us, affording us some insights into the beauty of its many intricate and orderly patterns.

# Phonological Description of Doyayo (Poli dialect)[1]

### Marinus and Elisabeth Wiering

*Doowaayąąyɔ* (literally, 'mouth of a child of man') is the language of the Dowayo people living in and around Poli, Department of the Benue, North Cameroon. The speakers of the language also call it *Doowaatyąąyɔ* ('mouth of children of men'), or *Dooyąąyɔ* ('mouth of man').

Tessmann (1932) and Greenberg (1963) call the language Namshi, in conformity with Fulani usage. However, according to Baudelaire (1944), Namshi (or Namci) includes two separate languages: Doyayo (or "Doayo") and the Duru-related language Duupa. Bohnhoff and Kraft (n.d.) similarly indicate that Duupa is related to Duru rather than to Doyayo.

In this article, the language will normally be referred to as Doyayo, and the people as the Dowayos.

Doyayo is classified in the Adamawa-Eastern language family, which, in turn, belongs to the Niger-Congo group (see Westerman and Bryan 1952).

---

[1]Translated and updated version of "Description phonologique du doowaayąąyɔ" published in ALCAM BULLETIN, 1976-2. We owe thanks to Mona Perrin for linguistic consultant help on this article.

## Geography and dialects

The area in which Doyayo is spoken can be delimited in relation to Poli:[2] to the east, Wanté, to the south, Sandé, Béré, and Boko, to the west, Salaki, Namji, Mayo Lanpté, Farkoumo, and Rogou, and to the north, Baandan, Doundé, Koné, Riga, and Badongo.

Doyayo can be divided into three distinct dialects (see appendix A): *Markɛ* of the plains, extending as far as Honlé and Koumdongo; Poli *Tɛɛrɛ*, with Kongle, Dakidongo, Boulko, and Marka as its boundaries; and Mountain *Tɛɛrɛ*, beginning at Mango. The data of this phonological description is based on the Poli dialect.

## Historical background

It must be emphasized that the present study is of a synchronic descriptive nature. It attempts to describe the phonology of present-day Doyayo. The absence of any written or taped material from the past makes a diachronic study virtually impossible.

Oral tradition designates first Voko and later Yola, Nigeria as the point of origin of the Dowayos. One can, indeed, identify a few loan words coming from Hausa or English.

(1)  *su:¹le³jɔ²*   (Hausa: *sule*)   'coin'
     *pi¹lo³jɔ²*                      'pillow'
     *le:³mu¹jɔ¹*                     'lemon'
     *bu³rɛd¹³jɔ²*                    'bread'

Loan words dating from the German occupation at the beginning of the century are rare, but one likely example was found.

(2)  *tɔs²lam¹³jɔ²*   'flashlight'
     German: *Taschenlampe* but note French *torche* and English *lamp!*

Most loan words are taken from Fulani, the trade language of Northern Cameroon, while French accounts for a good number of loans as well, especially among the better educated Dowayos. It is interesting to note that, since work was officially begun on the Doyayo language in 1971, there has been a progressive tendency on the part of native speakers,

---

[2] The spelling of the names of the villages listed follows the convention of the maps of the Tchamba and Poli regions (page 33-I and 33-II, respectively), published by the Geographic Institute of Yaoundé.

especially those learning to read their language, to purge all foreign elements and arrive at an unadulterated version. This seems to be the natural result of their increased acceptance of their identity as a people, somehow linked to the realization that their language is in no way inferior to others.

**Cultural background**

Most Dowayos are farmers. The main food products are guinea corn and peanuts, the main non-food products cotton and kapok. Dowayos also grow corn, manioc, rice, yams, sweet potatoes, papayas, bananas, okra, sesame seeds, and various leafy vegetables. They raise cattle, goats, chickens, and a few sheep, but the use of meat is restricted to special occasions, such as a funeral, a memorial or ritual feast, or a sacrifice ordered by the spirits.

On opposite poles of Dowayo society are two separate castes: at the top of the hierarchy, the rainmaker, living up in the mountains; and on the bottom, the smiths and potters of the plain. Strong taboos serve to perpetuate the separation of these two groups from the rest of Dowayo society.[3]

Dowayo culture is rich in traditional customs, like circumcision rites, burial rites, and skull ceremonies. Of particular interest is the little cone-shaped wooden flute used by the newly-circumcized for communication. During their 6-month initiation period, males may communicate with a woman only by means of this flute. They can make themselves understood using only the tones of the language because, with its two holes, the flute is able to reproduce the four level tones and all the glides described in §1.4.3. The flute is adequate for the greetings and simple conversations, but, appropriately, does not lend itself to deep dialogue. This phenomenon of communicating by using only tone is reminiscent of the whistle speech of the Mazatecos in Mexico reported by Cowan (1948).

# 1 The phonological hierarchy

The phonological hierarchy consists of six levels: discourse, phonological paragraph, phonological phrase, phonological word, syllable, and phoneme.

---

[3]Cf. Barley, 1983.

## 1.1 Discourse

The discourse is composed of phonological paragraphs. It is characterized by an opening and a closing formula. The opening formula can be simply the expression of the title or subject. The most common closing formulas are in (3).

(3)  $dḁ:^{23}dḁ^1mḁ:^{31}$   'It is finished now.'
     $dḁ:^{23}la^3bɔ:^{13}$   'That is how it ended.'
     $an^1bɔ^1la^3bɔ:^{13}$   'That is how it is.'

**Folk tales.** The opening formula can express the intention of telling a folk tale or simply name the title of the tale as in (4).

(4)  $wɛ^1ɓk^4bid^{41}jɔ^1$   'Let us tell a folk story.'
     $bid^{41}jɔ^1$           'A folk story'
     $kɔ^{23}ba^1hi^1rɔ^2mḁ:^{23}$  'The rooster and the hare'

The closing formula is usually one of those mentioned in (3), but occasionally it expresses the perpetuation of the final state. For example, after a great victory, in which a young man retrieves his three sisters out of the belly of a snake (a cannibal in disguise), the story of "Three Women" ends with the words, $siŋ^{23}tɔ^1ɔ:^1nɛ^1wɔ:r^{31}ma^{31}$ 'And so his sisters died', meaning that his sisters lived happily until they died. The story of the rooster and the hare, in which the panther ends up being thrown into a deep hole, ends with the words 'And the panther stayed in that hole forever'.

The experienced storyteller will articulate rapidly and use certain particles as well as the repetition of words like verbs and ideophones to heighten suspense and increase the vividness of his tale.

The best-loved stories are characterized by a musical refrain, woven into the plot and usually introduced about halfway through. Normally it simply identifies the theme of the story, but sometimes it signals the turning point in the plot. For example, the little boy chased away for letting his father's monkeys escape has to sing to the accompaniment of the drum, 'Beatin' beatin', my father beat me up, saying I let the animals get out'. As soon as he has sung this refrain two times, all the animals in the forest come and fall into the trap made for the monkeys.

The audience participates by laughing heartily at appropriate intervals and saying $hɔ:^4$ 'yes!'

# Phonological Description of Doyayo

**Narratives.** The opening formula may be a statement of the subject or a declaration such as, 'You asked me to recount to you...'.

The closing formula often brings the hearer back to the present: wi³gi²ma³re¹tin¹go³gɛ¹rɛ³ 'So here we are now, going along together'.

The articulation tends to be somewhat less rapid than in the folk story.

The listener encourages the narrator by saying "Yes!" periodically throughout the account.

**Procedural texts.** The opening formula, when it is not the expression of the subject, is in the order of, 'When you..., you...'.

The closing formula, again one of those in (3), is nearly always preceded or followed by the particle gɔ:¹³ 'There, there you are, that's it!'

There is abundant use of overlap. Each successive step in the procedure is introduced by a recap of the preceding one: gɔ²hi³dokt³ gi¹dạ:¹³, hi³wɛ:³-hi³lo:⁴daŋ²go³ 'When they finish washing (it), they take a knife'.

Procedural texts are normally characterized by their brevity.

## 1.2 The phonological paragraph

The phonological paragraph corresponds to the grammatical paragraph. It functions in the narrative discourse and is composed of phonological sentences.

At the beginning of a paragraph, one often finds one of the temporal particles gɔ², yɔ¹, and rɛ¹ 'when'. At crucial points in the discourse, the paragraph may begin with ja:¹la¹ 'suddenly'. The particle gɔ¹ 'all right, thus, then', having both an anaphoric and a deictic function, can either initiate or terminate a paragraph. The end of a paragraph is further marked by a pause.

## 1.3 The phonological phrase

The phonological phrase, or pause group, is that stretch of speech delimited by two pauses. It functions in the phonological paragraph and is composed of phonological words. The end of the phonological phrase, like that of the paragraph, is normally marked by a pause.

## 1.4 The phonological word

### 1.4.1 Definition.
The phonological word corresponds to the grammatical word. It functions in the phonological phrase and is composed of syllables. Compound words can attain a length of eight syllables, or seven in non-final position, but the maximum length for an uncompounded word is four

syllables. The usual number of syllables in pause-group final position is two or three.

The phonological word represents a rhythmic entity composed of a one- to two-syllable core and a periphery that is from one to three syllables long and normally follows the core. The tones of the syllables within a word are interdependent, while they are less dependent on the tones of other words within the phonological phrase.

Certain sounds only occur in word-initial position in (non-compound) words and thus help identify the initial boundary. The sounds in question are ʔ, ɓ, ɗ, kp, gb, and h. The glottal stop, being entirely predictable, is not described at phoneme level. Any word not beginning with a consonant begins with a glottal stop. For the sake of convenience, the glottal is therefore omitted from the phonetic notation. Where reduplication causes the glottal exceptionally to appear word-medial, its presence is indicated by a hyphen, which is maintained in the phonemic notation as well to signal the break between the vowels.

(5)  o:³ʔo¹           /o:³-o¹/            'he waited'
     ɛ⁴ʔɛ¹            /ɛ⁴-ɛ¹/             'no!'
     na̰⁴ʔa¹           /na̰⁴-a¹/            'Mommy'
     tɔ̰⁴ʔɔ̰⁴nɔ:¹jɔ¹    /tɔ̰⁴-ɔ̰⁴nɔ:¹jɔ¹/    'heron'
     ga̰⁴ʔa̰⁴ʔa̰⁴        /ga̰⁴-a̰⁴-a̰⁴/         'round and full' (ideophone)

The other sounds occur in word-medial position only in the event of reduplication of the first syllable:

(6)  dɛ³dɛŋ³jɔ²       /dɛ³dɛŋ³jɔ²/        'guitar-like musical instrument'
     hɔ¹hɔ²¹jɔ¹       /hɔ¹hɔ²¹jɔ¹/        'type of snake'

Length does not function in Doyayo consonants; there are no inherently long consonants in true Doyayo words. Phonetic consonant length is found only across morphological boundaries and in loan words of Fulani origin (Fulani being the trade language of northern Cameroon). Some examples can be seen in (7).

(7)  bɛt¹ 'well'                + -tɔ¹nɔ̰¹ 'very'  → bɛ¹t:ɔ¹nɔ̰¹ 'very well'
     lɛg²³ 'go down (sun)'      + gɛ¹ 'for him'    → lɛ²³g:ɛ¹ 'he's fine (this evening)!'
     dɔj² 'horse'               + -jɔ² 'INDF'      → dɔ²j:ɔ² 'a horse'
     kok¹ 'guinea corn stalk'   + ka:³lɛ² 'stalk'  → ko¹k:a:³lɛ² 'guinea corn stalk'

Some examples of Fulani loan words are in (8).

(8)  le²p:ol³jɔ²    /lep²pol³jɔ²/   'handkerchief'
     ba²g:o³jɔ²    /bag²go³jɔ²/    'drum'
     wa³d:i¹jɔ¹    /wad³di¹jɔ¹/    'perfume'

**1.4.2 Structure.** Given the large number of possible syllable patterns in Doyayo, it would be quite impractical to present an inventory of all the possible word patterns. However, some general remarks can be made.

As a rule, words not falling into the nominal or verbal category display a simple structure, usually consisting of a single syllable carrying high or mid-high tone and having the pattern V, CV, VC, or CVC. Some examples are in (9).

(9)  a¹       'he, she says, said'
     an¹      'if, so that, like'
     hi¹      'and, with'
     gɛ²      'not'
     hɛw³¹    'too, also, either'
     zaŋ¹     'true(ly), real(ly), not at all'

The disyllabics, much fewer in number, usually have the pattern CVCV, CVCCV, or CV:CV, as seen in (10).

(10) gɛ¹rɛ³   'here he is'
     bɔ¹rɔ¹   'that one'
     ge²ro³   'perhaps'
     kin¹sa¹  'maybe'
     ja:¹la¹  'suddenly'

As for nominals and verbals, it can be stated that, whenever they are followed by a pause, they must end in a vowel. Thus, the last syllable will be CV (or V, in the case of a reduplicated vowel). In medial (non-pause-group final) position, the vowel is dropped and the final consonant is moved to the previous syllable as seen in (11).

(11) Pause-group final    Pause-group medial

     ta:¹lɛ¹              ta:l¹              'scar'
     kun³dir³jɔ²          kun³dir³           'tortoise'
     ho¹bo¹               hob¹               'red'
     re³kɔ²               rek³               'go'
     nɔ:²ko³              nɔ:k²              'quickly'

In non-final position and in the absence of pause, a non-compound NOMINAL has the following structure:

- First syllable (monosyllabic): any pattern (see the inventory in §1.5.2) not ending in a sequence of more than two consonants.
- First syllable (polysyllabic): any pattern not ending in a consonant cluster.
- Second syllable (non-final): CV or CVC, as in $a^3ga^3tu^1$ 'net' and $riŋ^1tig^3ja^1$ 'tramp'.
- Second syllable (final) or third syllable (final): CN, CNC, CV, CV:, CVC, CV:C, CVCC, as in (12).

(12)  $tu^1tn^3$ or $tu^1tin^3$        /$tu^1tin^3$/       'entrance hut'
      $pɛ^1pɛ^1tn^3$ or $pɛ^1pɛ^1tin^3$  /$pɛ^1pɛ^1tin^3$/   'swallow (bird)'
      $mjp^1tns^3$ or $mjp^1tins^3$    /$mip^1tins^3$/     'cover (off pot)'
      $lɛ:^2lɛ^2$                                          'type of bird'
      $ʔa:^3ti^1$                                          'green beans'
      $kil^2bu^3$                                          'soda'
      $kpuk^1tum^{21}$                                     'cobra'
      $ti^1la:^{13}$                                       'marbles'
      $lu^3fir^3$                                          'flea(s)'
      $la^2ja:r^2$                                         'amulet'
      $kan^1durk^{21}$                                     'large snake'

A VERB in non-final position and in the absence of pause has the following structure:

- First syllable (monosyllabic): any syllable pattern (see the inventory under §1.5.2).
- First syllable (polysyllabic): any pattern not ending in a succession of more than three consonants.
- Second syllable: CV, CVC, CVCC, as in (13).

(13)  $re^3tn^1$ or $re^3tin^1$           'go together'
      $mjp^4tnz^1$ or $mjp^4tinz^1$       'just covered with something and came back'
      $sɛ:^4zi^1gɛ^1$                     'he looked at him'
      $bɛ^3si^3hi^3$                      'they like it'
      $zaŋ^1si^1mj^3$                     'he read for me'
      $hạ^3tir^1$                         'he destroyed (it)'
      $kam^1sim^{13}$                     'bring me!'
      $sɛ:brt^1sim^1$                     '(several) were split open for me'
      $hạ^3tirs^1$                        'destroy for'

Third syllable: CV, as in (14).

(14) ha¹tir¹go³ 'destroying'
 e⁴li¹hi¹ 'he called them'
 gbɛn¹tin¹go³ or gbɛn¹tn¹go³ 'seeing each other'

When the second syllable is closed by one or two consonants, an ensuing personal pronoun is not preceded by an epenthetic vowel and therefore cannot be abbreviated by dropping its final vowel, as this would yield an impermissible syllable pattern as in (15).

(15) ka⁴sin¹gɛ³, but not ka⁴sing¹³ 'he hoists him up with it'
 ha³tirs¹mį³, but not ha³tirsm¹³ 'he destroyed it for me'

Fourth syllable (relatively infrequent): CV, as in (16).

(16) w̃a:⁴si⁴mį⁴gɛ⁴ 'he caught him for me'
 el¹si¹mį³hi³ 'call them for me!'

**1.4.3 Tone.** Level tones are indicated by means of the raised numerals: ¹ high, ² mid-high, ³ mid, ⁴ low. Every syllable carries one tone or a sequence of tones. It seems probable that a diachronic study would reveal the absence of any true glides, as one observes a general pattern of syllable loss with the retention of tone, resulting in a tone sequence. Probably, tone is not linked to the syllable but to the word, a conjecture which is borne out by the fact that words can indeed be grouped according to the tonal patterns they display.

The absence of a true glide is corroborated by the fact that there are no words with a CV syllable pattern bearing a glide which is not clearly liable to interpretation as a tone sequence. While there are many verbs and nouns with a CV: pattern that carry a glide (for example, ga:²³ 'be bright'; ka:³¹ 'dog'), not one of the restricted number of verbs and nouns or the many words of other categories with a CV pattern bears a non-suspect sequence of tones. The ²³ glide on the verb *to* 'thatch the roof', for example, results from the optional loss of the final *b*, as illustrated by the examples in (17).

(17) to²³gɛ¹ 'he thatched it'
 to(b)²³luk¹bɔ:¹³ 'he thatched the house's roof'
 to²bɔ³, to:²³¹bɔ¹ 'he thatched it'

Another example of a glide resulting from the loss of a syllable is exhibited by the possessive article j̃a²³ 'their'. The semi-focal form of this adjective reveals the origin of both the glide and the nasalization: j̃an²³ (non-final) or j̃a²nɛ³ (final) 'their'.

The up- or downglide that occurs pause-group final, always accompanied by the lengthening of the vowel, on many words and particles is fully predictable in terms of the morphology.

(18)  rek³ra:¹du¹kɛ³nɛ¹, rek³ra:¹du:¹³   'he's gone home for now, he's gone home'
      ri:³ri¹mą³ja⁴, ri:³ri¹mą:³⁴          'is that enough?, that's enough?'
      ri:³ri¹mą:³¹                          'it's enough'

In ²³ verbs, one easily obtains a double (or three-tone) glide in pause-group final position, due to the lengthening of the vowel.

(19)  heg²³, he:g²³¹                       'put on (clothing)'
      gi¹he¹gɔ³, gi¹he:¹³¹gɔ¹              'he will put (it) on'
      kpɛ:n²³, kpɛ:n²³¹                    'he closed (it) with'

In the last phrase of (19), the vowel was already long, so only the upglide was added.

In nouns, most sequences of three tones are the result of syllable loss with the retention of tone. That is the case with each of the sequences in (20).

(20)  ¹³²          ta:¹³ro² 'there is not'    + ja⁴ 'INTRR'        → ta:r¹³² ja⁴ 'isn't there?'
      ³¹⁴          ka:³¹ 'dog'                + ja⁴ 'INTRR'        → ka:³¹ ja⁴/ka:³¹⁴ 'is it a dog?'
      ⁴¹⁴          sa:⁴¹ 'bag'                + ja⁴ 'INTRR'        → sa:⁴¹ja⁴/sa:⁴¹⁴ 'is it a bag?'
      ³¹²          ka:³¹ 'dog'                + -i² 'DEM'          → ka:³¹² 'this dog here'
      ²³²          wa:²³ 'child'              + -i² 'DEM'          → wa:²³² 'this child here'
      ⁴¹²          sa:⁴¹ 'bag'                + -i² 'DEM'          → sa:⁴¹² 'this bag here'
      ²¹², ²¹³, ²¹⁴  gi² 'it is'              + aj¹²/aj¹³/aj¹⁴ 'where?' → ga:j²¹²/ga:j²¹³/ga:j²¹⁴ 'where is it?'

A few nouns bearing a three-tone pattern have been observed to maintain all three tones in their abbreviated (monosyllabic) form. These all have the CV:C or CVCC syllable pattern, and their tonal pattern is either ²³¹ or ¹²¹. We shall examine these in (21) and (22).

(21)  ²³¹ pi:t²³¹jɔ¹ / pi:t²³¹ / pi:²³ti¹    'prop'
      lɛγ²³¹jɔ¹ / lɛγ²³¹ / lɛγ²³ri¹          'spider'

# Phonological Description of Doyayo

The $^{231}$ tonal pattern is inherent to the word meaning 'prop' and to the word meaning 'spider'. The tonal pattern must be maintained even when a syllable is lost due to the absence of pause. When demonstrative -jɔ is added to the shortened form, it takes a high tone under the influence of the preceding syllable. It is also interesting to note that syllable patterns appear to be closely related to tone change in the verb.[4] Similarly, the $^{23}$ sequence, restricted to syllables structuring CV, CV:, and CVC, seems clearly related to the $^{231}$ sequence, found only in syllables structuring CV:C and CVCC.

(22)  $^{121}$ za:l$^{121}$jɔ$^1$ / za:l$^{121}$ / za:$^{12}$li$^1$       'okra'
      fɛpt$^{121}$jɔ$^1$ / fɛpt$^{121}$ / fɛpt$^{12}$ti$^1$       'fish scale'
      gba:n$^{121}$jɔ$^1$ / gba:n$^{121}$ / gba:$^{12}$nį$^1$   'tree bark'

The $^{121}$ tonal pattern is inherent to the words meaning 'okra', 'fish scale', and 'tree bark', respectively, so the shortened form must contain the entire sequence of three tones. Here it is of interest to note that there are a considerable number of nouns bearing this same tone pattern, but having a disyllabic stem and exemplified in (23).

(23)  pa$^1$kir$^{21}$         'wing'
      kɔ$^1$kɔt$^{21}$         'butterfly, moth'
      kpuk$^1$tum$^{21}$       'cobra'
      nạ:$^{23}$ se:k$^1$le$^{21}$  'type of bird'

It is not inconceivable that CV:C$^{121}$ and CVCC$^{121}$ are the result of the loss of a syllable of what first was a disyllabic stem with the structure CV$^1$CVC$^{21}$, by the loss of either the middle consonant (yielding CV:C$^{121}$) or the second vowel (yielding CVCC$^{121}$). This would of course require that the two vowels in the first instance be identical or the second vowel be epenthetic, and the two consonants in the second instance be capable of uniting to make a cluster as in (24).

(24)  za$^1$wal$^{21}$ ∘ − w → za:l$^{121}$
      fɛ$^1$pɛt$^{21}$ ∘ / fɛ$^1$pit$^{21}$ ∘ − V → fɛpt$^{121}$

This theory is strengthened by the fact that the form za$^1$wal$^{21}$ has indeed been found to exist, in free variation with za:l$^{121}$.

If, then, one considers length as only a matter of vowel reduplication, one can posit a one-to-one relationship between the number of tonal units

---

[4]For a more detailed discussion of the tone system, see §8 of the following article.

in a word, on the one hand, and the number of syllables, on the other. Where this relationship is not manifested, one can surmise that the extra tone has resulted from the loss of a syllable due to the dropping of a vowel or consonant.

It is difficult to find four words of the same category to illustrate the contrast of the four level tones. High and mid-high tend to characterize nouns, while mid and low are more characteristic of verbs. One commonly finds contrasts like those in (25).

(25) ja:$^1$      'grandfather'
     ja:$^2$      'grandmother'
     ja:$^3$      'hide'
     ja:$^4$      'send'

     nạm$^1$      'blacksmith'
     nạm$^2$      'animal'
     nạm$^3$      'grind'
     nạm$^4$      'dance!'
     nạm$^{23}$   'move'

There is considerable evidence in the data to arouse suspicion about the contrast between high and mid-high tone, but adequate proof for uniting them has not yet been found. The semantic link between the high and mid-high examples above (note that the blacksmith, being an outcast, is probably not differentiated, in the minds of the Dowayos at large, from an animal) is seen in a small number of other pairs of nouns as in (26).

(26) ba:$^1$      'male'
     ba:$^2$      'father'

     gums$^1$     'conjunctivitis'
     gums$^2$     'illness'

     bεt$^1$      'beautiful'
     bεt$^2$      'heaven'

     wa:t$^1$     'kingdom'
     wa:t$^2$     'children'

In verbs, what arouses suspicion is the fact that high tone frequently functions as a detransitivizer as shown in (27).

(27)  hot³      'bathe (TR)'
      hot¹      'bathe (ITR)'

      hod³      'take off'
      hod¹      'come off'

      bid³      'turn inside out (TR)'
      bid¹      'turn inside out (ITR)'

      hạs³      'remove'
      hạs¹      'come off'

      mịd³      'find, discover'
      mịd¹      'be found, be revealed'

      zẹ:r⁴     'leave over, reserve'
      zẹ:r¹     'be left over'

However, these findings are not corroborated by the rest (that is, the greater part) of the data, making it impossible to posit a watertight theory about semantic conditioning of high tone in Doyayo.

There are a few verbs with high or mid-high tone and a somewhat comparable number of nouns with mid or low tone.[5]

(28)  zayl¹     'kneel, crawl'
      zaŋ¹      'read'
      jɛ²       'shoot (an arrow)'
      le²       'eat'
      keg³      'weevil'
      ro:b³     'leopard'
      kɔls⁴     'dried bean pods'
      nɔ:⁴kil⁴  'race'

*Verb tone.* Verbs can be divided into eight classes, according to their stem tone. They are the following, in the order of frequency of their occurrence: ³, ⁴, ²³, ¹, ², ³¹, ⁴¹, and ¹²/¹³. The ¹² and ¹³ patterns have been grouped together, because ¹² has been observed to occur on only one verb, *ta:¹²* 'not be', and it changes to ¹³ in the expression *ta:¹³ro²* 'there is (are) not'.

---

[5]For a fuller treatment of this phenomenon, see the second and third articles in this volume.

Tone $^2$ verbs all have the syllable pattern CV, though it is useful to note at this point that tone $^2$ functions grammatically in verbs in the negative aorist, replacing any non-high tone. This is shown in (29).

(29) rek$^3$ nɔ:$^2$ko$^3$           'he went fast'
     rek$^2$ nɔ:k$^2$ gɛ:$^{23}$     'he didn't go fast'
     mɔ$^3$ ga:m$^{41}$ tu$^2$sɛ$^3$ 'you gave me money'
     mɔ$^1$ ga:m$^{21}$ tus$^2$ gɛ:$^{23}$ 'you didn't give me money'

Tone $^1$, $^{31}$, and $^{41}$ verbs never have the CV: syllable pattern. Tone $^{12}$ and $^{13}$ verbs occur only in this pattern, and it seems reasonable to link them with the tone $^1$ verbs as being in complementary distribution with them. (Note that high tone nouns do manifest the CV: syllable pattern and this high tone changes to $^{13}$ in the relational form, i.e., before a secondary pause.) Examples of these tones are in (30).

(30) kpɛ:r$^1$                    'open'
     a:n$^{31}$                   'refuse, forbid'
     kan$^{41}$                   'bring up'
     sɔ:$^{13}$                   'anoint'
     go:$^1$jɔ$^1$                'It's a spear.'
     lo:m$^4$ go:$^{13}$, ta:$^2$bo$^3$ hi$^1$ se:$^{23}$  'Take a spear, a bow, and arrows.'

(31) High tone frame

     hi$^1$ **hot**$^1$ jo:$^1$si$^3$go$^3$      'They will **bathe** tomorrow.'
     hi$^1$ **hot**$^{13}$ jo:$^1$si$^3$go$^3$   'They will **rest** tomorrow.'
     hi$^1$ **hot**$^3$ jo:$^1$si$^3$go$^3$      'They will **bathe him** tomorrow.'
     hi$^1$ **hopt**$^4$ jo:$^1$si$^3$go$^3$     'They will **drink it all** tomorrow.'

(32) Mid-high tone frame

     gɔ$^2$ **ta**:$^{12}$ bak$^2$ du:$^{13}$    'He usually **isn't** in the garden.'
     gɔ$^2$ **ta**:$^{23}$ bak$^2$ du:$^{13}$   'It usually **tears** in the garden.'
     gɔ$^2$ **ta**:$^3$ bak$^2$ du:$^{13}$      'He usually **hunts** in the garden.'
     gɔ$^2$ **ta**:$^4$ bak$^2$ du:$^{13}$      'She usually **rams it** in the garden.'

     nis$^2$ **mat**$^1$ bak$^2$ du:$^{13}$     'A woman **fell** in the garden.'
     nis$^2$ **mat**$^{23}$ bak$^2$ du:$^{13}$  'A woman **tied them** in the garden.'
     nis$^2$ **mat**$^3$ bak$^2$ du:$^{13}$     'A woman **made him fall** in the garden.'
     nis$^2$ **kapt**$^4$ bak$^2$ du:$^{13}$    'A woman **caught them** in the garden.'

# Phonological Description of Doyayo

(33)    Mid tone frame

       mḭ³ hɛ:¹³ mą³ ɓɔ³rɔ³       'I finally **thrust it in**.'
       mḭ³ jɛ² mą³ ɓɔ³rɔ³        'I finally **shot (arrows)**.'
       mḭ³ hɛ:²³ mą³ ɓɔ³rɔ³      'I finally **went a different way**.'
       mḭ³ hɛ:³ mą³ ɓɔ³rɔ³       'I finally **diverted it**.'
       mḭ³ hɛ:⁴ mą³ ɓɔ³rɔ³       'I finally **cut it**.'

       hi³ sɔ:¹³ mą³ gɔ:¹³        'So they **anointed him**.'
       hi³ sɔ:²³ mą³ gɔ:¹³        'So they **moved him away**.'
       hi³ sɔ:³ mą³ gɔ:¹³         'So they **castrated him**.'
       hi³ sǫ:⁴ mą³ gɔ:¹³        'So they **looked at him**.'

(34)    Low tone frame

       hɔ:⁴ guβr¹ gbag⁴¹ du:¹³     'Yes, **it spilled** in the hangar.'
       hɔ:⁴ guβr²³ gbag⁴¹ du:¹³    'Yes, **it all spilled** in the hangar.'
       hɔ:⁴ gumb³ gbag⁴¹ du:¹³    'Yes, **he moved it all** in the hangar.'
       hɔ:⁴ guβr⁴ gbag⁴¹ du:¹³     'Yes, **he spilled it all** in the hangar.'

       wi³ ja:t¹ ną:⁴mḭ¹ lɛl²³ du:¹³    'We **hid** at my mother's.'
       wi³ jǫ² ną:⁴mḭ¹ lɛl²³ du:¹³    'We **drank (it)** at my mother's.'
       wi³ jɔ:²³ ną:⁴mḭ¹ lɛl²³ du:¹³   'We **painted** at my mother's.'
       wi³ ją:n³¹ ną:⁴mḭ¹ lɛl²³ du:¹³  'We **forbad it** at my mother's.'
       wi³ ja:t³ ną:⁴mḭ¹ lɛl²³ du:¹³    'We **hid it** at my mother's.'
       wi³ ja:t⁴ ną:⁴mḭ¹ lɛl²³ du:¹³    'We **sent them** at my mother's.'

*Nominal tone.* Noun stems manifest more variety in their basic structure than verb stems. While a verb stem cannot be longer than two syllables and is normally monosyllabic, disyllabic stems are common among nouns, and stems of three and even four syllables have been observed. This apparent imbalance between verbal and nominal length is, however, compensated for by the fact that the suffixed verb can attain a length of four syllables through the addition of an imperative subject and direct and indirect pronoun objects, thus often more than doubling its original length, while the noun stem can add only one syllable. Some examples are in (35).

(35)    hą³tir¹           'break, destroy'
       hą³tirs¹mḭ³ge³   'He destroyed it for me.'

       el⁴              'call'
       el¹si¹mḭ³ge³     'Call him for me!'

| | |
|---|---|
| *luk¹* | 'house' |
| *lu¹kɔ³* | 'his house' |
| *pɛ¹pɛ¹tin³wa:²³* | 'baby swallow' |
| *pɛ¹pɛ¹tin³wa:²jạ²³* | 'their baby swallow' |

Twenty different tone patterns have been observed on noun stems each of which is shown in (36)–(40) (a hyphen separates the stem tone from that of the suffix in each given pattern).

(36)  Level patterns

1 1

| | | | |
|---|---|---|---|
| *ti¹kɔ¹* | 'gourd' | *nạm¹rɛ¹* | 'laziness' |
| *hɛːl¹jɔ¹* | 'rock' | *raː¹jɔ¹* | 'compound' |
| *ga¹la¹jɔ¹* | 'injection' | *loː¹rɛ¹jɔ¹* | 'evil spirit' |

2 2

| | | | |
|---|---|---|---|
| *tar²jɔ²* | 'Fulani' | *nụːn²jɔ²* | 'big pot' |
| *lɛː²lɛ²jɔ²* | 'type of bird' | *gbuŋ²tuŋ²jɔ²* | 'type of pot' |

3 2

| | | | |
|---|---|---|---|
| *keg³jɔ²* | 'weevil' | *gba³jɔ³* / *gbar³jɔ²* | 'father-in-law' |
| *roːb³jɔ²* | 'leopard' | *riŋs³jɔ²* | 'for sale' |

4 2

| | | | |
|---|---|---|---|
| *gɛːl⁴jɔ²* | 'medicinal plant' | *kɔls⁴jɔ²* | 'dried bean pods' |
| *tu⁴ug⁴jɔ²* | 'loin-cloth' | *buː⁴bil⁴jɔ²* | 'large fish' |

(37)  Rising patterns

21 1

| | | | |
|---|---|---|---|
| *bạm²¹jɔ¹* | 'leprous spot' | *zɛn²¹jɔ¹* / *zɛnd²¹jc¹* | 'oyster' |
| *gbɔ²nɔ¹jɔ¹* | 'road' | | |

31 1

| | | | |
|---|---|---|---|
| *kel³¹jɔ¹* | 'scorpion' | *foː³¹jɔ¹* | 'reptile' |
| *kurk³¹jɔ¹* | 'snail' | *gu³tu¹jɔ¹* | 'pigeon' |
| *dɛ³rɛŋt³¹jɔ¹* | 'type of drum' | | |

41 1

| | | | |
|---|---|---|---|
| *bor⁴¹jɔ¹* | 'tadpole' | *lɔːd⁴¹jɔ¹* | 'slug' |
| *kɔlk⁴¹kɔ¹* / *kɔlk⁴¹jɔ¹* | 'throat' | *hɛ⁴kum¹jɔ¹* | 'oil pot' |

# Phonological Description of Doyayo

<sup>32 2</sup>
ba³nɛ²jɔ²　　　'ring'　　　　　　mạr³gan²jɔ²　　'neophyte switch for
kum³be²jɔ²　　'sweet potato'　　　　　　　　　　　chasing away women'

(38) Falling patterns

<sup>13 2</sup>
sɛs¹³jɔ²　　　'sorcery'　　　　　bu¹zum³jɔ²　　　'wild cucumber'
tun¹tig³jɔ²　　'pus'　　　　　　ti¹la:¹³jɔ²　　　'type of game'

<sup>14 2 (rare)</sup>
u:¹be⁴jɔ²　　　'circular dance'

<sup>23 2</sup>
ho:²³jɔ²　　　'guinea-fowl'　　　rɔ²mạ²³jɔ²　　　'hare'
dɛ:²si³jɔ²　　'type of lizard'

<sup>24 2 (rare)</sup>
wa²wa⁴jɔ²　　'girl'　　　　　　wa²la⁴jɔ²　　　'boy'

(39) Irregular patterns

<sup>3 2 / 23 2 (becomes ² or ²²)</sup>
to³to² (tot²)　　　　　'guinea corn'　　gạ:³to² (gạ.t²)　　'ocular discharge'
la²ja:³rɛ² (la²ja.r²)　'fetish, amulet'

<sup>3 2 / 4 2 (becomes ²)</sup>
dɔp³to² / dɔp⁴to²　　'wild yam'　　　wa:³to² / wa:⁴to²　'children'
(dɔpt²)　　　　　　　　　　　　　　(wa.t²)

<sup>4 2 (becomes ²³)</sup>
ka⁴rɛ² (kar²³)　　　'switch'　　　　ạ⁴rɔ² (ạr²³)　　　'water buffalo'
tạ⁴mɔ̣² (tạm²³)　　 'sheep'

(40) Complex patterns

<sup>121 1</sup>
paps¹²¹jɔ¹　　　'grasshopper'　　za:l¹²¹jɔ¹ / za¹wal²¹jɔ¹　'okra'
du¹kum²¹jɔ¹　　'lungs'　　　　　su¹sug²¹jɔ¹ / su¹su²¹go¹　'hair'

<sup>231 1</sup>
lɛyr²³¹jɔ¹　　　'spider'　　　　　pị.t²³¹jɔ¹　　　'prop'

<sup>4141 1 (only example)</sup>
bim⁴¹rud⁴¹jɔ¹　　'legendary
　　　　　　　　animal'

⁴¹¹³ ² (only example)
*gew⁴¹gew¹³jɔ²*        'type of drum'

¹¹⁴¹ ¹ (only example)
*ɓin¹di¹rik⁴¹jɔ¹*        'creeping bush'

*Minimal pairs*

| | | | |
|---|---|---|---|
| *ba:¹* | 'male' | *ga:s¹* | 'gift' |
| *ba:²* | 'father' | *ga:s³* | 'clean' |
| *ba:³* | 'dance (dirge)' | *ga:s⁴* | 'give for' |
| *ba:⁴* | 'pierce, sew' | *ga:s²³* | 'seem bright to' |
| *ba:¹³* | 'landlord' | | |
| *ba:²³* | 'be complete' | | |
| *ba:⁴¹* | 'sigh of fatigue' | *go:¹* | 'spear' |
| | | *go:⁴* | 'answer' |
| | | *go:²³* | 'try, measure' |
| *bɛt¹* | 'beautiful' | | |
| *bɛt²* | 'heaven, God' | | |
| *bɛt³* | '(they) are good' | *gums¹* | 'conjunctivitis' |
| | | *gums²* | 'illness' |
| | | *gums³²* | ⎫ 'be sick for' |
| *ɓa:t¹* | 'liver' | *gums³* | ⎭ |
| *ɓa:t³* | '(they) beat (him)' | | |
| *ɓa:t⁴* | '(they) beat (drums)' | | |
| *ɓa:t²³* | '(they) are expensive' | *gba:n³* | 'defend oneself with' |
| | | *gba:n⁴* | 'keep/put with' |
| | | *gba:n²³* | 'argue with' |
| *do:s¹* | 'emaciation' | *gba:n¹²¹* | 'bark (of tree)' |
| *do:s²* | 'formerly' | | |
| *do:s³* | 'lose weight for' | | |
| *do:s²³* | 'sting for' | *hɛ:l¹* | 'rock' |
| *do:s³¹* | 'first' | *hɛ:l³* | 'peel' |
| | | *hɛ:l⁴* | 'clean up excrements' |
| | | *hɛ:l²³* | 'diverge repeatedly' |
| *gaps¹* | 'mean' | | |
| *gaps²* | ⎫ 'fighting, danger' | | |
| *gaps³²* | ⎭ | *hi̧:t¹* | 'satiety' |
| *gaps⁴* | 'be mean for' | *hi̧:t²* | ⎫ 'fresh' |
| | | *hi̧:t³²* | ⎭ |
| | | *hi̧:t³* | 'be satiated repeatedly' |

## Phonological Description of Doyayo

| | | | |
|---|---|---|---|
| ga:l¹ | 'bright, light' | | |
| ga:l⁴ | 'give several th.' | | |
| ga̰:l¹³ | 'wild turnip' | kal¹ | 'crab, shelf' |
| ga:l²³ | '(they) shine' | kal²³ | } 'head load cushion' |
| ga:l³¹ | 'beehive' | kal⁴² | |
| ga:l² | } 'axe' | kal⁴¹ | 'of a head cushion' |
| ga:l³² | | | |
| hob¹ | 'red' | | |
| hob⁴ | 'drink all up' | ka̰:s¹ | } 'lees, dregs' |
| hob²³ | 'be(come) red' | ka̰:s² | |
| | | ka̰:s³² | 'lever' |
| | | ka̰:s²³ | 'give eyedrops' |
| | | ka̰:s³¹ | 'contrariness' |
| ja:¹ | 'grandfather' | | |
| ja:² | 'grandmother' | | |
| ja:³ | 'hide' | kɔt¹ | 'second yam harvest' |
| ja:⁴ | 'send, put' | kɔt⁴ | 'kiss' |
| ja:²³ | 'monkey, sorcerer' | kɔt⁴¹ | 'brave, courageous' |
| ja:³¹ | 'vulva' | kɔ:³ | 'rust' |
| ja̰:¹ | 'mouth, language' | kɔ:⁴ | 'rub between palms' |
| ja̰:³ | 'knead' | kɔ:²³ | 'chicken(s)' |
| ja̰:⁴ | 'be rare' | | |
| ja̰:²³ | 'dissolve, melt' | kpel¹ | 'become' |
| | | kpel⁴ | 'pour' |
| ja̰:n¹ | 'their (EM)' | kpel²³ | 'duck, swerve' |
| ja̰:n³ | 'knead with' | | |
| ja̰:n⁴ | 'be rare with' | | |
| ja̰:n²³ | 'dissolve with' | lu:r² | } 'theft' |
| ja̰:n³¹ | 'refuse to give' | lu:r³² | |
| | | lu:r²³ | 'kick up dust' |
| | | lu:r³¹ | 'thief' |
| jɛ̰:³ | '(four letter word)' | lu:r⁴¹ | 'whirlwind' |
| jɛ̰:⁴ | 'settle a matter' | | |
| jɛ̰:²³ | 'brother' | | |
| jɛ̰:³¹ | 'jester, clown' | | |
| | | ta:l¹ | 'scar' |
| | | ta:l² | } 'shoe(s)' |
| | | ta:l³² | |
| jɔ:s¹ | 'blindness' | ta:l³ | 'shoot many' |
| jɔ:s⁴ | 'finish, blind' | ta:l⁴ | 'ram many floors' |
| jɔ:s²³ | 'be blind for' | ta:l¹² | '(they) are not' |
| | | ta:l²³ | '(they) tear' |

| | | | |
|---|---|---|---|
| mạ:t¹ | 'yam' | | |
| mạ:t² | } 'deception' | | |
| mạ:t³² | | tot¹ | 'bend over' |
| mạ:t³ | 'trick, deceive' | tot² | } 'guinea corn' |
| mạ:t³¹ | 'sour yellow cherry' | tot³² | |
| | | tot³ | 'sting often' |
| | | tot²³ | '(they) cover' |
| nạm¹ | 'blacksmith' | | |
| nạm² | } 'animal, meat' | | |
| nạm³² | | to:s¹ | 'taxes' |
| nạm³ | 'grind' | to:s³ | 'sprinkle for' |
| nạm²³ | 'move' | to:s⁴ | 'pay for' |
| nạm⁴ | 'dance! circumcize!' | | |
| | | tus² | } 'money, metal' |
| nạ:² | 'brother-in-law' | tus³² | |
| nạ:³ | 'chat' | tus³ | 'spit' |
| nạ:⁴ | 'mother, aunt' | tus²³ | 'forge for' |
| nạ:⁴¹ | 'Mom, Mother, Madam' | | |
| nạ:²³ | 'cow, cattle' | | |
| | | wa:l¹ | 'country, world' |
| | | wa:l² | } 'skull house' |
| nį:³ | 'insult' | wa:l³² | |
| nį:⁴ | 'moisten, fold' | wa:l³ | '(they) live' |
| nį:²³ | 'be harmless' | | |
| | | wa:t¹ | 'kingdom' |
| nɔ:s² | } 'bird' | wa:t² | } 'children' |
| nɔ:s³² | | wa:t³² | |
| nɔ:s³ | 'vex for' | wa:t³ | 'water, rinse' |
| nɔ:s⁴ | 'run for' | | |
| | | za:s¹ | 'curse' |
| ra:¹ | 'compound' | za:s² | } 'cover (of pot)' |
| ra:³ | 'remove dead leaves' | za:s³² | |
| ra:²³ | 'say' | za:s³ | 'cover for' |
| | | za:s²³ | 'come for' |
| se:m¹ | 'shame' | | |
| se:m⁴ | 'look!' | zept¹ | 'flame' |
| se:m²³ | 'calm down!' | zept² | } 'medicinal plant' |
| | | zept³² | |
| | | zept⁴ | 'sell' |

# Phonological Description of Doyayo

| | | | |
|---|---|---|---|
| *ta:³* | 'kill (with arrow)' | | |
| *ta:⁴* | 'ram with stone' | | |
| *ta:¹²* | 'not be' | *zo:s²* | ⎫ |
| *ta:²³* | 'tear' | *zo:s³²* | ⎬ 'prey, game' |
| | | *zo:s³* | 'harvest honey for' |
| *zɔmt¹* | 'type of fruit tree' | *zo:s³¹* | 'fond of meat' |
| *zɔmt³* | 'lick one's fingers' | | |
| *zɔmt⁴* | 'pray repeatedly' | | |
| | | | |
| *zu̧:k¹* | 'pounded (AJ)' | | |
| *zu̧:k³* | 'drizzle for a long time' | | |
| *zu̧:k⁴* | 'pound lazily' | | |

## 1.5 The syllable

**1.5.1 Definition.** A syllable is a language segment composed of an obligatory vowel nucleus, optionally preceded and/or followed by a consonantal margin. The margin to the left of the nucleus contains at most one consonant; the right margin may contain a single consonant or a cluster of from 2 to 4 consonants. The vowel constituting the nucleus of the syllable may be short or long, oral or nasal: V, V:, Ṿ, Ṿ:. The boundary between syllables is always drawn within the adjoining margins before the last consonant as shown in (41).

(41)  *ko:⁴¹-tɔ¹*     'it is dry'
      *lag¹-rɛ¹*      'deaf people'
      *mi̧br⁴¹-zɔ³*   'he opened'

**1.5.2 Structure.** If we represent syllable structure in terms of the type of vowel in the nucleus (short, long, oral, nasal) and the number of consonants in the margin, we obtain the 40 potential patterns in (42).

(42)
| | | | | | | |
|---|---|---|---|---|---|---|
| V | *a¹* | 'he said' | CV | *jɔ¹* | 'here' |
| Ṿ | *ɔ̧²³* | 'his' | CṾ | *jɔ̧²* | 'drink' |
| V: | *a:²³* | 'be wide' | CV: | *da:³* | 'pass' |
| Ṿ: | *a̧:²³* | 'conceal' | CṾ: | *da̧:²³* | 'be finished' |
| VC | *or²³* | 'co-wife' | CVC | *hɛs³* | 'sweep up for' |
| ṾC | *a̧r²³* | 'buffalo' | CṾC | *hɛ̧s²* | 'seasoning' |
| V:C | *a:s²³* | 'seem wide to' | CV:C | *da:s³* | 'pass for' |
| Ṿ:C | *a̧:s²³* | 'conceal from' | CṾ:C | *da̧:s³* | 'finish' |
| VCC | *ɛrk¹* | 'asking' | CVCC | *ɓark⁴¹* | 'bell' |

| | | | | | | |
|---|---|---|---|---|---|---|
| γCC | ərk² | 'nail' | Cγcc | hɛpt² | | 'earth' |
| V:CC/ VCC | a.ts²³/ats²³ | 'open many for' | CV:CC/ CVCC | sɛ:βr³¹/sɛβr³¹ | | 'yell' |
| γ:CC/ γCC | a.ts²³/ats²³ | 'conceal many from' | Cγ:CC/ CγCC | pɛ:kt³¹/pɛkt³¹ | | 'often spread unwillingly' |
| VCCC | ɛylt³ | 'reach out (PL)' | CVCCC | dɛβrz¹ | | 'be partly cut off' |
| γCCC | ɛβrt⁴ | 'cave in (PL)' | CγCCC | tɛβrz³¹ | | 'have just strung' |
| V:CCC* | (not found) | | CV:CCC/ CVCCC | sɛ:βrs³¹/sɛβrs³¹ | | 'yell for' |
| γ:CCC* | (not found) | | Cγ:CCC/ CγCCC | sɛ:βrt¹/sɛβrt¹ | | 'split open' |
| VCCCC | ɛylts³¹ | 'reach out for (PL)' | CVCCCC | dɛβrts¹ | | 'be cut off for', 'yell often for' |
| γCCCC | ɛβrts⁴¹ | 'cave in for (PL)' | CγCCCC | tɛβrts³¹ | | 'string often for, split open for' |
| V:CCCC* | (not found) | | CV:CCCC* | (not found) | | |
| γ:CCCC* | (not found) | | Cγ:CCCC* | (not found) | | |

A consonant cluster closing a syllable results in the optional (in the case of a 4-consonant cluster, obligatory) shortening of the long vowel nucleus of that syllable. This explains the multiple forms and why some of the patterns have not been found.

## 2 The phoneme

The phoneme is composed of one or two phonetic realizations and functions in the syllable.

### 2.1 Interpretation

#### 2.1.1 Simple segments to be interpreted as either vowels (V) or consonants (C): *i/j, u/w*.
After a pause and before a consonant, after a consonant and before pause, or between two consonants, we interpret the simple segment as a vowel.

(43)  *il²³*   'be sticky, gluey'   *ul²³*   'whistle'
      *di¹*   'on, upon'           *du¹*   'in'
      *bid³*  'turn inside out'    *bud³*  'conceive'

In these positions, the segment constitutes the nucleus of the syllable and bears the tone.

After a pause and before a vowel, after a vowel and before a pause, and between two vowels, we interpret the segment as a consonant.

(44)  jɔ¹         'here, when'     wɔ¹        'those'
      lej¹        'be eaten'       sɛw³       'all'
      la:¹ja¹jɔ¹  'soldiers'       wa²wa⁴jɔ²  'little girl'

In these positions, the segment constitutes the margin and not the nucleus of the syllable, and thus is functioning as a consonant.

**2.1.2 Segments to be interpreted as either simple or complex: Ṽ, V:, Ṽ:.** Nasalization can affect any vowel except *e* or *o*. Nasalized vowels are not interpreted as a sequence of vowel plus nasal consonant (VC), because any nasal consonant can occupy the postnuclear margin, and this would therefore result in consonant clusters that are not permissible in Doyayo: hẹm⁴si¹gɛ¹ 'it tastes good to him'. (No consonant, be it nasal or oral, can precede *m* in a cluster.)

V and CV are common syllable patterns: a¹zɛ̣²hi¹gɛ:²³ /a¹zɛ̣²hi¹gɛ²/ 'He said, "He didn't find them."' Some unambiguous examples of nasalized vowels and nasal consonants are shown in (45).

(45)  kam³    'carry away, take along'
      kaŋ²³   'climb up with'
      kan⁴¹   'boa constrictor'
      kạm³¹   'he took me along'

The examples in (46) serve to illustrate the contrast between oral and nasal vowels.

(46)  i, ị    fikt³   'remove the moss'     fịkt³    'press many reluctantly'
      ɛ, ɛ̣   tɛk¹    'looking for'         tɛ̣k¹    'spinning (web)'
      a, ạ   hab²³   'pig'                 hạb²³    'tie up'
      ɔ, ɔ̣   zɔb⁴    'drip, flow'          zɔ̣b⁴    'pray, request'
      u, ụ   guj¹    'be spilled'          gụj¹    'hurt oneself'

However, as can be seen in the phonemic contrasts in §2.3, there is partial neutralization of contrast in the case of the closed vowels *i* and *u*.

Length can affect any and all vowels. As no "non-suspect" vowel sequences have been found, long vowels are not interpreted as VV.

The examples in (47) serve to illustrate the contrast between short and long vowels.

(47)  i, i:      gi¹          'he, and'              gi:¹         'he (EM)'
      i̧, i̧:     fi̧l³         'strangle (PL)'        fi̧:l³        'twine (PL)'
      e, e:     ɓez³         'seek quickly'         ɓe:z³        'just pouted'
      ɛ, ɛ:     gbɛn³        'see'                  gbɛ:n³       'cut with'
      ɛ̧, ɛ̧:    sɛ̧b⁴¹        'pepper'               sɛ̧:b³¹       'it's nearby'
      a, a:     war³         'ask'                  wa:r³        'take leave of'
      a̧, a̧:    ha̧k¹         'tying up'             ha̧:k¹        'wanting'
      ɔ, ɔ:     tɔs¹         'famine'               tɔ:s¹        'magic'
      ɔ̧, ɔ̧:    zɔ̧⁴          'pray'                 zɔ̧:⁴         'box'
      o, o:     hob¹         'red'                  ho:b¹        'fear'
      u, u:     tun²³        'forge with'           tu:n²³       'collect with'
      u̧, u̧:    gu̧³          'hurt'                 gu̧:³         'smell'

**2.1.3 Sequences amenable to interpretation as clusters or as simple segments.** Sequences *mb*, *nd*, and *ŋg*, which never occupy the prenuclear margin reserved for simple segments, are all interpreted as clusters of two separate phonemes, thus: *m* and *b*, *n* and *d*, *ŋ* and *g*. In every case, both the phonemes in question appear alone elsewhere.

(48)  gumb³        'put (PL) outside'       lɛnd¹    'cannibal'
      gum³         'hurt, be ill'           dɛd¹     'louse'
      gub⁴         'throw away'             hin¹     'thing'
      na̧ŋg³¹       'he grinds it'
      na̧n³         'fidget'
      na̧g⁴¹        'he circumcizes him'

**2.1.4 A simple segment that could be interpreted as a sequence of vowel plus nasal (Vn) or as a simple syllabic segment (n).** In a syllable beginning with an alveolar stop, *n* is interpreted as a sequence of vowel plus nasal consonant (Vn). This interpretation is supported, on the one hand, by the fact that all the corresponding words in the Markɛ dialect have a vowel plus nasal sequence, as, for example, *pɛ¹pɛ¹tin³jɔ²* 'swallow'; and on the other hand by the fact that in the verbs, syllabic *n* preceded by an alveolar stop corresponds to *in* preceded by any other sound.

(49)  hɛ̧:³mi̧n¹              'it tastes good with'
      ho³tn¹ / ho³tin¹       'bathe with'
      hɛ³din¹                'sweep with'
      ha̧³sin¹                'remove with'
      pa³tin³                'shell'
      ri:¹tins³              'resemblance'

# Phonological Description of Doyayo

## 2.2 Phonetic realizations

| Consonants | p | | t | k | kp |
|---|---|---|---|---|---|
| | b | | d | g | gp |
| | β | | | ɣ | |
| | ɓ | | ɗ | | |
| | | f | s | | h |
| | | v | z | | |
| | m | | n | ŋ | |
| | | | l | | |
| | | | r | | |
| | w | | j | | |
| | w̃ | | j̃ | | |

Vowels  i  i:  į  į:                u  u:  ų  ų:
         e  e:                       o  o:
         ɛ  ɛ:  ɛ̨  ɛ̨:                ɔ  ɔ:  ɔ̨  ɔ̨:
                  a  a:  ą  ą:

Tones   ¹high      ²mid-high      ³mid      ⁴low

Glides   12 13 14 23 24 42 41 32 31 21
         121 131 132 231 232
         212 213 214 312 314 412 414

## 2.3 Phonemic contrasts

### 2.3.1 Consonants

|  | p | | b | | ß/ɓ | |
|---|---|---|---|---|---|---|
| **INITIAL** | | | | | | |
| | pį:l¹ | 'trap' | bį:l² | 'morning' | ɓį:l² | 'not soil' |
| | pat³¹ | 'squirrel' | bat³ | 'weed' | ɓat¹ | 'big, strong' |
| | pu:²³ | 'be mealy' | bu:²³ | 'be white' | ɓu:²³ | 'spread out' |
| **MEDIAL** | | | | | | |
| | pa:³pe² | 'round dance' | pa¹bi¹ | 'uncle' | ——— | |
| **FINAL** | | | | | | |
| | zeps⁴ | 'buy for' | zeb⁴ | 'buy' | biβz⁴ | 'just wrapped' |
| | gupt⁴ | 'irrigate' | gub⁴ | 'throw out' | guβr⁴ | 'pour out' |

|  | t |  | d |  | ɗ |  |
|---|---|---|---|---|---|---|
| INITIAL |  |  |  |  |  |  |
|  | tɛː³ | 'braid' | dɛː³ | 'knock down' | ɗɛː²³ | 'be able' |
|  | tɔb⁴ | 'eat up' | dɔb⁴ | 'kick' | ɗɔb⁴ | 'be heavy' |
|  | tuβr¹ | 'clear up' | duβr²³ | 'be very deep' | ɗuβr³ | 'shake' |
| MEDIAL |  |  |  |  |  |  |
|  | dɛ¹ta⁴ | 'village name' | dɛ¹dɛ¹ | 'louse' | dɛː²³ɗɛ¹ | 'he can' |
| FINAL |  |  |  |  |  |  |
|  | bit³ | 'make sauce' | bid³ | 'turn inside out' | ——— |  |
|  | hot³ | 'bathe' | hod³ | 'take off' | ——— |  |

|  | k |  | g |  | ɣ |  |
|---|---|---|---|---|---|---|
| INITIAL |  |  |  |  |  |  |
|  | kɛː³ | 'multiply' | gɛː³ | 'divide' | ——— |  |
|  | kab⁴ | 'catch' | gab⁴ | 'be mean' | ——— |  |
|  | ko¹lɛ¹ | 'spirit' | go¹lɛ¹ | 'hill' | ——— |  |
| MEDIAL |  |  |  |  |  |  |
|  | da³kɔ³ | 'she sifts' | da³gɔ³ | 'she receives' | ——— |  |
| FINAL |  |  |  |  |  |  |
|  | kek³ | 'crow' | keg³ | 'weevil' | ——— |  |
|  | dak³ | 'sift' | dag³ | 'taste' | ——— |  |
|  | rɔks³ | 'cluck for, smooth for' | ——— |  | rɔɣz³ | 'just clucked, smoothed' |

|  | kp |  | gb |  |
|---|---|---|---|---|
| INITIAL |  |  |  |  |
|  | kpɛː²³ | 'close' | gbɛː²³ | 'go around' |
|  | kpor³ | 'stretched out' | gbor³ | 'go ahead and' |

|  | f |  | v |  |
|---|---|---|---|---|
| INITIAL |  |  |  |  |
|  | fikɪ³ | 'remove moss' | vikɪ³ | 'frown' |
|  | fɛŋ¹ | 'tiny' | vɛŋ¹ | 'fidgety' |
| MEDIAL |  |  |  |  |
|  | lu³fir³jɔ² | 'flea' | vɔ¹vɔr¹³jɔ² | 'gnat' |

|  | s |  | z |  |
|---|---|---|---|---|
| INITIAL |  |  |  |  |
|  | seb⁴ | 'serve' | zeb⁴ | 'buy' |
|  | sɛː²³ | 'moon, month' | zɛː²³ | 'river' |
|  | soːs² | 'string' | zoːs² | 'game, prey' |
| MEDIAL |  |  |  |  |
|  | soː³sɛ² | 'string' | soː¹zɛ⁴ | 'soldier' |
|  | bu³sum¹ | 'darken!' | bu³zum¹ | 'ant hill' |

# Phonological Description of Doyayo

**FINAL**
| | | | |
|---|---|---|---|
| hiʃ³ | 'pull out for' | hiʒ³ | 'pull out fast' |
| hɛʃ³ | 'swerve for' | hɛʒ³ | 'just swerved' |
| huʃ³ | 'rub for' | huʒ³ | 'rub quickly' |

**l**      **r**

**INITIAL**
| | | | |
|---|---|---|---|
| liβl²³ | 'singe' | riβl²³ | 'grow in clusters' |
| lag³ | 'hear' | rag³ | 'wash (grain, etc.)' |
| lu:²³ | 'tomorrow' | ru:²³ | 'adulterer' |

**MEDIAL**
| | | | |
|---|---|---|---|
| ta:¹lɛ¹ | 'scar' | ta:¹rɛ¹ | 'three' |

**FINAL**
| | | | |
|---|---|---|---|
| el⁴ | 'call' | er⁴ | 'stand' |
| wa:l¹ | 'country, world' | wa.r¹ | 'chief' |
| gul²³ | 'enter' | gur²³ | 'horn' |

**m**      **n**      **ŋ**

**INITIAL**
| | | | | | |
|---|---|---|---|---|---|
| mį:²³ | 'blow (nose), knot' | nį:²³ | 'be harmless' | — | |
| mą:³ | 'deceive' | ną:³ | 'chat, visit' | — | |

**MEDIAL**
| | | | | | |
|---|---|---|---|---|---|
| dɔ³mį¹ | 'circumcized person' | dɔ³nį¹ | 'cooking pot' | dɔŋ¹gij¹ | 'let them move' |

**FINAL**
| | | | | | |
|---|---|---|---|---|---|
| sim²³ | 'stub (toe)' | sin²³ | 'descend with' | siŋ²³ | 'sister' |
| tɔm³ | 'send on an errand' | tɔn²³ | 'set on fire' | tɔŋ³ | 'be many' |

**w**      **w̃**      **j**      **j̃**

**INITIAL**
| | | | | | | | |
|---|---|---|---|---|---|---|---|
| wɛkɩ³ | 'return (PL)' | w̃ękɩ³ | 'bestir' | jɛr²³ | 'inherit' | j̃ęr³ | 'crush' |
| wɛ:³ | 'return' | w̃ę:³ | 'bud' | ja:⁴ | 'send' | j̃ą:⁴ | 'be rare' |

**MEDIAL**
| | | | | | | | |
|---|---|---|---|---|---|---|---|
| za³we²jɔ² | 'ankle ring' | ną²w̃ą:³lɛ² | 'milk' | | | | |
| wa²wa⁴ | 'little girl' | | | ja²ja² | 'grandma' | | |

**FINAL**
| | | | | | | | |
|---|---|---|---|---|---|---|---|
| ga.w⁴ | 'give us' | ga.w̃³ | 'sprinkle us' | ga.j⁴ | 'give them' | gą.j̃³ | 'water them' |

**h**

**INITIAL**
| | |
|---|---|
| hį:³ | 'be satiated' |
| hakɩ³ | 'mend' |
| hʊr²³ | 'stink' |

**2.3.2 Vowels.** N.B. The glottal stop, automatic word-initial in the absence of any other consonant, has been omitted. Where two freely fluctuating forms of a word occur (~), one nasalized and the other non-nasalized, the translation accompanies the preferred form.

|  | i |  | į |  | i: |  | į: |  |
|---|---|---|---|---|---|---|---|---|
| INITIAL | | | | | | | | |
| | is³¹ | 'goat' | | | iːs³ | ~ | įːs³ | 'bury for' |
| | in²³ | 'refuse' | ~ įn²³ | | iːn³ | ~ | įːn³ | 'bury with' |
| | ij¹ | 'become gluey' | | | iːj¹ | ~ | įːj¹ | 'be buried' |
| MEDIAL | | | | | | | | |
| | pin²³ | 'sprout with' | | | piːn²³ | ~ | pįːn²³ | 'prop up!' |
| | kim³ | ~ | kįm³ | 'create' | kiːm⁴ | ~ | kįːm⁴ | 'touch!' |
| | fikɪ³ | 'remove moss' | ~ fįkɪ³ | 'press many reluctantly' | | | | |
| | sis³ | 'let down' | | | siːs³ | ~ | sįːs³ | 'throw plumb' |
| FINAL | | | | | | | | |
| | | | | | tiː²³ | ~ | tįː²³ | 'be salty' |
| | | | | | mį² | 'isn't it?' | mį:²³ | 'blow (nose)' |

|  | e |  | e: |  |
|---|---|---|---|---|
| INITIAL | | | | |
| | eˡsum¹ | 'set up!' | eː³sum¹ | 'second' |
| MEDIAL | | | | |
| | kel³¹ | 'scorpion' | keːl¹²¹ | 'denial' |
| | ses³ | 'notch, cut for' | seːs¹³ | 'sorcery' |
| FINAL | | | | |
| | se⁴ | 'take a helping' | seː⁴ | 'look' |
| | le² | 'eat' | leː²³ | 'starve' |

|  | ɛ |  | ę |  | ɛ: |  | ę: |  |
|---|---|---|---|---|---|---|---|---|
| INITIAL | | | | | | | | |
| | ɛs³ | 'seek for' | | | ɛːs³ | 'sing for' | ęːs³ | 'pour for' |
| | ɛm⁴ | 'walk' | | | ɛːm³ | 'sing!' | ęːm³ | 'pour!' |
| | ɛmb⁴ | 'walk' | ęmb²³ | 'cave in (PL)' | | | | |
| MEDIAL | | | | | | | | |
| | tɛk¹ | 'seeking' | tęk¹ | 'spinning' | tɛːk¹ | 'braiding' | tęːk¹ | 'skinning' |
| | kɛm²³ | ~ | kęm²³ | 'hear' | kɛːm³ | 'try your best' | kęːm³ | 'remove the roof' |
| | wɛj¹ | 'comb one's hair' | | | wɛːj¹ | 'come to one's self' | węːj¹ | 'open (bud)' |
| | jɛs¹ | 'shoot for' | jęs¹ | 'fragile' | jɛːs⁴ | 'judge for' | jęːs² | 'medicine' |

# Phonological Description of Doyayo

| | a | | ḁ | | a: | | ḁ: | |
|---|---|---|---|---|---|---|---|---|
| FINAL | tɛ⁴ | 'seek' | tɛ̣²³ | 'spin' | tɛː³ | 'braid (mat)' | tɛ̣ː⁴ | 'peel' |

| | a | | ḁ | | a: | | ḁ: | |
|---|---|---|---|---|---|---|---|---|
| INITIAL | | | ḁm²³ | 'scratch (PL)' | aːm³ | 'suck' | ḁːm²³ | 'conceal (PL)' |
| | am²³ ~ aj¹² | 'where?' | ḁm²³ ḁj¹ | 'to last' 'be scratched' | aːj¹ | 'widen' | ḁːj¹ | 'be concealed' |
| MEDIAL | gal¹ | 'pancreas' | gạl¹ | 'boil' | gaːl² | 'axe' | gạːl¹³ | 'turnip' |
| | has³ | 'please' | hạs³ | 'remove' | haːs³ | 'draw (water) for' | hạːs²³ | 'be sorry for' |
| | | | hạs¹ | 'come off' | | | | |
| | wal²³ | 'man' | w̃ạl²³ | 'cave' | waːl² | 'skull hut' | w̃ạːl² | 'milk' |
| FINAL | kaj¹ | 'be caught' | kạj¹ | 'be brought' | kaːj¹ | 'be lamented' | kạːj¹ | 'be folded' |

| | ɔ | | ɔ̣ | | ɔː | | ɔ̣ː | |
|---|---|---|---|---|---|---|---|---|
| INITIAL | ɔt³ ~ ɔːt³ | | ɔ̣t³¹ | 'day' | ɔːt³ | 'leave (PL)' | ɔ̣ːt³ | 'pinch (PL)' |
| | ɔn³ ~ ɔːn³ | | ɔ̣n²³ | 'his' | ɔːn³ | 'leave off!' | ɔ̣ːn³ | 'pinch!' |
| MEDIAL | 6ɔr³ | 'now, then' | 6ɔ̣r³ | 'kill' | | | 6ɔ̣ːr³ | 'squeeze all' |
| | kɔm⁴ | 'stay' | | | kɔːm⁴ | 'rub!' | kɔ̣ːm³ | 'dance!' |
| | sɔm³ ~ | | sɔ̣m³ | 'different' | sɔːm²³ | 'move over!' | sɔ̣ːm⁴ | 'look at many' |
| | hɔs³ | 'flay for' | hɔ̣rs¹ | 'mumble' | hɔːs³ | 'seem tall to' | hɔ̣ːs³ | 'dry a little' |
| FINAL | zɔ⁴ | 'flow' | zɔ̣⁴ | 'pray' | zɔː³ | 'sharpen' | zɔ̣ː⁴ | 'box' |
| | jɔ¹ | 'when' | j̃ɔ̣² | 'drink' | jɔː²³ | 'dye' | j̃ɔ̣ː²³ | 'be blind' |

| | o | | | | oː | | | |
|---|---|---|---|---|---|---|---|---|
| INITIAL | ok¹ | 'coagulating' | | | oːk¹ | 'waiting' | | |
| | on⁴ | 'bring back with' | | | oːn³ | 'wait!' | | |
| MEDIAL | kol¹ | 'spirit, heart' | | | koːl³ | 'go on a diet' | | |
| | gbol²³ | 'whistle' | | | gboːl²³ | 'close (PL)' | | |
| | hob¹ | 'red' | | | hoːb¹ | 'fear' | | |
| FINAL | ro⁴ | 'singe' | | | roː³ | 'trip up' | | |

|  | u |  | ụ |  | u: |  | ụ: |  |
|---|---|---|---|---|---|---|---|---|
| INITIAL | | | | | | | | |
| | un²³ | 'wash (face) with' | | | u.n²³ | 'smoke with' | | |
| | uj¹ | 'be washed' | | | u.j¹ | 'be smoked' | | |
| MEDIAL | | | | | | | | |
| | ɓul³ | 'prune' | — | | ɓu:l²³ | 'spread (PL)' | ɓụ:l²³ | 'hoe several places' |
| | guj¹ | 'be spilled' | gụj¹ | 'hurt one-self' | | | | |
| | sunt³ ~ sụnt³ | | sụnt³ | 'pierce (PL) with' | su.n³ | | sụ.n³ | 'pierce with' |
| | ruk¹ | 'slow' | | | ru:k¹ | 'waterpot' | | |
| FINAL | | | | | | | | |
| | du²³ | 'deepen' | | | du:² | 'type of bird' | | |
| | su²³ | 'slap hard' | — | | su:³ | | sụ:³ | 'pierce' |

## 2.4 Phonemes

### 2.4.1 Consonants

|  |  | labial | alveolar | post-alveolar | labio-velar |
|---|---|---|---|---|---|
| Stops | voiceless | p | t | k | kp |
| | voiced | b | d | g | gb |
| | implosive | ɓ | ɗ | | |
| Fricatives | voiceless | f | s | h | |
| | voiced | v | z | | |
| Nasals | | m | n | ŋ | |
| Laterals | | | l | | |
| Vibrants | | | r | | |
| Semivowels | | w | | j | |

### 2.4.2 Vowels

|  | front |  |  |  | central |  |  |  | back |  |  |  |
|---|---|---|---|---|---|---|---|---|---|---|---|---|
| close | i | ị | i: | ị: | | | | | u | ụ | u: | ụ: |
| close-mid | e | | e: | | | | | | o | | o: | |
| open-mid | ɛ | ɛ̣ | ɛ: | ɛ̣: | | | | | ɔ | ɔ̣ | ɔ: | ɔ̣: |
| open | | | | | a | ạ: | a: | ạ: | | | | |

The contrast between nasalized and non-nasalized close vowels is often neutralized.

## 2.4.3 Tone

high 1
mid-high 2
mid 3
low 4

## 2.5 Description of phonemes

### 2.5.1 Consonants

/p/ [p] voiceless bilabial stop
    [pa¹bi¹] /pa¹bi¹/ 'uncle'
    [rɔps¹jɔ¹] /rɔps¹jɔ¹/ 'blessing'

/b/ [β] voiced bilabial fricative; occurs initially in voiced consonant clusters, except when the following consonant is /d/
    [haβz⁴] /habz⁴/ 'perish quickly'
    [kiβl¹] /kibl¹/ 'roll on the ground'
  [b] voiced bilabial stop; occurs elsewhere
    [ba:³] /ba:³/ 'dance a dirge'
    [u:¹be⁴jɔ²] /u:¹be⁴jɔ²/ 'round dance'
    [gab⁴] /gab⁴/ 'be mean'

/ɓ/ [ɓ] voiced bilabial implosive
    [ɓa:³] /ɓa:³/ 'beat'

/kp/ [kp] voiceless labiovelar stop
    [kpa:³] /kpa:³/ 'mow'

/gb/ [gb] voiced labiovelar stop
    [gba:³] /gba:³/ 'deflect'

/t/ [t] voiceless alveolar stop
    [ta:³] /ta:³/ 'kill with arrows'
    [zu:³ta²jɔ²] /zu:³ta²jɔ²/ 'tucan'
    [hot¹] /hot¹/ 'bathe'

/d/ [d] voiced alveolar stop
    [da:³] /da:³/ 'pass'
    [bu:²dɛ³] /bu:²dɛ³/ 'white people'
    [hod¹] /hod¹/ 'come off'

/ɗ/ [ɗ] voiced alveolar implosive
   [ɗa:⁴]         /ɗa:⁴/         'help'
   [dɛ³ɗɛŋ³jɔ²]   /dɛ³ɗɛŋ³jɔ²/   'guitar-like instrument'

/k/ [k] voiceless velar stop
   [ka:³]         /ka:³/         'weep'
   [du¹kum²¹jc¹]  /du¹kum²¹jɔ¹/  'thorny tree'
   [dak³]         /dak³/         'sift'

/g/ [ɣ] voiced velar fricative; occurs initially in a voiced consonant cluster
   [daɣd³¹]       /dagd³¹/       'already got'
   [lɛɣr²³¹jɔ¹]   /lɛgr²³¹jɔ¹/   'spider's web'
   [zaɣl¹]        /zagl¹/        'kneel, crawl'

   [g] voiced velar stop; occurs elsewhere
   [ga:⁴]         /ga:⁴/         'give'
   [ja¹gi¹]       /ja¹gi¹/       'rat with bushy tail'
   [dag³]         /dag³/         'get, meet, taste'

/f/ [f] voiceless labiodental fricative
   [fa:³]         /fa:³/         'doubt, deny'
   [lu³fir³jɔ²]   /lu³fir³jɔ²/   'flea'

/v/ [v] voiced labiodental fricative
   [vikt³]        /vikt³/        'frown'
   [vɔ¹vɔr¹³jɔ²]  /vɔ¹vɔr¹³jɔ²/  'gnat'

/s/ [s] voiceless alveolar spirant
   [sa:³]         /sa:³/         'mock, despise'
   [dɛ:²si³jɔ²]   /dɛ:²si³jɔ²/   'type of lizard'
   [kas⁴]         /kas⁴/         'cause to climb'

/z/ [z] voiced alveolar spirant
   [za:³]         /za:³/         'rince'
   [lɛ²za¹jɔ¹]    /lɛ²za¹jc¹/    'last year'
   [kaz⁴¹]        /kaz⁴¹/        'climb up here'

N.B. There is considerable idiolectical variation as to the point of articulation of the spirants *s* and *z*. Some speakers even pronounce them as alveopalatal fricatives.

# Phonological Description of Doyayo

/m/ [m] voiced bilabial nasal
    [mã:³]    /ma:³/      'deceive'
    [bu¹mɛ̃¹]   /bu¹mɛ¹/    'beer'
    [lɔm³]     /lɔm³/      'bite'

N.B. Syllable-initially, *m* always causes nasalization of the ensuing vowel. This explains why *m* is never followed by a close-mid vowel (*e*, *e:*, *o*, or *o:*), which cannot be nasalized in Doyayo.

/n/ [n] voiced alveolar nasal
    [nã:³]      /na:³/      'chat, visit'
    [ku³nũ¹jɔ¹]   /ku³nu¹jɔ¹/   'dolomite'
    [lɔn³]     /lɔn³/      'be well twined'

N.B. Like *m*, *n* can only be followed by a nasalized vowel.

/ŋ/ [ŋ] voiced velar nasal; occurs only syllable final
    [lɔŋ²³]    /lɔŋ²³/     'be stuck in the throat'

/l/ [l] voiced alveolar lateral approximant
    [la:¹]      /la:¹/      'fire'
    [ta:¹lɛ¹]    /ta:¹lɛ¹/     'scar'
    [el⁴]      /el⁴/      'call'

/r/ [r] voiced alveolar flap
    [ra:¹]      /ra:¹/      'compound'
    [ta:¹rɛ¹]    /ta:¹rɛ¹/     'three'
    [er⁴]      /er⁴/      'stand'

/w/     voiced bilabial semivowel
    [w̃] nasalized; occurs in a syllable the nucleus of which is filled by a nasal vowel
        [w̃ã:⁴]     /wa:⁴/      'catch'
        [kãw̃³¹]     /kaw³¹/     'he took us'
    [w] non-nasalized; occurs elsewhere
        [wa:³]     /wa:³/      'live, stay, continue'
        [wa²wa⁴jɔ²]   /wa²wa⁴jɔ²/   'little girl'
        [sɛw³]     /sɛw³/      'all'

/j/     voiced palatal semivowel
    [j̃] nasalized; occurs in a syllable the nucleus of which is filled by a nasal vowel
        [j̃ã:³]     /ja:³/      'knead'
        [zɛj̃¹]      /zɛj¹/      'be found'

|   | [j] | non-nasalized; occurs elsewhere |   |   |
|---|---|---|---|---|
|   |   | [ja:³]      | /ja:³/      | 'hide' |
|   |   | [la²ja:³rɛ²] | /la²ja:³rɛ²/ | 'fetish' |
|   |   | [aj¹²]      | /aj¹²/      | 'where?' |

/h/ [h] voiceless glottal fricative
    [ha:³]    /ha:³/    'be sour'
    [hɔ¹hɔ²¹jɔ¹]    /hɔ¹hɔ²¹jɔ¹/    'big snake'

## 2.5.2 Vowels

/i/ [i] voiced close unrounded vowel
    [il²³]    /il²³/    'be gluey'
    [bid³]    /bid³/    'turn inside out'
    [gi²]    /gi²/    'be'

/i:/ [i:] voiced close unrounded long vowel
    [i:l²³¹]    /i:l²³¹/    'it's gluey (final)'
    [ti:s³]    /ti:s³/    'bring down'
    [ti:³]    /ti:³/    'descend'

/ĩ/ [ĩ] voiced close unrounded nasalized vowel
    [ĩj¹]    /ĩj¹/    'be submerged'
    [kĩb³¹]    /kĩb³¹/    'He created me'
    [kĩ³]    /kĩ³/    'he shaped'

/ĩ:/ [ĩ:] voiced close unrounded nasalized long vowel
    [ĩ:j¹]    /ĩ:j¹/    'be buried'
    [kĩ:b⁴¹]    /kĩ:b⁴¹/    'he touched me'
    [tĩ:³]    /tĩ:³/    'pitch dark'

/e/ [e] voiced close-mid unrounded vowel
    [el⁴]    /el⁴/    'call'
    [lel²³]    /lel²³/    'yesterday'
    [ge¹]    /ge¹/    'him, toward'

/e:/ [e:] voiced close-mid unrounded long vowel
    [e:r¹]    /e:r¹/    'two'
    [le:l²³]    /le:l²³/    'starve (PL)'
    [se:²³]    /se:²³/    'calm down'

Phonological Description of Doyayo 35

/ɛ/ [ɛ] voiced open-mid unrounded vowel
　　　[ɛl³]　　　/ɛl³/　　　'ask (PL)'
　　　[lɛl²³]　　/lɛl²³/　　'place'
　　　[gɛ¹]　　　/gɛ¹/　　　'here'

/ɛ:/ [ɛ:] voiced open-mid unrounded long vowel
　　　[ɛ:n³]　　　/ɛ:n³/　　　'sing!'
　　　[lɛ:l²³]　　/lɛ:l²³/　　'wander about'
　　　[sɛ:²³]　　 /sɛ:²³/　　 'moon'

/ɛ̃/ [ɛ̃] voiced open-mid unrounded nasal vowel
　　　[ɛ̃n²³]　　　/ɛ̃n²³/　　　'cave in with'
　　　[sɛ̃b⁴¹]　　/sɛ̃b⁴¹/　　'pepper'
　　　[tɛ̃²³]　　 /tɛ̃²³/　　 'spin (web)'

/ɛ̃:/ [ɛ̃:] voiced open-mid unrounded long nasal vowel
　　　[ɛ̃:n³]　　　/ɛ̃:n³/　　　'reach out!'
　　　[sɛ̃:b³]　　/sɛ̃:b³/　　'approach'
　　　[tɛ̃:²³]　　/tɛ̃:²³/　　'draw (line)'

/a/ [a] voiced open central vowel
　　　[a¹]　　　/a¹/　　　'he said'
　　　[gal¹]　　/gal¹/　　'pancreas'
　　　[ga¹]　　 /ga¹/　　 'it's he'

/a:/ [a:] voiced open central long vowel
　　　[a:²³]　　　/a:²³/　　　'be open, wide'
　　　[ga:l¹]　　/ga:l¹/　　'light, brightness'
　　　[za:²³]　　/za:²³/　　'come'

/ã/ [ã] voiced open central nasal vowel
　　　[ãn³]　　　/ãn³/　　　'dig up with'
　　　[gãl¹]　　/gãl¹/　　'boil'
　　　[zã⁴]　　 /zã⁴/　　 'eat (sauce)'

/ã:/ [ã:] voiced open central long nasal vowel
　　　[ã:n³¹]　　　/ã:n³¹/　　　'refuse'
　　　[gã:l¹³]　　/gã:l¹³/　　'type of turnip'
　　　[zã:²³]　　 /zã:²³/　　 'live, be saved, be healed'

/ɔ/ [ɔ] voiced open-mid back rounded vowel
  [ɔ³]      /ɔ³/       'hortatory'
  [gɔl¹]    /gɔl¹/     'mistreat'
  [zɔ⁴]     /zɔ⁴/      'drip, flow'

/ɔː/ [ɔː] voiced open-mid back rounded long vowel
  [ɔː³]     /ɔː³/      'leave'
  [gbɔːl¹]  /gbɔːl¹/   'big'
  [zɔː³]    /zɔː³/     'sharpen'

/ɔ̃/ [ɔ̃] voiced open-mid back rounded nasal vowel
  [ɔ̃²³]    /ɔ̃²³/     'his, her, its'
  [gbɔ̃j̃¹] /gbɔ̃j̃¹/  'be killed'
  [zɔ̃⁴]    /zɔ̃⁴/     'pray'

/ɔ̃ː/ [ɔ̃ː] voiced open-mid back rounded long nasal vowel
  [ɔ̃ː³]    /ɔ̃ː³/     'pinch'
  [tɔ̃ːk¹]  /tɔ̃ːk¹/   'pouring (liquid)'
  [zɔ̃ː⁴]   /zɔ̃ː⁴/    'box'

/o/ [o] voiced close-mid back rounded vowel
  [o⁴]      /o⁴/       'bring in (flock)'
  [gol¹]    /gol¹/     'hill'
  [to⁴]     /to⁴/      'make a roof for'

/oː/ [oː] voiced close-mid back rounded long vowel
  [oː⁴]     /oː⁴/      'well, all right then!'
  [toːk¹]   /toːk¹/    'paying'
  [toː³]    /toː³/     'pay'

/u/ [u] voiced close back rounded vowel
  [us²³]    /us²³/     'wash (face) for'
  [ɓul³]    /ɓul³/     'prune'
  [du²]     /du²/      'not deep'

/uː/ [uː] voiced close back rounded long vowel
  [uːs²³]   /uːs²³/    'smoke for'
  [ɓuːl²³]  /ɓuːl²³/   'spread out (PL)'
  [duː²]    /duː²/     'type of bird'

/ũ/ [ũ] voiced close back rounded nasal vowel
  [gũj̃¹]  /gũj̃¹/    'hurt oneself'

# Phonological Description of Doyayo

/ṵ:/ [ṵ:] voiced close back rounded long nasal vowel
    [ɓṵ:l²³]    /qṵ:l²³/    'hoe (PL)'
    [kṵ²³]    /kṵ:²³/    'back'

## 2.6 Phoneme distribution

**2.6.1 Consonant distribution.** In (50) the circle (∘) signifies that the consonant is found in (word-) medial position only in the case of reduplication or in a compound noun. "Initial" and "final" bears reference to either the syllable or the word.

In general, it can be stated that:

— Any consonant except *ŋ* can occur in word- or syllable-initial position.

(50) Occurrence of consonants in initial (prenuclear), medial (between two vowel nuclei), and final (postnuclear) position

|  | p | b | ɓ | t | d | ɗ | k | g | kp | gb | f | v | s | z | m | n | ŋ | l | r | w | j | h |
|---|---|---|---|---|---|---|---|---|---|---|---|---|---|---|---|---|---|---|---|---|---|---|
| initial | x | x | x | x | x | x | x | x | x | x | x | x | x | x | x | x |   | x | x | x | x | x |
| medial | x | x | ∘ | x | x | ∘ | x | x | ∘ | ∘ | x | ∘ | x | x | x | x |   | x | x | x | x | ∘ |
| final |   |   |   | x |   |   | x | x |   |   |   |   | x |   | x | x | x | x | x | x | x |   |

— *ɓ, ɗ, kp, gb, v,* and *h* occur only word initially. Their only occurrence in word-medial position is (syllable initial) within a compound noun or in a reduplicated syllable.
— Any consonant can occur in word- or syllable-final position except *p, ɓ, ɗ, kp, gb, v,* and *h*.
— *ŋ* only occurs syllable finally.

There are no restrictions on the occurrence of consonants together in any one phonological word, provided the restrictions applying to each consonant in particular are observed.

(51) Syllable-final clusters of two consonants in the verb

|   | p | b | ɓ | t | d | ɗ | k | g | kp | gb | f | v | s | z | m | n | l | r | w | j | h |
|---|---|---|---|---|---|---|---|---|---|---|---|---|---|---|---|---|---|---|---|---|---|
| p |   |   |   | x |   |   |   |   |   |   |   |   | x |   |   |   |   |   |   |   |   |
| b |   |   |   |   | x |   |   |   |   |   |   |   |   | x |   | x | x |   |   |   |   |
| t |   |   |   |   |   |   |   |   |   |   |   |   | x |   |   |   |   |   |   |   |   |
| d |   |   |   |   |   |   |   |   |   |   |   |   |   | x |   |   |   |   |   |   |   |
| k |   | x |   |   |   |   |   |   |   |   |   |   | x |   |   |   |   |   |   |   |   |
| g |   |   |   |   | x |   |   |   |   |   |   |   |   | x |   | x | x | x |   |   |   |
| s |   |   |   |   |   |   |   |   |   |   |   |   |   |   |   |   |   |   |   |   |   |
| z |   |   |   |   |   |   |   |   |   |   |   |   |   |   |   |   |   |   |   |   |   |
| m | x |   |   | x | x |   |   |   |   |   |   |   | x | x |   | x | x | x |   |   |   |
| n |   |   |   | x | x |   | x | (x) |   |   |   |   | x | x |   |   |   |   |   |   |   |
| ŋ |   |   |   | x | x |   | x | x |   |   |   |   | x | x |   | x | x | x |   |   |   |
| l |   |   |   | x | x |   | x | (x) |   |   |   |   | x | x |   |   |   |   |   |   |   |
| r |   |   |   | x | x |   | x | (x) |   |   |   |   | x | x |   |   |   |   |   |   |   |
| w |   |   |   |   |   |   |   |   |   |   |   |   |   |   |   |   |   |   |   |   |   |
| j |   |   |   |   |   |   |   |   |   |   |   |   |   |   |   |   |   |   |   |   |   |

In the verb, all consonant clusters cross morphological boundaries. Verbal suffixes -t(ɔ), -dir(o)/-d(o)/ -r(o), -k(ɔ), -k(o), -go, -s(ɔ), -z(ɔ), -n(ɔ)/-n(u), -l(ɔ), and -r(ɔ), when added to a verb already ending in a consonant, result in consonant clusters. Word final in the absence of pause, all the above-mentioned suffixes, except -go, drop their vowel, and the result is a word-final consonant cluster. In this position, the only cluster ending in g is ŋg, which results from adding the personal pronoun object suffix -ge 'third-person singular' to a verb ending in m.

Example (51) illustrates the following rules that apply to the formation of consonant clusters in the verb:

— The alveolar stops t and d, when added to a stop, cause the devoicing or voicing, respectively, of that stop. A cluster of two stops must be heterorganic and end in an alveolar stop.
— The sibilants s and z, when added to a stop, cause its devoicing or voicing, respectively. For example, dag³ 'receive' + -s = daks³ 'receive for/sift for'; dak³ 'sift' + -z = dagz³ 'sift quickly/receive quickly'.
— When n is preceded by a stop other than b, it is separated from that stop by i-epenthesis in slow speech, but in normal speech it becomes syllabic n. When it comes first in a cluster, the other consonant must be a homorganic stop or sibilant or k. Adding any other consonant results in obligatory i-epenthesis. k can be added with or without epenthesis.

# Phonological Description of Doyayo

- The only consonants that can precede *l* or *r* in a cluster are *b, g, m,* and *ŋ*. After any other consonant, there is obligatory *i*-epenthesis before *l* and *r*.
- *s* and *z* never occur initially in a cluster. *s + s = ts, s + z = dz*. Other consonants following *s* or *z* are separated from them by *i*-epenthesis.
- *m* never occurs finally in a consonant cluster. Sometimes it gains its initial position by means of metathesis with the final consonant of the verb to which it is suffixed, as in: *kab⁴* 'catch' + *-m* = *kamb⁴* 'catch many'.
- The clusters *mk* and *mg* do not occur, because there is automatic assimilation of the *m* of the verb stem to the point of articulation of the velar stop.
- There are no double consonants in syllable-final position.

In (52) the circle (°) marks clusters that occur only in certain Fulani loan words.

(52) Two-consonant clusters in medial position in nominals

|   | p | b | ɓ | t | d | ɗ | k | g | kp | gb | f | v | s | z | m | n | l | r | w | j | h |
|---|---|---|---|---|---|---|---|---|---|---|---|---|---|---|---|---|---|---|---|---|---|
| p | ° |   | x |   |   |   |   |   |   |   |   |   | x |   |   |   |   |   |   |   |   |
| b |   |   |   |   |   |   |   |   |   |   |   |   |   | x |   |   |   |   |   | x |   |
| t |   |   | x |   |   |   |   |   |   |   |   |   |   |   |   |   |   |   |   | x |   |
| d |   |   |   |   |   |   |   |   |   |   |   |   |   |   |   |   |   |   |   | x |   |
| k |   |   | x |   |   |   |   |   |   |   |   | x |   | x | x |   |   |   |   | x |   |
| g |   |   |   | x |   |   |   | ° |   |   |   |   |   | x | x |   |   |   |   | x |   |
| s |   |   |   |   |   |   |   |   |   |   |   |   |   |   |   |   |   |   |   | x |   |
| z |   |   |   |   |   |   |   |   |   |   |   |   |   |   |   |   |   |   |   |   |   |
| m | ° | x | x |   |   |   |   |   |   |   |   | x |   |   |   | x | x | x |   | x |   |
| n |   | x | x |   |   |   |   |   |   |   |   | x |   |   |   |   |   |   |   | x |   |
| ŋ |   | x | x |   |   |   | x | x | x |   |   | x |   |   |   |   | x |   |   | x |   |
| l |   | x |   | x | x | x |   |   |   |   |   | x |   |   |   |   |   |   |   | x |   |
| r |   |   |   |   | x | x |   |   |   |   |   | x |   |   |   |   |   |   | ° | x |   |
| w |   |   |   |   |   |   |   |   |   |   |   |   |   |   |   |   |   |   |   | x |   |
| j |   |   |   |   |   |   |   |   |   |   |   |   |   |   |   |   |   |   |   |   | x |

(53)   Two-consonant clusters in final position in nominals

|   | p | b | t | d | k | g | s | z | m | n | l | r |
|---|---|---|---|---|---|---|---|---|---|---|---|---|
| p |   |   | x |   |   |   | x |   |   |   |   |   |
| b |   |   |   |   |   |   |   |   |   | x |   |   |
| t |   |   |   |   |   |   |   |   |   |   |   |   |
| d |   |   |   |   |   |   |   |   |   |   |   |   |
| k |   |   | x |   |   |   | x |   |   |   |   |   |
| g |   |   |   |   |   |   |   |   |   |   | x | x |
| s |   |   |   |   |   |   |   |   |   |   |   |   |
| z |   |   |   |   |   |   |   |   |   |   |   |   |
| m |   |   | x | x |   |   |   |   |   |   | x | x |
| n |   |   | x | x |   | x |   |   |   |   |   |   |
| ŋ |   |   | x | x | x | x |   |   |   |   | x | x |
| l |   |   | x |   | x | x |   |   |   |   |   |   |
| r |   |   |   |   | x | x |   |   |   |   |   |   |

The following suffixes occur in nominals: *(-yɔ), -t(yɔ), -d(yɔ), -dɛ(yɔ), tɔnɔ(yɔ), (-ɔ), (-o), -t(o), -k(o), -g(o), (-ɛ), -l(ɛ), -n(ɛ), -r(ɛ)*, and *-s(ɛ)*.

In non-pause-group final position, where the element between parentheses is dropped, the consonantal suffixes, meeting a stem-final consonant, form a cluster with that consonant. All final consonant clusters in the nominal can be explained in this way. This leaves the word-medial clusters *mb, lb, ŋg, rg, kl, kr,* and *ŋgb* still unaccounted for. In the case of *ŋgb*, the presence of a morphological boundary imposes itself by virtue of the restrictions on the occurrence of *gb* word medially. *ŋg* can be explained because *ŋ* is not permitted to initiate a syllable. Thus, *g* has a transitional function. That the *b* of *mb* has the same function is substantiated by the word *kum³bil³yɔ²* 'twins', when one takes note of the fact that the word *kum³* 'to have twins', adds a transitional *b* when a suffix is to be added. Though no definite proof can be found concerning the other four clusters, *kl, kr, lb,* and *rg*, there is very good reason to assume that here, as well, morphological boundaries are involved.

Therefore, what was already said about verbs can be stated about nominals: CONSONANT CLUSTERS OCCUR ONLY ACROSS MORPHOLOGICAL BOUNDARIES.

In fact, what is said about consonant clusters in verbs and nominals can be said about consonant clusters in the Doyayo language as a whole, as there is virtually no clustering in words of other categories. We therefore conclude that THERE ARE NO TRUE CONSONANT CLUSTERS IN DOYAYO.

The restrictions on juxtaposition of consonants in final position in nominals are identical to those already mentioned for verbals.

# Phonological Description of Doyayo

— Of the consonants that can occur in the postnuclear margin, *s* and *z* cannot initiate a cluster.
— *m* and *ŋ* must initiate the cluster in which they occur.
— *t* and *s* cause the devoicing of the following stop; *d* and *z* cause the voicing of the following stop.
— *n* can only be preceded by *g* or by a heterorganic nasal.
— *g* and *k* cannot be preceded by *m* (the latter changes to *ŋ* before a velar stop).
— Double consonants are found only across morphological boundaries (i.e., length does not characterize consonants in Doyayo.)

(54) Three-consonant clusters in syllable-final position

| | t | d | s | z | | t | d | s | z | | t | d | s | z |
|---|---|---|---|---|---|---|---|---|---|---|---|---|---|---|
| pt | | | x | | mz | | | | | ŋz | | | | |
| ps | | | | | mn | x | x | x | x | ŋn | x | x | x | x |
| bd | | | | x | ml | x | x | x | x | ŋl | x | x | x | x |
| bz | | | | | mr | x | x | x | x | ŋr | x | x | x | x |
| bl | x | x | x | x | nt | | | x | | lt | | | x | |
| br | x | x | x | x | nd | | | | x | ld | | | | x |
| kt | | | x | | nk | | | | | lk | | | x | |
| ks | | | | | ns | | | | | ls | | | | |
| gd | | | | x | nz | | | | | lz | | | | |
| gz | | | | | ŋt | | | x | | rt | | | x | |
| gl | x | x | x | x | ŋd | | | | x | rd | | | | x |
| gr | x | x | x | x | ŋk | x | | x | | rk | | | x | |
| mt | | | x | | ŋg | | | | | rs | | | | |
| ms | | | | | ŋs | | | | | rz | | | | |

Three-consonant clusters occur only in verbs, where they result from the addition of several suffixes to a single stem. In word-medial position, the syllable break is made between the second and the third consonant.

For morphological reasons, the modal suffix *-k(o)* is not followed by other suffixes. The derivational *-k* suffix can be followed by *t* or *s*. For phonological reasons, the suffixes *-s* and *-z* cannot be followed by other suffixes, except by interposing an epenthetic *-i-;* they must always be final in a consonant cluster.

Any three-consonant cluster ending in the suffix *-t* can still take an *-s* or *-z* suffix. This gives twenty-two possible clusters of four consonants shown in (55).

(55)  blts   bldz   brts   brdz
      glts   gldz   grts   grdz
      mnts   mndz   mlts   mldz   mrts   mrdz
      ŋkts   ŋgdz   ŋnts   ŋndz   ŋlts   ŋldz   ŋrts   ŋrdz

(56) Consonant clusters[6]

|   | C | CC | | CCC | | | CCCC | | | |
|---|---|---|---|---|---|---|---|---|---|---|
|   | C1 | C2 | C3 | C4 | C5 | C6 | C7 | C8 | C9 | C10 |
| p |   |   |   |   |   |   |   |   |   |   |
| t | x | x | x |   | x | x |   | x |   |   |
| k | x | x |   | x |   |   |   |   |   |   |
| b | x | x |   | x |   |   | x |   |   |   |
| d | x | x | x |   | x | x |   | x |   |   |
| g | x | x |   | x |   |   | x |   |   |   |
| m | x | x |   | x |   |   | x |   |   |   |
| n | x | x | x | x |   |   |   |   |   |   |
| ŋ | x | x |   | x |   |   | x |   |   |   |
| s | x |   | x |   |   | x | x |   |   | x |
| z | x |   | x |   |   | x |   |   |   | x |
| l | x |   | x | x |   |   |   | x |   |   |
| r | x |   | x | x |   |   |   | x |   |   |
| w | x |   |   |   |   |   |   |   |   |   |
| j | x |   |   |   |   |   |   |   |   |   |

*Initial consonant*

— *b, g, m,* and *ŋ* initial in all consonant clusters (C, CC, CCC, CCCC).
— *k* and *n* initial only in C, CC and CCC.
— *t* and *d* initial only in C and CC.

*Final consonant*

— *s* and *z* final in all consonant clusters.
— *t* and *d* final in C, CC, CCC.
— *ŋ, l,* and *r* final in C and CC.
— All consonants except *p* final in C.

---

[6]For this table and the conclusions resulting from it, we wish to express our gratitude to Peter Kingston of SIL in England.

## Penultimate consonant

— *t* and *d* are penultimate in all consonant clusters.
— *l* and *r* are penultimate in CCC.

## Prepenultimate consonant

— *l* and *r* are prepenultimate in CCCC.

(57) Distribution of consonants that can occupy the postnuclear margin

| | |
|---|---|
| Class 1: only alone | *w, j* |
| Class 2: initial | |
|     2.1 in all clusters | *b, g, m, ŋ* |
|     2.2 in all except the four-consonant clusters; final preceded by a velar or a bilabial consonant | *n* |
|     2.3 in all clusters, but observing the morphophonemic restrictions applying in a four-consonant cluster | *k* |
| Class 3: second in all clusters (C, CC, CCC, CCCC) | *l, r* |
| Class 4: final in all consonant clusters (C, CC, CCC, CCCC) | *s, z* |

**2.6.2 Co-occurrence of consonants and vowels.** The following observations can be made as to the co-occurrence of consonants and vowels within a syllable:

*m* or *n* in the prenuclear margin cause (automatic) nasalization of the vowel nucleus: [mɛ̃:³] /mɛ:³/ 'know', [nɔ̃:⁴] /nɔ:⁴/ 'run'. As *e* and *o* have no nasal counterparts, they are never found in a syllable beginning with a nasal consonant.

*l* never initiates a syllable with a nasal vowel as the nucleus.

*r* never initiates a syllable with a close nasal vowel as the nucleus, that is: *į̃, į̃:, ų̃,* or *ų̃:*.

These restrictions on the occurrence of vowels and consonants in Doyayo closely resemble patterns observed in several Kwa languages, which also have no open-mid nasal vowels.[7]

---

[7]Cf. Hyman, 1972.

**2.6.3 Vowel distribution.** In general, the vowels *i*, *ɛ*, and *o* in word-final position tend to characterize nominals, while *ɔ* is more typical of verbal forms.

(58) Occurrence of vowels in compound nouns having the syllable patterns CVCV, CVCVC, and CVVCV in non-pause-group final position

|   | i | e | ɛ | a | ɔ | o | u |
|---|---|---|---|---|---|---|---|
| i | x |   | x | x |   |   |   |
| e | x |   |   |   |   |   |   |
| ɛ | x |   | x | x | x | x | x |
| a | x | x | x | x | x | x | x |
| ɔ | x |   | x | x | x |   |   |
| o | x |   |   |   |   | x | x |
| u | x | x |   | x | x |   |   |

The mid-close vowels *e* and *o* are neither preceded nor followed by mid-open vowel *ɛ* or *ɔ*. *e* and *o* seldom occur in any but the first syllable of a word.

Long vowels occur either in the first or the second syllable but (except in a few compound nouns) never in a later syllable: *a:³ti¹jɔ¹* 'type of green beans', *lɛ:²lɛ²jɔ²* 'kind of bird', *ti¹la:¹³jɔ²* 'children's game', *ɔ:³mɔ³ge³* 'leave him alone!'.

Except in the case of compound nouns, or of syllable reduplication, or suffixation of the third person-possessive adjective *-ɔ²³* or *-jã²³*, nasal vowels occur in the first syllable only: *hẽ¹tum¹jɔ¹* 'of the bush' and *fã:⁴sɛ²* 'glue'.

## Appendix A

### Doyayo dialects

Doyayo has three dialects, considered by the Dowayos as being very different, but found to be quite mutually comprehensible: Markɛ of the plains, Poli of the plateau, and mountain Tɛɛrɛ. Usually the Poli dialect is grouped together with that of the mountains under the name Tɛɛrɛ, because these two dialects resemble each other more than they resemble Markɛ. However, as the Markɛ and the Poli dialects are considered more prestigious than the speech of the mountain people, it was deemed preferable to maintain a three-way distinction for the purpose of the survey.

# Phonological Description of Doyayo

The table of dialects below contains a list of 70 words. The first 49 were taken from the first 200 words on the list drawn up by the linguist Swadesh, numbers 50–52 from his supplementary questionnaire of idiomatic expressions, and numbers 53–70 from a word list based on our Doyayo texts. Tone, if marked, would undoubtedly have brought out further distinctions between the dialects. There appear to be five level tones in Markɛ (Bohnhoff ms.), the fifth being lower than the others and causing speakers of the Poli dialect to remark, "The Markɛ people talk way down low!"

| | Reference | | Markɛ | Poli | Mountain |
|---|---|---|---|---|---|
| 1. | I, me | Sw 1 | mi̧/mi̧ga | mi̧/mi̧ja | mi̧/mi̧ga |
| 2. | you (SG) | Sw 2 | mɔ/mɔga | mɔ̧/mɔ̧ja | mɔ̧/mɔ̧ga |
| 3. | this | Sw 4 | jɛrɛ | jɛrɛ | jɔrɛ |
| 4. | that | Sw 5 | bɛrɛ | bɔrɔ | bɔrɛ |
| 5. | small | Sw 15 | wɛnsɛ | w̧ansɛ | wansɛ |
| 6. | louse | Sw 22 | ɗɛdɛ | ɗɛdɛ | ɗɛdo |
| 7. | seed | Sw 24 | niŋsɛ | lɛŋsɛ | lɛŋsɛ |
| 8. | root | Sw 26 | tɛɛ̧ jɛɛ̧sɛ̧ | tɛɛ̧ jɛɛ̧sɛ | tɛɛ jɛɛ̧sɛ |
| 9. | bark | Sw 27 | pokiljɔ | pokiljɔ | pɔgljɔ |
| 10. | bone | Sw 31 | niŋko | lɛŋko | lɛŋko |
| 11. | egg | S2 33 | baarɛ | ba̧a̧rɛ | ba̧a̧rɛ |
| 12. | horn | Sw 34 | gulɛ | gurɛ | gurɛ |
| 13. | hair | Sw 37 | suksjɔ | susugjɔ | susugjɔ |
| 14. | eye | Sw 40 | lɛlɛ | lɔlɛ/jɔlɛ | jɔlɛ/njɔlɛ |
| 15. | moth | Sw 44 | ja̧a̧jɔ | ja̧a̧jɔ | nja̧a̧jɔ |
| 16. | drink | Sw 54 | jɔ̧ɔ̧kjɔ | jɔkjɔ | njɔkjɔ |
| 17. | eat | Sw 55 | leekjɔ | lekjɔ | lekjɔ |
| 18. | sleep | Sw 60 | jookjɔ | jokjɔ | jokjɔ |
| 19. | swim | Sw 63 | mɛm fɨkjɔ | fɨkjɔ | fɨkjɔ |
| 20. | fly | Sw 64 | ɗukikjɔ | ɗukigjɔ | ɗukigjɔ |
| 21. | lie | Sw 67 | kosikjɔ | kusigjɔ | kusikjɔ |
| 22. | sit | Sw 68 | dɔɔtikjɔ | dɔɔtigjɔ | dɔɔtikjɔ |
| 23. | stone | Sw 77 | beto | beto | bito |
| 24. | earth | Sw 79 | hɛpto | hɛpto | hɛpto |
| 25. | ash | Sw 83 | tamɛ | tamɔ̧ | tamɔ̧ |
| 26. | road | Sw 85 | gbanajɔ | gbɔnɔ̧jɔ | gbɔnɔ̧jɔ |
| 27. | red | Sw 87 | hɔbɔ | hobo | hoobo |
| 28. | night | Sw 92 | jɛmsɛ | jɛ̧msɛ | njɛ̧msɛ |
| 29. | new | Sw 96 | sɛgɔ | sego | sego |
| 30. | you (PL) | Sw 101 | nɛ/nɛɛga | nɛ/nɛja | nɛ/nɛga |
| 31. | he/him | Sw 102 | gi/giga | gi/gija | gi/giga |
| 32. | a little | Sw 113 | kaasi/kansi | kaasi | kaasi |
| 33. | sky | Sw 114 | bɛtha | bɛtha | bɛtka |
| 34. | wash | Sw 123 | doktiljɔ | doktigjɔ | doptikjɔ |

| | | | | | |
|---|---|---|---|---|---|
| 35. | arm | Sw 127 | naanɛ | nąanɛ | nąanɛ |
| 36. | intestine | Sw 133 | hadɛ | hadɛ | hado |
| 37. | grass | Sw 138 | hɛto | hɛto | hɛto |
| 38. | far | Sw 156 | hɛlba | hɛmlɔ | hɛemlɔ |
| 39. | near | Sw 157 | sɛɛba | sɛɛbɔ | sɛɛbɔ |
| 40. | thick | Sw 158 | naaba | nąabɔ | nąabɔ |
| 41. | short | Sw 160 | lɔɔba | lɔɔbɔ | lɔɔbɔ |
| 42. | bad | Sw 165 | bɔptinɛ | bɔptinɛ | bɔptilɛ |
| 43. | straight | Sw 168 | eera | eerɔ | eerɔ |
| 44. | push | Sw 175 | jarkjɔ | jaarikjɔ | jaarigjɔ |
| 45. | throw | Sw 176 | bisikjɔ | bisigjɔ | bisigjɔ |
| 46. | fall | Sw 183 | mątikjɔ | mątigjɔ | mątigjɔ |
| 47. | fill | Sw 184 | hįįsikjɔ | hįįsigjɔ | hįįsigjɔ |
| 48. | think | Sw 185 | mɔkikjɔ | mɔkigjɔ | mɔkikjɔ |
| 49. | blow | Sw 190 | ulkjɔ | ulkjɔ/ulikjɔ | uligjɔ |
| 50. | I saw you (SG) | Sw S 72 | mį gbɛnmɔ | mį gbɛnįmɔ | mį gbɛnįmɔ |
| 51. | I saw him | Sw S 73 | mį gbɛnge | mį gbɛnįge | mį gbɛnįge |
| 52. | he was called | Sw S 97 | hi elik ela | hi elig elɔ | hi elig elɔ |
| 53. | he lies down | T 73 | kosa | kusɔ | kusɔ |
| 54. | he descends | T 118 | tiiza | tiizɔ | tiizi |
| 55. | he arrives | T 129 | tuura | tuurɔ/mųzɔ | mųzi |
| 56. | seeing | T 87 | gbɛŋko | gbɛnįko | gbɛnįko |
| 57. | stay! | T 90 | kɔmmɔ | kɔmbimɔ | kɔmbimɔ |
| 58. | arrive | T 98 | tuurkjɔ | tuurikjɔ | tuurikjɔ |
| 59. | multiple of ten | T 31 | dumble | dumbeli | dumbili |
| 60. | I (EM QUOT) | T 145 | bee | bee | bii |
| 61. | thing | T 125 | hinɛ | hinɛ | hɛnɛ |
| 62. | pray | T 9 | zɔb | zɔb | zɔb |
| 63. | first | T 28 | kɛti | kete/kɛnɛ | kɛnɛ |
| 64. | in the middle | T 148 | tɛɛs du | tees du | tee du |
| 65. | not straight | T 141 | gbɛɛti | gbeeti | gbeeti |
| 66. | do something else | T 143 | zɛj̃ | zej | zɛɛj̃ |
| 67. | wash (face) | T 4 | ul | ur | ul |
| 68. | theft | T 53 | luulɛ | luurɛ | luurɛ |
| 69. | soil | T 66 | wąąsɛ | wiisɛ | wiiko |
| 70. | firewood | T 55 | ranto | rɛnto | lɛnto |

Some of the differences shown in the above chart are regular, others are less so or not at all.

**Regular divergencies between the dialects.** While Poli and mountain speakers often use *g* in the infinitive (45), those of Markɛ consistently use *k* (45). See also (20)–(23), (34), (44), and (46)–(49). In this regard, the mountain dialect sometimes groups with Poli and sometimes with Markɛ.

# Phonological Description of Doyayo

The nominoverbal ending -ɔ of the Poli and mountain dialects regularly changes to -a in Markɛ. See (38)–(41), (43), and (53)–(55). This same ending sometimes changes to -i in mountain speech (see (54)–(55)).

Verbs of the limited group bearing a CV pattern in the aorist have a long vowel in the infinitive in the Markɛ dialect (see (16)–(18)). Note that the verb 'swim' in (19), having a CVC pattern in the aorist, does not lengthen its vowel in Markɛ.

**More or less characteristic divergencies** Vowels that are nasal in Poli and mountain speech are often oral in Markɛ, which has less nasalization than the other dialects. See (10), (11), (14), (24), (28), (35), (37), (62), and (69).

Markɛ seems to have a greater predilection for consonant clusters than the other two dialects, making less use of the epenthetic vowel. See (13), (44), (50), (51), (56)–(59).

The Markɛ dialect often but not always replaces r with l, as in (12), (67), and (68). Note, however, that in (70), it is the mountain dialect that gives preference to the l.

**Irregular divergencies.** There are other differences only applying to isolated cases, as in (3), (4), (19), (34), (35), etc.

## Appendix B

**Doyayo orthography**

| Phoneme | p | t | k | kp | b | d | g | gb | ɓ | ɗ | f | s | h | v | s | m | n | ŋ | l | r | w | j |
|---|---|---|---|---|---|---|---|---|---|---|---|---|---|---|---|---|---|---|---|---|---|---|
| Spelling | p | t | k | kp | b | d | g | gb | ɓ | ɗ | f | s | h | v | s | m | n | ng | l | r | w | j |

| | | | | | | | |
|---|---|---|---|---|---|---|---|
| Phoneme | i | e | ɛ | a | ɔ | o | u |
| Spelling | i | e | ɛ | a | ɔ | o | u |
| Long vowels | i: | e: | ɛ: | a: | ɔ: | o: | u: |
| Spelling | ii | ee | ɛɛ | aa | ɔɔ | oo | uu |
| Short nasal vowels | ĩ | | ɛ̃ | ã | ɔ̃ | | ũ |
| Spelling | i̧ | | ɛ̧ | a̧ | ɔ̧ | | u̧ |
| Long nasal vowels | ĩ: | | ɛ̃: | ã: | ɔ̃: | | ũ: |
| Spelling | i̧i̧ | | ɛ̧ɛ̧ | a̧a̧ | ɔ̧ɔ̧ | | u̧u̧ |

| Level tones | 1 | 2 | 3 | 4 |
|---|---|---|---|---|
| Spelling | ´ | - | ǀ | ` |

The above orthography has been developed in conformity with the guidelines set up at the C.E.R.E.L.T.R.A. orthography conference held in Yaoundé, Cameroon, in March 1979. The guidelines were designed to promote uniformity in the transcription of the many languages of Cameroon and thus serve the interests of national unity while at the same time facilitating the job of linguists and others making the transition between two or more languages. The decision was opportune, because just around that time, the computer became a general commodity. It made the typewriter with all its limitations obsolete, so that our original orthography, which had incorporated some digraphs (reducing readability) could be discarded without regret.

There is minimal tone representation in the orthography now being employed, by the express wish of the readers, who prefer to rely on the context wherever possible rather than on diacritic markings. Tone is marked primarily on minimal pairs (that is, on the less frequent member of the set; as, for example, on *wáát* 'kingdom' and not on *wāāt* 'children'; and on *wāāl* 'skull hut' rather than on *wáál* 'world'. It is also marked on subject pronouns or verbs in a negative or initial subordinate clause, where the immediate context does not provide an adequate clue to the tonal situation. Where a glide occurring on a short vowel has to be marked, only the first element of the glide is represented, as in /mɔ$^1$ kạb$^{21}$ mɛm$^1$lɛl$^{23}$ gɛ$^2$ be$^2$/ *mɔ́ kāb mɛmlɛl gɛ be* 'you didn't take me to a place where there's water'.

## Appendix C

### Doyayo Text

In this short story, every set of three lines includes, at the top, the phonemic transcription, then the spelling, and below that, a word-for-word translation. A free translation is given after the story.

kɔ$^{23}$ba$^1$  hi$^1$   rɔ$^2$ma$^{23}$
kɔba      hi    rɔma
cock      and   hare

1. rɔ$^2$ma$^{23}$ ra:$^{23}$    kɔ$^{23}$ba$^1$ a$^1$   pa$^1$bi$^1$  wɛ$^1$  hag$^3$ sum$^3$lɛ$^2$.  2. hi$^3$
   Rɔma      raa       kɔba     a     "Pabi,   wɛ    hag    sumlɛ."         Hi
   hare      heˆsaid   cock     QUOT  "uncle   weˆFUT make   tom-tom."       they

# Phonological Description of Doyayo

rɛ³tn¹nu³    hi¹    kɔ²³ba:¹³   3. hi³   rɛ³kɔ²   4. a¹    jɛ³    wɛ¹   hag³   suml²
retinu    hi    kɔba.     Hi    rekɔ.     A    "Yɛ   wɛ   hag   suml
went^together with cock.    they went.    QUOT "HRT we make tom-tom

a¹    hɛt¹   du:¹³
a     hɛt    du.
LOC grass in.

5. kɔ²³ba¹   gɔ²    hag³   suml²    bɔ:¹³   rɔ²ma²³   hagz³    ɔ²nɛ³   bɔ¹    nɔ:k²tɔ¹nɔ:¹³
Kɔba     gɔ    hag    suml     bɔ,    rɔma     hagz     ɔnɛ    bɔ    nɔɔktɔnɔ;
cock   when made tom-tom that,   hare   he^made his   that quickly^very;

za:²³    a¹    wa.r¹   gɛ:¹³   6. za:²³    6a:⁴    a¹    kpuk³   kpuk³   ụ⁴hụ¹³hụ¹
zaa     a    waar   ge.     Zaa    6aa    a    "Kpuk   kpuk,   ụhụhụ;
he^came LOC chief SPEC.   he^came he^beat CIT "capook capook oohoohoo;

kpuk³   kpuk³   ụ⁴hụ¹³hụ¹    7. rɔ²ma²³   geps²    ɔ²nɛ³   bɔ¹    rɔb¹tɔ¹nɔ¹   gɛ:²³
kpuk    kpuk    ụhụhụ."      Rɔma    gēbs    ɔnɛ    bɔ    rɔbtɔnɔ    gɛ.
capook capook oohoohoo."   hare   didn't^fix his   that well^very not.

8. kɔ²³ba¹   geps⁴    ɔ²nɛ³   bɔ¹    rɔb¹tɔ¹nɔ:¹³   za:²³    kụ:²³   du¹   6a:⁴    gɔ:¹³
Kɔba    gèbs    ɔnɛ    bɔ    rɔbtɔnɔ;    zaa    kụụ   du   6aa    gɔ:
cock    he^fixed his   that well^very;   he^came after in   he^beat then:

zɛ¹leŋ¹   zɛ²leŋ²   zɛ³leŋ³   mi¹   ti:³    tar²jɔ²   zɛ¹leŋ¹   zɛ²leŋ²   zɛ³leŋ³   zɛ⁴leŋ⁴   zɛ³leŋ³
"Zɛleŋ   zeleŋ   zeleŋ,   mi    tii    taryɔ,    zeleŋ    zeleŋ;    zeleŋ   zeleŋ   zeleŋ
"zeleng zeleng zeleng, I^FUT descend Fulani, zeleng, zeleng; zeleng zeleng zeleng

zɛ⁴leŋ⁴   mi¹    9. ti:³    tar²jɔ²   zɛ³leŋ³
zeleŋ,   mi     tii    taryɔ,    zeleŋ."
zeleng, I^FUT   descend Fulani, zeleng."

10. wa.r¹   bɔ¹   lag³     gɔ¹   la³bɔ:¹³   11. hi³    pub⁴    rɔ²ma²³   gɔ:¹³    12. le:s¹
Waar   bɔ    lag     gɔ   labɔ.     Hi    pub     rɔma     gɔ.      Lees
chief that he^heard so   thus.    they dumped hare   so^then.   food

wɔ¹    sɛw³   hi³   ga:⁴   kɔ²³ba¹   gi¹ja:¹³   13. kok²    wɛ:¹³,   bis¹    wɛ:¹³,   hin¹
wɔ     sɛw    hi    gaa    kɔba     giya.      Kok      wɛ,     bis     wɛ,    hin
those   all    they gave cock   him.      couscous these, sauce these thing

za:¹dɛ³    wɛ¹    sɔm³sɔm³   hi³   ga:⁴    kɔ²³ba¹   gi:¹     sɛw³
zaadɛ     wɛ    sɔmsɔm,    hi    gaa    kɔba     gii     sɛw.
other(PL) these various,   they gave cock   him(EM) all.

14. rɔ²ma²³   gbɛn²     an¹bɔ¹    rɛ¹    a¹    kɔ²³ba¹   gi²   be¹    da:¹rik¹
Rɔma    gbēn     anbɔ    rɛ     a    "Kɔba    gi   be    daarik
hare    when^he^saw like^that SUBCJ QUOT "cock he^is me surpassing

da:¹rɔ¹.   15. jɛ:l⁴      gaps³² ma:³¹
daarɔ."        Yɛɛl       gabs   ma.
RDP"           he^began   fight  and^so.

16. wa.r¹  bɔ¹   kar⁴        dɔj²ɔ³       bɔ¹  ha:¹³ ra:²³  a¹   nɛ¹
    Waar   bo    kar         dɔyɔ         bɔ   ha;   raa    a    "Nɛ
    chief  that  he^mounted  horse^his    that on;   he^said QUOT "you(PL)

ti:³tn¹             bak² jɔ:l²   di¹sɛ³
tiitin              bak  yɔ̧ɔ̧l    disɛ."
descend^together   field behind below."

17. hi³   rek³   hi³    zɛm²³   na:³mi¹  hi³   ja⁴ri⁴ge⁴  a¹  sa̧:l²  du:¹³  18. na:m³¹
    Hi    rek    hi     zɛm     naami    hi    yaarige    a   sa̧a̧l    du.        Naam
    they  went   they   found   panther  they  pushed^it  LOC hole    in.        panther

bɔ¹  dɔts⁴       ma⁴  ga:¹ti¹  a¹   sa̧:l²  du  hɔ:¹³.
bɔ   dɔts        ma   gaati    a    sa̧a̧l    du  hɔ.
that it^sat^INTS so   for^good LOC  hole   in  over^there.

N.B. The lengthening of the vowel in particles in pause-group final position is fully automatic and therefore not reflected in the spelling.

### The cock and the hare

The hare said to the cock, "Uncle, let's go and make some tom-toms." They went off together. (They left.) The hare said, "Let's make tom-toms out in the bush."

While the cock was busy making his tom-tom, the hare quickly made his. He came to the chief and played, "Pook, pook, oo-hoohoo; pook, pook, oo-hoohoo." The hare hadn't made his drum very well.

The cock made his very well. He came afterwards and played, "Zeleng, zeleng, zeleng, I will go down to the Fulani, zeleng, zeleng. Zeleng, zeleng, zeleng, zeleng, I will go down to the Fulani, zeleng."

This is what the chief heard; and so they dismissed the hare. All the prepared food they gave to the cock. The various dishes of couscous, the sauces, and all the many other foods, all went to the cock.

When the hare saw this, he thought, "The cock is surpassing me." He started picking a fight.

The chief mounted his horse and said, "Go down to the end of the field."

They went and found the panther there. They pushed it into a hole. And the panther stayed in that hole forever.

## References

Barley, Nigel. 1983. Symbolic structures: An exploration of the culture of the Dowayos. Cambridge: CUP.

Baudelaire. 1944. La numération de 1 à 10 dans les dialectes. Habé de Garona, Guider-Poli, et Rey-Bouba. BSEC 5:25–300.

Bohnhoff, Lee E. Dooyaayo grammar. ms.

────── and Charles H. Kraft. n.d. An initial comparison of Duru, Duupa and Doyayo (Namshi). ms.

Cowan, George M. 1948. Mazateco whistle speech. Language 24:280–86.

Greenberg, Joseph H. 1963. The languages of Africa. The Hague: Mouton.

Hyman, Larry M. 1972. Nasals and nasalization in Kwa. Studies in African Linguistics 3(2).

Tessmann, Günther. 1932. Die Völker und Sprachen Kameruns. Sonderabdruck aus Petermanns Mitteilungen Doppelhefte 5/6, 7/8. Gotha: Justus Perthes.

Westerman, Diedrich and Margaret A. Bryan. 1952. Languages of West Africa. Handbook of African languages. London: Oxford University Press.

Wiering, Elisabeth. 1974. The indicative verb in Doowaayaayo. Linguistics 124:33–55.

# The Indicative Verb in Doyayo[1]

### Elisabeth Wiering

The purpose of this paper is to examine the composition and structure of the verb word that functions as head of the verbal phrase in the affirmative indicative mood in Doowaayaayɔ.[2] The investigation was undertaken primarily to determine restrictions on the occurrence of suffixes, rules for the insertion of a vowel epenthesis, and changes in the tonal pattern resulting from suffixation.

The verb word at the head of the verbal phrase may be a simple root in its minimal form, or it may be a stem with one or more modificational suffixes followed by a personal pronoun or a tense marker. When both an object pronoun and a tense marker are present, an overload mechanism frontshifts the pronoun onto a preceding auxiliary. The maximum expansions of the verb that have been observed in unelicited data include (after the root) (1) two modificational suffixes with one personal pronoun, (2) one modificational suffix with two personal pronouns, or (3) one modificational suffix with one tense marker.

---

[1] Updated version of "The Indicative Verb in Doowaayaayɔ" published in Linguistics 124, March 15, 1976.

[2] This paper was produced at a workshop of the Institute of Linguistics held in Miango, Nigeria, from October to December, 1972, under the direction of Dr. Joseph E. Grimes, and partially supported by National Science Foundation grant GS–3180A–1. I wish to express my appreciation to Dr. Grimes for his many helpful suggestions both in the analysis of the data and in the preparation of the manuscript.

## 1 Tense and mode

The signalling system of the tenses and modes presents a rather diversified picture in Doowaayaayɔ. The aorist and the remote future tenses are marked only by tone, the proximate and present tense by tone plus a verbal suffix, and the various modes by tone plus tense plus a clause-initial particle. A brief discussion of the tenses and modes follows.

**Aorist.** The aorist tense has a completive and a gnomic aspect. It refers to an action, process, or state completed or existing in the past (with or without repercussions in the present) on the one hand, or regularly taking place or existing in the present on the other. In this tense, the subject pronoun and the verb maintain their base of lexical tones and the third-person singular is a zero morpheme:[3] $mi^3$ $kpe^4lɔ^4$ 'I pour(ed)', $kpe^4lɔ^4$ 'he pours (poured)', $mi^3$ $tɔɔ^3$ $tɔ^1$ 'I grew (am) big', $tɔɔ^3$ $tɔ^1$ 'he grew (is) big'.

**Remote Future.** The remote future tense refers to an action, process, or state that is to be performed, to happen, or to exist in the not immediate future. This tense is marked by a high tone on the subject pronoun. The stem normally maintains its lexical tone: $mi^1$ $kpe^4lɔ^4$ 'I will pour', $gi^1kpe^4lɔ^4$ 'he will pour', $mi^1$ $tɔɔ^3tɔ^1$ 'I will grow (be) big', $gi^1$ $tɔɔ^3tɔ^1$ 'he will grow (be) big'. In the case of tone $^{23}$ verbs like $il^{23}$ 'be sticky', however, the tone on the stem changes to $^{13}$: $gi^1$ $i^1lɔ^3$ 'it will be sticky'. When used in conjunction with second-person singular $mɔ$ or second-person plural $nɛ$, the remote future also functions as an indirect imperative. Thus, the form $mɔ^1$ $kpe^4lɔ^4$ can mean either 'you will pour' or 'pour!'. Any imperative that is non-initial in a sentence takes the indirect form: $re^3k$-$u^1$-$mɔ^1$ $mɔ^1$ $kam$-$s^3$ $gɔn^{23}$ $be^1$, $gi^1$ $rek^3$ $gi^1$ $goo^{13}$ $ɓɛ^1$ (go-EP-you you-FUT take-BEN mother-in-law my, she-FUT go she-FUT try again) 'Go (direct) take (indirect) it to my mother-in-law, let her go (indirect) and try (indirect) again.'

**Present.** This tense refers to an action or process taking place at the moment of speaking. The present is characterized by the subject pronoun maintaining its lexical tone, the auxiliary $gi^2$ being optionally present, and the tone of the stem changing to high. The present tense suffix -$ko^3$ (with

---

[3]For details about the phonemes of Poli Tɛɛrɛ Doowaayaayo see the previous article.

# The Indicative Verb in Doyayo

allomorphs -$k^1$, -$g^1$, -$ko^1$, -$go^1$, -$ko^3$, and -$go^3$)[4] s, or z, except for $dund^3$ 'get up', $hɛd^3$ 'sweep', and $baks^1$ 'allign', and two-syllable stems ending in a modificational suffix. Two other irregular verbs that take only g are $maat^1$ 'deceive', and $rek^3$ 'go' in its use with epenthesis. All other verbs have a free choice between k and g. is added to the verb stem, and the stem is optionally repeated (unless a noun phrase precedes the verb head) at the end of the clause in the intermediate form described in the next §, but with tone 1: $mi^3$ ($gi^2$) $kpel$-$k^1$ $mɛm^1$ ($kpe^1lɔ^1$) (I (be) pour-PRES water (pour-intermediate) 'I am pouring water', $mi^3$ ($gi^2$) $luk^1$ $hɛ^1d$-$i^1$-$go^3$ (I (be) house sweep-EP-PRES) 'I am sweeping house', $mi^3$ ($gi^2$) $tɔɔ$-$k^1$ $tɔ^1$ or $mi^3$ $gi^2$ $tɔɔ^1$-$ko^1$ 'I am growing'. When the proximate and the present are identical in their surface structure, the context of the discourse in which they occur provides the clue for distinguishing them. For example, in a subordinate clause, where the tone of the subject pronoun perturbs to high if it is not already high tone.

**Proximate.** This tense refers to an action, process, or state that is to come about in the immediate future, or that will be going on when something else intervenes(-ed). It is characterized by the addition of the suffix -ko (with allomorphs -$k^1$, -$g^1$, -$ko^1$, -$go^1$, -$ko^3$, and -$go^3$) to the verb stem, the tone of the stem thereby changing to high. The subject pronoun takes high tone and the auxiliary $gi^2$ 'be' is optionally added between the pronoun and the verb: $mi^1$ ($gi^2$) $kpel^1$-$ko^1$ 'I am going to pour', $mɛm^1$ $bɔ^1$ $gi^1$ ($gi^2$) $saa^1$-$ko^1$ (water DEM it will-be get-hot-PROX) 'the water is going to get hot'.

---

[4]The distribution of the allomorphs of the proximate/present suffix -ko is according to the following rules: First, -k and -g occur only clause medially, and all other allomorphs clause finally, except in the case of a two-syllable stem ending in a modificational suffix. The latter always takes -$ko^3$ or -$go^3$: $i^1n$-$i$-$l^1$-$ko^3$ 'refusing several things', $ha^1tir^1$-$go^3$ 'mutilating'. Secondly, in clause-final position -$ko^3$ or -$go^3$ is used when the verb is preceded by the negative auxiliary $taa^{13}$ or by a noun phrase, otherwise -$ko^1$ or -$go^1$ is used. Thirdly, the choice between the allomorphs involving k and those involving g is made on the basis of the syllable pattern of the verb. Only k is permitted with CV and (C)VV roots and with roots and stems patterning (C)VC where the final consonant is not t, d, k, s, or z, except irregular $zaŋ^1$ 'read', $gben^3$ 'see', and $el^4$ 'call'. Three other irregular roots that take only k are $haam^1$ 'yawn', $baar^4$ 'begin', and $zagl^1$ 'crawl'. Only g is permitted with (C)VC and (C)VCC roots and stems ending in d, k, s, or z, except for $dund^3$ 'get up', $hɛd^3$ 'sweep', and $baks^1$ 'align', and two-syllable stems ending in a modificational suffix. Two other irregular verbs that take only g are $maat^1$ 'deceive', and $rek^3$ 'go' in its use with epenthesis. All other verbs have a free choice between k and g.

**Mode.** The various modes, with the exception of the negative and imperative (described briefly in §9), are built on one of the above patterns. Each involves a clause- or sentence-level modal or adverbial element. They are summarized briefly in (1).

(1)  Mode                    Preceding   Construction              Clause-final
                              element     corresponding to          element
  Dependent
  a. conditional 1            $an^1$      aorist
  b. conditional 2            $a^4$       aorist negative
  c. conditional 3            $gɔ^2$      proximate (pronoun¹)
  d. conditional 4            $yɔ^1$      proximate (pronoun¹)
  e. anterior aorist          $(yɔ^1)$    aorist negative
  f. anterior future          $gɔ^2$      future
  g. temporal                             aorist negative           $rɛ^1$
  h. subjunctive              $an^1$      future

  Independent
  i. consequential            $yɔ^1$      aorist (pronoun³)
  j. normative                $gɔ^2$      aorist

a. $an^1$ $wɛ^3$ $mɛɛ^3$ $yɔ^2$ $yɔ^1$ $wɛ^3$ $tɔ^2$ $gɛɛ^{23}$
   if   we   knew  INTS  RES  we   eat  not
   If we had known, we wouldn't have eaten (it).

b. $a^4$ $be^1$ $aas^2$ $yɔ^1$ $mɔ^3$ $tuu^4$ $tu^1$
   if  I  open  RES  you  go^out  [RDP]
   If I open it, you will go out.

c. $gɔ^2$ $nɛ^1$ $yɛɛ$-$k^1$ $ri^1$ $nɛ^1$ $yɛɛ^1$-$ko^3$ $bee^1$ $be^3$
   when  you^PL  judge-PROX  how  you  judge-PROX  I^EM  I
   $ree^{31}$-$kɔ^1$
   left-LGTH
   If that's the way you're going to argue the matter, I'm leaving.

d. $yɔ^1$ $mɔ^1$ $gi^2$ $re$-$k^1$ $ma^3$ $mɔ^3$ $re$-$k^1$ $rii^{13}$
   when  you  be  go-PROX  DEIC  you  go-PROX  how
   If you really think you're going then, how are you going?

e. $rek^2$ $gi^1$ $gbɔŋ^3$-$ge^1$ $nis^2$ $tɔ^1$ $wɛɛ^3$ $la^3gɔ^3$ $a^1$
   had^gone  he^will  kill-him  wife^his  returned  heard  that
   When he had gone to kill him, his wife heard that...

# The Indicative Verb in Doyayo

f.  *gɔ² mɔ¹ re³-kɔ² mi¹ bḭḭ¹³ lɛɛ¹tre³ mii¹³*
    when you^FUT go-I2    I^FUT write letter my
    When you have gone, I will write my letter.

g.  *lug² rɛ¹ pir² gɛɛ²³*
    had^planted when sprouted not
    When he planted it, it didn't sprout.

h.  *gi² an¹ mɔ¹ kɛ¹mɔ³*
    be that you^will understand
    It is necessary that you understand.

i.  *yɔ¹ mi³ tuu² gɛɛ²³*
    RES I went^out not
    I won't (wouldn't) go out.

j.  *gɔ² hi³ yaa⁴ bis¹ duu¹³*
    HAB they send sauce in
    It is put in sauce.

## 2 Lengthening and elision

Before going into the internal composition of verb words, it needs to be pointed out that most verb words in Doowaayaa̰yɔ have several forms depending on their position in an utterance. There may be from one to three intermediate clause-final forms, differing one from another only as to the tone of the final syllable. Any one of these can be used to obtain the short clause-medial form or the lengthened utterance-final form. The difference between the intermediate forms is not immediately apparent, though it can be observed that the second and third alternatives, call them I2 and I3, tend to pattern closer to the end of an utterance than I1: *re³k-ɔ³*, *rek³ lu³g-ɔ²* 'he went (I1), went (short) planted (I2)'.

Example (2) shows that simple rules may be stated for shortening and lengthening a verb word. The shortened form is obtained from one of the intermediate forms by dropping the final vowel or, in the case of the reduplicating verbs, the reduplicated element. The tone of the dropped vowel is lost unless it is ³ preceded by ², as in *i²l-ɔ³*, *il²³* 'be sticky'. In this case, the tone ³ joins the tone of the first syllable to make a ²³ glide. If the dropping of the vowel of the intermediate form would yield a short form ending in a doubled consonant or a bilabial or velar nasal plus a homorganic (epenthetic) stop, the last consonant is dropped as well. Thus, for the intermediate forms $dɔ-y^1-y-ɔ^3$, $ɛm^4-b-ɔ^2$, and $zaŋ^1-g-ɔ^3$, we obtain $dɔ-y^1$, $ɛm^4$, and $zaŋ^1$ respectively.

The lengthened form of the verb word is obtained by lengthening and upgliding to the high vowel of the first syllable of the intermediate form, then changing the tone of the remaining syllables to high. When the tone of the first syllable is already high, as in $haa^1m-ɔ^3$, an upglide is obtained by beginning at level $^2$: $haa^{21}m-ɔ^1$.

(2)

| | Short | Intermediate 1 2 3 | Long | Gloss |
|---|---|---|---|---|
| a. | $sɛɛ^1b-i-k^1$ | $sɛɛ^1b-i^1-ko^3$ | | 'he is approaching' |
| b. | $e^4l-i-g^4$ | $e^4l-i^4-ge^4$ | | 'he called him' |
| c. | $aa^{23}$ | $aa^{23}\ a^1$ | | 'it is wide' |
| d. | $gɔ^2$ | $gɔ^2\ gɔ^1$ | | 'he made' |
| e. | $haam^1$ | $haa^1m-ɔ^3$ | $haa^{21}m-ɔ^1$ | 'he yawned' |
| f. | $dɔ-y^1$ | $dɔ-y^1-y-ɔ^3$ | $dɔɔ-y^{21}-y-ɔ^1$ | 'he kicked' |
| g. | $zaŋ^1$ | $zaŋ^1-g-ɔ^3$ | $zaaŋ^{21}-g-ɔ^1$ | 'he read' |
| h. | $kad-z^{41}$ | $kad^{41}-z-ɔ^3$ | $kaad^{41}-z-ɔ^1$ | 'he rolled up' |
| i. | $ka^4t-i-l^1$ | $ka^4t-i^1-lo^3$ | $kaa^{41}t-i^1-lo^1$ | 'he rolled up several things' |
| j. | $sɔɔ^3t-i-n^1$ | $sɔɔ^3t-i^1-nu^3$ | $sɔɔ^3t-i^1-nu^1$ | 'he excited with' |
| k. | $ɛm^4$ | $ɛm^4-b-ɔ^4$, $ɛm^4-b-ɔ^2$ | $ɛɛm^{41}-b-ɔ^1$ | 'he walked' |
| l. | $fɔb^4$ | $fɔb^4-ɔ^4$, $fɔ^4b-ɔ^2$ | $fɔɔ^{41}b-ɔ^1$ | 'he followed' |
| m. | $fɔb-z^4$ | $fɔb^4-z-ɔ^4$, $fɔb^4-z-ɔ^2$ | $fɔɔb^{41}-z-ɔ^1$ | 'he followed quickly' |
| n. | $dir^3$ | $di^3r-ɔ^3$, $di^3r-ɔ^2$ | $dii^{31}r-ɔ^1$ | 'he pulled' |
| o. | $sɛp-t^3$ | $sɛp^3-t-ɔ^3$, $sɛp-t-ɔ^2$ | $sɛɛp^{31}-t-ɔ^1$ | 'he approached several times' |
| p. | $il^{23}$ | $i^2l-ɔ^3$, $i^{23}l-ɔ^2$, $i^{23}l-ɔ^1$ | $ii^{231}l-ɔ^1$ | 'it is sticky' |

(2) shows that suffixation, verb type (reduplicating vs. nonreduplicating verbs), and tone play a part in determining how many forms a verb word may have. We may summarize the relationship as follows:

— any verb suffixed with a tense marker (present or proximate, as (a)) or a personal pronoun (b) and any open-syllable reduplicating verb (c and d) has two forms only, the longer of which functions in both clause- and utterance-final position.

— any verb with high tone (e, f, and g) or an upglide to high (h) on the first syllable, and any verb containing a second syllable with a vowel epenthesis (i and j) has a short form, a long form, and one intermediate form.

— any nonreduplicating verb stem with low tone or mid tone and no epenthetic vowel (k–o) has a short form, a long form, and two intermediate forms.

# The Indicative Verb in Doyayo

— any nonreduplicating verb stem carrying the tonal sequence mid-high mid (p) has a short form, a lengthened form, and three intermediate forms.

When one considers the behavior of mid-high tone within the tone system, where it often neutralizes contrasts,[5] one is inclined to regard it as a sort of neutral tone. This would explain the use of mid-high in the I2 form, as no contrast is needed in the final syllable. Perhaps high tone in the I3 form can be regarded as a compensation for the preceding downglide.

## 3 The verb root

The initial element of any verb word in Doowaayąąyo is the verb root or stem. This forms the nucleus to which various suffixes may optionally be added. The ROOT is defined as the minimal meaningful nuclear segment of the verb word. A STEM is a root together with one or more modificational suffixes that have become closely associated with the root in common usage. The verb $gb\varepsilon\varepsilon^3$ 'cut' has given rise to two stems, $gb\varepsilon\varepsilon\text{-}r^3$ (cut-INTS) 'slaughter' and $gb\varepsilon\varepsilon\text{-}l^3$ (cut-DIST) 'cut up', which are in common use. The first suffix acts like a derivational suffix, giving a stem. Other modificational suffixes can be added to that derived stem: $gb\varepsilon\varepsilon^3\text{-}r\text{-}i\text{-}l^1$ (cut-INTS-EP-DIST) 'slaughter several animals' and $gb\varepsilon\varepsilon\text{-}l\text{-}s^3$ (cut-DIST-BEN) 'cut up for someone'.

While stems may attain two syllables even in their shortened form, roots are always monosyllabic. There is a small number of stems which appear not to be reducible to a monosyllabic root, but their structure is so exactly parallel to that of a root plus suffix that they can be analyzed as stems containing a deponent root: $paa^1sin^1$ (*$paa^1$ -s CAUS -i EP -n ACC) 'iron (clothes)', $h\underline{a}^3tir^1$ (*$ham^3$ or *$h\underline{a}^3$ -t ITER -i EP -r INTS) 'ruin, mutilate'.

Verb roots and stems may be broadly divided into two categories, reduplicating or vowel-final (with the syllable patterns $CV^2$ and $(C)VV^{23/2/4}$) and nonreduplicating or consonant-final (with the syllable patterns (C)VC, (C)VVC, and (C)VCC(C)). The nonreduplicating verbs are characterized by an -ɔ suffix in their intermediate form, as $ɓb^4$, $ɓ^4b\text{-}ɔ^4$ 'follow'. The reduplicating verbs, however, cannot take this suffix, for they already end in a vowel and no uninterrupted sequence of two distinct vowels is permitted within a word. Instead, the root itself is repeated with

---

[5]See the following article for further discussion on tone patterns.

a short vowel and high tone in the repeated element: $le^2$, $le^2$-$le^1$ 'eat'; $gaa^{23}$, $gaa^{23}$-$ga^1$ 'be clear'.

A further classification by tones and syllable patterns may be made of the nonreduplicating roots and monosyllabic complex stems, none of which reduplicate because their suffixes are consonantal. The majority of nonreduplicating stems carry tone $^3$, tone $^4$, or tone $^{23}$. All the nonreduplicating syllable patterns, (C)VC, (C)VCC, and (C)VCC(C)C, are found in tone $^3$ and tone $^4$ verbs, as well as in a small class of tone $^1$ verbs. Tone $^{23}$ verbs have only one nonreduplicating pattern, (C)VC. As for other nonreduplicating stems, the only ones with an upglide are $aan^{31}$ and $yaan^{31}$, both meaning 'forbid'. All other upglides to $^1$ in a monosyllabic stem result from suffixation, as in $kem$-$d^{231}$ (hear-PREPC) 'already heard'. The relationship between tones and syllable patterns is summarized in (3).

(3)                       Reduplicating

| Tone | 1 | 2 | 3 | 4 | 23 | 31 |
|---|---|---|---|---|---|---|
| | — | CV | (C)VV | (C)VV | (C)VV | — |

Nonreduplicating

| Tone | 1 | 2 | 3 | 4 | 23 | 31 | 41 |
|---|---|---|---|---|---|---|---|
| | (C)VC | — | (C)VC | (C)VC | (C)VC | — | — |
| | (C)VVC | — | (C)VVC | (C)VVC | — | (C)VVC | (C)VVC |
| | (C)VCC(C) | — | (C)VCC | (C)VCC | — | — | (C)VCC(C) |

## 4 Modificational suffixes

Doowaayąąyɔ has a set of eleven suffixes used to modify the verb in some way. They behave like derivational affixes in some cases, but in others they merely modify the meaning of the root or stem without affecting its privileges of occurrence. They are -$m$ augmentative, -$l$ distributive, -$t$ iterative, -$r$ intensive, -$s$ causative, -$s$ benefactive, -$n$ accessory, -$tn$ associative, -$d$ prepunctive, -$z$ immediate, and -$y$ resultative.

There is some overlap of meaning among the first three suffixes, -$m$, -$l$, and -$t$. In some cases, when one of the three has been used to form a stem with a specialized meaning that is normally associated with one of the others, there can be a complete interchange of meaning. Thus, -$l$ with the stem $mib$-$r^4$ 'open' has idiomatically taken on the iterative meaning usually associated with -$t$: $mib^4$-$r$-$i$-$l^1$ 'open several times'; but with that stem -$t$ assumes the distributive meaning usually attributed to -$l$: $mib$-$r$-$t^4$ 'open

## The Indicative Verb in Doyayo

several things'. However, a basic area of meaning can be designated for each suffix that characterizes its nonidiomatic use.

**Augmentative** *-m* carries primarily the connotation of plurality, signalling the involvement of several objects or patients as in (4).

(4)  εε³       'sing'       εε-m³       'sing (many songs)'
     tɔɔ³      'grow'       tɔɔ-m³      '(several things or people) grow'
     haa³      'be sour'    haa-m³      '(several things) are sour'

With verbs of motion *-m* functions as iterative as in (5).

(5)  wεε³      'return'     wεε-m³      'return several times'

Phonological restrictions (/m/ must be initial in any consonant cluster in which it occurs) and the fact that augmentative *-m* placed after an epenthetic vowel would be confused with the clause-medial form of the first- and second-person singular suffix, *-m*, combine to require that augmentative *-m* always be suffixed directly to the root of the verb. It is never joined to a verb ending in *m*, or *ŋ*, or to a consonant cluster. When added to a root ending in a single consonant, it either occasions the removal of the consonant or, in the case of final *s*, interchanges with it as in (6)

(6)  εr³       'ask'        ε-m³        'ask (many questions)'
     zįįb³     'be long'    zįį-m³      '(several things) are long'
     tus³      'spit'       tu-m-s³     'spit out (several things)'

When added to one of the CV² verbs, augmentative *-m* brings about both the lengthening of the vowel and a change of tone, resulting in CVVm³ as in (7).

(7)  yɔ²       'drink'      yɔɔ-m³      'drink (many drinks)'

There is one exception to the lengthening rule, however, in (8).

(8)  gɔ²       'make, do'   gɔ-m¹       'do (many things)'

**The distributive suffix** *-l* has a locative and a temporal connotation, as well as involving the notion of plurality. It indicates that the action, process, or state in question affects several objects or patients in several places or over a period of time. The broadness of its meaning may explain why this suffix in contrast to all others often occurs twice on the same stem as seen in (9).

(9)  εε³      'sing'        εε-m-l¹      'sing several songs (-m) over a
                                          period of time (-l)'
     dak³     'sift'        da³k-i-l¹    'sift several kinds of flour'
                            dak³-l-i-l¹  'sift several kinds of flour several
                                          times each (over a period of time)'
     mɔk⁴     'think'       mɔ⁴k-i-l¹    'think day after day'
     her³     'choose'      he-l³        'choose a little here, a little there'
     tɔɔ³     'grow'        tɔɔ-l³       '(several things/people) grow'

Sometimes *-l* confers a derogatory meaning to the verb, as illustrated in (10).

(10) bɟɟ²³    'write'       bɟɟ-l²³      'scrawl'
     ɓuu²³    'spread out'  ɓuu-l²³      'spread out helter skelter'

**Iterative** *-t* normally refers to an action being repeated several times as in (11).

(11) baa⁴    'sew'          baa-t⁴       'sew several times'
     aam³    'suck'         aam-t³       'suck several times'
     kar⁴    'climb'        ka-t⁴        'climb several times'

In its idiomatic use, however, it may assume a wide variety of other meanings shown in (12).

(12) mɔk⁴    'think'        mɔk-t⁴       'think all day long'
     ɓuu²³   'spread out'   ɓuu-t²³      'spread out (several mats)'
     her³    'choose'       he-t³        'choose many out of one place'
     fɔb⁴    'follow'       fɔp-t⁴       'follow fast and furiously'

In process verbs the iterative meaning is often accompanied by a weakening of the sense of the verb as in (13).

(13) tɔr²³   'starve'       tɔ-t²³       'almost starve several times'

Similarly, a diminutive connotation is noted in the stative verbs, but the iterative meaning gives way to a distributive one as in (14).

(14) haa³    'be sour'      haa-t³       '(several things) are a little sour'
     sa̠a̠³   'be hot'       sa̠a̠-t³      '(several things) are warm'

# The Indicative Verb in Doyayo

**Intensive -r** refers to an action being done completely, perfectly, or forcefully, or to a process or state that is extremely advanced or surpasses all others as in (15).

(15) baa⁴ 'pierce'     baa-r⁴ 'pierce completely'
     ɓaa³ 'beat'       ɓaa-r³ 'beat (a dog) to death'
     zaŋ¹ 'read'       zaŋ-r¹ 'read all'
     wɔm³ 'be old'     wɔm-r³ 'be excessively old (and frail)'

Intensive -r rarely occurs with roots or stems ending in an alveolar stop or sibilant, because the prepunctive suffix -d, unlimited in its distribution, is realized as r after these sounds. The two forms would thus be easily confused. One exception is luk³-t-i-r¹ (plant-ITER-EP-INTS/PREPC), which can be interpreted as either 'plant all several times' or 'already planted several times'. Sometimes -r has a special idiomatic meaning, as in (16).

(16) zɛm²³ 'find'      zɛm-r³ 'translate'
     fɔb⁴ 'follow'     fɔb-r⁴ 'resemble'

There is also a small group of verbs which, with the addition of -r, reverse their meaning as in (17).

(17) kpɛɛ⁴ 'close (a door)'        kpɛɛ-r⁴ 'open (a door)'
     mipt⁴ 'cover (a pot)'         mib-r⁴  'uncover (a pot)'
     zug²³ 'close up (a hole)'     zug-r³  'open up (a hole)'
     tuu⁴  'go out, leave'         tuu-r⁴  'arrive'
     zeb⁴  'buy'                   zeb-r⁴  'sell'
     lag³  'hear'                  lag-r³  'be deaf'
     gub⁴  'throw away (solids)'   gub-r⁴  'throw away (liquids)'

The only tone change associated with the -r suffix is that of ²³ in a consonant-final stem, which changes to ³.

**Causative -s** transforms an intransitive root into a transitive stem. Its use is restricted to the stative verbs and to a few verbs of motion. In verbs with the syllable pattern (C)VVC, the addition of an -s or -z suffix brings about the shortening of the vowel as seen in (18).

(18) zɛɛr⁴   'remain'
     zɛr-s⁴  'cause to remain'       (remain-CAUS)
     zɛr-s⁴  'remain for someone'    (remain-BEN)
     zɛrz⁴   'just remained'         (remain-IMM)

When added to a root carrying tone ²³, it changes the tone to ³ or, exceptionally, ⁴ as in (19).

(19)    ɓaa²³    'be tough, hard'    ɓaa-s³    'make tough or hard'
       gul²³    'enter'    gu-s³    'cause to enter'
       mɛɛ²³    'drop (ITR)'    mɛɛ-s⁴    'cause to drop'
       zaa²³    'fall'    zaa-s⁴    'cause to fall'

Causative, like augmentative, with which it is mutually exclusive, always occupies the position next to the root, belonging to the inner layer of suffixes.

**Benefactive** *-s*, suffixed to a verb of action, indicates that something is being done for the benefit of another person as in (20).

(20)    zaŋ¹    'read'    zaŋ-s¹    'read for (or to) someone'
       ɓb⁴    'follow'    ɓp-s⁴    'follow for someone'

In verbs of process or state, someone is still involved as a receptor, or one might say experiencer, but the element of purpose or design commonly associated with benefactives is lacking. Thus, *wɔ³-s-i³-mi³* (die-BEN-EP-me) should not be translated 'he died for me' but 'he died on me (in my presence, and in spite of all my efforts to help him)'. Similarly, *bɛ³-s-i³-mi³* (be-good-BEN-EP-me) does not mean 'it is good for me' or 'he is good to me', but rather 'it (he) appeals to me, I like it (him)'. Benefactive *-s* belongs to the outer or inflectional layer of modificational suffixes. When it occurs immediately following the causative or a root-final *s*, there is an upglide of the preceding syllable to tone ¹ and phonological rules change the first *s* to *t* as seen in (21).

(21)    gaa-s³        +   -s    >    ga-t-s³¹    'brighten for someone'
       be^bright-CAUS       BEN

       tus³   +   -s    >    tu-t-s³¹        'spit for someone'
       spit       BEN

**Accessory** *-n* indicates instrument, conveyance, or accompaniment. In verbs of action it is instrumental as in (22).

(22)    hag-n³    kun¹sig³yɔ²
       make-ACC thread
       He makes it with thread.

## The Indicative Verb in Doyayo

$le\text{-}n^1 \quad naa^2n\varepsilon^3$
eat-ACC hand
He eats with his hands.

In motion verbs it signals either the use of a vehicle or the conveyance of an object as in (23).

(23) $mi^3 \quad re\text{-}n^3 \quad d\mathfrak{o}y^2y\mathfrak{o}^2$
 I go-ACC horse
 I went on horseback.

$loo^4 \quad g\mathfrak{o}\mathfrak{o}^{23} \quad w\mathfrak{o}^1 \quad ka\text{-}n^4 \quad t\varepsilon\varepsilon^1 \quad ha^{13}$
take peanut PL^DEM climb-ACC tree on
He took the peanuts and climbed up a tree with them.

When used with verbs of state or process, the *-n* suffix can indicate accompaniment of two (or more) objects, manner, or non-instigative cause as in (24).

(24) $haa\text{-}n^3 \quad zam^3s\varepsilon^2$
 be^sour-ACC tamarind
 It is sour with tamarind.

 $t\mathfrak{o}\mathfrak{o}n^3 \quad h\mathfrak{o}n^1til^3y\mathfrak{o}^2$
 grow^ACC weakness
 He grew up with weakness.

 $w\mathfrak{o}\text{-}n^3 \quad gum^1s\varepsilon^3$
 die-ACC illness
 He died of an illness.

**Associated suffix *-tn¹*** (*-tin¹* in slow speech) expresses pure accompaniment of persons, and occasionally of objects as well. Though it resembles the combination of iterative *-t* and accessory *-n*, *-tn* is a suffix in its own right and acts as a unit grammatically. The consonants are never separated by another suffix, nor can their order be reserved without a change of meaning. *-tn* always requires a plural subject as seen in (25).

(25) $wi^3 \quad le^1\text{-}tn^1 \quad hi^1 \quad baa^2 \quad mi^1$
 we ate-ASS with father my
 I ate with my father.

*hi³ wɔm³-tn¹u³*
they grow^old-ASS^INTM^form
They grew old together.

*wi³ haa³-tn¹    le²lɔ³*
we be^sour-ASS yesterday
We quarrelled together yesterday.

*lees² wɔ¹    hi³    haa³-tn¹u³*
food PL^DEM they be^sour-ASS^INTM^form
All these foods are sour.

Note that while *wi³ le¹-tn¹* can be translated 'we ate together', *wi³ le-n-t¹* would mean 'we ate several things (using a previously-named instrument)'.

**Prepunctive** *-d¹* indicates that the action, process, or state spoken of in the verb has already (or, in the negative, not yet) come about. It may be applied to any verb root or stem. If the resultant short form is monosyllabic there is an upglide to tone ¹ as in (26).

(26)  *hag³*   'he made'       *hag-d³¹*   'he already made'
      *le²*    'he ate'        *le-d²¹*    'he already ate'
      *wɔr³*   'he died'       *wɔ-d³¹*    'he already died'
      *zoob⁴*  'it is bitter'  *zoob-d⁴¹*  'it is already bitter'

The *-d¹* suffix has an allomorph *-r¹*, used with *i*-epenthesis after roots and other affixes ending in an alveolar stop or sibilant or *k*. The *-d* allomorph is also permitted in this environment as shown in (27), but its use is rare.

(27)  *hɔnt³*            'he roasted'
      *hɔn³t-i-r¹*       'he already roasted' (preferred to *hɔn³t-i-d¹*)

      *yɔɔ-s³*           'he finished'
      be^finished-CAUS
      *yɔɔ³-s-i-r¹*      'he already finished' (preferred to *yɔɔ³-s-i-d¹*)

**Immediate** *-z* has both a temporal and a directional connotation. Like *-d*, it belongs to the outer layer of modificational suffixes and is compatible with any verb. However, the meaning varies according to the type of verb modified. When referring to an action or a motion, *-z* indicates one or a combination of the following: rapid execution, proximity in time to the present moment, something done or begun elsewhere with results directed

## The Indicative Verb in Doyayo

at and shortly to reach the speaker. Rapid execution and proximity to the present apply also to verbs of process as shown in (28).

(28) kam-z³    waa²³    bɔ¹    raa¹    duu¹³
carry-DIR^to speaker child that home^in
He brought the child home.
(in contrast to 'he took the child home')

nɔɔ⁴¹-z-ɔ¹
run-IMM-long^form
He ran quickly.

mi¹ dag-z²  hin¹ za¹  gɛɛ²³
I    get-IMM thing other not
I couldn't get anything just now.

tɔɔ-z³    nɔɔ²ko³
grow-IMM quickly
He certainly has grown up quickly.

In stative verbs, -z still indicates rapidity and proximity to the present moment, but in addition it converts the state into a process as in (29).

(29) haa³  'be sour'           haa-z³  'turn sour (rapidly, recently/soon)'
    saạ³  'be hot, difficult'  saạ-z³  'get hot, become difficult'

**Resultative** *-y¹*, suffixed to verbs of action, yields a passive construction. Normally it is a nonagentive passive, but occasionally the agent or non-instigative cause is expressed, as in (30).

(30) kok²          bɔ¹   le-y¹   a¹ zaạn¹  zaa¹³
thick^porridge DEM eat-RES at person other
The thick porridge was eaten by someone else.

bak² mi¹ dɔɔ¹-s-i-y¹         a¹ nam²    za¹  naan² duu¹³
field my  burn-CAUS-EP-RES at neighbor other hand  in
My field got burned by a neighbor.

dɔɔ¹ mi¹ baa¹-y-i-t¹       kops² dɔŋ²go³
leg  my  pierce-RES-EP-ITER thorn by^reason^of
My leg is pierced by many thorns.

Stative verbs use $-y^1$ to indicate the state that results from the process counterpart of the root, but not, as in the case of $-z$, with any temporal connotation. Rather they carry an idea of completeness or quality as in (31).

(31)  haa³ 'be sour'  haa-y¹  'be (have become) sour'
      bɛr³ 'be beautiful'  bɛ-y¹ ~ bɛ¹r-i-y¹  'be extremely beautiful'

The addition of the $-y^1$ suffix to any stem results in tone ¹ on the entire short form of the stem. The intermediate form, like that of all tone ¹ verbs, has tone ³ on its final syllable. When $-y$ is added to roots of the pattern (C)VC not containing another suffix, the additional changes are noted: final $b$ drops as in (32).

(32)  ɓb⁴ 'follow'  ɓ-y¹-y-ɔ³ 'he is followed (short, INTM)'

Final $\eta$ requires the addition of a transitional $g$ or $n$ as in (33).

(33)  zaŋ¹ 'read'  zaŋ¹-g-i-y¹ ~ zaŋ¹-n-i-y¹ 'it is read (short)'

Final $g$, $r$, $l$, $m$, and $n$ are optionally dropped, but the dropping of the nasals results in the nasalization of the vowel as in (34).

(34)  lug³ 'plant'  lu-y¹ ~ lu¹g-i-y¹  'it is planted'
      kar⁴ 'climb'  ka-y¹ ~ ka¹r-i-y¹  'it is climbed'
      kpel⁴ 'pour'  kpe-y¹ ~ kpe¹l-i-y¹  'it is poured'
      kam³ 'take'  ka̧-y¹ ~ ka¹m-i-y¹  'it is taken'
      gbɛn³ 'see'  gbɛ̧-y¹ ~ gbɛ¹n-i-y¹  'it (he) is seen'

The number of modificational suffixes joined to any one verb is usually quite limited. Though one may elicit forms like baa-r⁴t-i-l-s¹ (pierce-INTS-ITER-EP-DIST-BEN) 'pierce several things through several times for someone' and baa-r¹-d-z-i-y¹ (pierce-INTS-ITER-IMM-EP-RES) 'it was pierced through several times just now', it is unusual for more than one or two of the suffixes to appear on a single stem. In fact, in over 100 pages of text scanned, not one case was noted in which the number of modificational suffixes exceeded two. We conclude, then, that while four suffixes are theoretically possible, usage generally limits the number to two.

None of the suffixes are mutually exclusive except augmentative $-m$ and causative $-s$. These exclude each other by their position, since neither allows any other suffix to come between itself and the verb root. Apart from augmentative and causative, which form an inner layer of suffixation

# The Indicative Verb in Doyayo

immediately following the root, there appears to be no inherent fixed order for the modificational suffixes. Note the alternate forms in (35).

(35)  *kam-n-d³¹*   ~  *kam³-d-i-n¹*
take-ACC-PREPC      take-PREPC-EP^ACC
He already took (using a previously-named instrument).

*kam¹-n-i-y¹*   ~  *ka¹m-i-y-n¹*
take-ACC-EP-RES      take-EP-RES-ACC
He was taken (in a previously named vehicle).

*ka⁴-n-i-l¹*   ~  *ka⁴-l-i-n¹*
climb-ACC-EP-DIST    climb-DIS-EP-ACC
He climbed up with several things (using a previously-named instrument).

However, occasionally the position of a suffix affects its meaning, as in (36).

(36)  *baa¹-t-i-y¹*   'it is pierced many times'
*baa¹-y-i-t¹*   'it is pierced by many things'

By far the most significant factors in the ordering of the suffixes are phonological restrictions. The chart in (37) presents the two-consonant clusters that have been found in Doowaayąąyo. It is significant, first of all, that there are no consonant clusters beginning with *s* or *z*.

(37)

|   | p | b | t | d | k | g | s | z | l | r | m | n | ŋ | y |
|---|---|---|---|---|---|---|---|---|---|---|---|---|---|---|
| p |   |   | x |   |   |   | x |   |   |   |   |   |   |   |
| b |   |   |   | x |   |   | x | x | x |   |   |   |   |   |
| t |   |   |   |   |   |   | x |   |   |   |   |   |   |   |
| d |   |   |   |   |   |   | x |   |   |   |   |   |   |   |
| k | x |   |   |   |   |   | x |   |   |   |   |   |   |   |
| g |   |   |   | x |   |   | x | x | x |   |   |   | x |   |
| s |   |   |   |   |   |   |   |   |   |   |   |   |   |   |
| z |   |   |   |   |   |   |   |   |   |   |   |   |   |   |
| l | x | x | x |   |   |   | x | x |   |   |   |   |   |   |
| r | x | x | x |   |   |   | x | x |   |   |   |   |   |   |
| m | x | x |   |   |   |   | x | x | x | x |   |   | x |   |
| n | x | x |   |   |   |   | x | x |   |   |   |   |   |   |
| ŋ | x | x | x | x |   |   | x | x | x | x |   |   | x |   |
| y | x | x |   |   |   |   | x | x |   |   |   |   |   |   |

Disregarding the consonants that do not correspond to one of the suffixes, one can observe that *m* has the greatest potential for initiating a cluster; even though it follows only *ŋ*, it can be followed by *t, d, s, z, l, r,* or *n*. In addition, *l, r, n,* and *y* can each combine only with following *t, d, s,* or *z; t* can be followed only by *s*, and *d* only by *z*. Thus, if we give the suffixes a relative ranking in terms of the likelihood of their occurrence at the beginning or the end of a cluster, we obtain (1) *-m*, (2) *-l, -r, -n,* and *-y*, (3) *-t* and *-d*, and (4) *-s* and *-z*.

(38) illustrates what happens when one of the suffixes is added to a stem ending in a single or double consonant. Only the last consonant of the stem is shown on the vertical axis, and this may or may not be a suffix.

(38)

|   | t | d | s | z | l | r | m | n | y |
|---|---|---|---|---|---|---|---|---|---|
| p | — | — | — | — | — | — | — | — | — |
| b | pt | bd | ps | bz | bl | br | m | mn/bin | y/biy |
| t | — | tir~tid | ts | dz | til | tir | m | tin | tiy |
| d | — | dir~did | ts | dz | dil | dir | m | din | diy |
| k | kt | gd | ks | gz | kil | kir | m | kin | kiy |
| g | kt | gd | ks | gz | gl | gr | m | gn/gin | y/giy |
| s | — | sir~sid | ts | dz | ls/sil | sir | ms | sin | siy |
| z | — | zir~zid | — | — | zil | zir | — | zin | ziy |
| l | t/lt | d/ld | s/ls | z/lz | lil | lir | m | n/lin | y/liy |
| r | t/rt | d/rd | s/rs | z/rz | l/ril | — | m | n/rin | y/riy |
| m | mt | md~mir | ms | mz | ml/mil | mr/mir | — | mn/min | y/miy |
| n | nt | nd | ns | nz | nil | nir | m | nin | y/niy |
| ŋ | ŋt | ŋd | ŋs | ŋz | ŋgil~ŋnil | ŋr~ŋgir~ŋnir | m | ŋgin~ŋnin | ŋgiy~ŋniy |
| y | yt/yit | yd/yid | ys | yz | yil | yir | — | yin | |

All the consonants on the horizontal axis represent suffixes. Where two alternate forms appear in the columns, separated by a slanted line, either one may be chosen for joining a suffix to a (C)VC stem, but only the second (longer) form is permitted for joining a suffix to a stem patterning (C)VVC or (C)VCC. Thus, *her³* 'choose' plus iterative *-t* results in either *het³* or *hert³* 'choose many times', the *r* being optionally dropped, while *gbɛɛr³* 'slaughter' with *-t* must retain the *r* with, however, an optional abbreviation of the vowel: *gbɛɛrt³* or *gbɛrt³* 'slaughter many times'. Usually, where two alternative forms exist for the suffixation of the same stem, the shorter one is preferred. Thus, *het³* is preferred to *hert³* and *hey¹* 'it is chosen' to *he¹riy¹*. The shorter forms occur more frequently in both elicited and unelicited data. Similarly, other factors being equal, *-ns* (*-n* plus *-s*) is

# The Indicative Verb in Doyayo

preferred to *-sin*, *-nd* to *-din*, *-rs* to *-sir*, *-ld* to *-dil*, and so on. It can be seen, then, that in spite of the possibilities offered by the epenthetic vowel (discussed in §5), the order of the suffixes is influenced by the rules of clustering.

## 5 Rules of vowel epenthesis

Any verb form may have at most one insertion of *i* in the suffix string. The placement of epenthetic *i* is related to the clustering of consonants that results from the addition of suffixes to the root or stem. The epenthesis is used to separate a nonpermissible sequence of consonants.

The clusters that are not permitted syllable finally, and must therefore be separated by the insertion of an *i*-epenthetic vowel, are (C)VC, (C)VVC, or (C)VCC roots or stems.

When the root or stem being suffixed has the syllable pattern (C)VC:

— any sequence in which the second consonant, i.e., the suffix being added, is *l, r, n,* or *y*, except when the final consonant of the stem is *b, g, l* (before *n* or *y*), *r,* or *m*. All these including *l* drop before a *y* suffix; *l* and *r* drop before *n* also;
— any sequence in which the first consonant is a sibilant: *ḥas³* 'remove', *ḥas-i-n¹* 'remove (using a previously named instrument)'; *ka⁴-z-i-d¹* (climb-IMM-EP-PREPC) 'he already climbed up just now'; and
— any sequence of two alveolar stops: *ka⁴t-i-d¹* (roll-EP-PREPC) 'he already rolled it up'.

When the stem being suffixed has the syllable pattern (C)VVC or (C)VCC, the following must be separated:

— any sequence in which the second consonant is a liquid or semivowel, except the sequences *bl, br, gl,* or *gr*. When the suffix is *-n*, the use of epenthesis alternates freely with the use of syllabic nasal as in (39);

(39) *sɛɛ³b-i-n¹* ~ *sɛɛ³b-n¹* 'approach with it (previously named object)'

    *koo⁴t-i-l¹*         '(several things) are dry'
    be^dry-EP-DIST

    *dak³-t-i-r¹*        'he already sifted several times'
    sift-ITER-EP-PREPC

baa³-t-i-y¹      'it is pierced by several things'
pierce-ITER-EP-RES

— any sequence in which the first consonant is a sibilant as in (40);

(40)   yɔɔ³-s-i-l¹      'he finished several things'
      be^finished-CAUS-EP-DIST

      ɓb⁴-z-i-d¹      'he already followed just now'
      follow-IMM-EP-PREPC

— any sequence of two alveolar stops as in (41); and

(41)   baa⁴-t-i-d¹      'he has already sewed several times'
      sew-ITER-EP-PREPC

— the clusters *ld*, *rd*, and *dz* may also be optionally separated by *i*-epenthesis as in (42).

(42)   gbɛɛ-l-d³¹   ~   gbɛɛ³-l-i-d¹      'he already cut in pieces'
      cut-DIST-PREPC

      gbɛɛ-r-d³¹   ~   gbɛɛ³-r-i-d¹      'he already slaughtered'
      cut-INTS-PREPC

      kam-d-z³¹   ~   kam³-d-i-z¹      'he has already brought it here'
      take-PREPC-IMM

It should be noted that the syllable that contains the epenthetic vowel may begin with a consonant, so that a sequence such as *kl*, which is not permissible at the end or beginning of a syllable, is quite acceptable across syllable boundaries as shown in (43).

(43)   da³k-i-l¹      'sift several kinds of flour'
      dak³-l-i-l¹      'sift several kinds of flour several times each'

When the suffix to be added is a personal pronoun or one of the tense markers, the rules for epenthesis are somewhat different. With a root or stem of the pattern (C)VVC or (C)VCC, an epenthetic vowel is always required. When the syllable pattern of the root or stem is (C)VC:

# The Indicative Verb in Doyayo

— an epenthetic vowel must be added before the pronoun unless the final consonant of the stem is *b*, which drops out, or *m*, which changes to *ŋ* before *g* and drops out elsewhere leaving behind nasalization of the stem vowel as in (44); and

(44) ɓɔb⁴ 'follow'    ɓɔ⁴-gе¹ 'he follows him'
      kɛm²³ 'understand'    kɛŋ²³-ge¹ 'he understands him'
                                    kɛ̃²³-hi¹ 'he understands them'

— an epenthetic vowel must be added before the proximate suffix -*ko* or the present suffix -*ko*, unless the final consonant of the stem is *b*, *g*, or *k*, all of which drop, or *m* which changes to *ŋ* as in (45).

(45) zɔb⁴ 'drip'    gi² zɔ-k¹    zɔ¹bɔ¹ 'it's dripping'
                    be drip-PRES drip

      lug³ 'plant'    hi¹ gi² lu¹-ko¹ 'they are going to plant'
                    they be plant-PROX

      kɛm²³ 'listen'    mi³ kɛŋ-k¹    kɛ¹mɔ¹ 'I am listening'
                    I    listen-PRES listen

The *i*-epenthesis rule also gives two alternate forms *ɛ* and *u*, which fluctuate with epenthetic *i* in certain environments. The *ɛ* occurs only before the first-person plural inclusive pronoun -*wɛ*, where it is preferred to *i*. In fact, the *ɛ*-epenthesis is so characteristic of that person that often the -*wɛ* suffix itself is dropped, its tone being added, however, to the epenthetic syllable as in (46).

(46) sɔɔ³t-ɛ³-wɛ³ ~ sɔɔ³t-ɛ³    'he excited us'
      dɔt⁴-s-ɛ¹-wɛ³ ~ dɔt⁴-s-ɛ¹³    'he tied for us'

Epenthetic *u* obligatorily replaces *i* in the second-person singular of the imperative as in *da²g-u³-mɔ³* (taste-EP-you) 'taste (it)!'. It fluctuates freely with *i* before the first-person singular -*mi*, second-person singular -*mɔ*, and first-person plural inclusive and exclusive -*wɛ* and -*wi* after all roots and stems except the irregular forms in (47).

(47) zaŋ¹ 'read'
      a̧r³ 'dig up'                 a̧-s³ 'dig up for someone'
      ɛr³ 'ask'                    ɛ-s³ 'ask (something) for someone'
      leg-l²³ '(many) are trapped'    leg-r²³ 'he is in a bad mess'

Compare the examples in (48).

(48)  gbɛ³n-i¹-mi¹  ~  gbɛ³n-u¹-mi¹          'he saw me'
      gbɛ³n-i¹-wɛ¹  ~  gbɛ³n-ɛ¹-wɛ¹  ~
         gbɛ³n-ɛ¹  ~  gbɛ³n-u¹-wɛ¹          'he saw us'

      ɛ³r-i¹-mi¹                              'he asked me'
      ɛ³r-i¹-wɛ¹  ~  ɛ³r-ɛ¹-wɛ¹  ~  ɛ³r-ɛ¹   'he asked us'

Epenthetic *u* also alternates freely with *i* before the present suffix *-ko* (in any of its allomorphs) in any root of stem where the vowel of the nuclear syllable is a back vowel. Compare the examples in (49).

(49)  dun¹d-i-k¹  ~  dun¹d-u-k¹     'he is rising'
      aa¹n-i-k¹                      'he is forbidding'
      bi¹s-i-g¹                      'he is leaving (something)'

As exceptions to this rule, *bal³* 'cultivate' and *hạ³tir¹* 'ruin' allow the same alternation, *hạ¹tir¹-go³* ~ *hạ¹tur¹-go³* 'he is ruining (something)'.

Stems with the syllable pattern (C)VVC sand (C)VCC where the final consonant is *l* are also irregular, as they do not permit the alternation: *mɔg¹l-i-k¹* 'is assembling'.

Epenthetic *u* alternates freely with *i* before the proximate suffix *-ko* (in any of its allomorphs) in any root or stem except those in (50), in which epenthesis itself is optional.

(50)  rek³                    'go'                  (*u* or no epenthesis)
      re¹-ko¹  ~  re¹k-u¹-go¹  'is about to go'

      il²³, ạr³, ɛr³, and er⁴                        (*i* or no epenthesis)
      er¹-ko¹  ~  e¹r-i¹-ko¹   'is going to stand'

## 6 Personal pronoun suffixes

There are eight personal pronoun suffixes in Doowaayạạyɔ. They are first-person singular *-mi* 'me' (direct speech) and *-be* 'me' (indirect speech), second-person singular *-mɔ* 'you', third-person singular *-ge* 'him, her, or it', first-person plural inclusive *-wɛ* 'us (all)', first-person exclusive *-wi* 'us (as opposed to you)', second-person plural *-ne* 'you (PL)', and third-person plural *-hi* 'them'. Each of these pronouns can function as either direct or

# The Indicative Verb in Doyayo

indirect object. The second- and third-persons singular and plural also function as the suffixed subject in the direct imperative.

The personal pronoun object never determines the tone of the verb word, nor does it maintain a fixed tone itself. Instead, its tone is determined by the tonal pattern on the verb (to be discussed in §7). If both an indirect and a direct object are present in one stem, they carry the same tone, which is either $^3$ or $^4$, and the indirect object requires the presence of benefactive -s as shown in (51).

(51)  $ok^2$-s-$i^3$-$mi^3$-$g^3$
block-BEN-EP-me-him
He stood in his way for me.

$gu$-$t^3$-s-$i^1$-$mi^3$-$ge^3$
enter-CAUS-BEN-EP-me-him
He caused him to enter for me.

$hi^3$  $waa^4$-s-$i^4$-$mi^4$-$ge^4$
they catch-BEN-EP-me-him
They caught him for me.

When both BEN -s and an object pronoun (direct, indirect, or both) are present in the verb, the remote future tense is signalled in the epenthetic vowel by a high tone as in $gi^1$ $ok^2$-s-$i^1$-$mi^3$-$ge^3$ 'he ($gi^1$) will stand in his way for me'.

The presence of proximate -ko or present -ko on the verb head frontshifts both the objects and the BEN to the preceding auxiliary $gi^2$, which in this case becomes obligatory as in (52).

(52)  $hi^1$   $gi^2$-s-$i^1$-$mi^3$-$ge^3$    $waa^1$-$ko^3$
they be-BEN-EP-me-him   catch-PROX
They will be catching him for me.

$mi^3$  $gi^2$-s-i-$g^1$           $kaa^1$-$ko^1$
I    be-BEN-EP-him^short  weep-PRES
I'm crying to him.

## 7 Tone patterns of the suffixed verb word

This section attempts to present rules for determining the tone pattern of the first intermediate form of the suffixed verb word. The tone of both the short and the lengthened form follows regularly from it, as described in §2. All rules apply only to the affirmative indicative. The rules are tried in order, and as soon as one rule succeeds all the remaining ones are disregarded.

1. When a -*ko* suffix is present, not immediately preceded by a closed syllable with *i*-epenthesis, and the verb itself is not preceded by a noun phrase object, the tone pattern of the verb word is $^{11}$ or $^{111}$ (depending on the number of syllables) as in (53).

(53)  *mi¹ kaa¹-ko¹*
      I    weep-PROX
      I am going to cry.

      *mi³ gi² dɛɛ¹-l-i¹-ko¹*
      I  be  cut-DIST-EP-PRES
      I am cutting something in pieces.

2. If the verb root or stem carries a high tone, as *zaŋ¹* 'read' and *dɔ-y¹* 'kick'; or if a -*ko* suffix occurs immediately preceded by a closed syllable with an epenthetic vowel or preceded in the clause by a noun phrase object, the tone pattern of the verb word is $^{13}$ or $^{113}$ as in (54).

(54)  *zaŋ¹-g-ɔ³*
      read-EP-INTM
      read

      *dɔ-y¹-y-ɔ³*
      kick (*dɔb⁴*)-RES-EP-INTM
      kick about

      *zagl¹*        *zagl¹-s-i¹-mi³*
      crawl        crawl-BEN-EP-me
                    He crawled for me.

      *el⁴*          *e¹l-i-n¹-go³*
      call          call-EP-ACC-PRES
                    He is calling about the matter.

      *mi³ gi² mɛm¹ kpel¹-ko³*   ∼   *mi³ gi² mɛm¹ kpe¹l-i¹ko³*
      I   be  water  pour-(EP)-PRES
      I am pouring water.

# The Indicative Verb in Doyayo

Note that this rule applies to all stems affected by a resultative *-y*, as these automatically fall into the group of high tone stems.

3. If *i*-epenthesis is followed by a modificational suffix, the tone pattern of the word is $^{X13}$ (where $^X$ represents the tone of the verb root) as in (55).

(55) $i^{23}n\text{-}i^1\text{-}l\text{-}o^3$
refuse-EP-DIST-INTM
He refused several things.

$luk^3\text{-}t\text{-}i^1\text{-}r\text{-}o^3$
plant-ITER-EP-PREPC-INTM
He has already planted several times.

$da^3k\text{-}i\text{-}l\text{-}s^1\text{-}ge^3$
sift-EP-DIST-BEN-him
He sifted several kinds of flour for him.

4. If the prepunctive suffix *-d* occurs between the verb root and epenthetic *i*, the tone pattern is also $^{X13}$. If there is no epenthetic vowel, this pattern contracts to $^{X\_1\ 3}$ as in (56)

(56) $el^4\text{-}d\text{-}i^1\text{-}wi^3$
call-PREPC-EP-us
He has already called us.

$\mathit{fob}^{41}\text{-}d\text{-}o^3$
follow-PREPC-INTM
He already followed.

5. If the benefactive suffix *-s* occurs immediately preceding vowel epenthesis, the tone pattern for all stems in the FUTURE is $^{X13}$ or (if two objects are present) $^{X133}$ as in (57).

(57) $wɔɔl^3$  'take by force'
$gi^1\ wɔl^3\text{-}s\text{-}i^1\text{-}wi^3\text{-}ge^3$  'he will catch him for us'
(he^FUT take^by^force-BEN-EP-us-him)

In the AORIST, there are three possible tone patterns, depending on the syllable structure of the root or stem preceding the *-s*:

a. All tone $^4$ verbs except those patterning (C)VC with *b* as the final consonant, and all tone $^3$ verbs with the syllable pattern

(C)VVC (before shortening of the vowel), (C)VCC, and (C)VC with final *d, k,* or *s*, take the pattern $^{X_{13}} \sim {}^{X_{133}}$ as in (58);

(58) *waar³*     'say good-bye'
    *war³-s-i¹-hi³*
    say^goodbye-BEN-EP-them
    He said good-bye to them for someone.

    *hod³*     'take off'
    *hot³-si¹-mi³-ge³*
    He took it off for me.

b.   all other tone ³ and tone ⁴ verbs pattern $^{XXX}$ in the aorist as in (59); and

(59)  *lug³*  'plant'   *luk³-s-i³-mi³-hi³*   'he planted them for me'
    *dir³*  'pull'    *di³-s-i³-hi³*      'he pulled them for someone'
    *fɔb⁴*  'follow'  *fɔb⁴-s-ɛ⁴-wɛ⁴*     'he followed us (all) for someone'
    *wa̰a̰⁴*  'catch'   *wa̰a̰⁴-s-i⁴-mi⁴-ge⁴*  'he caught him for me'

c.   the tone ² and the tone ²³ verbs pattern $^{233}$ and $^{2333}$ as in (60).

(60)  *gɔ²*  'make, do'  *gɔ²-s-i³-mi³-ge³*  'he did it for me'
    *in²³*  'refuse'    *in²-s-i³-mi³*      'he refused someone for me, me
                                               for someone'
                       *in²-s-i³-mi³-ge³*  'he refused him (it) for me'

6. If either the immediate suffix *-z* or the causative suffix *-s* is present before the epenthetic vowel, the tone pattern of the verb word is $^{X_{11}}$ as in (61).

(61)  *el⁴*    'call'       *el⁴-z-i¹-ge¹*  'he called him just now'
    *dir³*   'pull'       *di³-z-i¹-mi¹*  'he pulled me here'
    *leg²³*  'be stuck'   *lek³-s-i¹-hi¹*  'he caused them to be stuck'
    *sɛɛb³*  'be near'   *sɛp³-s-i¹-wi¹*  'he brought us near'

7. If one of the suffixes *-m, -l, -r, -t,* or nonsyllabic *-n* occurs before the epenthetic vowel and the verb stem has a level tone, the verb word has the pattern $^{XXX}$ as in (62).

# The Indicative Verb in Doyayo

(62)  $el^4$   'call'   $el^4$-$t$-$i^4$-$mi^4$   'he called me several times'

 $kam^3$   'carry'   $kam^3$-$l$-$i^3$-$ge^3$   'he took him to several places'

 $fob^4$   'follow'   $fom^4$-$n$-$\varepsilon^4$-$w\varepsilon^4$ or $fom^4n\varepsilon^4$   'he followed us with it'

With those same suffixes, if the stem has a glide, a spreading principle[6] places the last tone of the glide on the epenthetic vowel, and the third (last) syllable carries tone $^3$ as in (63).

(63)  $in^{23}$   'refuse'   $in^2$-$r$-$i^3$-$mi^3$   'he refused me completely'

 $aan^{31}$   'forbid'   $aan^3$-$t$-$i^1$-$ge^3$   'he forbade it several times'

If there is no epenthetic vowel, the second tone of the $^{23}$ glide goes to the second syllable as in (63), giving $in^2$-$r$-$ɔ^3$ 'refuse completely'; but with all upglides the pattern is $^{X1\ 3}$ as in $aan^{31}$-$t$-$ɔ^3$ 'forbid several times'.

8. If only a pronoun object is suffixed to the verb, the tone of the verb word is $^{X1}$ for all roots patterning CV, (C)VV, (C)VC (where the final consonant is $b$ or $m$) as in (64).

(64)  $y\varepsilon^2$   'shot'   $y\varepsilon^2$-$hi^1$   'he shot them'

 $oo^3$   'wait'   $oo^3$-$ge^1$   'he waited for him'

 $mɔɔ^{23}$   'give birth'   $mɔɔ^{23}$-$hi^1$   'she gave birth to them'

 $fob^4$   'follow'   $fo^4$-$ge^1$   'he followed him'

 $k\varepsilon m^{23}$   'listen, understand'   $k\varepsilon\eta^{23}$-$ge^1$   'he understands him'

    $k\underset{\cdot}{\varepsilon}^{23}$-$mi^1$   'he understands me'

With stem patterning (C)VC$^3$ (where the final consonant is not $b$, $m$, or $d$) and (C)V$g^{23}$, the tone is $^{X11}$ as in (65).

(65)  $nin^3$   'pursue'

 $ni^3n$-$i^1$-$hi^1$   'he pursued them'

 $og^{23}$   'solidify, stand in someone's way'

 $o^{23}g$-$i^1$-$wi^1$   'he stood in our way'

The verb $re\eta s^3$ 'come in the absence of someone', which also takes the patterns $^{X11}$, should probably be analyzed as a deponent root with a causative suffix as shown in $re\eta^3$-$s$-$i^1$-$mi^1$ (◦deponent^root-CAUS-EP-me) 'he

---

[6]For further discussion of this tone pattern see the following article, §3.2.

came in my absence'. All other tone ³ and tone ⁴ verbs take the tonal pattern ˣˣˣ as in (66).

(66)  maat³   'deceive'   maa³t-i³-wi³   'he deceived us'
      mɔk⁴    'think'     mɔ⁴k-i⁴-ge⁴    'he thinks of him'
      zɛbr⁴   'visit'     zɛb⁴r-i⁴-nɛ⁴   'he visited you'

All remaining ²³ verbs (i.e., those whose final consonant is not b, m, or g) take the tone pattern ²³² as in (67).

(67)  in²³   'refuse'   i²n-i³-wi²   'he refused us'

## 8 Negatives and imperatives

This paper examines the verb word only in the affirmative indicative. A few observations can be made, however, about the negative and the imperative.

There are three negative constructions. The first corresponds to the aorist tense and is formed by the addition of the negative particle gɛ² 'not' at the end of the verbal phrase. The subject pronoun takes tone ¹, the third-person singular being a zero morpheme. The verb takes tone ² on its nuclear syllable, tone ¹ on the second syllable, if any, and tone ³ on the third syllable, if any. Compare the expressions in (68) in the affirmative and negative.

(68)  zaa²³-za¹/zaa² gɛɛ²³           'he came/he didn't come'
      (Note the loss of reduplication, since the verb itself is never in clause-final position in the negative.)

      mi³ gbɛ³n-i¹-ge¹/mi¹ gb-ɛ²n-i-g¹ gɛɛ²³   'I saw him/I didn't see him'
      (Note the shortening of the pronoun in clause-medial position.)

      hi³ waa̰⁴-s-i⁴-mi⁴-ge⁴/hi¹ waa̰²-s-i¹-mi-g³ gɛɛ²³
      they catch-BEN-EP-me-him (not)
      They caught him for me./They didn't catch him for me.

Sometimes multiple embedding within the verb phrase places several other verbs between gɛ² and the verb that is being negated. Sentences like those in (69) are not unusual.

# The Indicative Verb in Doyayo

(69)   wal²³ yɛ¹rɛ¹-yɔ¹   be¹   mɛɛ²   hi¹n-ɔ³   an¹   gɔ²   be¹
       man this-here   I   know   thing-its   that   when   I
       gɔ¹-s-i¹-ge¹       an¹   gi¹       ɔɔ³   hin¹   hạạl²   wɔ¹
       do-BEN-EP-him   soˆthat   heˆFUT   leave   thing   bad   DEMˆPL
       woo¹-k-ɔ¹³                   a¹   sɛ²gbar²³yɔ¹              du¹   ge¹   gɛɛ²³
       word-PRES-inˆthatˆway   at   oldˆmen'sˆtalkingˆplace   in   it   not
       I don't know what I can do to him so that he may stop doing those
       bad things in the compound.

The second negative construction is used for the incomplete (non-aorist) tenses, remote future, proximate, and present, the remote/proximate/present distinction being neutralized in the negative, so that all three have the same form. The negative resembles quite closely the proximate, with the subject pronoun, however, taking high tone, the negative auxiliary $taa^{12}$ 'be not' replacing the normal $gi^2$ 'be', and the -ko suffix always carrying tone 3 as in (70).

(70)   hi¹   taa¹²   zaa¹-ko³
       they   beˆnot   come-TNS
       They will not come, are not coming, are not going to come.

       mi¹   taa¹²   wɛɛ¹-z-i¹-go³
       I   beˆnot   return-IMM-EP-TNS
       I will not return, am not returning, am not going to return.

The third negative construction is the negative imperative. It is formed with the interdictory word $bɔ^2$ followed by the pronoun and verb with the tones of the remote future tense as in (71).

(71)   bɔ²   mɔ¹   re³k-ɔ³          'don't go!'
       INTDC   youˆSG   go-INTM
       bɔ²   wɛ¹   le¹g-ɔ³           'let's not get stuck!'
       bɔ²   hi¹   fɔ⁴-ge¹           'let them not follow him!'

There are two main types of imperative in the affirmative. One, the indirect imperative, is morphologically identical with the remote future tense and could be considered a specialized use of it. As mentioned earlier, the use of the indirect imperative is obligatory in the second part of a double imperative as in (72).

(72)  rɛ³k-u-m¹  mɔ¹       loo⁴
      go-EP-you you^INDR take
      Go get it!

In contrast to the remote future, the reduplicating root *loo⁴* is not repeated in its imperative use, however, even though it is in clause-final position.

The second type of imperative is the direct imperative. It is formed in the second and third persons by removing the subject pronoun from its normal position before the verb and adding it to the verb as a suffix as in (73).

(73)  hɛ³d-u¹-mɔ¹    'sweep! (you SG)'
      hɛ³d-i¹-nɛ¹    'sweep! (you PL)'
      hɛ³d-i¹-ge¹    'let him sweep!'
      hɛ³d-i¹-hi¹    'let them sweep!'

The same rules that bring about changes in certain stems in the indicative before a personal pronoun suffix (§6) apply also in the imperative as in (74).

(74)  nam²³         'move'
      na̰²³-mɔ²      'move! (you SG)'
      naŋ²³-ge¹     'let him move!'

Though its structure resembles that of a verb with an object pronoun in the indicative, the imperative has its own tonal pattern, making it clearly distinguishable. The chart in (75) compares a few of the indicative tonal patterns with the corresponding patterns in the imperative.

(75) No object

| INDC | | IMP | |
|---|---|---|---|
| 3 3 | | 3 1 1 | |
| maa³t-ɔ³ | 'he deceived' | maa³t-u¹-mɔ¹ | 'deceive!' |
| 3 3 | | 3 3 2 | |
| la³g-ɔ³ | 'he heard' | la³g-u³-mɔ² | 'hear!' |
| 4 4 | | 4 1 1 | |
| zɛb⁴r-ɔ⁴ | 'he visited' | zɛb⁴r-u¹-mɔ¹ | 'visit!' |
| 4 4 | | 4 2 | |
| fɔ⁴bɔ⁴ | 'he followed' | fɔ⁴-mɔ² | 'follow!' |
| 2-3 1 | | 2-3 2 | |
| tuu²³-tu¹ | 'he collected' | tuu²³-mɔ² | 'collect!' |

# The Indicative Verb in Doyayo

(76) **One object**

| INDC | | IMP | |
|---|---|---|---|
| 3 3 3 | | 3 1 3 3 | |
| $maa^3t$-$i$-$g^3$/ $maa^3t$-$i^3$-$ge^3$ | 'he deceived him' | $maa^3t$-$u^1$-$mɔ^3$-$ge^3$ | 'deceive him!' |
| 3 1 1 | | 3 1 3 3 | |
| $la^3g$-$i^1$-$ge^1$ | 'he heard him' | $la^3g$-$u^1$-$mɔ^3$-$ge^3$ | 'hear him!' |
| 4 4 4 | | 4 1 3 3 | |
| $zẹb^4r$-$i^4$-$ge^4$ | 'he visited him' | $zẹb^4r$-$u^1$-$mɔ^3$-$ge^3$ | 'visit him!' |
| 4 1 | | 4 4 4 | |
| $fɔ^4$-$ge^1$ | 'he followed him' | $fɔ^4$-$mɔ^4$-$ge^4$ | 'follow him!' |
| 2–3 1 | | 2–3 3 3 | |
| $tuu^{23}$-$ge^1$ | 'he collected him' | $tuu^{23}$-$mɔ^3$-$ge^3$ | 'collect him!' |

(77) **Two objects**

| INDC | | IMP | |
|---|---|---|---|
| 3 1 3 3 | | 1 1 3 3 | |
| $mat^3$-$s$-$i^1$-$mi^3$-$ge^3$ | 'he deceived him for me' | $mat^1$-$s$-$i^1$-$mi^3$-$ge^3$ | 'deceive him for me!' |
| 3 1 3 3 | | 1 1 3 3 | |
| $lak^3$-$s$-$i^1$-$mi^3$-$ge^3$ | 'he heard him for me' | $lak^1$-$s$-$i^1$-$mi^3$-$ge^3$ | 'hear him for me!' |
| 4 1 3 3 | | 1 1 3 3 | |
| $zẹbr^4$-$s$-$i^1$-$mi^3$-$ge^3$ | 'he visited him for me' | $zẹbr^1$-$s$-$i^1$-$mi^3$-$ge^3$ | 'visit him for me!' |
| 4 1 3 3 | | 1 1 3 3 | |
| $fɔp^4$-$s$-$i^1$-$mi^3$-$ge^3$ | 'he followed him for me' | $fɔp^1$-$s$-$i^1$-$mi^3$-$ge^3$ | 'follow him for me!' |
| 2–3 1 3 3 | | 1 1 3 3 | |
| $tuu^{23}$-$s$-$i^1$-$mi^3$-$ge^3$ | 'he collected him for me' | $tuu^1$-$s$-$i^1 mi^3$-$ge^3$ | 'collect him for me!' |

If an object pronoun is present in the imperative, it follows the subject pronoun as in (78).

(78) $fɔ^4$-$mɔ^4$-$ge^4$
follow-you-him
Follow him!

$kam^3$-$z$-$u^1$-$mɔ^3$-$ge^3$
take-IMM-EP-you-him
Bring him here!

If both a direct and an indirect object are involved in the command, the subject pronoun is replaced in the construction by the indirect object with benefactive -*s* preceding it. This imperative is dintinguished from the indicative form it resembles by the changing of the tone of the nuclear syllable to high. Compare the examples in (79).

(79)  el⁴-s-i¹-mi³-hi³          'he called them for me'
      call-BEN-EP-me-them

      el¹-s-i¹-mi³-hi³          'call them for me!'

Two other imperative constructions have been found, both of which are restricted to the first person. On the one hand, they resemble the indirect imperative by their use of the remote future form; and on the other hand, they would appear to complete the direct imperative paradigm, which has no first-person form. The more common of these two first-person imperatives consists of ɔ³ 'let' (only in this contruction) plus future as in (80).

(80)  ɔ³ mi¹ ka³m-ɔ³           'let me carry it!'
      ɔ³ be¹ wɛɛ¹-z-a³          'let me (go and) return! (indirect discourse)'
      ɔ³ wi¹ le²                'let's eat!'
      ɔ³ we¹ ɓk⁴ bid⁴¹yɔ¹       'let's tell a story!'

The other first-person imperative is restricted to the plural inclusive pronoun wɛ. It consists of dɛ⁴ 'go, begin' (found only in this construction) plus future. The first-person plural inclusive wɛ, however, is so intimately associated with this construction that it becomes an optional element in the surface structure as shown in (81).

(81)  dɛ⁴ wɛ¹ le² ~ dɛɛ⁴¹ le² ~ dɛ⁴ le²
      'let's go eat, let's start eating!'

      dɛ⁴ wɛ¹ kaŋ³-ge¹ ~ dɛɛ⁴¹ kaŋ³-ge¹ ~ dɛ⁴ kaŋ³-ge¹
      'let's take him away!'

# Tone Patterns of Nominals in Doyayo[1]

### Marinus Wiering

Traditional phonemics used to confine its area of research strictly to phonological phonemena. Modern trends have been to view language rather as an indivisible whole, in which for example grammatical categories can play a part in a phonological description. The cataloguing of mere phonological contracts is no longer considered the end of the linguist's investigation of a sound system.

---

[1]An earlier draft of this paper was produced at a workshop of the Institute of Linguistics, held in Miango, Nigeria, from October to December 1972, under the direction of Joseph E. Grimes, and partially supported by National Science Foundation grant GS–1380A–1. I am indebted to Dr. Grimes for many helpful suggestions in regard to the analysis of the data, as well as to the preparation of the manuscript. I also want to thank my friends, Philip A. Noss and Piet van Reenen, and my colleagues Mona Perrin and John Watters, for some helpful comments and criticisms and my wife, Elisabeth Wiering, for her contribution to the organization and analysis of the data.

Field notes for the present study, completed in 1976, were taken, within the framework of a cooperative agreement between the Summer Institute of Linguistics and the University of Yaoundé, by the author and his wife during a thirty-two-month stay in Poli and Gare in the period of June 1971 to March 1974 and from May 1975 to December 1975 under the auspices of the National Office for Scientific and Technological Research (ONAREST) of Cameroon. Our language assistant, Mr. Pascal Djataou, who has learned to write his language, including the tone, very accurately, accompanied us to the workshop, and has from the beginning participated in the project.

This paper was prepared with the aid of an alphabetical concordance and a reverse concordance (based on tone) produced at the University of Oklahoma Computer Laboratory under a project partially funded by National Science Foundation grant GS–1605.

The purpose of this paper is to give a description of Dooyaayɔ tone patterns with special reference to tone changes on nominals.

The four contrastive level tones of Dooyaayɔ can combine within a syllable into two-tone and three-tone glides. Within the word the level tones and glides combine according to certain regular patterns.[2]

As shown in the tables in (12) and (33), the distribution of tone is restricted by three factors: (1) the grammatical category of the word, (2) the shape of the syllable of its stem, and in the case of nominals, (3) the particular suffix that a certain stem takes in pause-group final position.

The choice of this suffix is limited by the tone pattern and the final consonant of the stem. The tone on the suffixes can be predicted from the tone of the last syllable of the stem according to two general rules (cf. §2.1). The tone on the plural suffix marker can also be predicted from the stem tone (cf. §3.2). These rules are summarized in the table in (37).

Dooyaayɔ nominals have both a lexical and a relational form. This latter form is used in co-ordinate constructions and often has a distinctive suffix and tone pattern. Another distinction that can be made is between definite and indefinite forms of nominals, each having their particular tone patterns (cf. (60)).

Tone patterns of demonstrative and vocative forms follow ad hoc rules which do not seem to fit a larger pattern.

## 1 The structure of the tone system

In Dooyaayɔ tone is a feature of the phonological word. The tone of syllables within a word stem is determined by a limited set of inherent patterns in which certain sequences occur and others are absent. Post stem syllables take their tone from the stem. In a limited number of cases the tone of the stem is affected by its position in the sentence.

There are four contrastive level tones in Dooyaayɔ: high, medium high, mid, and low. They will be symbolized[3] respectively as $^1$, $^2$, $^3$, and $^4$ as in *yaa$^1$* 'grandfather', *yaa$^2$* 'grandmother', *yaa$^3$* 'to hide', and *yaa$^4$* 'to send'. Consecutive tones may be of equal or of different pitch. Every syllable bears either one level tone or a sequence of level tones.

---

[2]An interesting object of the Doowaayɔ culture is a wooden flute, about 15 centimeters (6 inches) long, which is used for communication. During their initiation period the young men are not supposed to talk to any woman, except by means of this flute. The flute has two holes and can produce all the pitches and glides described in this paper. The men play the tones that accompany the segments of the languages and are thus able to communicate, in a way similar to Mazateco whistle speech (cf. Cowan 1948).

[3]For a description of the phonemes of Poli Tɛɛrɛ Dooyaayɔ see the first article in this volume.

# Tone Patterns of Nominals in Doyayo

**1.1 Combinations of two level tones.** This interpretation considers length as a duplication of the vowel and sees a close correspondence between the number of tonal suprasegmental units on the one hand, and the number of vocalic segmental units on the other. When this correspondence fails to manifest itself, which is rare, one may assume that there has been elision or contraction of segmental units with retention of the tone.

Tonal 'glides' are interpreted as sequences of level tones resulting from the loss of a syllable or from the lengthening of a vowel, as shown in (1)–(3). The proposition that tonemic glides do not exist in Dooyąąyɔ is corroborated by the virtual absence of glides on CV shaped words,[4] whereas glides on CVV words like $kaa^{31}$ 'dog' and $gaa^{23}$ 'to be clear' are frequent.

Affirmative sentences ending in certain particles (e.g., $du^1$ 'in, into' and $gɛ^2$ 'not') have an automatic downglide to $^3$ on the last word. In case this last word already bears tone $^3$, as with the particle $ma^3$ 'then', the tone glides up to $^1$ to provide a contrast, since it cannot glide down farther to $^4$, as this would convert the affirmative statement into a question (cf. §5).

This up- or downgliding before a pause is always accompanied by a lengthening of the final vowel. Compare the *du* in (1), the *gɛ* in (2), and the *ma* in (3).

(1)  $rek^3\ raa^1\ du^1\ kɛ^3nɛ^1$   'he has gone home for the moment'
     $rek^3\ raa^1\ du{:}^{13}$      'he has gone home'

(2)  $nɔɔs^2\ gɛ^2\ ya^4$   'is it not a bird?'
     $nɔɔs^2\ gɛ{:}^{23}$   'it is not a bird'

(3)  $rii^3ri^1\ ma^3\ ya^4$   'is this enough?'
     $rii^3ri^1\ ma{:}^{31}$   'that's enough'

There are eleven different two-way glides.[5] Examples of downglides are in (4) and upglides in (5).

---

[4]Verbs for example that are CV shaped only have the level tone $^2$, like $le^2$ 'to eat'. Occasionally one comes across verbs of the $^{23}$ pattern that have the CV$^{23}$ form in certain contexts, but this results from the loss of the final *b*, as in $to^{23}\ ge^1$ 'he makes the skeleton of the roof', $to^{23}\ luk^1\ bɔ{:}^{13}$ or $tob^{23}\ luk^1\ bɔ{:}^{13}$ 'he makes the skeleton of the roof of the house'. For a fuller treatment of the verb structure including its tone patterns, see the second article in this volume.

[5]For simplicity's sake we are using the term GLIDE, although strictly speaking it is rather a TONAL SEQUENCE. The combinations listed present eleven out of the twelve possible sequences. The sequence $^{43}$ never occurs and $^{34}$ occurs only in ideophones.

(4) Downglides

|    |                                  |                          |
|----|----------------------------------|--------------------------|
| 12 | ɬaa¹²                            | 'not be'                 |
|    | ay¹²                             | 'where?'⁶                |
| 13 | sees¹³                           | 'sorcery'                |
|    | gaal¹³                           | 'wild turnip'            |
|    | leg¹³ < le¹ gɔ³                  | 'will get stuck'         |
|    | sil¹³ < si¹lɔ³                   | 'will get down'          |
| 14 | ay¹⁴                             | 'where? (EM)'            |
|    | ge¹⁴ < ge:¹⁴                     | 'him?'                   |
|    | du¹⁴ < du:¹⁴                     | 'in?'                    |
| 23 | waa²³                            | 'child'                  |
|    | kɔɔ²³                            | 'chicken'                |
|    | sil²³ < si²lɔ³                   | 'get down'               |
|    | leg²³ < le²gɔ³                   | 'get stuck'              |
| 24 | nɔ²⁴ < nɔ:²⁴                     | 'what?, why? (EM)'       |
| 34 | maa³⁴                            | 'sound made by cow (ID)' |

(5) Upglides

|    |                                  |                      |
|----|----------------------------------|----------------------|
| 21 | maal²¹ < maa²li¹                 | 'chimpanzee'         |
|    | bạm²¹ < bạ²mi¹                   | 'leprous spot'       |
|    | zɛnd²¹ < zɛn²di¹                 | 'oyster'             |
| 31 | foo³¹                            | 'species of lizard'  |
|    | kaa³¹                            | 'dog'                |
|    | kel³¹ < ke³li¹                   | 'scorpion'           |
|    | kurk³¹ < kur³ki¹                 | 'snail'              |
| 32 | baar³² < baa³rɛ²                 | 'egg'                |
|    | suml³² < sum³lɛ²                 | 'drum'               |
| 41 | saa⁴¹                            | 'sack'               |
|    | gaat⁴¹                           | 'hill'               |
|    | bips⁴¹ < bip⁴si¹                 | 'corn'               |
|    | kɔlk⁴¹ < kɔl⁴ki¹                 | 'throat'             |
| 42 | kar⁴² < ka⁴rɛ²                   | 'stick, rod'         |
|    | daŋ⁴² < daŋ⁴go²                  | 'knife'              |
|    | wal⁴² < wa⁴lɔ²                   | 'man'                |

**1.2 Combinations of three level tones.** With the ²³ verbs one may find a sequence of three tones on the same syllable, resulting from the lengthening of the vowel in phrase final position, as in (6). The vowel in the last word, being long already, does not change. Only the tone changes.

---

⁶For those examples which are taken out of a question context, cf. §5.

## Tone Patterns of Nominals in Doyayo

(6) $heg^{23}/heg^{231}$      'to don'
     $gi^1\ he^2g\mathfrak{o}^3/gi^1\ he{:}^{231}g\mathfrak{o}^1$      'he will don'
     $kp\varepsilon\varepsilon n^{23}/kp\varepsilon\varepsilon n^{231}$      'shut with'

With the nominals and a few verbals the majority of three-tone sequences result from the loss of a syllable with retention of the tone. This happens in the case of all the sequences in (7).[7]

(7)   $taar^{132}$   <   $taa^{13}ro^2$                    'there-is-not'

    $kaa^{314}$   <   $kaa^{31}$   +   $ya^4$        'Is it a dog?'
                         dog        Q PART

    $saa^{414}$   <   $saa^{41}$   +   $ya^4$        'Is it a sack?'
                         sack       ?

    $gaay^{212}$   <   $gi^2$   +   $ay^{12}$        'Where is he?'
                        it-is      where?

    $gaay^{213}$   <   $gi^2$   +   $ay^{13}$        'Where is he?'
                        it-is      where? (repeated)

    $gaay^{214}$   <   $gi^2$   +   $ay^{14}$        'Where is he??'
                        'it-is'     where? (EM)

    $kaa^{312}$   <   $kaa^{31}$   +   $-i^2$        'This dog here.'
                         dog        DEM

    $saa^{412}$   <   $saa^{41}$   +   $-i^2$        'This sack here.'
                         sack       DEM

    $waa^{232}$   <   $waa^{23}$   +   $-i^2$        'This child here.'
                         child      DEM

    $n\varepsilon\varepsilon k^{232}$   <   $n\varepsilon\varepsilon^{23}ko^2$                     'today'

Certain nominals always have a three-tone pattern in their roots, which are shaped either CVVC or CVCC.[8] There are some with the pattern $^{231}$

---

[7]There are thirty-one possibilities to form three-way glides in a four-tone system: 121, 123*, 124*, 131, 132, 134*, 141, 142, 143, 212, 213, 214, 231, 232, 234*, 241, 242, 312, 313, 314, 321*, 323, 324, 412, 413, 414, 421*, 423, 424, 431*, and 432*. The eight combinations that are marked with an asterisk can be left out of consideration, because they are not phonetically distinguishable from two-way glides. Note that only the $^{121}$ and $^{231}$ patterns are inherent to nominals. The combinations in the other examples result from contraction of tones.

[8]One can observe a certain correspondence between syllable structure and tonal behavior in verbs. (See the second article in this volume.) Similarly, one might well assume that there is a relationship between the tone pattern $^{23}$, which is restricted to the syllable patterns CVV and CVC, and the tone pattern $^{231}$ which is restricted to the syllable patterns CVVC and CVCC.

in (8) and others with the patterns $^{121}$ in (9). The shortened form shows the loss of the suffix -*i*, but not of its tone.

(8)    $^{231}pi̱i̱t^{231}$    <    $pi̱i̱^{23}ti^1$    'prop'
       $lɛgr^{231}$    <    $lɛg^{23}ri^1$    'spider's nest'

(9)    $^{121}zaal^{121}$    <    $zaa^{12}li^1$    'okra'
       $fɛpt^{121}$    <    $fɛp^{12}ti^1$    'fish scale'

The patterns $^{231}$ and $^{121}$ are inherent to the words meaning 'prop' and 'spider's nest' and to the words meaning 'okra' and 'fish scale' respectively. The shortened form therefore has the complete pattern of three tones.[9]

**1.3 Tonal contrasts.** It is difficult to find words of the same grammatical category to illustrate the contrast among the level tones and glides. In general, tones $^1$ and $^2$ are represented by nouns, while tones $^3$ and $^4$ are characteristic of verbs, though there are a limited number of exceptions[10] to this rule.

Tone $^2$ acts as a kind of 'neutral' tone. For example, although tone $^1$ verbs remain unchanged, all tone $^{23}$, tone $^3$, and tone $^4$ verbs change their tones to $^2$ when the negative particle $gɛ^2$ 'not' is introduced.

(10)    $mɔ^3$    $loo^4$    $wɔd^{23}$    $mi^1$    $ya^4$
       you^SG take^AOR thing(s) my Q
       Did you take my things?

       $ɛ^{3'}ɛ^1$    $mi^1$    $loo^2$    $gɛ^{23}$
       no I take^AOR not
       No, I did not take them.

---

[9]There are a considerable number of nominals with this tone pattern, but with a disyllabic root like $pa^1kir^{21}$ 'wing', $kɔ^1kɔt^{21}$ 'butterfly', $kpuk^1tum^{21}$ 'cobra', $naa^{23}seek^1le^{21}$ 'species of bird'. It is not unreasonable to assume that the form $CVVC^{121}$ and $CVCC^{121}$ could have resulted from the shortening of the disyllabic form $CV^1CVC^{21}$; either from the loss of the middle consonant (giving $CVVC^{121}$), or from the loss of the second vowel (giving $CVCC^{121}$), which would require that the second and third consonant could come together to form a cluster. For example, $za^1wal^{21}*$ could have given $zaal^{121}$ from the loss of the $w$; $fɛ^1pet^{21}*$ could have given $fɛpt^{121}$, from the loss of the second vowel.

[10]There are a small number of verbs with tone $^1$ and $^2$, and a small number of nouns with tone $^3$. Monosyllabic nouns with tone $^4$ are rare. The only examples found thus far are $mukt^4$ 'kind of grass', $gɛɛl^4$ 'plant used as medicine', and $kɔls^4$ 'leaf of dry bean'. Disyllabic nouns with tone $^4$ are a little more frequent.

# Tone Patterns of Nominals in Doyayo

The $^{23}$, $^{31}$, and $^{41}$ glides occur both on nominals and verbs; $^{32}$ and $^{42}$ occurring on nominals can be nuance expressing variations of $^{2}$ and $^{23}$. These variations will be treated in §4. Apart from the grammatical restrictions, which are shown in (12), the level tones and glides contrast with one another as shown in (11).

(11)  $baa^1$  'male'                              $yaa^1$  'grandfather'
      $baa^2$  'father'                            $yaa^2$  'grandmother'
      $baa^3$  'to dance a death dance'            $yaa^3$  'to hide'
      $baa^4$  'to pierce, sew'                    $yaa^4$  'to send, put'
      $baa^{13}$ 'proprietor'                      $yaa^{23}$ 'monkey, sorceror'
      $baa^{23}$ 'to be complete'                  $yaa^{31}$ 'vagina'
      $baa^{41}$ 'expression of fatigue'

  $tot^1$                'to bend'
  $tot^2 \sim tot^{32}$  'guinea corn'
  $tot^3$                'to sting several times'
  $tot^{23}$             'several people make the scaffolding of the roof'

  $luur^2 \sim luur^{32}$  'theft'
  $luur^{23}$              'to make a lot of dust'
  $luur^{31}$              'thief'
  $luur^{41}$              'whirlwind'

(12) Tonal restrictions in one syllable stems on grammatical classes in Dooyąąyɔ[11]

| Tone | N     | V   | Q     | I   | A   |
|------|-------|-----|-------|-----|-----|
| 1    | x     | x   | ((x)) | x   | x   |
| 2    | x     | (x) | ((x)) | (x) | x   |
| 3    | (x)   | x   | ((x)) | x   | x   |
| 4    | ((x)) | x   | x     | x   | (x) |
| 12   |       | (x) | ((x)) |     | (x) |
| 13   | x     | x   | ((x)) |     | x   |
| 14   |       |     | (x)   |     |     |
| 23   | x     | x   |       |     | x   |
| 24   |       |     | (x)   |     |     |
| 34   |       |     |       | x   |     |

---

[11] $N$ stands for nominal, $V$ for verb, $Q$ for question word, or nominal in question context, $I$ for ideophone, and $A$ for other words (like numerals, particles, etc.). $X$ indicates occurrence of tone. Parentheses indicate limited distribution, double parentheses indicate very restricted distribution.

| Tone | N | V | Q | I | A |
|---|---|---|---|---|---|
| 21 | x | x | | | |
| 31 | x | x | | x | x |
| 41 | x | x | | | x |
| 32 | x | | | | x |
| 42 | x | | | | |
| 121 | (x) | | | | |
| 231 | (x) | x | | | |
| 232 | | | ((x)) | | x |
| 131 | | x | | | |

**1.4 Word tone patterns.** Although the majority of the nominals have a monosyllabic root, one also finds a large number of bisyllabic and even some trisyllable roots, which yield level, rising, falling, complex, and alternating word tone patterns as shown in (13)–(17). Nominals in (17)[12] have two alternating tone patterns in the stem, which are determined by the context (see §5.1).

(13) Level patterns
  1 $tik^1$ 'gourd' $namr^1$ 'laziness'
    $hɛɛl^1$ 'rock' $raa^1$ 'compound'
    $loo^1rɛ^1$ 'ancestor spirit'

  2 $tar^2$ 'Fulani' $nuun^2$ 'big pot'
    $lɛɛ^2lɛ^2$ 'redshank' $gbuŋ^2tuŋ^2$ 'kind of pot'

  3 $keg^3$ 'weevil' $gbar^3$ 'father-in-law'
    $roob^3$ 'leopard' $riŋs^3$ 'sale'

  4 $gɛɛl^4$ 'plant used as medicine' $kɔls^4$ 'leaf of dry bean'
    $tu^4tug^4$ 'loin-cloth' $buu^4bil^4$ 'big fish'

(14) Rising patterns[13]
  21 $bạm^{21}$ 'leprous spot' $zɛnd^{21}$ 'oyster'
     $gbɔ^2nɔ^1$ 'road'

  31 $kel^{31}$ 'scorpion' $gu^3tu^1$ 'pigeon'
     $dɛ^3rɛŋt^{31}$ 'type of drum'

---

[12]Thus far only one example of a different irregular pattern has been found: ($^2$ ~ ($^{32}$ ~ $^{42}$)) $duul^2$ ~ ($duul^{32}$ ~ $duul^{42}$) 'rest, remainder'.

[13]Note the absence of $^{42}$ patterns.

# Tone Patterns of Nominals in Doyayo

    41  $bor^{41}$   'tadpole'              $lɔɔd^{41}$   'slug'
        $hɛ^4kum^1$  'oil jug'

    32  $ba^3nɛ^2$  'ring'            $kum^3be^2$  'sweet potato'
        $mar^3gan^2$  'circumcized man's switch for chasing women away'

(15)  Falling patterns
    13  $sees^{13}$   'sorcery'        $bu^1zum^3$   'wild cucumber'
        $tun^1tig^3$  'pus'            $ti^1laa^{13}$   'children's game'
        $tu^1tin^3$   'entrance hut'  $foo^1tin^3$   'tick, blood-sucking insect'

    14  $uu^1be^4$  'round dance' (rare)

    23  $hoo^{23}$   'guinea fowl'     $rɔ^2ma^{23}$  'hare'
        $dɛɛ^2si^3$  'type of lizard'

    24  $wa^2wa^4$  'young girl' (rare)

(16)  Complex patterns[14]
    121  $paps^{121}$   'locust'        $zaal^{121}$  'okra'
         $du^1kum^{21}$  'lung'         $su^1sug^{21}$  'hair'

    231  $lɛgr^{231}$  'spider's nest'  $pįį̨t^{231}$  'prop'

    4141  $ɓim^{41}rud^{41}$  'legendary animal'

    4113  $gew^{41}gew^{13}$  'type of drum'

    1141  $ɓin^1di^1rik^{41}$  'type of vine'

(17)  Alternating patterns
    2 ~ 32/42  $tot^2 \sim tot^{32}$           'guinea corn'
              $gaat^2 \sim gaat^{32}$     'mucous of the eye'
              $la^2yaar^2 \sim la^2yaar^{32}$  'amulet, fetish'
              $taal^2 \sim taal^{42}$      'shoe'
              $yɛɛs^2 \sim yɛɛs^{42}$     'medicine'
              $dapt^2 \sim dapt^{42}$     'skirt made of leaves'

---

[14] The examples given of the last three patterns are the only ones found thus far.

| | | |
|---|---|---|
| 23 ~ 42 | dɛl²³ ~ dɛl⁴² | 'basket' |
| | bam²³ ~ bam⁴² | 'big watersnake' |
| 42 ~ 432 | ku⁴dɔɔl² ~ ku⁴dɔɔl³² | 'heat of the day' |
| | ku⁴saal² ~ ku⁴saal³² | 'morning (8–11 a.m.)' |

## 2 Nominals in non-final and final position

As is the case in many African languages, there are hardly any phonological features or inherent criteria in words which would help us to distinguish between nouns and adjectives in Dooyaayɔ. Such distinctions are made on the basis of structural behavior. Since these 'nouns' and 'adjectives' follow the same tonal rules in Dooyaayɔ, with only a few exceptions, they are treated here in one category.

Most Dooyaayɔ words have a short and long form. The long form is obligatory in pause-group final position. It is obtained from the short form by adding a suffix.[15] In the case of nouns, the meaning of this suffix is more or less equivalent to the indefinite article in English.

For the majority of nominals the suffix is -yɔ, which can follow any sound that occurs stem-finally in nominals,[16] and follows stems that have either a level or gliding tone pattern. The other three suffixes: -ɛ, -o, and -ɔ[17] can only be preceded by stems that end in certain consonants and have a level tone on their last syllable. Glides on certain nominals change to level tones when the nominal is suffixed.

-ɛ occurs following the continuants /s m n l r/; -o following the stops /t k b d g/;[18] -ɔ following the liquids /m n l r/. There is overlap between the

---

[15]One might also argue the other way round of course, and say that the long form is the lexical form, which is shortened in pause-group medial position. The choice is arbitrary, except that starting from the suffixes, it is impossible to formulate adequate rules to predict the tone on the stem, since the group of tone ³ and tone ⁴ nouns, although small, is too large to be left out of consideration.

[16]All nominals that take the -yɔ suffix and whose stem ends in a consonant have an alternative suffix -i, which indicates the relational form (see §4). The tone on the -i suffix follows the spreading principle, which is discussed in §3 on the formation of plurals.

[17]Thus far only two examples have been found of a fifth suffix -u: du¹tu¹ 'fish' and hu¹tu¹ 'excrement'. It seems that -u must be regarded as an allomorph of -o, which occurs following -ut and harmonizes with the preceding short vowel as contrasted by muut²/muu³to² 'face' and tut¹/tut¹yɔ¹ 'knife-edge'.

[18]g is inserted between ŋ and -o, because /ŋ/ never occurs syllable initially, as in siŋ²³/siŋ⁴go² 'sister'.

# Tone Patterns of Nominals in Doyayo

consonants that can precede -ɛ and -ɔ and often there is free variation between the two as shown in (18).

(18)  sɔ$^1$mɛ$^1$ ~ sɔ$^1$mɔ$^1$   'type of antelope'
      wa̰$^4$lɛ$^2$ ~ wa̰$^4$lɔ$^2$   'cave'
      ka$^4$rɛ$^2$ ~ ka$^4$rɔ$^2$   'stick, rod'

Fluctuation also occurs between the -yɔ ending and -ɛ and -ɔ,[19] as in (19).

(19)  rɔbs$^1$yɔ$^1$ ~ rɔb$^1$sɛ$^1$   'blessing, gift'
      duk$^1$yɔ$^1$ ~ du$^1$kɔ$^1$   'knee'

Apart from the phonological restrictions mentioned, the suffix does not follow a regular pattern. Attempts to classify the stems semantically, to show which suffixes they take, lead into a blind alley, as can be seen from the examples.[20]

The suffixes of nouns and adjectives in a sentence show no concord relationships to each other, although when a plural form exists nouns and adjectives do agree as to number. It is interesting that certain stems when used as nouns, take a suffix different from the one that the same stem takes as adjective: gap$^4$sɛ$^2$ 'riot', gaps$^{41}$yɔ$^1$ 'roguish'. Different types of nouns may also be assigned different suffixes: zoo$^3$sɛ$^2$ 'prey' (patient noun), zoos$^{31}$yɔ$^1$ 'person who likes meat' (attributive noun).

**2.1 Tone patterns of the long form.** The tones on the suffixes -yɔ, -ɛ, and -ɔ can be predicted:[21] (1) If the level tone, or the last element of a glide on the last syllable of the stem is tone $^1$, the suffix takes tone $^1$ as in

---

[19]It is hard to find an example of -yɔ fluctuating with -ɔ. The only example found thus far is gbar$^3$yɔ$^2$ ~ gba$^3$rɔ$^3$ 'father-in-law'.

[20]All French and most Fulani loan words take the -yɔ suffix like va$^3$ran$^1$da$^4$yɔ$^2$ 'verandah', may$^3$to$^3$fon$^{13}$yɔ$^2$ 'tape recorder', sal$^3$te$^3$yɔ$^2$ 'dust bin', bor$^3$dɛl$^{13}$yɔ$^2$ 'prostitute'; a$^3$sa$^1$na$^1$yɔ$^1$ 'match', kɔr$^2$wol$^3$yɔ$^2$ 'chair', bas$^1$kur$^{13}$yɔ$^2$ 'bike'. Some Fulani loan words ending in -r, however, take the -ɛ suffix, like ma$^2$loo$^3$rɛ$^2$ 'rice'.

[21]No exceptions to these rules have been found within the category of nominals that take -yɔ. Among those that take one of the other suffixes the following three exceptions have been found, each one of them also being peculiar in other ways: gbar$^3$/gba$^3$rɔ$^3$ ~ gbar$^3$yɔ$^2$ 'father-in-law' (cf. footnote 19); ka$^2$siŋ$^{23}$/ka$^2$siŋ$^{23}$yɔ$^2$ ~ ka$^2$siŋ$^4$go$^2$ ~ ka$^2$siŋ$^2$gɛ$^3$ 'river bank'; lɛɛ$^1$sig$^3$/lɛɛ$^1$sig$^3$yɔ$^2$ ~ lɛɛ$^1$si$^3$go$^3$ ~ lɛɛ$^1$si$^3$gɛ$^3$ 'afternoon'. Note that gba$^3$rɔ$^3$ and lɛɛ$^1$si$^3$gɛ$^3$ also form an exception to the restriction that -ɛ, -o, and -ɔ suffixes do not carry the same tone as the last syllable of the stem, unless this bears tone $^1$. (Cf. footnote 26.)

(20), or (2) if the level tone or the last element of a glide on the last syllable of the stem is any tone lower than ¹, the suffix takes tone ² as in (21).

(20)  laa¹/laa¹yɔ¹         'fire'              hɛɛl¹/hɛɛl¹yɔ¹        'rock'
      loo¹rɛ¹/loo¹rɛ¹yɔ¹    'ancestor spirit'   ba̰m²¹/ba̰m²¹yɔ¹        'leprous spot'
      kel³¹/kel³¹yɔ¹        'scorpion'          bid⁴¹/bid⁴¹yɔ¹         'story'
      paps¹²¹/paps¹²¹yɔ¹    'locust'            lɛgr²³¹/lɛgr²³¹yɔ¹     'spider's nest'
      uus¹/uu¹sɛ¹           'smoke'             hob¹/ho¹bo¹            'red'
      hoob¹/hoo¹bo¹         'fear'              nam¹/na¹mɔ¹            'blacksmith'

(21)  dɔy²/dɔy²yɔ²                         'horse'
      lɛɛ²lɛ²/lɛɛ²lɛ²yɔ²                   'redshank'
      riŋs³/riŋs³yɔ²                       'sale'
      kɔls⁴/kɔls⁴yɔ² ~ kɔl⁴sɛ²             'leaf of dry bean'
      kum³be²/kum³be²yɔ²                   'sweet potato'
      sees¹³/sees¹³yɔ²                     'sorcery'
      tun¹tig³/tun¹tig³yɔ²                 'pus'
      rɔ²ma²³/rɔ²ma²³yɔ²                   'hare'
      zḭḭ²³/zḭḭ²³yɔ²                       'long'
      nii⁴til⁴/nii⁴til⁴yɔ²                 'bent'²²

The suffixes -ɛ, -o, and -ɔ are not only restricted in relation to the sounds that they can follow, but also in relation to the stem tone patterns. The examples above show that these three suffixes are only preceded by level stem tones.²³ Similarly, nominals with an unchanging stem tone lower than ¹ that are not followed by -yɔ are virtually absent. Nominals which have a ²³ glide or tone ² on the stem in the short form change their stem tone to ⁴ and ³ or ⁴ respectively when they are suffixed by -ɛ, -o, or -ɔ, as shown below.

The contrast between tone ² and ²³ is minimal in nominals, since the distribution of these tones is entirely determined by the shape of the stem of the nominal in the case of (C)VC stems and almost wholly in the case of CVV stems.

In (C)VC stems taking -ɛ, -ɔ, or -o the occurrence of tone ² is limited to stems ending in a voiceless consonant as in (22).

---

²² To elicit examples of the short form, the frame X taa¹³ ro² 'X there-is-not' can be used, and for the long form the frame gaa⁴ mi⁴ X 'give me X!'

²³The only exceptions consist in a limited number of nouns having two alternate forms, one ending in -yɔ, the other in -ɛ, -o, or -ɔ. Examples include kɔlk⁴¹yɔ¹ ~ kol⁴¹ko¹ 'throat' and ho²lum²³yɔ² ~ ho²lu²³mɛ² 'rest, vacation'.

# Tone Patterns of Nominals in Doyayo 97

(22) *tus²* 'money'
  *wit²* 'sesame'
  *bak²* 'field'

Tone ²³ on the other hand appears with (C)VC stems only if the stem ends in a voiced consonant as in (23).

(23) *dɛl²³* 'basket'    *hab²³* 'pig'
  *a̰r²³* 'buffalo'    *bam²³* 'watersnake'
  *tun²³* 'deer'    *siŋ²³* 'sister'
  *wɔd²³* 'thing, container'    *seg²³* 'new'

In CVV stems taking the *-yɔ* suffix we do find ² and ²³ in contrast, but only with open vowels and close back vowels as in (24).

(24) *naa²* 'friend, brother-in-law'    *naa²³* 'cow'
  *buu²* 'species of bird'    *buu²³* 'white, a white person'

When a (C)VC² nominal takes its long form, the stem-tone changes to ³ as in (25).

(25) *tus²/tu³sɛ²*    'money'
  *bak²/ba³ko²*    'field'
  *wit²/wi³to²*    'sesame'²⁴

When a (C)VC²⁵ nominal takes its long form, the tone on the stem ²³ changes to ⁴ as in (26).

(26) *dɛl²³/dɛ⁴lɛ²*    'basket'
  *hab²³/ha⁴bo²*    'pig'
  *a̰r²³/a̰⁴rɔ²*    'buffalo'
  *bam²³/ba⁴mɔ²*    'watersnake'
  *tun²³/tu⁴nɔ²*    'deer'
  *siŋ²³/siŋ⁴go²*    'sister'
  *wɔd²³/wɔ⁴dɛ² ~ wɔ⁴dɔ²*    'thing, container'
  *seg²³/se⁴go²*    'new'

---

²⁴As the stems of these examples all end in a voiceless consonant, only long forms with -ɛ and -o are to be found, because the -ɔ suffix must be preceded by a liquid consonant. Cf. §2.

²⁵Some speakers, probably being influenced by the Markɛ dialect, optionally use a tone ³ instead of a tone ⁴ on the stem: *dɛl²³/dɛ⁴lɛ² ~ dɛ³lɛ²* 'basket'.

When a CVCC² nominal ending in the cluster -pt or -ps takes its long form, the stem-tone changes to ⁴ as in (27).

(27)  dapt²/dap⁴to²   'skirt made of leaves'
      kops²/kop⁴sɛ²   'thorn'

If the CVCC²³ nominal ends in -ŋk, -rk, -lk; -ŋs, -ns, -ms, -rs, -ls, -ks; -kt, -nt, -mt; -gl or -ml the tone on the stem changes to ³ when the nominal takes its long form as in (28).

(28)  baŋk²/baŋ³ko²   'shoulder'         bɛrk²/bɛr³ko²    'side'
      belk²/bel³ko²   'debt'             lɛns²/lɛŋ³sɛ²    'seed'
      kans²/kan³sɛ²   'kind of hammer'   gums²/gum³sɛ²    'conjunctivitis'
      gɛrs²/gɛr³sɛ²   'miracle'          wils²/wil³sɛ²    'blackmaking'
      muks²/muk³sɛ²   'indifferent hair' wɛkt²/wɛk³to²    'cheek'
      rɛnt²/rɛn³to²   'firewood'         mimt²/mim³to²    'sad(ness)'
      dɔgl²/dɔg³lɛ²   'word'             saml²/sam³lɛ²    'red powder'

When a CVVC² nominal ending in -k, -t, -b, -r, or -n takes its long form, the stem-tone changes to ³ as in (29).

(29)  yaak²/yaa³ko²    'death chant'
      hɔɔt²/hɔɔ³to²    'baby's excrement'
      zeeb²/zee³bo²    'mouse'
      kɔɔr²/kɔɔ³rɛ²    'blossom, flower'
      naan²/naa³nɛ²    'hand, arm'

When a CVVC² nominal ending in -s, -l, or -m takes its long form, the stem-tone changes either to ³ or ⁴. As the forms are phonetically very similar, the tonal changes do not seem to follow a regular pattern, so that the different forms will have to be listed in the dictionary. In some cases there is free fluctuation between tone ³ and ⁴ on the stem. Examples of CVVC² nominals changing to ³ in the long form are in (30).

(30)  pa̰a̰s²/pa̰a̰³sɛ²   'cheated husband'
      zoos²/zoo³sɛ²   'prey'
      zɔɔl²/zɔɔ³lɛ²   'whetstone'
      riim²/rii³mɛ²   'spider's web'

Examples of CVVC² nominals changing to ⁴ in the long form are in (31).

(31)  fạas²/fạa⁴sɛ²      'glue'
      zool²/zoo⁴lɛ²      'hide'
      zɔɔm²/zɔɔ⁴mɛ²     'salty liquid'

Examples of CVVC² nominals changing to ³ ~ ⁴ in the long form are in (32).

(32)  duul²/duu³lɛ² ~ duu⁴lɛ²     'person who is resting'
      yɔɔl²/yɔɔ³lɛ² ~ yɔɔ⁴lɛ²     'anus'

The relationship between the stem tone patterns, the suffixes, and the syllable shape of the stem in pause-group final position are summarized in the table in (33).[26]

(33)
| Tone | CVV | CVC | | CVVC | | CVCC | |
|---|---|---|---|---|---|---|---|
| 1      | A    | A   | B      | A    | B | A   | B    |
| 2      | Aᵃ   | ((A)) |      | (A)  |   | —   |      |
| 2 = 3/4 | —   |     | Bᵃ     |      | B |     | B    |
| 3      | —    | (A) | (((B))) | (A) |   |     |      |
| 4      | ((A)) | —  |        | (A)  |   | (A) | ((B)) |
| 13     | —    | —   |        | A    |   | —   |      |
| 23     | Aᵃ   | —   |        | —    |   | —   |      |
| 23 = 4 | —    |     | Bᵃ     | —    |   | —   |      |
| 32     | —    | A   |        | A    |   | A   |      |
| 31     | A    | A   |        | A    |   | A   |      |
| 41     | A    | A   |        | A    |   | A   |      |
| 121    | —    | ((A)) |      | (A)  |   | (A) |      |
| 231    | —    | —   |        | A    |   | A   |      |

---

[26] A stands for any stem followed by -yɔ, B stands for any stem followed by -ɛ, -o, or -ɔ. Parentheses indicate low frequency. ᵃ indicates that the contrast between the tone patterns of the stems preceding this suffix is minimal, because the stem final sounds are almost in complementary distribution.
  Taking this pattern and the factor of low frequency into account, it can be said that tones ²/²¹/²³/²³¹, ³/³¹, and ⁴/⁴¹ nearly complement one another's respective distribution.
  Note the absence of tone ² on the stem before -ɛ, -o, and -ɔ. This is also illustrated by some nouns that have a stem with tone ² on the last syllable and can take either -yɔ or -ɛ, -o and -ɔ. When the noun takes one of the latter three suffixes the tone of the last syllable of the stem changes: nuun²/nuun²yɔ² ~ nuu³nɛ² 'big cooking pot', gbuŋ²tuŋ²/gbuŋ²tuŋ²yɔ² ~ gbuŋ²tuŋ³go² 'clay pot used for storage'.

## 3 Formation of plurals

It is possible to treat nouns and adjectives in the same section, because adjectives can be pluralized with or without the presence of the noun that they qualify: $ho^1bo^1$ 'red'/$hin\ ho^1bɛ^1 \sim ho^1bɛ^1$ 'red things'. It is difficult to establish rules to determine whether or not a nominal can be pluralized in Dooyąąyɔ. From a phonological point of view the division seems elusive. There are only a few observations that can be made: No nouns which originate from a root ending in a vowel and which denote non-humans are found in the plural.[27]

Tonal restrictions on pluralization of nominals are that no plurals are found with stems having an unchanging level pattern, nor with stems having a complex tone pattern: upglide, downglide or vice versa. Also, plurals rarely occur on nominals with an irregular stem tone pattern, which changes from $^2$ to $^{32}$ (cf. §1).

From a semantic point of view it can be said that nouns referring to human beings take plural, although there are some exceptions as $hin^3da^1yɔ^1$ 'older brother or sister' and $bam^2ba^2dɛ^3yɔ^2$ 'musician', which cannot be pluralized. Looking at other categories like animate, inanimate, animals, objects, etc. one can find many contradictory indications as in (34).

(34)    $damt^{31}yɔ^1$                  $dam^3tɛ^1yɔ^1$       'hedgehog(s)'
        $bar̪^{21}yɔ^1$                   —                'mountain hedgehog' (no plural)
        $su^1mɛ^1 \sim su^1mɔ^1$    $su^1mɛ^1yɔ^1$       'partition(s) of a granary'
        $bi^4lɛ^2$                         —                'granary' (no plural)
        $par^{31}yɔ^1$                   —                'partition of a granary' (no plural)

However, so far no plurals have been found in the areas of clothing, disease, reptiles, or nouns expressing feeling.

The pluralizer that occurs most often is $-ɛ$ with tone $^1$, $^2$, or $^3$. A few words take $-o$ with tones $^1$ or $^2$. Many plural markers are optional. For example it is grammatically correct in Dooyąąyɔ to say either $bid^{41}\ taa^1rɛ^1$ or $bi^4dɛ^1\ taa^1rɛ^1$ 'three stories'.[28]

**3.1 Transition features.** If the stem ends in a vowel, $d$, or sometimes $t$ is inserted to make the transition to plural $-ɛ$ as in (35). (35b) is an exception where the final vowel of the stem is dropped when the plural

---

[27]The two exceptions to this rule both have an irregular plural: $kal^1baa^1/kal^1baa^1dɛ^3$ 'type of small monkey', $raa^1/raa^1to^1$ 'compound(s)'.

[28]The question whether or not plural markers are obligatory may involve factors of style, which still have to be investigated.

marker is added. If the stem ends in -ŋ, d or g is inserted as in (35c). If the stem ends in -m, b is sometimes inserted as in (35d). Thus far only one case, (35e), of vowel shifting in the plural has been found.

(35) a. buu²³/buu²dɛ³              'white person(s)'
     zįį²³/zįį²dɛ³                  'long thing(s)'
   b. nɛɛ¹raa¹³/nɛɛ¹rɛ¹            'shepherd(s)'
   c. waŋ²³/waŋ²gɛ³ ~ waŋ²dɛ³      'sibling(s)'
   d. bam²¹/bam²bɛ¹                'leprous spot(s)'
   e. ząąn¹/zę¹nɛ³                 'person(s)'

With some adjectives ending in -il we notice a special phenomenon: l is replaced by the plural suffix -ɛ and the epenthetic[29] i drops out as in (36).

(36) nii⁴til⁴/nii¹tɛ¹              'bent thing(s)'
     dag¹til³ ~ dag¹tɛ¹            'light thing(s)'
     bɔŋ⁴til⁴/bɔɔ⁴tɛ¹ ~ bɔŋ¹tɛ¹    'arrow thing(s)'

**3.2 Tonal features of pluralization.** With the majority of nouns the tone on the pluralizer is determined by the SPREADING PRINCIPLE, which is the third major rule to predict the tone on a nominal suffix in Dooyąąyɔ (cf. §2.1 and the table in (37)). This principle can be formulated as follows: The tone on the suffix is identical to the tone on the last syllable of the stem, or the last element of a glide on the last syllable of the stem is transferred to the appended syllable. The vast majority of pluralized nouns follow this rule.[30] Examples are shown in (38) and exceptions in (39).

(37) Tonal rules of suffixes of Dooyąąyɔ nominals

| Rule | Tone on stem-final syllable | Tone on suffix |
|---|---|---|
| i | 1 | 1 |
| ii | 2/3/4 | 2 |
| iii | X | X |
|  | G | LG |

---

[29]The epenthetic -i is inserted between two consonants which cannot form a cluster in Dooyąąyɔ. It often occurs in verb forms. See §5 of the second article in this volume.

[30]Rules i and ii relate to the formation of suffixes in pause-group final position, rule iii (spreading principle) applies mainly to plural suffixes. X stands for any level tone, although no instances of tone ⁴ spreading to the appended syllable have been found as yet. G stands for any two- or three-way glide. LG stands for the last element of the glide.

(38) $tut^1/tu^1tɛ^1$ 'knife-edge(s)'
　　 $gaak^1/gaa^1kɛ^1$ 'dry season(s)'
　　 $dɛnt^1/dɛn^1tɛ^1$ 'old man/men'
　　 $kpaar^3/kpaa^3rɛ^3$ 'uncircumcized person(s)'
　　 $gum^{21}/gum^2bɛ^1$ 'grasshopper(s)'
　　 $aab^{31}/aa^3bɛ^1$ 'mistake(s)'
　　 $nɛs^{31}/nɛ^3sɛ^1$ 'relative(s)'
　　 $naad^{41}/naa^4dɛ^1$ 'old woman/women'
　　 $bips^{41}/bip^4sɛ^1$ 'corn'
　　 $buu^{23}/buu^2dɛ^3$ 'white person(s)'
　　 $gɛr^{23}/gɛ^2rɛ^3$ 'healer(s)'
　　 $bɛɛg^{121}/bɛɛ^{12}gɛ^1$ 'fruitbearing vine(s)'
　　 $pii̯t^{231}/pii̯^{23}tɛ^1$ 'prop'

(39) $tar^2/ta^2rɛ^{23}$ 'Fulani(s)'
　　 $kops^2/kop^4sɛ^1$ 'thorn'
　　 $baa^1/baa^1dɛ^3$ 'male(s)'
　　 $baa^2/baa^3bɛ^1$ 'father(s)'
　　 $nɔɔ^1/nɔɔ^1dɛ^3$ 'female(s), mother(s)'
　　 $laa^1ya^1/laa^1yaa^1dɛ^3$ 'soldier(s)'
　　 $zaan^1/zɛ^1nɛ^3$ 'person(s)'
　　 $nɛɛ^1raa^{13}/nɛɛ^1rɛ^1$ 'shepherd(s)'
　　 $yaa^1boon^2/yaa^1boo^2nɛ^3$ 'language(s)'

Adjectives which can be followed by the suffix -yɔ also follow the spreading rule as in (40).

(40) $fɛɛt^1/fɛɛ^1tɛ^1$ 'wide thing(s)'
　　 $gaps^{41}/gap^4sɛ^1$ 'dangerous things'

Adjectives which take -ɛ, -o, and -ɔ form their plurals according to the spreading principle, but the tone pattern on the stem is the one of the relational form, which will be discussed in §4. In (41) the long and relational forms are stated for comparison.

(41) 　　　　　　Long　　　Relational
　　 $rɔb^1$　　$rɔ^1bɛ^3$　$rɔ^1bɔ^1, rɔ^1bo^3$　'good thing(s)'
　　 $kimt^2$　$kim^2tɛ^3$　$kim^3to^2, kim^2to^3$　'round thing(s)'
　　 $wil^{23}$　$wi^2lɛ^3$　$wi^4lɔ^2, wi^2lɔ^3$　'dark thing(s)'

**3.3 Plurals in pause-group final position.** Plurals in final position invariably take the suffix -yɔ, which follows the pluralizer as shown in (42).

Tone Patterns of Nominals in Doyayo

The tone on the suffix is determined according to the two rules for tone on suffixes given in §2.1.

(42)  aa³bɛ¹      aa³bɛ¹yɔ¹     'mistakes'
      buu²dɛ³     buu²dɛ³yɔ²    'white persons'
      dɛn¹tɛ¹     dɛn¹tɛ¹yɔ¹    'old men'

## 4 Relational versus independent forms of nominals

In adddition to its lexical form, each nominal has an enumerative, or *relational* form, as first element in coordinate phrases, and when the nominal stands in an antecedent relationship to the following clause.[31] For example, to³to² 'guinea corn' has its relational form to²to³ which is used as ENUMERATION as in (43a), COORDINATE PHRASE as in (43b), and ANTECEDENT as in (43c).

(43)  a. mi³ gbɛn³ to²to³, nam²bo³, kɔl⁴si² hi¹ zaa¹²li¹
         'I saw guinea corn, meat, dried bean leaves and okra.'

      b. hi³ gaam⁴¹ to²to³ hi¹ nam²bo³
         'They gave me guinea corn and meat.'

      c. hi³ gaam⁴¹ to²to³, mi³ ren³ gɔ¹
         'They gave me guinea corn, so I took it with me.'

         hi³ gaam⁴¹ to²to³ hi¹ nam²bo³, mi³ ren³ gɔ¹³
         'They gave me guinea corn and meat, which I took along.'

         mɔ¹ gbɛn² to²to³, mɔ¹ raa¹si³mi³
         'If you see guinea corn, tell me.'

The relational form is obtained from the long form as follows:

— Nominals whose stems end in an open syllable and have tone ¹, drop the -yɔ suffix and add a tone ³, so as to form a downglide.

---

[31] The relational form also serves to indicate desirability versus non-desirability in certain contexts. For example yɔ¹ gaam⁴¹ to²to³ 'he would give me guinea corn' would imply that the speaker would be happy with gift, whereas yɔ¹ gaam⁴¹ to³to² would indicate that he would prefer to receive something else.

(44)  $tɛɛ^1yɔ^1/tɛɛ^{13}$          'tree'
      $laa^1yɔ^1/laa^{13}$          'fire'

— Nominals whose stems end in an open syllable and have a tone lower than $^1$ or a glide, only drop the -yɔ suffix.

(45)  $lɛɛ^2lɛ^2yɔ^2/lɛɛ^2lɛ^2$       'redshank'
      $kaa^{31}yɔ^1/kaa^{31}$         'dog'
      $saa^{41}yɔ^1/saa^{41}$         'sack'
      $kɔɔ^{23}yɔ^2/kɔɔ^{23}$         'chicken'

— Nominals, whose stem ends in a consonant or consonant cluster and has an upglide to $^1$, change the -yɔ suffix to an -i suffix,[32] which takes a tone according to the spreading principle discussed in §3.2.

(46)  $bar^{21}yɔ^1/ba^2ri^1$            'mountain hedgehog'
      $po^1kil^{21}yɔ^1/po^1ki^2li^1$    'bark of the tree'
      $is^{31}yɔ^1/i^3si^1$             'goat'
      $gbag^{41}yɔ^1/gba^4gi^1$         'shelter'
      $zaal^{121}yɔ^1/zaa^{12}li^1$     'okra'
      $kpand^{121}yɔ^1/kpan^{12}di^1$   'trap'
      $pịịt^{231}yɔ^1/pịị^{23}ti^1$     'prop'

— Other nominals ending in -yɔ simply change the suffix to -i while maintaining its tone (which is derived from the stem according to the two rules given in §2.1).

(47)  $fur^1yɔ^1/fu^1ri^1$              'hoe'
      $dɔy^2yɔ^2/dɔy^2yi^2$             'horse'
      $to^3tor^3yɔ^2/to^3to^3ri^2$      'type of ant'
      $ɛm^4bil^4yɔ^2/ɛm^4bi^4li^2$      'walk'
      $sees^{13}yɔ^2/see^{13}si^2$      'sorcery'

— Tone $^1$ nominals ending in -ɛ, -o, or -ɔ retain their endings, but the tone of the ending changes from $^1$ to $^3$.

(48)  $taa^1lɛ^1/taa^1lɛ^3$             'scar'
      $lu^1ko^1/lu^1ko^3$               'house'
      $na^1mɔ^1/na^1mɔ^3$               'blacksmith'

---

[32] Another way to look at this phenomenon is to say that the final vowel of the nominal is deleted and the y shifts to i becoming the nucleus of the last syllable.

# Tone Patterns of Nominals in Doyayo

— Nominals which have tone ³ or tone ⁴ on the stem in the long form and end in -ɛ, -o, or -ɔ retain their endings, but the tone of the ending changes from ² to ³ and the tone of the last syllable of the stem changes to ².

(49) kɔ⁴lɛ²/kɔ²lɛ³        'nape of the neck'
     la²yaa³rɛ²/la²yaa²rɛ³  'fetish'
     to³to²/to²to³         'guinea corn'
     daŋ⁴go²/daŋ²go³       'cactus'
     wa⁴lɔ²/wa²lɔ³         'man'

## 5 Nominals in questions

Questions in Dooyaayɔ are formed in two ways. First, they are formed by means of the question particle *ya⁴* at the end of the question. Another possibility is to use the tone of the question particle, letting the voice drop to ⁴ at the end of the question.[33] Compare the clauses in (50).

(50) mɔ¹    reek³¹   ya⁴
     you^SG go^FUT  Q
     Are you going?

     mɔ¹    ree³¹kɔ¹⁴
     you^SG go^FUT-INTRR
     You are going?

The dropping of the voice to ⁴ with the question particle or with the last word can hardly be called a feature of question intonation. As shown in §§1.1 and 1.2, the voice often automatically goes either up or down in pause-group final position. When listening to angry, agitated speech one gets the impression that the final glides are being shortened, whereas in affectionate speech, to children for instance, the glides tend to become more prominent. Pike (1948:16–17) points out that tone languages have

---

[33] The question particle *ya⁴* does not make the question more emphatic (as is the case with the interrogative *nde* in Gbaya, cf. Noss 1973:200), except that leaving out the question particle and adding the tone ⁴ to the final syllable of the last word of the sentence is a feature of fast rather than of slow speech.

The particle *ma³* 'just, then' in questions changes its tone to ⁴, because the sequence ³⁴ is only permitted in ideophones. Thus it becomes very similar to a question particle: *mɔ³ rek¹ raa¹ ma³ ya⁴* (you go-PRES home then Q) 'Are you going home then?', *mɔ³ rek¹ raa¹ ma⁴* (you go-PRES home then-Q) 'You are going home then?'

not been reported to have "a highly organised contrastive system with a limited number of relative levels controlling the formation of intonations that carry shades of meaning." In Dooyaayɔ intonation seems to be only of the emotional type.

**5.1 Indefinite short form.** The form which results when the nominal is put in a question context with the question particle $ya^4$ is isomorphic with the form we find in participial constructions as in (51) and (52).

(51)   $mi^3$  $rek^1$       $maa^2li^1$  $ze^1ko^3$
       I    go^PRES  monkey    buying
       I am going to buy a monkey

(52)   $see^1to^1$  $zerk^2$       $bo^1$  $gi^1$  $zaa^{13}$   $mi^1$  $ɔɔ^3$   $tot^{32}$
       till    rainy^season   the    it   will^come   I    leave   guinea^corn
       $lu^1ko^3$
       planting
       I am not going to plant guinea corn before the rainy season comes.

We will call this form, which occurs both in questions and in participial constructions, the INDEFINITE SHORT FORM.

**5.2 Nominals in questions with question particle.** When we examine the changes that occur when nominals are placed in the context of a question that uses the question particle, we observe that nominals which end in a vowel, like $raa^1$ 'home, compound', and $tɛɛ^1$ 'tree' remain unchanged.[34] Nominals, which take the -yɔ suffix and end in a consonant, change to their relational form as shown in (53).[35]

(53)   $ʔt^{31}/ʔ^3ti^1$         'day'
       $paps^{121}/pap^{12}si^1$  'locust'
       $maal^{21}/maa^2li^1$     'chimpanzee'
       $kel^{31}/ke^3li^1$        'scorpion'
       $bid^{41}/bi^4di^1$        'story'
       $gaps^{41}/gap^4si^1$      'roguish'
       $nii^4til^4/nii^4ti^4li^2$ 'bent'

---

[34]Nominals ending in a vowel with a $^{23}$ pattern have an optional upglide to $^2$ in the indefinite form: $zɛɛ^{23}$ ~ $zɛɛ^{232}$ 'river'. Nominals with tone $^2$ and ending in a semivowel change their tone pattern to $^{32}$ in the indefinite form: $dɔy^2/dɔy^{32}$ 'horse'.

[35]To elicit these examples the frames $mɔ^3$ $raa^{23}$ $X$ $ya^4$ 'did you say X?' or the frame $mɔ^3$ $raa^{23}$ $X$ $ma^4$ 'you said X then?' can be used.

# Tone Patterns of Nominals in Doyayo

Nominals ending in -ɛ, -o, or -ɔ, which have an unchanging level pattern like *uus¹* 'cloud', *luk¹* 'house', and *nam¹* 'blacksmith' remain unchanged. Nominals with an irregular pattern change to the tone pattern of the long form which is imposed on their short form. In the examples given in (54) the long form is stated in parentheses for comparison.

(54)  gaps²/gaps⁴²     (gap⁴sɛ²)      'riot'
      bak²/bak³²        (ba³ko²)       'field'
      wal²/wal⁴²        (wa⁴lɔ²)       'cave'
      dɛl²³/dɛl⁴²       (dɛ⁴lɛ²)       'basket'
      bam²³/bam⁴²       (ba⁴mɔ²)       'big water snake'
      siŋ²³/siŋ⁴²       (siŋ⁴go²)      'sister'

**5.3 Nominals in questions without question particle.** As stated, the tone on the question particle is ⁴. If the question particle is left out, one of the following[36] tone changes takes place:

— If the nominal has a stem ending in an open syllable, bearing a level tone, or upglide to ¹ the tone ⁴ is added to form a downglide as in (55a). If the syllable bears a downglide, the tone ⁴ supplants the second element of the glide as in (55b).

(55)  a. laa¹/laa¹⁴      'fire(?)'
         kaa³¹/kaa³¹⁴    'dog(?)'
         saa⁴¹/saa⁴¹⁴    'sack(?)'

      b. zɛɛ²³/zɛɛ²⁴     'river(?)'
         lɔɔ²³/lɔɔ²⁴     'short(?)'

— If the nominal belongs to the category that changes to its relational form in questions, then the tone ⁴ is added to the -i ending as in (56).

(56)  ɔt³¹/ɔ³ti¹⁴       'day(?)'
      bid⁴¹/bi⁴di¹⁴     'story(?)'

— In the remaining cases the tone ⁴ is added to the long form of the nominal as in (57).

---

[36] For these examples a frame like *mɔ³ gin²¹ X* 'you have X?' must be used, since it is not possible to ask the question without question marker using the verb *raa²³* 'say' which is used in the frames mentioned in footnote 33.

(57)  uus¹/uu¹sɛ¹⁴        'smoke(?)'
      bak²/ba³ko²⁴        'field(?)'
      dɛl²³/ dɛ⁴lɛ²⁴      'basket(?)'

**5.4 Plurals in questions.** When placed in a question and preceded by a question marker, the plural nominal generally remains unchanged. Exceptions to this rule are given in (58).

(58)  waa³to²/waat³² ~ waa²taa⁴²   'children(?)'
      doo³dɛ²/dood³²              'people(?)'

If the question is asked without a question marker, the plural nominal adds tone ⁴ to its last syllable as in (59a). If, however, the last syllable bears tone ³, it is changed to ² before ⁴ as in (59b). (The sequence ³⁴ is limited to ideophones.)

(59) a.  aa³bɛ¹/aa³bɛ¹⁴       'mistakes(?)'
         bi⁴dɛ¹/bi⁴dɛ¹⁴       'stories(?)'

     b.  wa²lɛ³/wa²lɛ²⁴       'men(?)'
         zɛɛ²dɛ³/zɛɛ²dɛ²⁴     'rivers(?)'

The tone patterns of the long, definite short (as opposed to indefinite short) and relational forms are summarized in the table in (60).³⁷

(60)

| Category of nominal | | Long | | Definite short | | Indefinite short | | Relational | |
|---|---|---|---|---|---|---|---|---|---|
| −V¹ | −A | 1 | −A¹ | 1 | − | 1 | − | 13 | − |
| −V⁺ ↗↘ | −A | ⁺↗↘ | −A² | ⁺↗↘ | − | ⁺↗↘ | − | ⁺↗↘ | − |
| −C↗¹ | −A | ↗¹ | −A¹ | ↗¹ | − | → | −i¹ | → | −i¹ |
| −C¹⁺ ↘ | −A | 1⁺↘ | −A¹ᐟ² | 1⁺↘ | − | 1⁺↘ | −i¹ᐟ² | 1⁺↘ | −i¹ᐟ² |
| 1 | −B | 1 | −B¹ | 1 | − | 1 | − | 1 | −B³ |
| 2⁼³ᐟ⁴ | −B | 3/4 | −B² | 2 | − | 32/42 | − | 2 | −B³ |
| 23⁼⁴ | −B | 4 | −B² | 2 | − | 42 | − | 2 | −B³ |

---

³⁷A stands for -yɔ, B for -ɛ, -o, or -ɔ (cf. the table in (33)), + indicates any level tone lower than ¹, ↗ indicates upglide, ↗¹ upglide ending in ¹, ↘ downglide; → indicates spreading principle.

Tone Patterns of Nominals in Doyayo                                    109

## 6 Demonstrative forms

There are several ways to indicate a demonstrative in Dooyaayɔ. Most common is the set in (61) which follow the noun.

(61)  yɛ$^1$rɛ$^1$    'this'       bɔ$^1$rɔ$^1$    'that'
      wɛ$^1$rɛ$^1$   'these'      wɔ$^1$rɔ$^1$   'those'

In addition there are four other demonstrative forms.[38] First, it is possible to place the yɔ$^1$ 'here' after the noun: seem$^4$ luk$^1$ yɔ:$^{13}$ (see-IMP house here) 'look at this house'. This yɔ$^1$ invariably carries tone $^1$, which, however, downglides to $^3$ in pause-group final position.

Secondly, it is possible to add the demonstrative to the noun. This may be done with yɔ$^1$, which basically shifts to -i or -ii and sometimes is indicated by a zero marker, or by allomorphs.

The third possibility of a bound demonstrative is the suffix -ɔ, which may be added to the noun. (The -ɔ suffix is identical to the third-person singular possessive, including its tone pattern.)

### 6.1 Short bound demonstrative with -i.
In many cases this form is identical to the relational form discussed in §4. Examples include nouns ending in -yɔ having a level stem tone other than $^1$ (62a), and those that have a closed-syllable stem carrying a downglide (62b), a one-step upglide ($^{21}$) (62c), or a complex (down-up) glide (62d).

(62)  a. baa$^2$           'father'               baa$^2$           'this father'
         lɛɛ$^2$/s$^2$     'redshank'             lɛɛ$^2$lɛ$^2$     'this redshank'
         kɛɛ$^3$kɛ$^3$     'bluebird'             kɛɛ$^3$kɛ$^3$     'this bluebird'
         tar$^2$           'Fulani'               ta$^2$ri$^2$      'this Fulani'
         gban$^3$          'dress'                gba$^3$ni$^2$     'this dress'
         kɔls$^4$          'dried bean-leaves'    kɔl$^4$si$^2$     'these dried bean
                                                                    leaves'

      b. sees$^{13}$       'sorcery'              see$^{13}$si$^2$  'this sorcery'

      c. bar̰$^{21}$        'mountain hedgehog'    ba̰$^2$ri$^1$      'this mountain
                                                                    hedgehog'

         po$^1$kil$^{21}$  'bark'                 po$^1$ki$^2$li$^1$ 'this bark'

      d. mark$^{231}$      'plainsman'            mar$^{23}$ki$^1$  'this plainsman'

---

[38]The semantic difference between these demonstratives is elusive. All that can be said at this point is that those with yɔ$^1$, -i, -ii, and -ɔ are used anaphorically.

Nouns ending in -yɔ with an open-syllable stem carrying tone $^1$ form the demonstrative by means of a downglide to $^2$ followed by a return to $^1$ as in (63).

(63)   tɛɛ$^1$     'tree'        tɛɛ$^{121}$    'this tree'

In -yɔ nouns with open-syllable stems carrying a glide, the demonstrative is obtained by the addition of a tone $^2$, resulting in a three-way glide shown in (64).

(64)   saa$^{41}$    'bag'      saa$^{412}$    'this bag'
       kaa$^{31}$    'dog'      kaa$^{312}$    'this dog'
       waa$^{23}$    'child'    waa$^{232}$    'this child'

-yɔ nouns with closed-syllable stems carrying a $^{31}$ or $^{41}$ glide, drop the second element of the glide and add -i$^2$ as in (65).

(65)   gbag$^{41}$   'shelter'  gba$^4$gi$^2$   'this shelter'
       is$^{31}$     'goat'     i$^3$si$^2$     'this goat'

Nouns ending in -ɛ, -o, or -ɔ having tone $^1$ on the stem, obtain their demonstrative form by the addition of -i$^2$ as shown in (66a). If the tone on the stem is lower than $^1$, the demonstrative is formed with the suffix -i and the tone pattern of the relational form as in (66b).

(66)  a. luk$^1$     'house'       lu$^1$ki$^2$   'this house'

      b. tot$^2$     'guinea corn' to$^2$ti$^3$   'this guinea corn'
         lɛl$^{23}$  'place'       lɛ$^2$li$^3$   'this place'

**6.2 Long bound demonstrative.** The bound long form is obtained by lengthening the final vowel of the short demonstrative form and upgliding to $^1$ (where the suffix tone is not already $^1$) as in (67a). When there is already a three-way glide, the long form is identical with the short in (67b). When -i$^2$ is preceded in the short form by tone $^2$ on the stem, the tone of the ending descends to $^3$ before upgliding to $^1$ as in (67c).

Tone Patterns of Nominals in Doyayo

(67) a. kɛɛ³kɛ³/kɛɛ³kɛɛ³¹     'this bluebird'
gba³ni²/ gba³nii²¹     'this dress'
gba⁴gi²/gba⁴gii²¹     'this shelter'
ba̧²ri¹/ ba̧²rii¹     'this mountain hedgehog'
mar²³ki¹/mar²³kii¹     'this plainsman'
po¹ki²li¹/po¹ki²lii¹     'this bark'

b. waa²³²/waa²³²     'this child'

c. ta²ri²/ta²rii³¹     'this Fulani'
nuu²ni²/nuu²nii³¹     'this cooking pot'

**6.3 Use of the short versus long bound demonstrative.** The short form is obligatory in pause-group final position. Before a locational particle (in, on, under, etc.), either the short or the long form may be used as in (68a). Elsewhere, the long form is obligatory. When used as subject, this demonstrative always neutralizes the tone of the verb, changing it to ² as in (68b).

(68) a. mi³gbɛn³ a¹ lu¹ki² ~ lu¹kii²¹ du¹³
I saw it in this house (that you told me about)

taa¹² a¹ gba⁴gi² ~ gba⁴gii²¹ ha¹³
It's not on this shelter (that we've been talking about).

b. hi¹nii²¹    dɛɛ̧r²       ma³ baa² mi¹ gaps²     yɔ¹ ya⁴
thing^this put^a^stop^to then father my viciousness this Q
Could anything put a stop to my father's viciousness?

buu²³²    zaa²   gi¹   dɛɛ̧⁴ro²
white^this came he put^a^stop^to
This white man came and put a stop to it.

**6.4 Demonstrative and third singular possessive with -ɔ.** The tone on the -ɔ suffix is either ²³ or ³. After multisyllable stems, the suffix takes ²³, except when the stem throughout bears tone ¹ shown in (69).

(69) to³tor³    'ant'      to³to³rɔ²³    'that/his ant'
su¹sug²¹    'hair'      su¹su²¹gɔ²³    'that/his hair'
maa²lɛ¹    'chimpanzees'      maa²lɛ¹ɔ²³    'those/his chimpanzees'
nɛ³sɛ¹    'relatives'      nɛ³sɛ¹ɔ³    'those/his relatives'
waa¹wa¹    'circular dance'      waa¹wa¹ɔ³    'that/his dance'
la¹gɛ¹    'deaf persons'      la¹gɛ¹ɔ³    'those/his deaf persons'

Monosyllabic nouns with tone ¹ or a three-way glide ending in ¹ on the stem take -ɔ³ as in (70).

(70)  luk¹         'house'         lu¹kɔ³         'that/his house'
      tɛɛ¹         'tree'          tɛɛ¹ɔ³         'that/his tree'
      kpand¹²¹     'trap'          kpan¹²¹dɔ³     'that/his trap'
      mark²³¹      'plainsman'     mar²³¹kɔ³      'that/his plainsman'

If the stem has tone ² or a downglide, the suffix takes tone ³ as in (71). (Note that with the ²³ glides the second element of the glide is lost in the demonstrative form.)

(71)  tar²         'Fulani'        ta²rɔ³         'that/his Fulani'
      tot²         'guinea corn'   to²tɔ³         'that/his guinea corn'
      nɛɛd²        'women'         nɛɛ²dɔ³        'those/his children'
      sees¹³       'sorcery'       see¹³sɔ³       'that/his sorcery'
      kɔɔ²³        'chicken'       kɔɔ²ɔ³         'that/his chicken'

If the stem has tone ³ or ⁴ or an upglide, the suffix takes ²³. The high element of the upglide is lost, except in the case of ²¹ shown in (72).

(72)  gbar³        'father-in-law'        gba³rɔ²³       'that/his father-in-law'
      kɔls⁴        'dried bean-leaf'      kɔl⁴sɔ²³       'that/his dried bean leaf'
      kaa³¹        'dog'                  kaa³ɔ²³        'that/his dog'
      is³¹         'goat'                 i³sɔ²³         'that/his goat'
      saa⁴¹        'sack'                 saa⁴ɔ²³        'that/his sack'
      gbag⁴¹       'shelter'              gba⁴gɔ²³       'that/his shelter'
      bar̰²¹        'mountain hedgehog'    ba̰²¹rɔ²³       'that/his mountain hedgehog'

### 7 Vocative forms

There are two types of vocative, the polite and the familiar, which will be treated in this section.

**7.1 Polite vocative.** The polite vocative has two freely alternating forms in the singular, one being identical with the relational form of the noun and shown in (73a). The other form is obtained by the addition of yɔɔ¹³ to the short definite form of the noun as in (73b).

# Tone Patterns of Nominals in Doyayo

(73) a. na¹mɔ¹        'blacksmith'           na¹mɔ³      'blacksmith!'
      lɛnd¹yɔ¹        'cannibal'             lɛn¹di¹     'cannibal!'
      naad⁴¹yɔ¹       'old woman'            naa⁴di¹     'old woman!'
      wa⁴lɔ²          'man'                  wa²lɔ³      'man!'

   b. nam¹yɔɔ¹³       'blacksmith!'
      lɛnd¹yɔɔ¹³      'cannibal!'
      naad⁴¹yɔɔ¹³     'old woman!'
      wal²³yɔɔ¹³      'man!'

In the plural, whenever the -ɛ of the plural form does not take tone ¹, the vocative is isomorphic with the relational form as shown in (74a). When the -ɛ of the plural form has tone ¹, the vocative is obtained by lengthening the -ɛ and downgliding to ³ as in (74b).

(74) a. la¹yaa¹dɛ³yɔ²   'soldiers'              la¹yaa¹dɛ³     'soldiers!'
        kpaa³rɛ³yɔ²    'uncircumcized men'     kpaa³rɛ³       'uncircumcized men!'

        nɛɛ³dɛ²        'women'                 nɛɛ²dɛ³        'women!'
        waa⁴to²        'children'              waa²to³        'children!'

    b.  dɛn¹tɛ¹yɔ¹     'old men'               dɛn¹tɛɛ¹³      'old men!'
        mar²³kɛ¹yɔ¹    'plainsmen'             mar²³kɛɛ¹³     'plainsmen!'
        naa⁴dɛ¹yɔ¹     'old women'             naa⁴dɛɛ¹³      'old women!'

Another form of the polite vocative in the plural, which freely alternates with the above, is obtained by the addition of the plural demonstrative wɛɛ¹³ < wɛ¹rɛ¹ 'these', which in non-final position is realized as wɛ¹. wɛɛ¹³ is added to the short plural form of the noun shown in (75).

(75) dɛn¹tɛ¹wɛɛ¹³     'old men!'
     kpaa³rɛ³wɛɛ¹³    'uncircumcized men!'
     nɛɛ²dɛ³wɛɛ¹³     'women!'

This form is obligatory in a few cases if one wants to avoid ambiguity, where the other form could indicate either the vocative of the singular or the vocative of the plural as shown in (76).

(76) gɛ²rɛ³          'medicine man/men!'    gɛ²rɛ³wɛɛ¹³    'medicine men!'
     ɔ²rɛ³           'co-wife/wives!'        ɔ²rɛ³wɛɛ¹³     'co-wives!'

**7.2 Familiar vocative.** The familiar vocative is obtained by the addition of -$yoo^3$ to the short definite form of the noun in (77).

(77)    $baa^2 \sim baa^2ba^2$    'father'
       $baa^2yoo^3 \sim baa^2ba^2yoo^3$    'Daddy!'

       $gbaag^{31}$    'fiancee'
       $gbaag^{31}yoo^3$    '(my) fiancee!'

       $dɛnt^1$    'old man'
       $dɛnt^1yoo^3$    '(my) old man!'

This vocative can also be added to Dooyaayɔ proper names and foreign origin as shown in (78). The familiar vocative does not exist in the plural.

(78)    $ɔɔm^{31}waa^3yoo^3\ zaa^{23}\ mɔ^2$    'Let-Me-Live (dog's name), come!'
       $an^1maa^3ri^1yoo^3$    'Annemarie!'

An alternative form of the familiar vocative, which is limited, however, to proper names, is obtained by the addition of the ending -$ii^2$ to the short form of the name. This form of the vocative is applicable to names of foreign origin ending in a consonant (79), as well as to many Fulani or true Dooyaayɔ names, where it supplants the final vowel (80).

(79)    $zil^3bɛ^{23}rii^2$    'Gilbert!'
       $ra^3sɛ^{13}lii^2$    'Rachel!'

(80)    $zaa^3taw^{13}yɔ^2$    'Rather Light-Skinned Person'    $zaa^3ta^{13}wii^2$
       $ɓɛɛ^3di^2bɔ^3$    'He Looks for a Dowry Cloth'    $ɓɛɛ^3di^{23}bii^2$
       $bɛt^1ki̠^3mɔ^3$    'God Created'    $bɛt^1ki̠^3mii^2$

## References

Bohnhoff, Lee E. and Charles H. Kraft. n.d. An initial comparison of Duru, Duupa, and Doyayo (Namshi). ms.

Cowen, George M. 1948. Mazateco whistle speech. Language 24:280–86.

Greenberg, Joseph H. (1963) 1966. The languages of Africa. The Hague: Mouton.

Noss, Philip A. 1973. Introduction to Gbaya. Meiganga (Cameroon).

Pike, Kenneth L. 1948. Tone languages. Ann Arbor: University of Michigan.
Tessmann, Günther. 1932. Die Völker und Sprachen Kameruns. Sondernabdruck aus Petermanns Mitteilungen. Doppelhefte 5/6, 7/8. Gotha: Justus Perthes.
Westermann, Dietrich and Margaret Bryan. 1952. Languages of West Africa. Handbook of African Languages 2. Oxford: OUP.
Wiering, Marinus and Elisabeth Wiering. 1976. Description phonologique du doohwaayããyo. Parler do Poli. Yaoundé: ALCAM 1976/2.

# Some Major Structures of Doyayo Syntax

## Elisabeth Wiering

The purpose of this study[1] is to present some of the major structures of the syntax of Dooyąąyɔ,[2] within the framework of the tagmemic model.[3]

A hierarchy consisting of seven levels has been set up to facilitate the analysis. They are discourse, sentence, clause, phrase, word, stem and morpheme level.

---

[1]This study reflects research done in Poli and Gare, Cameroon, by the author and her husband between 1971 and 1979, under the auspices of the Summer Institute of Linguistics and within the framework of a cooperative agreement with the University of Yaoundé and the National Office of Scientific and Technological Research (ONAREST) of Cameroon.

A sincere debt of gratitude is owed to Pascal Djataou for his patient help with the gathering and checking of data on his language. Furthermore, I am indebted to Mona Perrin, Ursula Wiesemann, and Don Burquest for consultant help at different stages of the analysis and write-up.

[2]The present study is based on the Tɛɛrɛ dialect of Poli. The symbolization in this paper is a phonemic transcription. For a more detailed description of Dooyąąyɔ phonology see the first article in this volume. Pause-group final morphophonemic changes in the form of vowel length and tonal up- or downglides have been omitted in the examples in this article.

[3]For a full description of the theoretical ramifications of this model, see K. L. Pike, *Language in Relation to a Unified Theory of the Structure of Human Behaviour* (The Hague: Mouton, 1967).

## 1 The morpheme

The morpheme functions within the stem and at word level and is, by definition, indivisible. It is the smallest meaningful unit of the grammar.

There are two kinds of morphemes: FREE (an open class) and BOUND (a closed class). Free morphemes are those minimal, meaningful units that can stand alone, while bound morphemes can only occur affixed to a free morpheme. Many roots, and the so-called particles, are free morphemes because they can function at word level without the addition of any other morphemes. For example, the *loo⁴* of *loo⁴ti¹nu³* 'marry' is a root or free morpheme meaning 'take'. The *-t*, *-n*, and *-u* are bound morphemes. They cannot occur by themselves, even though each has a meaning (*-t* ITERATIVE, *-n* ACCESSORY, *-u* INFLEXIONAL), but must be affixed to a root or stem.

### 1.1 Free morphemes

The types of roots, in the approximate order of their relative frequency, are verbs, nouns, ideophones, adverbs, numerals, and adjectives. Verbs far outnumber other kinds of roots, and there are far more nouns and adjectives formed by derivation from verb roots than there are true nouns or adjectives based on a nominal or adjectival root. In fact, a single verb root usually gives rise to a number of derived nouns and adjectives as shown in (1).

(1) wɔr³ 'die'  
    wɔr³ko²      'death, corpse'  
    wɔrk³¹yɔ¹      'dead'  
    wɔ¹lɛ¹      'paralyzed'  
    wɔ¹sɛ¹      'epidemic'  
    wcr³kil¹yɔ¹      'dead'  
    wc³tig¹yɔ¹      'anguish, extreme anxiety'

(2) gaa²³ 'shine, be bright'  
    gaa¹to¹, gaat¹yc¹      'clean'  
    gaa¹lɛ¹      'bright'  
    gaa¹tig¹yɔ¹      'cleanliness'  
    gaa¹kil³yɔ²      'brightness, daylight'  
    gaa¹ki¹      'very bright'

Though it is sometimes difficult to ascertain the precise meaning and form of a root, there is considerable evidence to suggest that all roots are monosyllabic in Doowaayaayɔ. Any word can be broken down into one or more monosyllabic roots with derivational and other affixes.

# Some Major Structures of Doyayo Syntax

Furthermore, true roots occur in only two major syllable patterns, (C)VC and (C)VV, and one minor syllable pattern, CV, restricted to the small group of tone 2 verbs. The very common (C)VCC and (C)VVC patterns are not considered to represent true roots because not a single instance has been observed where the pattern was not suspect of being interpreted as root + derivational suffix, thus making a stem.

(3)  (C)VCC or (C)VVC stem                Root

| | | | |
|---|---|---|---|
| waal$^1$ | 'country' | waa$^3$ | 'live, inhabit' |
| yɔɔr$^1$ | 'blind person' | yɔɔ$^{23}$ | 'be blind' |
| zaas$^2$ | 'cover (of pot)' | zaa$^3$ | 'cover (v)' |
| toos$^1$ | 'taxes' | too$^4$ | 'pay (v)' |
| piit$^{231}$ | 'prop (N)' | pii$^{23}$ | 'prop (v)' |
| gbɛɛr$^3$ | 'slaughter (v)' | gbɛɛ$^3$ | 'cut (v)' |
| tuur$^4$ | 'arrive' | tuu$^4$ | 'go out' |
| piil$^1$ | 'trap (N)' | pii$^{23}$ | 'prop (v)' |
| miil$^2$ | 'nostril' | mii$^{23}$ | 'blow one's nose' |
| luur$^{41}$ | 'dust-devil' | luu$^{23}$ | 'kick up dust' |
| maat$^3$ | 'trick, fool (v)' | maa$^3$ | 'deceive' |
| maat$^2$ | 'deception, trickery' | maa$^3$ | 'deceive' |
| gums$^1$ | 'sickness' | gum$^3$ | 'hurt' |
| gums$^2$ | 'conjunctivitis' | gum$^3$ | 'hurt' |
| gabs$^2$ | 'strife, danger' | gab$^4$ | 'fight, be mean, belligerent' |
| gabs$^{41}$ | 'mean (AJ)' | gab$^4$ | 'fight, be mean, belligerent' |
| gubr$^4$ | 'pour out, spill completely' | gub$^{23}$ | 'pour, spill (ITR)' |
| | | gub$^4$ | 'pour, spill (TR)' |
| dɔgl$^2$ | 'word, matter, business' | dɔg$^{23}$ | 'speak' |
| ribl$^2$ | 'bunch (of fruit)' | rib$^{23}$ | 'grow in a bunch' |
| wɔrk$^2$ | 'death' | wɔr$^3$ | 'die' |
| wɔms$^1$ | 'old age' | wɔm$^3$ | 'be/grow old' |
| wɔmt$^1$ | 'wall' | wɔm$^3$ | 'build' |
| zugr$^3$ | 'unplug' | zug$^{23}$ | 'plug up' |
| dikt$^{31}$ | 'quickly' | dig$^3$ | 'hurry' |
| nɔɔk$^2$ | 'quickly' | nɔɔ$^4$ | 'run' |

One other instance of a CVCC pattern is observed, and this concerns the homorganic consonant clusters *mb, nd,* and *ŋg*. The stops are usually optional, except when followed by a vowel, so they are considered basically transitional. Thus, we are not dealing here with true clusters.

(4) No transition
    kam³; kaŋk¹ ka¹mɔ¹           'carrying'
    zeṅ²³; zɛ¹nik¹ zɛ¹nɔ¹         'forgetting'

(5) Transition
    kɔm(b)⁴; kɔm¹bik¹ kɔm¹bɔ¹    'staying'
    dun(d)³; dun¹dik¹ dun¹dɔ¹    'rising'
    zaŋ(g)¹; zaŋ¹gik¹ zaŋ¹gɔ¹    'reading'

**1.1.1 Verb roots.** Verb roots occur in the two main syllable patterns, (C)VC and (C)VV. The parentheses here indicate that the initial consonant occurs in some roots and not in others, but its presence or absence has no effect whatever on the tone pattern of the verb word.

As previously mentioned, verbs have a third syllable pattern, CV, which is restricted to the very small class of tone ² roots.

There are five etic tone patterns of verb roots: ¹, ², ²³, ³, and ⁴. The patterns ²³, ³, and ⁴ are the most common, with the tone ³ verbs far outnumbering all others. The limited class of tone ² roots, though numbering less than a dozen, includes such common verbs as le² 'eat', yɔ² 'drink', yo² 'sleep', and gi² 'be'. A closer examination of tone ¹ verbs reveals that there are no non-suspect examples of verb roots with high tone. The vast majority of these forms are, in fact, stems formed by a perturbation to high tone to indicate a change from transitivity to intransitivity or from active to passive as shown in (6).

(6) hod³   'take off (clothing)'    hod¹   'come off (clothing)'
    hot³   'bathe someone'          hot¹   'take a bath'
    bis⁴   'throw away'             bis¹   'be thrown away'
    hạs³   'remove'                 hạs¹   'come off'

The verbs kpel¹ 'become', tot¹ 'bend', and a few others, may possibly be true roots, but the l of kpel¹ and the final t of tot¹ could easily represent the distributive and the iterative suffix respectively, thus making these forms highly suspicious, even though an actual root cannot be traced.

(7)–(9) give examples of the most common classes of verb roots.

(7) Tone ³
    oo³    'wait, keep'       baa³   'dance for a dead person'
    ɛr³    'ask'              nam³   'grind'
    ịị³    'bury'             hɛd³   'sweep'
    ɛɛ³    'sing'             gụụ³   'smell'
    wɛɛ³   'return'           dig³   'hurry'

Some Major Structures of Doyayo Syntax

(8) Tone ²³
| | | | |
|---|---|---|---|
| aa²³ | 'be wide/open' | baa²³ | 'produce (vegetation)' |
| ii²³ | 'exchange' | bii²³ | 'write' |
| uu²³ | 'emit smoke' | tuu²³ | 'sweep/gather up' |
| ur²³ | 'wash (face)' | gul²³ | 'enter' |
| am²³ | 'take/be long' | nam²³ | 'move' |
| ɔg²³ | 'jell, solidify' | dɔg²³ | 'speak/say' |
| ɛb²³ | 'crumble'⁴ | tɛb²³ | 'spin' |

(9) Tone ⁴
| | | | |
|---|---|---|---|
| ii⁴ | 'lick' | kii⁴ | 'touch' |
| ob⁴ | 'bring in (the flock)' | nab⁴ | 'dance' |
| er⁴ | 'stand, stop' | kpel⁴ | 'pour' |
| ɛm⁴ | 'walk' | kɔm⁴ | 'stay' |
| baa⁴ | 'pierce, sew' | dɔb⁴ | 'kick' |

**1.1.2 Noun roots.** True noun roots occur in the two basic syllable patterns, (C)VC and (C)VV, but they have nearly twice as many etic tone patterns as the verb roots. However, if one posits a basic opposition between intrinsically high and intrinsically non-high noun roots, the eight patterns can be broken down into four emic patterns, namely: ¹, ², ³, and ⁴. This observation is borne out by the charts of the etic tone patterns of noun roots in (10) and (11). The figures on the left indicate the emic, or underlying, tone patterns, while those along the top show the suffix tone. All the upglides to high tone occur on roots that take the high-tone -yɔ suffix.

(10)

| underlying root tone | suffix -yɔ¹ | -yɔ² | | |
|---|---|---|---|---|
| | 1 | 1 | 13X | X only (C)VV roots |
| | 2 | 21 | 23X/2Y | Y only (C)VC roots |
| | 3 | 31 | 3Y | |
| | 4 | 41 | 4Y | |

---

⁴Verb roots patterning (C)VC, where the last C is b drop the final consonant before all but the simple -ɔ suffix.

(11)  -ε/-ɔ/-o suffix:    High    Mid-High    Mid[c5]

    root:
       High                     1
       Mid-High                         42a/23b
                                        32a/2b
       Mid                                         3

N.B. Note that roots taking the -ε/-ɔ/-o suffix never have a (C)VV pattern.

The most common tone patterns of (unsuffixed) noun roots are [1], [2], and [23]. Examples of noun roots are given in (12)–(16) and are in their relational form.

(12) **High tone roots**

| -yɔ[1] | | -yɔ[2] | | -ε/-ɔ/-o/(-u) | |
|---|---|---|---|---|---|
| tot[1] | 'razor blade' | | | duk[1] | 'knee' |
| dak[1] | 'calabash' | | | nam[1] | 'blacksmith, potter' |
| fur[1] | 'hoe' | | | tam[1] | 'ashes' |
| baa[1] | 'male' | | | dut[1] | 'fish' |
| goo[1] | 'spear' | | | | |

(13) **Tone [2] noun roots**

| -yɔ[1] | | -yɔ[2] | | -ε/-ɔ/-o/(-u) | |
|---|---|---|---|---|---|
| bạr[21] | 'hedgehog' | tar[2] | 'Fulani' | nam[2] | 'animal, meat' |
| gum[21] | 'locust' | dɔy[2] | 'horse' | bak[2] | 'field, garden' |
| bam[21] | 'leprous spot' | baa[2] | 'father' | tus[2] | 'metal, money' |
| | | | | tot[2] | 'sorghum' |
| | | | | duk[2] | 'bag, thousand' |

---

[5]Where (a) independent, or lexical form of the noun; (b) relational (= narrative or enumerative) form; and (c) only one example of a tone [3] suffix has been observed in Doyayo: gba³rɔ³/gbar³yɔ² 'father-in-law'. It should be noted that, on phonological grounds, the pattern (C)VV does not occur on -ε/-ɔ/-o nouns. The [42/23] patterning is mutually exclusive with the [32/2] patterning, the latter affecting (C)VC noun roots ending in t, k, or s sounds that seem to have the propensity of raising the tone. All mid-high -ε/-ɔ/-o noun stems patterning (C)VVC and (C)VCC also take [32/2].

# Some Major Structures of Doyayo Syntax

(14) Tone $^{23}$ noun roots

| -yɔ¹ | -yɔ² | | -ɛ/-ɔ/-o/(-u) | |
|---|---|---|---|---|
| | waa²³ | 'child' | tam²³ | 'sheep' |
| | doo²³ | 'human being' | gum²³ | 'owl' |
| | kɔɔ²³ | 'chicken' | ạr²³ | 'water buffalo' |
| | gɔ̧ɔ̧²³ | 'peanuts' | lɛl²³ | 'place' |
| | nɛɛ²³ | 'woman' | hab²³ | 'boar' |

(15) Tone $^3$ noun roots

| -yɔ¹ | | -yɔ² | | -ɛ/-ɔ/-o/(-u) | |
|---|---|---|---|---|---|
| ɔ̧t³¹ | 'day, sun' | gban³ | 'robe' | | |
| is³¹ | 'goat' | gbar³ | = | gbar³ | 'father-in-law' |
| taw³¹ | 'ankle-bell' | mag³ | 'type of bird' | | |
| kaa³¹ | 'dog' | keg³ | 'weevil' | | |
| dɔm³¹ | 'circumcized person' | | | | |

(16) Tone $^4$ noun roots

| -yɔ¹ | | -yɔ² | | -ɛ/-ɔ/-o/(-u) |
|---|---|---|---|---|
| gbag⁴¹ | 'shelter' | kɔls⁴ | 'dried black-eyed pea leaves' | |
| bɔk⁴¹ | 'sling' | | | |
| saa⁴¹ | 'bag' | | | |
| hɛɛ⁴¹ | 'type of sesame' | | | |

## 1.2 Bound morphemes

**1.2.1 Derivational suffixes.** Derivational suffixes are suffixes that are added to roots to convert them into stems of the same or another class. For example, verb roots can be converted into verb stems, noun stems, adjective stems, or adverb stems. Noun and adjective roots can be converted into noun or adjective stems and, less commonly, into verb stems.

*Verbal derivational suffixes.* There are fourteen common derivational suffixes resulting in verb stems. These are listed in (17) according to their estimated relative frequency of occurrence, beginning with the most frequent.

(17)

| | | | | |
|---|---|---|---|---|
| | ɓaa²³ | 'be hard' | kar⁴ | 'climb' |
| benefactive -s | ɓaas²³ | 'seem hard to someone' | kas⁴¹ | 'climb for someone' |
| immediate -z | ɓaaz²³ | 'be hard just now' | kaz⁴¹ | 'climb this way, i.e., toward speaker' |
| | ɓaa²³ | 'be hard' | kar⁴ | 'climb' |
| accessory -n | ɓaan²³ | 'be hard with' | kan⁴¹ | 'climb with' |
| prepunctive -d/-dir | ɓaad²³¹/ ɓaa²³dir¹ | 'already be hard' | kard⁴¹/ kad⁴¹ | 'already have climbed' |
| reciprocal -tin | ɓaa²³tin¹ | 'all be hard' | kar⁴tin¹/ ka⁴tin¹ | 'climb together' |
| intensive/ durative -s/-sig | ɓaas²³¹ | 'be so hard' | ka⁴sig¹ | 'keep on climbing' |
| | ɓaa²³sig¹ | 'stay so hard' | | |
| causative -s | ɓaas³ | 'harden, strengthen' | kas⁴ | 'bring up, cause to mount' |
| | kpɛɛ²³ | 'close' | | |
| passive -y | kpɛɛy¹ | 'be closed' | kay¹/ka¹riy¹ | 'be climbed, mounted' |
| iterative -t | ɓaat²³ | 'several are hard' | kat⁴ | 'climb many times' |
| distributive -l | ɓaal²³ | 'be hard in several places' | ka⁴ril¹ | 'climb many trees' |
| | | | ka⁴til¹ | 'many people climb (many) trees' |
| intensive/ reversive -r | kpɛɛr⁴ | 'open' | gub⁴ gubr⁴ | 'pour out, spill' 'spill completely' |
| augmentative -m | zįį²³ zįįm³ | 'long (AJ)' 'be long (PL S)' | tus³ tums³ | 'spit' 'spit out (PL O)' |
| pejorative -k | gbaa⁴ gbaak⁴ | 'put, keep' 'put down keep in disorder' | kol¹ kolk³ | 'be healthy' 'cough' |
| | lɔɔ²³ | 'short (AJ)' | zoo³ | 'remove the honey from' |
| intensive -b | lɔɔb³ | 'be/become short' | zoob⁴ | 'be/become bitter' |

The first four suffixes listed in (17) (benefective -s, immediate -z, accessory -n, and prepunctive -d/-dir) are the most common and least restricted of all the suffixes, because they can occur with any verb root or stem. The causative -s and passive -y are restricted semantically, the former occurring

# Some Major Structures of Doyayo Syntax

almost exclusively with intransitive roots or stems and the latter nearly always with transitives. The suffix -n sometimes functions as a causative, as in *len¹* 'feed' (from *le²* eat') and *wɛɛn³* 'give back, return (TR)' (from *wɛɛ³* 'return (ITR)'). There is considerable overlap of function between iterative -t, distributive -l, and augmentative -m. Sometimes even -n functions distributively.

As many as four verbal derivational suffixes can occur with a single root. A sequence of four derivational suffixes in a verb stem is rare, but three are not uncommon (see the second article in this volume for further discussion). Some examples of roots with more than one derivational suffix are in (18).[6]

(18)
| Root | | Derived stem | |
|---|---|---|---|
| mɔk⁴ | 'think' | mɔk⁴til¹ | 'think all day every day' |
| el⁴ | 'call' | el¹diy¹ | 'already be called' |
| gbɛɛ³ | 'cut' | gbɛlts³¹ | 'cut up into small pieces for someone' |
| | | gbɛɛl³nins¹ | 'cut up many things with something for someone' |
| ar³ | 'scrape up, dig up' | at³sin¹ | 'scrape up for someone with something (PL S)' |
| fɔb⁴ | 'follow' | fɔpts⁴ | 'pursue for someone' |
| | | fɔmndz⁴¹ | 'have followed with something already just now this way (toward speaker)' |
| lug³ | 'plant' | luys¹ | 'be planted for someone' |
| baa⁴ | 'sew' | baa⁴lilt¹ | 'sew very poorly (PL O)'[7] |
| yɛɛ⁴ | '(deponent root)' | yɛɛl⁴tir¹ | 'already have started many times' |
| yɔ² | 'drink' | yɔɔ³mins¹ | 'drink (PL O) with something for someone' |

*Nominal and adjectival derivational suffixes.* There is considerable overlap of function between derivational suffixes that create nouns and those that create adjectives. In fact, with verbal roots, only a few of the suffixes are strictly nominal or adjectival; the majority can perform either function, depending on the root they are modifying.

*Conversion of nouns/adjectives into other noun/adjectives.* Derivational suffixes that convert nouns or adjectives into other nouns or adjectives are shown in (19)–(24). Inflexional suffixes are separated from the stem by a hyphen.

---

[6] Multiple suffixation usually results in addition of -i- epenthesis and thus of a syllable.

[7] Here the first -l is functioning pejoratively.

(19) Abstract -s, -ums          Derived noun

| | | | |
|---|---|---|---|
| tɛɛ¹-yɔ¹ | 'tree' | tɛs¹-ɛ¹ | 'forest' |
| gɛr⁴-ɔ² | 'healer' | gɛrs³-ɛ² | 'miracle' |
| rɔb⁴¹-yɔ¹ | 'foreign' | rɔbs⁴¹-ɛ¹/-yɔ¹ | 'journey' |
| sąąm³¹-ɔ¹ | 'friend' | sąms³¹-ɛ¹/-yɔ¹ | 'friendship' |
| lagr¹-yɔ¹ | 'deaf' | lag¹rums¹-ɛ¹/-yɔ¹ | 'deafness' |
| nɛs³-ɛ² | 'relative' | nɛ³sums¹-ɛ¹/-yɔ¹ | 'relatives' |
| waar¹-yɔ¹ | 'chief' | waa¹rums¹-ɛ¹/-yɔ¹ | 'kingdom' |
| gbɔɔl¹-ɛ¹ | 'big' | gbɔ¹lums¹-ɛ¹/-yɔ¹ | 'greatness' |

(20) Partitive -d or -um/-im/-dum or -in

| | | | |
|---|---|---|---|
| kųų²³-yɔ² | 'back' | kųųd³¹-yɔ¹ | 'last' |
| kɔl⁴-ɛ² | 'neck' | kɔl⁴-um¹-yɔ¹ | 'of the neck' |
| hɛt¹-o¹ | 'grass/ bush-bush' | hɛt¹um¹-yɔ¹ | 'wild' |
| buu¹-yɔ¹ | 'belly' | buu¹dum¹-yɔ¹ | 'internal' |
| fab¹-o¹ | 'uncle' | fab¹in¹yɔ¹ | 'of the uncle' |

(21) Diminutive -d or -l/-dil

| | | | |
|---|---|---|---|
| naa⁴¹-yɔ¹ | 'mother' | naad⁴¹-yɔ¹ | 'little mother' |
| sum⁴-ɔ² | 'big drum' | suml³-ɛ² | 'tom-tom' |
| gban³-yɔ² | 'robe' | gban³dil³-ɛ²/-yɔ² | 'clothes' |

(22) Diminutive -a

| | | | |
|---|---|---|---|
| oor¹-yɔ¹ | 'babysitter' | oo¹ra¹⁴-yɔ² | 'young babysitter' |
| wal⁴-ɔ² | 'man' | wa²la⁴-yɔ² | 'boy' |
| rɔm⁴-ɔ² | 'rabbit' | rɔ²ma¹⁴-yɔ² | 'hare' |
| dɛnt¹-yɔ¹ | 'old man' | dɛn¹ta⁴-yɔ² | 'little old man' |

(23) Augmentative -tɔ

| | | | |
|---|---|---|---|
| hɛb⁴¹-yɔ¹ | 'saucepot' | hɛb⁴¹tɔ¹-yɔ¹ | 'beer tub' |
| wal⁴-ɔ² | 'man' | wal⁴¹tɔ¹-yɔ¹ | 'male' |
| dɔm³¹-yɔ¹ | 'circumcized person' | dɔm³tɔ¹-yɔ¹ | 'first-circumcized person' |

# Some Major Structures of Doyayo Syntax

(24) Functional *-ya*

| | | | |
|---|---|---|---|
| *dobᶠtilᶠ-yɔ²* | 'leprosy' | *dobᶠtilᶠyaᶦ-yɔᶦ* | 'leper' |
| *ramsᶦ-εᶦ* | 'message' | *ramsᶦyaᶦ-yɔᶦ* | 'messenger' |
| *gɔɔ²³ sąkᶦ -yɔᶦ* | 'peanut butter' | *gɔɔ²³sąkᶦyaᶦ-yɔᶦ* | 'maker or seller of peanut butter' |
| *biᶦsεᶦ* | 'sauce' | *bisᶦyaᶦ-yɔᶦ* | 'of the sauce' |

*Conversion of verbs into nouns or adjectives.* Derivational suffixes that convert verbs into nouns, adjectives, or adverbs are listed in (25)–(39). (The vowels *-i-* and *-u-* within the suffix are always epenthetic.)

(25) Abstract *-s*                Derived noun

| | | | |
|---|---|---|---|
| *wɔr³* | 'die' | *wɔsᶦ-εᶦ* | 'epidemic' |
| *rɔb⁴* | 'be gracious' | *rɔbsᶦ-εᶦ* | 'blessing' |
| *saŋ³* | 'be cold' | *saŋs³-yɔ²* | 'cold(ness)' |
| *bit³* | 'reconstitute, add liquid' | *bisᶦ-εᶦ* | 'sauce' |
| *dor³* | 'precede' | *doos³¹-yɔᶦ* | 'first (AJ)' |
| | | *doos³-εᶦ* | 'previously, earlier, in the past' |
| | | *woos⁴¹-yɔᶦ* | 'diligent, hard-working' |
| *woo⁴* | 'work' | *woos⁴-ε²* | 'work (N)' |
| *gab⁴* | 'be mean; pick a fight' | *gaps⁴-ε²* | 'trouble, fighting danger' |
| | | *gaps⁴¹-yɔᶦ* | 'aggressive, querrulous' |
| *doo³* | 'lose weight, get thin' | *doosᶦ-εᶦ* | 'weight loss, thinness' |

(26) Nominal *-d*

| | | | |
|---|---|---|---|
| *hąs³* | 'remove' | *hądᶦ-εᶦ* | 'intestines' |
| *hɔɔm⁴* | 'suck' | *hɔd⁴-ε²* | 'bee' |
| — | (root unknown) | *dεdᶦ-εᶦ* | 'louse' |
| — | | *budᶦ-εᶦ* | 'fly' |
| — | | *diid³¹-yɔᶦ* | 'small wasp' |
| — | | *dood³¹-yɔᶦ* | 'boogeyman' |
| *bid⁴¹* | 'unfold, open up' | *bid⁴¹ yɔᶦ* | 'story, folktale' |

(27) Functional *-kya( ~ -ikya ~ -igya)*[8]

| | | | |
|---|---|---|---|
| *zεε⁴* | 'dig' | *zεεkᶦyaᶦ-yɔᶦ* | 'digger' |
| *woon⁴* | 'work with' | *wookᶦyaᶦ-yɔᶦ* | 'worker' |

---

[8]The resultant form is inherently an adjective, but it functions frequently as a noun.

| | | | |
|---|---|---|---|
| zaas³ | 'save' | zaa¹sig¹ya¹-yɔ¹ | 'savior' |
| bal³ | 'cultivate' | balk¹ya¹-yɔ¹ | 'farmer' |
| ban³ | 'cultivate with' | ba¹nik¹ya¹-yɔ¹ | 'for cultivating (AJ)' |

(28) Nominal -tin (= -t + EP + n)

| | | | |
|---|---|---|---|
| foo²³ | 'burst' | foo¹tin³-yɔ² | 'tic' |
| tuu⁴ | 'go out' | tu¹tin³-yɔ² | 'entrance hut' |
| mɛɛ²³ | 'fall, drop' | mɛ¹tin³-yɔ¹ | 'urine' |
| pɛɛ⁴ | 'lift' | pɛ¹pɛ¹tin³-yɔ² | 'swallow (bird)' |

(29) Nominal -(i)r

| | | | |
|---|---|---|---|
| kɔɔ³ | 'bloom' | kɔɔr³-ɛ² | 'flower' |
| tuu²³ | 'collect, sweep together' | tuur¹-ɛ¹ | 'mound' |
| dɔɔ²³ | 'burn' | dɔɔr¹-ɛ¹/-yɔ¹ | 'stake, execution pole' |
| dund³ | 'rise' | dun³dir¹-yɔ¹ | 'plateau' |
| kaps⁴ | 'light (a fire)' | kap¹sir³-yɔ² | 'pins-and-needles sensation' |
| ʔʔ³ | 'pinch' | ʔ³tir¹-yɔ¹ | 'ant' |

(30) Nominal -tig

| | | | |
|---|---|---|---|
| rɔb⁴ | 'be generous' | rɔb¹tig⁴-yɔ² | 'generosity' |
| wɔr³ | 'die' | wɔ³tig¹-yɔ¹ | 'anguish, extreme anxiety' |
| hɛɛm⁴ | 'be sweet, savory' | hɛm¹tig³-yɔ² | 'flavor, sweetness, savor' |
| tuun⁴ | 'go out with' | tun¹tig³-yɔ² | 'pus' |
| bɛn³ | 'be beautiful with' | bɛn¹tig³-yɔ² | 'feathers' |

(31) Nomino-adjectival -t

| | | | |
|---|---|---|---|
| er⁴ | 'stop, stand' | ert⁴-yɔ² | 'halt, stance' |
| dɛŋl³ | 'swear' | dɛŋlt³-yɔ² | 'oath' |
| gaa²³ | 'shine' | gaat¹-yɔ¹ | 'clean' |
| bɛr³ | 'be beautiful' | bɛt¹yɔ¹ | 'beautiful' |
| hol²³ | 'breathe' | hot¹-o¹ | 'breath, breathing' |
| baa³ | 'dance for the dead' | baat¹-o¹ | 'poor man's death dance' |
| dɛɛ⁴ | 'be short' | dɛɛt¹-o¹ | 'short, small' |
| ɔɔ³ | 'leave' | ɔɔ¹t-o¹ | 'gleanings' |
| ʔʔ³ | 'pinch' | ʔʔ¹t-o¹ | 'pinch, mouthful (between fingers)' |

Some Major Structures of Doyayo Syntax                              129

      *kim³*          'shape into a ball, create'    *kimt¹-o¹*      'round'

      *dɔɔ²³*         'sow'                      *dɔɔt¹-o¹*      'seed'

(32) Nomino-adjectival -*l*

| | | | |
|---|---|---|---|
| *taa³* | 'shoot' | *taal¹-ε¹* | 'scar' |
| *hɛd³* | 'sweep' | *hɛl⁴-ε²* | 'broom' |
| *wɔr³* | 'die' | *wɔl¹-ε¹* | 'paralyzed' |
| *gaa²³* | 'shine' | *gaal¹-ε¹* | 'bright' |
| *hɔɔ²³* | 'dry in sun' | *hɔɔl⁴-ε²* | 'sand' |
| *bib⁴* | 'cover, envelop' | *bil⁴-ε²* | 'granary' |

(33) Nomino-adjectival -*il* (~*bil*~*kil*~*til*~*sil*)

| | | | |
|---|---|---|---|
| *fɔk⁴* | 'tell (story)' | *fɔ⁴kil⁴-yɔ²* | 'story, account' |
| *tɔɔ³* | 'grow' | *tɔɔ³bil³-yɔ²/-ε²* | 'growth' |
| *nɔɔ⁴* | 'run' | *nɔɔ⁴kil⁴-yɔ²/-ε²* | 'race' |
| *wɔr³* | 'die' | *wɔr³kil¹-yɔ¹* | 'mortal' |
| *haŋ³* | 'wear out' | *haŋ¹sil³-yɔ²* | 'worn-out (rag) for cleaning' |
| *kum(b)³* | 'have twins' | *kum³bil³-yɔ²* | 'twin' |
| *gum³* (AJ) | 'hurt' | *gum¹til³-yɔ²* | 'sick person' |
| *haa³* | 'be sour' | *haa¹til³-yɔ²* | 'type of sour vegetable' |
| *kɔɔb³* | 'eat dry bread/couscous' | *kɔɔ³bil¹-yɔ¹/ε¹* | 'dry bread/couscous' |

(34) Nomino-adjectival -*(i)k*

| | | | |
|---|---|---|---|
| *gbugl³* | 'bark' | *gbug¹lik¹-yɔ¹* | 'barking' |
| *kar⁴* | 'climb' | *kark¹-yɔ¹* | 'steep' |
| *kɔb⁴* | 'draw (water)' | *kɔk¹-o¹* | 'drinkable' |
| *wɔr³* | 'die' | *wɔrk³-o²* | 'death; corpse' |
| *sąb⁴* | 'squish' | *sąk¹-yɔ¹* | 'paste' |

(35) Nomino-adjectival -*m*

| | | | |
|---|---|---|---|
| *yo²* | 'sleep' | *yoo¹m-ε¹* | 'sleep' |
| *bɔɔ⁴* | 'soak' | *bɔɔm⁴-ε²* | 'sponge' |
| *see²³* | 'be quiet' | *seem¹-ε¹* | 'shame' |
| *gąą³* | 'sprinkle' | *gąąm⁴-ε²* | 'blood' |
| *kur³* | 'squeeze' | *kum¹-ε¹* | 'oil' |

(36) Nomino-adjectival *-n*

| | | | |
|---|---|---|---|
| *εε³* | 'sing' | *εε³-n-ε²* | 'for singing'(AJ) |
| *gum³* | 'hurt' | *gum³n-ε²* | 'hurting (AJ)' |
| *dɔb⁴* | 'be heavy' | *dɔm⁴n-ε²* | 'heavy' |

(37) Nomino-adjectival *-n* (± vowel abbreviation and tone change)

| | | | |
|---|---|---|---|
| *naa³* | 'converse' | *naan³-ε²* | 'hand' |
| *nuu³* | 'prepare, cook (couscous)' | *nuun³-ε²* | 'big pot for preparing couscous' |
| *zaa²³* | 'live, be alive' | *zaan³-ε²/yɔ²* | 'person' |
| *dɔɔ⁴* | 'prepare, cook' | *dɔn³-ε¹/dɔn³¹yɔ¹* | 'cooking pot' |
| *maa³* | 'fool, cheat' | *man³-yɔ²* | 'lover, concubine' |
| *boo³(yaa¹yɔ¹)* | 'speak (mouth)' | *yaa¹boon³-ε²* | 'language, speech' |

(38) Nomino-adjectival # (length or tone)

| | | | |
|---|---|---|---|
| *luu(r)³* | 'steal' | *luur³-ε²* | 'theft' |
| | | *luur³¹-yɔ¹* | 'thief' |
| *hoo(b)³* | 'be afraid' | *hoob¹-o¹* | 'fear' |
| *rɔb⁴* | 'be true' | *rɔb¹-o¹* | 'true; truth' |
| *zɔb⁴* | 'pray' | *zɔɔb⁴-o²* | 'prayer' |
| *zoob⁴* | 'be bitter' | *zoob⁴¹-yɔ¹* | 'bitter type of vegetable' |
| *keg³* | 'gnaw, nibble' | *keg³-yɔ²* | 'weevil' |
| *yεs³* | 'worsen' | *yεs³¹-yɔ¹* | 'worse' |
| *ged⁴* | 'tell on someone' | *ged¹-yɔ¹* | 'habit of telling on people' |
| *nab⁴* | 'dance; celebrate' | *naa³b-o²* | 'dance, celebration' |

(39) Nominal *-(s)um*

| | | | |
|---|---|---|---|
| *tεb²³* | 'spin(web)' | *tεb⁴sum⁴-yɔ²/-ε²* | 'spider's web' |
| *hol²³* | 'rest' | *ho²lum²³-yɔ²/-ε²* | 'vacation' |
| *ruut⁴* | 'bud (v)' | *ruu⁴tum⁴-yɔ²/-ε²* | 'budding' |
| *daks³* | 'join' | *dak³sum³-yɔ²/-ε²* | 'crossing' |
| *kur³* | 'squeeze' | *ku¹rum³-yɔ³/-ε²* | 'oil' |

**1.2.2 Pluralizing suffixes.**[9] Most adjectives in Dooyaayɔ can take a plural suffix. By contrast, only a limited number of nouns, mostly human,

---

[9] What is given here is a brief summary, for the sake of clarity. For a more thorough treatment of this subject, see the third article of this volume.

# Some Major Structures of Doyayo Syntax

have a plural form. The plural suffix is ε, with allomorphs -ε, -d, -dε, -t, and VV→V + -ε. The plural suffix functions at stem level in the HEAD MODIFIER slot of the noun or adjective as shown in (40).

(40) doo-d² gbɔl¹-ε³ hi¹ waa²-t-o³
    human-PL big-PL and child-PL-INFL
    grown-ups and children

(41) daŋ²³ zįį²-dε³ wans¹-ε¹ eer¹-ε¹
    knife long-PL small-PL two-INFL
    two small swords

(42) mi³ gbɛn³ maal²-ε¹ kit²-ε¹ a¹ hɛt¹ du¹
    I saw chimpanzee-PL many-PL LOC grass in
    I saw many chimpanzees in the bush-bush.

**1.2.3 Inflexional suffixes.** Inflexional suffixes are the endings normally taken by nouns and adjectives. This is a closed class with only ten members: -yɔ¹, -yɔ², -ε¹, -ɔ¹, -o¹, (-u¹), -ε², -ɔ², -o², and -ɔ³. The inflexional suffix functions at word level in the POSITION MARKER slot of the noun or adjective. For examples, see (19)–(39).

**1.2.4 Possessive suffixes.** The possessive suffix functions at word level in the *root polarizer* slot of the noun. This is a closed class, with the eight members in (43).

(43)   -mi¹   'my'         -wi¹   'our (EXCL)'
      -be¹   'my (CIT)'   -wε¹   'our (INCL)'
      -mɔ¹   'your (SG)'   -nε¹   'your'
      -ɔ²³   'his/her/its'   -yạ²³   'their'

Each of these forms has an allomorph which can replace it with the noun that functions in the head slot of the CP (circumstantial phrase). The allomorph is a free form that precedes the noun rather than being suffixed to it and is identical in form, except in the third person, where -ɔ²³ becomes gi¹ and -yạ²³ becomes hi¹.

**1.2.5 Demonstrative suffixes.** The demonstrative suffix functions at word level in the ROOT POLARIZER slot of the noun.

This is a closed class with two members: remote -ɔ 'that', and proximal -i 'this'. The remote suffix has the allomorphs -ɔ²³ and -ɔ³ and is mutually exclusive with the free remote demonstrative form bɔ¹, which functions at phrase level. The proximal suffix has the allomorphs -$i^1$, -$i^2$, and -$i^3$ (non-emphatic) and -$ii^{21}$ (emphatic) with closed-syllable nouns and ±LENGTH$^{21}$ or ±LENGTH$^2$ in open syllable nouns. It is mutually exclusive with proximal demonstrative -$yɔ^1$, which functions at phrase level.

For examples of the demonstrative suffixes, see §3.1.1. For a discussion of the tone patterns on these suffixes, see §3.1.4. 'Tone of nominal forms'.

## 2 The stem

The stem functions at word level and is potentially composed of one or more roots, one or more root converters (with $i$-epenthesis where applicable), and one stem modifier. The three major types of stems are the noun stem, the adjective stem, and the verb stem.

The stem is set up as a separate hierarchical level for Doowaayaayɔ because the derivational suffixes and plural, augmentative, and diminutive suffixes have been observed to be far more intimately related to the root and to have more stringent rules governing their use than any of the other suffixes.[10]

### 2.1 Noun stems

The noun stem is that unit which normally fills the head slot of the noun word. It is potentially composed of one or two roots, from one to four derivational suffixes, and one stem modifier.

There are three main types of noun stems, the simple noun stem, the compounded noun stem, and the duplicative noun stem.

**2.1.1 The simple noun stem.** The simple noun stem has the structure shown in (44).

(44)
$$+ \text{ hd: } \begin{Bmatrix} \text{v rt} \\ \text{n rt} \\ \text{aj rt} \end{Bmatrix} \pm \text{ rt cnv}_{(4)}: \begin{Bmatrix} \text{drv sf} \\ \text{tn} \\ \text{lgth/sht} \end{Bmatrix} \pm \text{ hd mod: } \begin{Bmatrix} \text{pl} \\ \text{aug} \\ \text{dim} \end{Bmatrix}$$

The simple noun has three tagmemes:

---

[10]For a detailed discussion of derivational (there referred to as "modificational") suffixes in the verb, see the second article in this volume.

# Some Major Structures of Doyayo Syntax

— an obligatory HEAD slot, filled by a verb root, a noun root, or an adjective root; and at least one of the following:
— an optional ROOT CONVERTER, with up to four occurrences, filled by a derivational suffix, a change of the root tone, or lengthening/shortening of the root vowel; and
— an optional HEAD MODIFIER slot, filled by a plural, augmentative, or diminutive suffix.

(45)    $ha\text{-}t^1\text{-}o^1$
please(V)^TN-DRV-INFL
love, joy

$h\varepsilon^4\text{-}l\text{-}\varepsilon^2$
sweep^TN-DRV-INFL
broom

$dund^3\text{-}i\text{-}r^1\text{-}yɔ^1$
rise-EP-DRV-INFL
plateau

$lee\text{-}s^1\text{-}\varepsilon^1$
eat^LGTH^TN-DRV-INFL
food

$lag^1\text{-}r\text{-}u\text{-}m\text{-}s^1\text{-}\varepsilon^1$
hear^TN-DRV-EP-DRV-DRV-INFL
deafness

$mip^1\text{-}t\text{-}i\text{-}n\text{-}s^3\text{-}\varepsilon^2$
cover(V)^TN-DRV-EP-DRV-DRV-INFL
cover (of pot or receptacle)

$tɔɔ^3\text{-}b\text{-}i\text{-}l^3\text{-}yɔ^2$
grow-DRV-EP-DRV-INFL
growth

$naab^3\text{-}o^2$
dance(V)^LGTH^TN-INFL
dance

$g\varepsilon r^3\text{-}s\text{-}\varepsilon^2$
healer^TN-DRV-INFL
miracle, strange event

$gban^3\text{-}d\text{-}i\text{-}l^3\text{-}yɔ^2$
robe-DRV-EP-DRV-INFL
clothes

$sam^{31}\text{-}s\text{-}\varepsilon^1$
friend^SHT-DRV-INFL
friendship

$waa^1\text{-}r\text{-}u\text{-}m^1\text{-}s\text{-}\varepsilon^1$
chief-EP-DRV-DRV-INFL
chieftainship

$gbɔl^1\text{-}u\text{-}m^1\text{-}s\text{-}\varepsilon^1$
big^SHT-EP-DRV-DRV-INFL
greatness

$rɔp\text{-}s^{41}\text{-}yɔ^1$
foreign-DRV-INFL
journey, trip

$wal^2\text{-}\varepsilon^3\text{-}yɔ^2$
men-PL-INFL
men

$d\varepsilon nt^1\text{-}\varepsilon^1$
oldman-PL
old men

$doo^3\text{-}d\text{-}\varepsilon^2$
human^TN-PL-INFL
people

$waa^2\text{-}t\text{-}o^3$
child^TN-PL-INFL
children

$maal^2\text{-}\varepsilon^1\text{-}yɔ^1$
chimpanzee-PL-INFL
chimpanzees

$raa^1\text{-}t\text{-}\varepsilon^1\text{-}yɔ^1$
compound-DRV-PL-INFL
families, villages

*wal²-a⁴-yɔ²*
man-dim-INFL
boy

*dɛnt¹-a¹⁴   za¹*
oldman-DIM other
a little old man

*oo¹-r-a¹⁴-yɔ²*
keep^TN-DRV-DIM-INFL
little babysitter

*nɔɔs²-a⁴*
bird-DIM
little bird

*rɔm²-a¹⁴*
hare^TN-DIM
rabbit

*wal⁴¹-tɔ¹-yɔ¹*
man-AUG-INFL
male

*hɛp⁴¹-tɔ¹-yɔ¹*
saucepot-AUG-INFL
beer tub

*dɔm³¹-tɔ¹-yɔ¹*
circumcised^person-AUG-INFL
first-circumcized person

The very limited class[11] of nouns and the somewhat more extensive class of adjectives that have a plural form can be divided into four subclasses according to their plural ending: (1) those ending in *-d* (the most restricted group), (2) those taking *-t*, (3) those taking *-dɛ*, and (4) all others *-ɛ*.

**Subclass 1.** This subclass of open-syllable roots forms the plural by adding *-d*. No adjectives have been found with this ending. Only two nouns, both very common, have been observed to take this suffix, namely *doo²³* 'human being' and *nɛɛ²³* 'woman, wife'. Other nominals taking this suffix were found to be basically adjectival, *nɔɔ¹* 'female', or verbal, *buu²³* 'white, be white'. See also §3.2.

(46)   *nɛɛ-d³²        gu²bsɛ¹*
       woman-PL(INDP) pour^BEN^us
       The women poured it for us.

       *doo-d²    taa¹r-ɛ¹*
       human-PL three-INFL
       three people

**Subclass 2.** This subclass of open-syllable roots forms the plural by adding *-t*. Only two nouns have been observed to fall into this category, namely *raa¹* 'home, compound' and *waa²³* 'child'. All adjective stems ending in diminutive *-aa⁴* form their plural with the *-t* suffix. Those ending in

---

[11]This is just a brief summary. For a further discussion of pluralization of nouns and adjectives, see the third article of this volume.

augmentative -tɔɔ¹ optionally add -t + V SHT in combination with preceding -ɛ or -dɛ, which is obligatory.

(47) waa-t² ee¹r-ɛ¹
child-PL two-INFL
two children

naa²³waa-t² doo¹til³-aa⁴-t-o²
cow^child-PL thin-DIM-PL-INF
thin little calves

buu²-dɛ²-tɔɔ¹-nɔ¹/ buu²-dɛ³-tɔ-t¹-nɔ¹
white-PL-AUG-AUG/ white-PL-AUG-PL-AUG
very white (PL)

**Subclass 3.** All other pluralizing nominal roots or stems ending in an open syllable or in -iŋ form the plural by adding -dɛ as shown in (48).

(48) naa²³-baa¹-dɛ³
cow-male-PL
bulls

waa-t²siŋ²-dɛ³-yɔ²
child-PL-sister-PL-INF
daughters

buu²-dɛ³
white-PL
white men

**Subclass 4.** All pluralizing nominals ending in a closed syllable where the last consonant is not -ŋ, add the suffix -ɛ to form the plural as shown in (49).

(49) wal²-ɛ³ rɔb¹-ɛ³
man-PL good-PL
good men

kʉʉd³-ɛ¹ wɔ¹
last-PL those
the last ones

**2.1.2 The compounded noun stem.** The compounded noun stem has the structure shown in (50).

(50)
$$+ \text{hd}_1: \begin{Bmatrix} \text{n rt/stm} \\ \text{v rt/stm} \end{Bmatrix} \pm \begin{bmatrix} \text{cmpd}: \begin{Bmatrix} \text{lgthV/shtV} \\ \text{assC/lossC} \\ \text{tn} \end{Bmatrix} \end{bmatrix}_{(3)} + \text{hd}_2: \begin{Bmatrix} \text{n rt/stm} \\ \text{aj rt/stm} \end{Bmatrix}$$

The compounded noun stem has three tagmemes:

— an obligatory HEAD$_1$ slot, filled by a noun root or stem or a verb root or stem;
— an optional COMPOUNDER slot with up to three occurrences, filled by lengthening or shortening of the previous vowel, loss or assimilation of the preceding (head, final) or following (head, initial) consonant, or a tonal change; and
— an obligatory HEAD$_2$ slot, filled by a noun root or stem or an adjective root[12] or stem.

(51)  **na²-waal³-ɛ²**
      cow^TN^SHT-milk-INFL
      cow's milk

   **dɔɔ¹-lɔl¹-ɛ¹**
   leg-eye-INFL
   ankle

   **bɛl²-laŋs¹-yɔ¹**
   rain^TN-LOSSC^water(rained)-INFL
   rain water

   **fu¹-dɔɔ¹-yɔ¹**
   hoe^LOSSC-foot-INFL
   old, worn-out hoe

   **hɛ²-zum¹-yɔ¹**
   sweep^TN^LOSSC-flour-INFL
   flour brush

   **kɔɔ²³-naal³-ɛ²**
   chicken-grindingstone-INFL
   gizzard

   **bi²-dɔng⁴-o²**
   granary^TN^LOSSC-side-INFL
   space below granary

   **bit¹-zul¹-ɛ¹**
   sauce^ASSC-head-INFL
   dried okra

   **kaa³¹-nuŋg⁴-o²**
   dog-tooth-INFL
   canine tooth

   **pɛɛ⁴-zum¹-yɔ¹**
   lift-flour-INFL
   donkey

---

[12]The adjective root cannot occur with a verb root, but requires that the filler of the head$_1$ slot be a noun root.

*kɔ²-bis¹-ɛ¹*
draw^TN^LOSSC-sauce-INFL
ladle

*hɔɔm⁴-dɔ¹t-o¹*
suck-nectar-INFL
humming-bird

*kaŋ¹-kol¹-yɔ¹*
carry-soul-INFL
dancing-bell

*kɔ²-buu²³-yɔ²*
chicken^TN^SHT-white-INFL
egret

*wal²³-hob¹-o¹*
man-red-INFL
bright red weaverbird

*wal²³-sɛr¹-ɔ¹*
man-young
disciple, aide

The criterion used to distinguish true compounded noun stems from noun phrases is indivisibility, as demonstrated by the fact that no possessive adjective suffix, or any noun phrase element, may come between the first and the second root or stem. Many of what appear to be compound stems with *baa¹* 'male, AUG', *nɔɔ¹* 'female, AUG', and *waa²³* 'young' do not meet this condition. The line of demarcation is often thin.

(52)    *dak¹-mi¹*    *nɔɔ¹*    *bɔ¹*
calabash-my female DEM
my big calabash

*tɛb⁴sum⁴-nɔɔ¹-mi¹*
web(DRV^STM)-female-my
my spider

*naa²³-mi¹ baa¹ yɛ¹rɛ¹*
cow-my    male this
this bull of mine

*taa¹rum³-baa¹-dɛ³*    *wɛ¹*
shooter-male^PL-our (INCL)
our hunters

*kɔɔ²³-wi¹*    *waa-t²*    *wɔ¹*
chicken-our(EXCL) child-PL DEM
our chicks

*doo²-waa-t²-wi¹*
human-child-PL-our(EXCL)
we Dowayos

dɛnt¹-a¹³   za¹   waa²³
old^man-DIM other child
a little old man

wal²-ɛ³-sɛ¹rɛ³   ɲɲ²³   wɔ¹
men-young-PL his   DEM
his disciples

**2.1.3 The duplicative noun stem.** The duplicative noun stem has the structure shown in (53).

(53)   + hd: rdp rt/stm ± rt cnv: drv sf

The duplicative noun stem has two tagmemes:

— an obligatory HEAD slot, filled by a reduplicated root or stem; and
— an optional ROOT CONVERTER slot, filled by a derivational suffix.

The reduplicated root consists of a basic syllable that is repeated. This syllable is often onomatopoetic. In disyllabic stems, when the basic syllable has the pattern $C_1VC_2$ (where $C_2$ is not a semivowel), the first C of the resulting medial cluster is dropped (i.e., $C_1VC_2C_1VC_2$ becomes $C_1VC_1VC_2$). In the few instances where this consonant was found to be retained, the second consonant of the cluster was changed (i.e., $C_1VC_2C_1VC_2$ became $C_1VC_2C_3VC_2$). Trisyllabic stems seem to have a CVV syllable as their basic syllable, either initially or finally. Only the vowel is reduplicated consistently, though without length. Any two of the syllable-initial consonants of the stem are identical. A four-syllable reduplicative stem results from the reduplication of a disyllabic derived noun stem. Tone is not considered in the present discussion.

(54)   su¹-sug³¹ / su¹-sug-s³¹         vɔ¹-vɔr¹³
       (RT)-(RT) (RT)-(RT)-DRV         (RT)-(RT)
       hair                            gnat

       kɔ¹-kɔt³¹                       to³-tor³
       hug-hug                         bite-bite
       butterfly                       small biting ant

       kɔ²-kɔr²                        ba¹-bal¹³
       (RT)-(RT)                       (RT)-(RT)
       bobbin                          tuberculosis

pɛ¹-pɛt¹-i-n³
(lift)-(lift)^DRV-EP-DRV
swallow

gew⁴¹-gew¹³
(id)-(id)
type of drum

bak¹-rak¹
(RT)-(RT)
rabies

kąą¹-kąą²¹
fold-fold
praying-mantis

lɛɛ²-lɛ²
err about-err about
type of bird

bi¹-ti¹-tii³¹
black(triple)
wild olive

gaa³ni³-gaa¹ni³
(DRV STM)-(DRV STM)
crow

ga³-gaŋ-s³
(RT)-(RT)-DRV
horsefly

ɛl⁴-d-ɛl⁴ / ɛl²-d-ɛl²
beg-(TR)-beg
old hag

gbuŋ²-tuŋ(g)³
(RT)-(RT)
saucepot

gbɛ¹-gbɛɛ-k³
cut-cut-DRV
sharp-bladed grass

see³-re¹-re¹
look-go-go
hawk

kee³rum³-kee¹rum¹
(DRV STM)-(DRV STM)
skirt made of wood fiber

## 2.2 Adjective stems

The adjective stem is that unit which normally fills the head slot of the adjective phrase or the qualifier slot of the modified noun phrase.

**2.2.1 Derived adjective stem.** The derived adjective stem has the structure shown in (55).

(55) 
$$+ \text{hd}: \begin{Bmatrix} \text{v rt/stm} \\ \text{n rt} \\ \text{aj rt} \end{Bmatrix} + \text{rt cnv}_{(3)}: \begin{Bmatrix} \text{drv sf} \\ \text{tn} \\ \text{lgth} \end{Bmatrix} \pm \text{hd mod}_1: \text{pl sf}$$

$$\pm \left[ + \text{ints}_{(3)}: \begin{Bmatrix} \text{dim sf} \\ \text{aug sf} \end{Bmatrix} \pm \text{hd mod}_2: \text{pl sf} \right]$$

The derived adjective stem has five tagmemes:

— an obligatory HEAD slot, filled by a verb root or stem, a noun root, or an adjective root;
— an obligatory ROOT CONVERTER slot, with up to three occurrences, filled by a derivational suffix, a change of tone on the root or stem, or a lengthening of the root vowel;
— an optional HEAD MODIFIER$_1$ slot, filled by a pluralizing suffix;
— optionally followed by an INTENSIFIER slot, with up to three occurrences, filled by a diminutive or augmentative suffix; which function in turn may be pluralized; through
— a HEAD MODIFIER$_2$ slot, filled by a pluralizing suffix.

Though the majority of derivational suffixes function in both the noun and the adjective stem, some are strictly nominal or adjectival. An upglide on a noun root yields an adjective, as does the addition to a noun root of the sequence -(d)-u-m, where -d and -m are derivational and -u- is an epenthetic vowel. Some examples are shown in (56) and (57).

(56)  *gum-n²*  
     hurt^TN-DRV  
     painful

     *gaa¹-t-ɛ¹*  
     shine^TN-DRV-PL  
     clean (PL)

     *doo¹-t-i¹-l-aa-t⁴*  
     lose^weight-DRV-EP-DRV-PL^DIM-PL  
     thin little (PL)

     *buu²-dɛ³-tɔɔ¹-nɔ¹*  
     be^white-PL-AUG-AUG  
     exceedingly white (PL)

     *hịị¹-s-i-l³*  
     be^full^TN-DRV-EP-DRV  
     full

     *woo⁴¹-s-a¹³*  
     work(v)^TN-DRV-DIM  
     diligent little

     *bɛ-t¹-tɔ¹-nɔ¹*  
     be^good^TN-DRV-AUG-AUG  
     very good

     *dɔɔ¹-d-u-m¹*  
     leg-DRV-EP-DRV  
     of the leg

Some Major Structures of Doyayo Syntax         141

*hɛ¹t-i-m¹*
grass-EP-DRV
wild

*hɛb⁴t-u-m¹*
earth-EP-DRV
earthy, of the land

*fa¹b-i-n³*
uncle-EP-DRV
of an uncle

*tee⁴¹*
middle^TN
middle (AJ)

*gbun¹-s-i-m³*
one-DRV-EP-DRV
one and only

*hɔr¹-s-u-m³-yɔ²*
scrape^TN-DRV-EP-DRV-INFL
last

*kʉʉ³-d-ɛ¹*
back-DRV-PL
last (PL)

(57)  *kʉʉ-d³¹-yɔ¹*            'last'
      *kɔ⁴l-u-m¹-yɔ¹*          'of the neck'
      *hɛ¹t-i-m¹-yɔ¹*          'wild'
      *buu¹-d-u-m¹-yɔ¹*        'internal'
      *fa¹b-i-n³-yɔ²*          'of an uncle'

      *nis² gɔɔ²³-sa̱-k¹-ya¹-yɔ¹*   'peanut butter lady'
      *bis¹-ya¹-yɔ¹*               'of the sauce'

      *doo-s³¹-yɔ¹*            'first'
      *woo-s⁴¹-yɔ¹*            'diligent'
      *gab-s⁴¹-yɔ¹*            'mean, belligerent, quarrelsome'

      *ɛɛ-n³-ɛ²*               'vocal, for singing'
      *gum³-n-ɛ²*              'painful'
      *dɔm⁴-n-ɛ²*              'grave, serious'

      *hin¹ zɛɛ-k¹-ya¹*            'thing for digging'
      *hin¹ woo¹-n-i-k¹-ya¹*       'tool'
      *za̱a̱¹-s-i-g¹-ya¹-yɔ¹*        'savior'
      *doo²³ bal-k¹-ya¹-yɔ¹*       'farmer'
      *hin¹ ba¹-n-i-k¹-ya¹-yɔ¹*    'garden tool'

      *gaa-t¹-yɔ¹*             'clean, shining'
      *bɛ-t¹-yɔ¹*              'beautiful'
      *dɛɛ¹-t-o¹*              'small'

| | |
|---|---|
| *kim³-t-o²* | 'round' |
| *wɔ¹-l-ɛ¹* | 'paralyzed' |
| *gaa¹-l-ɛ¹* | 'bright' |
| | |
| *wɔr¹-k-i-l³-yɔ²* | 'dead' |
| *haŋ¹-s-i-l³-yɔ²* | 'old, worn-out' |
| *kum³-b-i-l³-yɔ²* | 'twin' |
| *gum¹-t-i-l³-yɔ²* | 'sick' |
| *haa¹-t-i-l³-yɔ²* | 'sour' |
| | |
| *kar-k¹-yɔ¹* | 'ascending' |
| *kɔ-k¹-yɔ¹* | 'for drinking, drinkable' |
| *wɔr-k¹-yɔ¹* | 'dead' |
| *gaa-m⁴¹-yɔ¹* | 'bloody' |
| | |
| *hoob¹-yɔ¹* | 'fearful' |
| *rɔ¹b-o¹* | 'true, real' |
| *yɛs¹-yɔ¹* | 'too much' |

**2.2.2 Functional adjective stem.** The functional adjective stem has the structure shown in (58).

(58)
$$+ \text{ hd: } \begin{Bmatrix} \text{n stm} \\ \text{qlf n} \\ \text{gen NP} \\ \text{pred NP} \end{Bmatrix} + \text{func: } \begin{Bmatrix} \text{-}ya^1 \\ \text{-}yaa^1d\varepsilon^3 \end{Bmatrix}$$

The functional adjective stem has two tagmemes:

— an obligatory HEAD slot, filled by a noun stem, a qualified noun, a genitival noun phrase, or a predicative noun phrase; and
— an obligatory FUNCTIONALIZER slot, filled by the derivational suffix *-ya* (SG)/*-yaadɛ* (PL).

**Derived from noun stems.** Functional adjective stems derived from noun stems are shown in (59).

(59) *naab²-yaa¹-dɛ³*
    dance-FUNC-PL
    dancers

*dood² nam²-ya¹*
people meat-FUNC
the meat-eaters

*dopᵗtil⁴-ya¹   bɔ¹*
leprosy-FUNC DEM
the leper

*gbaat²-ya¹*
fight(N)-FUNC
a matter of fighting

*bil²³   kubl²-ya¹-yɔ¹*
granary attic-FUNC-INFL
a granary with an attic

*nɛɛ²³   yaar¹-ya¹-waa²³*
woman poverty-FUNC-DIM
a poor little old lady

*nɛɛ²³   yɛ¹rɛ¹   yaar¹-ya¹-yɔ¹*
woman this   poverty-FUNC-INFL
This woman is poor.

*hi¹   dood²   rɔɔs²-ya¹-yɔ¹*
they people wealth-FUNC-INFL
They are rich people.

*mɔɔ¹   yɔ¹ mɔ¹ gi² yaar¹-ya¹*
you^EM as   you are poverty-FUNC
You who are poor . . .

*wal²³ wɔrk²-ya¹   yɔ¹*
man corpse-FUNC DEM
the man with the corpse

*zaan¹   vaam²de³-ya¹*
person donkey-FUNC
the one who wanted the donkey

**Derived from qualified nouns.** Functional adjective stems derived from qualified nouns are shown in (60).

(60) tam²³ dɔɔ¹-ɓɛr¹kil³-ya¹   bɔ¹
sheep leg-broken-FUNC DEM
the lame sheep

dɔɔ¹-ɓɛr¹kil³-ya¹   bɔ¹
leg-broken-FUNC DEM
the lame

loo¹rɛ¹-hạạl²-ya¹ bɔ¹
spirit-evil-FUNC DEM
the demoniac

**Derived from genitival noun phrases.** Functional adjective stems derived from genitival noun phrases are shown in (61).

(61) nis²   gɔɔ²³-sạk¹-ya¹   bɔ¹
woman peanut-paste-FUNC DEM
the peanut butter lady

zạạn¹   wɔrk²-zul¹-ya¹   bɔ¹
person corpse-head-FUNC DEM
the man who takes the head off the corpse

**Derived from predicative noun phrases.** Functional adjective stems derived from predicative noun phrases are shown in (62).

(62) sɛ n³yɛl¹ suml²-baak¹-ya¹   bɔ¹
Samuel drum-beating-FUNC DEM
Samuel, the drummer

zạạn¹   zul¹-look¹-ya¹   bɔ¹
person head-taking-FUNC DEM
the decapitator

hin¹   mɛ¹tin³-guk¹-ya¹   hi¹   hut¹-hịịk¹-ya¹
thing urine-pouting-FUNC and stool-passing-FUNC
toilet; receptacle for urinating and passing stools

zạạn¹   bak²-balk¹-ya¹
person garden-cultivating-FUNC
gardener

*hin¹ balk¹-yaa¹-dɛ³*
thing tilling-FUNC-PL
tilling instruments

*doo²³ hin¹-zaŋ¹gig¹-ya¹-yɔ¹*
human thing-reading-FUNC-INFL
reader

*zɛɛk¹-ya¹    gii²¹ro¹*
digging-FUNC there^is^EM
There *is* a digger.

## 3 The word

The word functions at phrase level and is normally composed of a single monosyllabic root, or a monosyllabic or polysyllabic stem, potentially preceded by one pronominal prefix (verbs only) and followed by an inflexional, a demonstrative or (again, in verbs only) up to three pronominal suffixes.

There are two types of words: major and minor. Major words are open classes and, with the exception of ideophones, are characterized by their ability to take at least one affix. Minor words are closed classes and usually consist of a single open syllable which becomes lengthened and/or incorporates an up- or downglide in pause-group final position. The personal pronouns constitute an exception, being usually disyllabic in pause-group final position because of the addition of an inflexional suffix.

### 3.1 Nouns

A noun is the word that normally fills the head slot of the noun phrase as shown in (63). As such, it can be modified by possessive adjectives, qualifiers, quantifiers, and demonstrative adjectives. It can also function in the adverbial phrase and in the vocative phrase as shown in (64).

(63)     mNP                              mNP        CP

*wal¹ za¹  gi² be² gɔ² gi² zɛɛ¹zig¹ maat¹    luur²*
man other is CUM HAB is  digging  cocoyam  theft
Now there was a man who was always digging up...

(64)     VocP
         ⌒
         $a^1$  $lɛn^1di^1$  $nɔ^2$?
         CIT cannibal what
         She said, "What's the matter, cannibal?"

The noun word has the structure shown in (65).

(65)
$$+ \text{ hd: n rt/stm} \left[ \pm \text{ r pol:} \begin{Bmatrix} \text{poss sf} \\ \text{dem sf} \\ \text{voc sf} \end{Bmatrix} \pm \text{ pos mkr: infl sf} \right]$$

The noun word has three tagmemes, the last two of which are mutually exclusive:

— an obligatory HEAD slot, filled by a noun root or a noun stem;
— *either:* an optional POLARIZER slot, filled by a possessive suffix, a demonstrative suffix or a vocative suffix;
— *or:* an optional POSITION MARKER slot, filled by an inflexional suffix.

(66)   $waa^{23}$-$yɔ^2$              $wa^4l$-$ɔ^2$
       child-INFL                    man-INFL
       child                         man

       $ni^3s$-$ɛ^2$                 $tɛɛ^1$-$yɔ^1$
       woman-INFL                    tree-INFL
       woman                         tree

       $hɔ^4d$-$ɛ^2$                 $bɛ^3t$-$o^2$
       bee-INFL                      DRV^STM-INFL
       bee                           sky, God

       $ta^1m$-$ɔ^1$                 $su^1sug^{31}$-$yɔ^1$
       ashes-INFL                    DPL^STM-INFL
       ashes, cinders                hair

       $see^3re^1re^1$-$yɔ^1$        $ba^3k$-$o^2$
       DPL^STM-INFL                  DRV-STM-INFL
       hawk                          garden

# Some Major Structures of Doyayo Syntax

*gbɔ¹lum¹s-ɛ¹*
DRV^STM-INFL
greatness

*ɓ⁴ki⁴l-i²*
DRV^STM-INFL
account

*bɛl²laŋs¹-yɔ¹*
CMPD^STM-INFL
rain water

*kɔ²bi¹s-ɛ¹*
CMPD^STM-INFL
ladle

*kɔ²buu²³-yɔ²*
CMPD^STM-INFL
egret

The head modifier function (see under stem, §2.1.2 and §2.2) is restricted to a limited number of nominals, mostly animate.

(67)  *wa²lɛ³-yɔ²*
man-INFL
men

*dɛn¹tɛ¹-wɛ¹*
old^man-our (INCL)
our old men

*dood²-yą²³*
human-POSS/DEM
their folks/those people

*maa²lɛ¹-yɔ¹*
chimpanzee-INFL
chimpanzees

*raa¹tɛ¹-yɔ¹*
village-INFL
villages

*oo¹rɛ³-wɛ¹³*
babysitter-VOC (literally 'our')
babysitters (VOC)

*wa²la⁴-yɔ²*
young^man-INF
boy

*dɛn¹ta¹³-yoo³*
little^old^man-VOC
little old man (VOC)

*oo¹ra¹³-yą²³*
young^babysitter-their
their little babysitter

*nɔɔ¹sa¹³-yɔ²*
little^bird-INFL
little bird

*rɔ²ma²³-yɔ²*
rabbit-INFL
rabbit

*wal⁴¹tɔ¹-yɔ¹*
big^man-INFL
man, male

*hɛp⁴¹tɔ¹-yɔ¹*
big^pot-INFL
beer tub

*dɔm³¹tɔ¹-yɔ¹*
first^circumcized^person-INFL
first-circumcized person

$wa^2lɛ^3sɛ^1rɛ^3$-$yą^{23}$
CMPD^N^STM-DEM/POSS
those/their disciples

**3.1.1 Classes of nouns.**[13] Nouns are divided into seven etic classes according to their tone pattern. These classes are given with their subclasses.

**Class 1.** High, closed-syllable stems (or roots) with -$yɔ^1$ ($^1$, $^{21}$, $^{31}$, $^{41}$, $^{121}$, $^{231}$). These nouns follow the SPREADING PRINCIPLE in the pause-group final narrative form. This class is subdivided according to the tone patterns of the demonstrative form.

*Subclass 1.* Stems bearing the upglide $^{21}$ add the suffix -$ɔ^{23}$ and -$i^1$/-$ii^1$ as shown in (68a).

*Subclass 2.* Upgliding stems $^{31}$ and $^{41}$ lose their upglide before the demonstrative endings -$ɔ^{23}$ and -$i^2$/-$ii^{21}$ as shown in (68b).

*Subclass 3.* Stems with a high level tone add the suffix -$ɔ^3$ and -$i^2$/ -$ii^{21}$ as shown in (68c).

*Subclass 4.* Stems with a two-way glide on the stem of the independent form add -$ɔ^3$ and -$i^1$/-$ii^{11}$ in the demonstrative as shown in (68d).

(68)
|   | INDEPENDENT | RELATIONAL | DEMONSTRATIVE |   |
|---|---|---|---|---|
| a. | $bą^{21}yɔ^1$ | $bą^2ri^1$ | $bą^{21}rɔ^{23}$, $bą^2ri^1$, $bą^2rii^1$ | 'hedgehog' |
| b. | $is^{31}yɔ^1$ | $i^3si^1$ | $i^3sɔ^{23}$, $i^3si^2$, $i^3sii^{21}$ | 'goat' |
|   | $bid^{41}yɔ^1$ | $bi^4di^1$ | $bi^4dɔ^{23}$, $bi^4di^2$, $bi^4dii^{21}$ | 'folktale' |
| c. | $fur^1yɔ^1$ | $fu^1ri^1$ | $fu^1rɔ^3$, $fu^1ri^2$, $fu^1rii^{21}$ | 'hoe' |
| d. | $kpand^{121}yɔ^1$ | $kpan^{12}di^1$ | $kpan^{121}dɔ^3$, $kpan^{12}di^1$, $kpan^{12}dii^1$ | 'mouse-trap' |
|   | $mark^{231}yɔ^1$ | $mar^{23}ki^1$ | $mar^{231}kɔ^3$, $mar^{23}ki^1$, $mar^{23}kii^1$ | 'plainsman' |

**Class 2.** Non-high closed-syllable stems with -$yɔ^2$. ($^{13}$, $^{223}$, $^2$, $^3$, $^4$). The tone pattern on the stems of these nouns remains constant in all forms. This class is subdivided into three subclasses according to the tone patterns of the demonstratized forms.

*Subclass 1* Tone $^2$ stems add -$ɔ^3$ and -$i^2$/-$ii^{31}$ in the demonstrative as shown in (69a).

---

[13] In this section, the designation STEM refers to roots or stems.

# Some Major Structures of Doyayo Syntax

*Subclass 2.* Stems with a $^{13}$ glide take -$ɔ^3$ and -$i^2/ii^{21}$ in the demonstrative as shown in (69b).

*Subclass 3* All other stems of this class (i.e., tone $^3$ and tone $^4$ stems) add -$ɔ^{23}$ and -$i^2$-$i^{21}$ in the demonstrativeas shown in (69c).

(69) a. *tar³yɔ²*   *ta²ri²*   *ta²rɔ³, ta²ri², ta²rii³¹*   'Fulani'
    b. *sees¹³yɔ²*   *see¹³si²*   *see¹³sɔ³, see¹³si², see¹³sii²¹*   'sorcery'
    c. *kɔls⁴yɔ²*   *kɔl⁴si²*   *kɔl⁴sɔ²³, kɔl⁴si², kɔl⁴sii²¹*   'dried blackeye pea leaves'
       *gban³yɔ²*   *gba³ni²*   *gba³nɔ²³, gba³ni², gba³nii²¹*   'robe'

**Class 3.** High stems with -$ε^1$, -$ɔ^1$, or -$o^1$ endings in the declarative maintain these endings, with a mid tone, in the narrative form and take -$ɔ^3$ and -$i^2/-ii^{21}$ in the demonstrative as shown in (70).

(70) *taa¹lɛ¹*   *taa¹lɛ³*   *taa¹lɔ³, taa¹li², taa¹lii²¹*   'scar'
       *na¹mɔ¹*   *na¹mɔ³*   *na¹mɔ³, na¹mi², na¹mii²¹*   'potter/blacksmith'
       *lu¹ko¹*   *lu¹ko³*   *lu¹kɔ³, lu¹ki², lu¹kii²¹*   'house'

**Class 4.** Tone $^3$ and $^4$ with -$ε^2$, -$ɔ^2$, and -$o^2$ endings in the declarative, except (C)VC stems where the final C is voiced, change the stem tone to $^2$ in all other forms and add -$ɔ^3/-ii^{31}$ in the demonstrative as shown in (71).

(71) *kuu³sɛ²*   *kuus²/kuu²sɛ³*   *kuu²sɔ³, kuu²si³, kuu²sii³¹*   'cloud'
       *gap⁴sɛ²*   *gaps²/gap²sɛ³*   *gap²sɔ³, gap²si³, gap²sii³¹*   'strife'
       *to³to²*   *tot²/to²to³*   *to²tɔ³, to²ti³, to²tii³¹*   'sorghum'

**Class 5.** Tone $^4$ stems with -$ε^2$, -$ɔ^2$, or -$o^2$ endings in the declarative that have the syllable pattern (C)VC, where the final C is voiced, pattern like stems of class 4, except in the short narrative form, which carries a $^{23}$ glide rather than a level tone as shown in (72).

(72) *ta⁴mɔ²*   *tam²³/ta²mɔ³*   *ta²mɔ³, ta²mi³, ta²mii³¹*   'sheep'
       *lɛ⁴lɛ²*   *lɛl²³/lɛ²lɛ³*   *lɛ²lɔ³, lɛ²li³, lɛ²lii³¹*   'place'

**Class 6.** High open stems with -$yɔ^1$ are divided into two subclasses.

*Subclass 1.* Stems with a level high tone are monosyllabic and have a downglide in the unshortened narrative form, and pattern $^{13}$ and $^{121}$ in the demonstrative (the latter consisting of just the stem plus tone, and no -*i* suffix; thus, also monosyllabic, and with no short-long distinction).

(73)  $t\varepsilon\varepsilon^1y\mathrm{ɔ}^1$   $t\varepsilon\varepsilon^{13}$   $t\varepsilon\varepsilon^1\mathrm{ɔ}^3$, $t\varepsilon\varepsilon^{121}$   'tree'
      $laa^1y\mathrm{ɔ}^1$   $laa^{13}$   $laa^1\mathrm{ɔ}^3$, $laa^{121}$   'fire'

*Subclass 2.* Stems with an upglide to high ($^{41}$ and $^{31}$) are also monosyllabic in the narrative and near demonstrative forms, and they neutralize the short-long distinction in both of these forms. They pattern $^{X23}$ and $^{X12}$ in the demonstrative (where $^X$ represents the initial tone of the stem glide).

(74)  $saa^{41}y\mathrm{ɔ}^1$   $saa^{41}$   $saa^4\mathrm{ɔ}^{23}$, $saa^{412}$   'handbag'
      $kaa^{31}y\mathrm{ɔ}^1$   $kaa^{31}$   $kaa^3\mathrm{ɔ}^{23}$, $kaa^{312}$   'dog'

**Class 7.** Non-high open stems with -$y\mathrm{ɔ}^2$ ($^{23}$, $^{2\text{-}2}$, and $^{3\text{-}3}$) fall into two subclasses.

*Subclass 1.* Monosyllabic stems of this class, with a $^{23}$ glide, neutralize the short-long distinction in the narrative and near demonstrative forms. The narrative form is identical with the stem, the remote demonstrative follows the spreading principle, and the near demonstrative is the stem with an upglide to high tone as shown in (75).

(75)  $waa^{23}y\mathrm{ɔ}^2$   $waa^{23}$   $waa^2\mathrm{ɔ}^3$, $waa^{231}$   'child'
      $doo^{23}y\mathrm{ɔ}^2$   $doo^{23}$   $doo^2\mathrm{ɔ}^3$, $doo^{231}$   'human being'

*Subclass 2.* Disyllabic and polysyllabic noun stems. Disyllabic reduplicating stems of this class with a level tone $^2$ or $^3$ maintain the stem tone in all forms and add $^{23}$ in the remote demonstrative and high tone plus vowel length in the proximal demonstrative as shown in (76).

(76)  $l\varepsilon\varepsilon^2l\varepsilon^3y\mathrm{ɔ}^2$   $l\varepsilon\varepsilon^2l\varepsilon^2$   $l\varepsilon\varepsilon^2l\varepsilon^2\mathrm{ɔ}^{23}$, $l\varepsilon\varepsilon^2l\varepsilon\varepsilon^{21}$   'species of bird'
      $k\varepsilon\varepsilon^3k\varepsilon^3y\mathrm{ɔ}^2$   $k\varepsilon\varepsilon^3k\varepsilon^3$   $k\varepsilon\varepsilon^3k\varepsilon^3\mathrm{ɔ}^{23}$, $k\varepsilon\varepsilon^3k\varepsilon\varepsilon^{21}$   'species of bird'

**3.1.2 Nominal forms.** A noun can have four demonstrative forms (cf. §4.1.4, The demonstratized noun). All non-demonstratized nouns have two basic forms, both of which have a long (pause-group final) and a short (non-pause-group final) realization: the INDEPENDENT form and the RELATIONAL form.

*The independent noun.* (RLN = relational, INDP = independent) The independent form of the noun occurs in a context of finality, uniqueness, or unrelatedness to other nouns, or for emphasis of an unmodified noun.

For example, the following specific environments have been noted:

# Some Major Structures of Doyayo Syntax

*Affirmative stative clause*

(77)　yɔ¹　dɔɔz²　bi¹sɛ³,　kam³zɔ²
　　　when sheˆprepared sauce(RLN) (she)ˆbrought
　　　　nam³bo²
　　　　(itˆwas)ˆmeatˆINDP
　　　When she had made sauce, she brought it. It was meat.

(78)　gi¹ lɛn¹di¹　　sįį³　gii¹　gi¹　　loo⁴be¹
　　　he cannibal(RLN) evenˆif heˆEM heˆ(will) takeˆme
　　　Even if he is a cannibal, he's the one who will marry me.

*One-sentence discourse*

(79)　a　be³　wąą⁴　ta²mɔ³　luu³rɛ²
　　　CIT I　seized sheepˆhis theftˆINDP
　　　He said I stole his sheep.

(80)　a¹　naa⁴¹　zoos² bɔ¹　boo³　yąą¹yɔ¹
　　　CIT mother　prey DEM speak mouthˆINDP
　　　He said, "Mother, the prey said something."

(81)　mi³ rek¹　tot³²　　ze¹ko³
　　　Iˆ# going sorghumˆINDP buying
　　　I am going to buy sorghum. (response to question)

(82)　gi² kɛŋk¹　tɔ¹nɛ¹
　　　is listening earˆINDP
　　　He is listening. (narrator's aside comment)

(83)　kaa³¹ baa¹dɛ³　hi³　gi²　di¹hɛ¹　be³ tuuk¹　　mɛ¹tin³yɔ²　hi¹
　　　dog maleˆPL they are here I　goingˆout urine　　　they
　　　　za¹　hi¹　zaa¹³　hi¹　lɔ³mɔ¹
　　　　POT they come they biteˆyou
　　　There are male dogs here—I'm going out to urinate—they might come and bite you. (interjected information)

*Mutually exclusive (non-cumulative) list*

(84)　ɛr³　　to³to²　　　　kɔɔ²³yɔ²　　ɛr³　　hin　za　lɛ³
　　　(heˆ)asks sorghumˆINDP chickenˆINDP (heˆ)asks thing other thus
　　　He demands sorghum or a chicken, or something like that.

*Emphasis of an unmodified noun*

(85)     $a^1$    $lɛn^1di^1$                $tɔ^2ge^1$
        CIT cannibal(INDP^SHT) devour^her
        "A cannibal ate her up," he said.

(86)     $nɛɛd^{32}$                $gub^2sɛ^1$
        woman^PL(INDP^SHT) pour^BEN^us(INCL)
        It's the women who pour it for us.

*Unique item, with no choice involved, and a slight overtone of undesirability*

(87)     $yɔ^1$    $gaa^4mi^1$    $to^3to^2$
        RES give^me sorghum^INDP
        She would give me sorghum.

**Relational noun.** The relational form of the noun occurs in all contexts that do not call for the independent form, i.e., it is in complementary distribution with the latter.[14]

(88)     $mi^3hɛd^3$    $lu^1ko^3$    $mi^3$    $kɔbz^4$    $mɛ^1mɛ^3$
        I^swept house I     drew water
        I swept the house and drew water. (non-EM narrative seq)

(89)     $loo^4$    $gban^3di^3li^2$    $taa^2lɛ^3$    $bɛ^1to^3$    $saa^4bu^1lu^3$
        took clothing     shoe     stone    soap
        She took some clothes, shoes, a stone, and soap. (CUM enumeration)

(90)     $hi^3$    $wɛɛ^3$    $hi^3$    $re^3ka^2$    $a^1$    $hi^1$    $lɛ^2lɛ^3$
        they return they go     at they place
        Then they went home. (circumstantial phrase)

(91)     $siŋ^{23}tɔ^1$    $bɛr^1kɔɔ^{13}$         $an^1$    $buu^{23}$
        sister^his be^beautiful^DEM like white
        His sister was as beautiful as a white woman. (comparative)

(92)     $a^1$    $bɔ^2$    $be^1$    $lil^3$    $hi^1nɛ^3$
        CIT INTDC I    fast thing
        He said I shouldn't fast. (negative)

---

[14]All bold italicized forms in this section are relationals.

(93)  mɔ³ zeb⁴  tot²  zeb¹ ya⁴
you bought sorghum RDP Q
Did you *buy* sorghum? (focus elsewhere)

(94)  a¹  lɛn¹di¹  nɔ²
CIT cannibal what
She said, "What's the matter, cannibal?" (vocative)

(95)  yɔ¹  gaa⁴mi¹  to²to³
RES give^me sorghum
She would give me sorghum. (choice from inventory, implying desirability)

When a given environment presents criteria for both the independent and the relational form, the independent form is preferred.

(96)  zaa̰¹nɔ³  gi¹ wɛɛ³  nɛ¹  mɛ¹mɛ¹
person^DEM he become ANT water^INDP
If that fellow has changed into water... (stative clause versus subordinant clause of sentence)

(97)  hin¹  yɔ¹  hi¹  el²  a¹  nam³bo²  hi³  zaa²³
thing REL they call CIT meat^INDP they came
Everything you could call an animal came...

**Demonstratized noun.** There are four different demonstrative forms of any noun (open-syllable stems have only three—see the proximal demonstrative nouns in (113)), one of which, the *-ɔ* form, is remote, and the other three, the *-yɔ, -i,* and *-ii* forms, are proximal. The tone of proximal *-yɔ* is invariably high, while the tone of the other three demonstrative endings is determined by the noun they modify.

This area needs more study and conclusions drawn in this section must be considered somewhat tentative, especially regarding the differences between the three proximal forms.

It should be noted here that there is also a set of independent demonstratives not covered in this article.

*Proximal forms.* The proximal forms of the demonstrative are used to refer to an object near the speaker or for extra vividness of style. There appears to be free variation between the forms, the only restriction being that the long *-ii* form cannot occur pause-group finally.

(98)  seem⁴           tɔ²ti³
      look^you^IMP sorghum^DEM^SHT
      Look at this sorghum.

(99)  mi³ gbɛn³ daŋ²gii³¹        luk¹   du¹
      I   saw   knife^DEM^LGTH house in
      I found this knife in the house.

(100) zaa¹yɔ¹    gɔ²  gi¹ sid¹za³         dɔɔ¹yɔ¹  lɛ³  dąą⁴
      other^DEM POT he come^down^OPT leg^DEM thus trample
          wɔrk³¹-yɔ¹   gii¹
          corpse-DEM it^EM
      This one fellow, when he started putting his foot down like this,
      stepped right on the corpse...

*Remote form.* The remote form of the demonstrative is used to refer to an object not near the speaker or to refer back to a previously mentioned object.

(101) mɔ³ gi²  look¹  kɔ²kɔ³        nɔ²
      you are taking sorghum^DEM why
      Why are you taking that couscous?

(102) hi¹nɔ³      hi³  gi²  buu²dɛ³tɔɔ¹nɔ¹
      thing^DEM they are  white^PL^INTS
      Those things are very, very white.

(103) nɔ²  nam²bɔ³   nɔ²
      what meat^DEM INTRR^REINF
      What kind of animal was it (that)?

Both the proximal and the remote form occur as head of the relative clause.

(104) saa³ɔ²³    mɔ¹   raa²  gaay²¹³
      bag^DEM  you say where^is
      Where is that bag you spoke of?

(105) hi¹nɔ³     mi¹  wa²rim¹  gii¹  bɔ¹
      thing^DEM I    ask^you it^EM DEM
      That's the very thing I was asking you about.

Some Major Structures of Doyayo Syntax 155

(106) bɔ² mɔ¹ ɓ⁴ gbɔ²nɔ¹yɔ¹ ɓ² naan² yɛ³li¹
INTDC you follow way^DEM follow hand left
Don't take the path that goes to the left.

(107) du¹tii²¹ mi¹ wąą̌² mi³ gaa⁴ doo²³yɔ²
fish^DEM I seize I gave person
The fish I caught I gave away.

**Tone of nominal forms.** The following charts are an attempt to summarize what has been said about the tone patterns of the different nominal forms, in terms of stem and suffix.

*Independent noun patterns.* Given the stem, the independent noun has a very simple rule governing the choice of its inflectional suffix. High stems and stems ending in high tone take a high tone suffix, while all stems ending in a tone lower than high take a tone 2 suffix. (ⁿ = non-high)

(108)

| last tone of stem | suffix tone 1 | 2 | |
|---|---|---|---|
| 1 | x | | (class 1, 3, and 6 nouns) |
| n | | x | (class 2, 4, 5, and 7 nouns) |

*Relational tone patterns.* The tone patterns of the relational form of the noun are best summarized in three separate charts.

— Relational tone patterns for classes 1 and 2 (closed stems with -yɔ¹) are shown in (109).[15]

(109)

| | -i¹ | -i² | |
|---|---|---|---|
| 1 | x | | (class 1: subcl. 3) |
| n(1) | | x | (class 1: subcl. 1, 2, 4) |
| n | | x | (class 2) |

— Relational tone patterns for classes 3, 4, and 5 (stems with -ɛ, -ɔ, -o). All stems of class 3 maintain the high tone on the stem and take a mid tone on the suffix. All stems of classes 4 and 5 retain only the mid-high tone on the stem (i.e., tone 2) and take a mid tone on the suffix as shown in (110).

---

[15]Parentheses in first column indicate that this tone is not retained when the suffix is added.

(110)  -ε³/-ɔ³/-o³

|   |   |
|---|---|
| ¹ n | x (class 3) |
|   | x (class 4 and 5) |

— Relational tone patterns for classes 6 and 7 (open stems with -yɔ). These stems are unsuffixed in the relational form. Open stems with a level high tone add a downglide to mid on the stem, while all other open stems remain unchanged.

(111)

|   | 3 | # |   |
|---|---|---|---|
| ¹ | x |   | (class 6, subcl. 1) |
| ¹ |   | x | (class 6, subcl. 2 and class 7) |

*Remote demonstrative noun patterns (nouns with -ɔ).*

(112)

|           | ₋³ | ₋²³ |              |                            |
|-----------|----|-----|--------------|----------------------------|
| level ¹/² | x  |     | lu¹kɔ³       | 'that house'               |
| downglide | x  |     | see¹³sɔ³     | 'that sorcery'             |
| 2-way gl. | x  |     | zaa¹²¹lɔ³    | 'that okra'                |
| upglide   |    | x   | gum²¹bɔ²³    | 'that locust'              |
| level ³/⁴ |    | x   | kpaa³rɔ²³    | 'that uncircumcized person'|
| polysyl.  |    | x   | ho²lu²³mɔ²³  | 'that vacation'            |

*Proximal demonstrative noun patterns (nouns with -i, -ii, or -yɔ).*

— The -yɔ¹ suffix presents no problem, as its tone is invariable and it is simply suffixed to the short relational form of the noun. In pause-group final position, the -yɔ¹ suffix lengthens and glides down to ³ thus: -yɔɔ¹³.

(113)

|          | INDEPENDENT | SHORT RELATIONAL | DEMONSTRATIVE | DEMONSTRATIVE FINAL |
|----------|-------------|------------------|---------------|---------------------|
| calabash | dak¹yɔ¹     | dak¹             | dak¹yɔ¹       | dak¹yɔɔ¹³           |
| house    | lu¹ko¹      | luk¹             | luk¹yɔ¹       | luk¹yɔɔ¹³           |
| Fulani   | tar³yɔ²     | tar²             | tar²yɔ¹       | tar²yɔɔ¹³           |
| sorghum  | to³to²      | tot²             | tot²yɔ¹       | tot²yɔɔ¹³           |
| place    | lɛ⁴lɛ²      | lɛl²³            | lɛl²³yɔ¹      | lɛl²³yɔɔ¹³          |
| goat     | is³¹yɔ¹     | is³¹             | is³¹yɔ¹       | is³¹yɔɔ¹³           |
| sorcery  | sees¹³yɔ²   | sees¹³           | sees¹³yɔ¹     | sees¹³yɔɔ¹³         |
| child    | waa²³yɔ²    | waa²³            | waa²³yɔ¹      | waa²³yɔɔ¹³          |

— The -i/-ii suffix has a suprasegmental allomorph of just tone on open stems. This can be represented as in (114). The numbers to the left

Some Major Structures of Doyayo Syntax

of the charts refer to the stem tone of the short relational form and those along the top refer to the tone or tones added to the stem.

(114)

| Class | Stem tone | Tone added | | | | |
|---|---|---|---|---|---|---|
| | | 1 | 21 | 2 | | |
| 7 | 2(polysyl)/23 | x | | | $waa^{231}$ | 'this child' |
| $6_1$ | 1 | | x | | $t\varepsilon\varepsilon^{121}$ | 'this tree' |
| $6_2$ | 31/41 | | | x | $kaa^{312}$ | 'this dog' |

— The tone patterns of closed stems with the -i/-ii suffix can be summarized as in (115). The numbers to the left of the chart refer to the stem tone of the shortened relational form, with parentheses indicating that a given tone is dropped before addition of the -i/-ii suffix, and those across the top refer to the suffixes with their different tone patterns. All stems lose their upglide before the -i/-ii suffix.

(115)

| Class | Stem tone | $-i^1/-ii^1$ | $-i^2/-ii^{21}$ | $-i^3/-ii^{31}$ | | |
|---|---|---|---|---|---|---|
| 4; 5 | $2/2(^3)$ | | | x | $l\varepsilon^2li^3/l\varepsilon^2lii^{31}$ | 'this place' |
| 1.1, 4 | $2(^1)/^{12}(^1)/^{23}(^1)$ | x | | | $zaa^{12}li^1/zaa^{12}lii^1$ | 'this okra' |
| 1.2, 1.3; 2; 3 | other | | x | | $d\mathrm{o}^3yi^2/d\mathrm{o}^3yii^{21}$ | 'this horse' |

**Possessive forms.** The possessed noun functions in the head of the modified noun phrase (mNP) and the definite noun phrase (defNP) in mutual exclusion with the simple relational noun word. It takes the possessive endings $-mi^1$ 'my', $-be^1$ 'my (CIT)', $-m\mathrm{o}^1$ 'your (SG)', $-\mathrm{o}^{23}/-\mathrm{o}^3/-\mathrm{o}^1$ 'his, her, its', $-wi^1$ 'our (EXCL)', $-w\varepsilon^1$ 'our (INCL)', $-n\varepsilon^1$ 'your (PL)', and $-ya^{23}$ 'their'. The tone is invariable in all except the third-person singular form, which is identical with the remote demonstrative. The third-person singular also has an invariable lengthened form in non-pause-group final position, which can function in the head slot of the definite noun phrase.

(116) $vaam^2de^3$ $\mathrm{oo}^{23}$ $b\mathrm{o}^1$ $gii^1$ $gu\eta^2ge^1$
    donkey his that she^EM she^hurt^him
    It's his donkey he's got a crush on.

(117) $d\mathrm{o}y^2h\varepsilon t^1be^1$          $z\varepsilon n^{23}m\mathrm{o}^1$ $b\mathrm{o}^1$
    horse^grass^my^CIT        root^your ART
    my grass                  your root

> *da³nɛ¹mi¹ bɔ¹*  
> hat^my  ART  
> my hat
>
> *baa²mɔ¹*  
> father^your  
> your father
>
> *sąąm³¹mi¹*  
> friend^my  
> my friend
>
> *hin¹ya²³ bɔ¹*  
> thing^their ART  
> their thing

## 3.2 Adjectives

An adjective is the word that normally fills the qualifier slot of the modified noun phrase. It also fills the head slot of the adjective phrase.

(118) *be³ zaa²³ wal²³sɛr¹ tɛ¹ko³*  
I came man^young looking^for  
I came to look for a young man.

(119) *nɛɛ²³ bɔ¹ be² lag¹yɔ¹*  
woman DEM CUM deaf  
Now, the woman was deaf.

(120) *dɔ²yɔ³ buu²³ an¹bɔ¹ fɛd¹fɛd¹*  
horse^his white like^that ID  
His horse was dazzling white.

(121) *kar⁴ dɔ²yɔ³ buu²³ bɔ¹ gɔ¹*  
climbed horse^his white DEM ANA  
He mounted his white horse.

(122) *luk¹ zaa¹ yɔ¹ rɔb¹tɔ¹nɔ¹ so³sor³ be²*  
house other LOC good^very ID CUM  
This is such a fine house.

The structure of the adjective is very similar to that of the noun, in that most of the nominal suffixes occur in the adjective as well. The most striking difference is that, while only a restricted number of nouns are capable of pluralization (of stem), diminution, or augmentation, there is relatively little restriction for adjectives. Furthermore, the reinforcer *-nɔ¹* can be added to either the diminutive or the augmentative, resulting in a form that is characteristically adjectival (though this *waa²³nɔ¹* or *-tɔ¹nɔ¹* form is also used adverbially).

# Some Major Structures of Doyayo Syntax

Basically, the adjective is composed of a root or stem, potentially followed by one or more root converters, a root modifier, and a polarizer or position marker. Two basic types of adjectives have been observed: the *simple* adjective and the *augmented* adjective. Note that the plural ending -$\varepsilon$ has several morphophonemic variants (see (130)).

**3.2.1 The simple adjective** has the structure shown in (123).

(123)
$$+ \text{hd:} \begin{Bmatrix} \text{aj rt} \\ \text{aj stm} \end{Bmatrix} \pm \text{pl: pl sf -}\varepsilon \pm \text{pol:} \begin{Bmatrix} \text{infl sf} \\ \text{dem sf} \\ \text{voc sf} \end{Bmatrix}$$

The simple adjective has three tagmemes:

— an obligatory HEAD slot, filled by an adjective root or stem,
— an optional PLURALIZER slot, filled by the pluralizing suffix -$\varepsilon$,[16] and
— an optional POLARIZER slot filled by an inflexional suffix.

**3.2.2 The augmented adjective** has the structure shown in (124).

(124)
$$+ \text{hd:} \begin{Bmatrix} \text{aj rt} \\ \text{aj stm} \end{Bmatrix} \pm \text{spec:} \begin{Bmatrix} \text{pl sf} \\ \text{dim-}a^4 \end{Bmatrix} \pm \text{ints}_1\text{:} \begin{Bmatrix} t\mathrm{ɔɔ}^1 \\ waa^{23} \end{Bmatrix} \pm \text{pl}_1\text{: pl-}t(o)$$
$$\pm \text{ints}_2\text{: } n\mathrm{ɔɔ} \pm \text{pl}_2\text{: pl sf -}d\varepsilon \pm \text{term: infl sf -}y\mathrm{ɔ}$$

The *augmented* adjective has seven tagmemes:

— an obligatory HEAD slot, filled by an adjective root or stem,
— an optional SPECIFIER slot, filled by a pluralizing suffix or diminutive -$a^4$,
— an optional INTENSIFIER$_1$ slot, filled by either -$t\mathrm{ɔɔ}^1$ or -$waa^{23}$,
— an optional PLURALIZER$_1$ slot, filled by the pluralizing suffix -$t(o)$,
— an optional INTENSIFIER$_2$ slot, filled by -$n\mathrm{ɔɔ}^1$,
— an optional PLURALIZER$_2$ slot, filled by the pluralizing suffix -$d\varepsilon$, and
— an optional TERMINAL slot, filled by an inflexional suffix.

---

[16]The pluralizing suffix -$\varepsilon$ is used when a derived simple adjective stem fills the head slot$_1$.

(125) nɛɛ²³   sɛr¹   zaa¹   bɔ¹   bɛr¹kɔɔ¹³
woman young other DEM be^good^DEM
One of the young women/The other young woman was very beautiful.

(126) zaa¹-ɔ³      gaay²¹⁴   ma³
other^DEM where^is DEIC
Where's that other one?

(127) bɔ²   mɔ¹   ɓ⁴   gbɔ²nɔ¹yɔ¹   ɓ²   naan²   yɛ³li¹
INTDC you follow way^DEM follows hand left
Don't take the path that goes to the left.

(128) hi³   baa⁴   gban³ya̰²³   sɛ²g-o³
they sewed robe^their new^INFL
They sewed new clothes for themselves.

(129) gbɔ²nɔ¹   rɔ¹b-o³      hi¹   gbɔ²nɔ¹   ha̰a̰²l-ɛ³
way      true-INFL and way      evil-INFL
a good way and a bad way

(130) Doo²³   gbɔɔl¹-ɛ¹
human big-INFL
He's a big shot.

doo²³   wil²³   za¹   gi²ro³
human black other exists
There are some Blacks...

wal²³   sɛr¹yɔɔ¹³
man young^VOC
Young man,...

naan²   yɛ³l-i¹
hand left-INFL
left, left hand

hab²³   kit²-tɔ¹-nɔ¹
pig    many-INTS-REINF
very many pigs

waa²-ɔ³   yɔ¹   namr¹-yɔ¹
child-his DEM lazy-INFL
This child of his is lazy.

buu²dɛ³-tɔɔ¹-nɔ¹
white-PL^AUG-REINF
very, very white

gbɔɔl¹-ɛ¹
big-INFL
big

gbɔɔl¹-tɔ¹
big-AUG
very big

gbɔɔl¹-tɔ¹-nɔ¹
big-AUG-REINF
very, very big/much

# Some Major Structures of Doyayo Syntax

gbɔ¹l-ɛ³-yɔ²
big-PL-AUG-PL-REINF
big (PL)

gbɔ¹l-e³-tɔt¹-nɔ¹
big-PL-AUG-PL-REINF
very, very big (PL)

gbɔ¹l-a¹⁴-yɔ²
big-DIM-INFL
rather big

gbɔ¹l-a¹⁴-nɔ¹ / gbɔ¹l-a¹⁴waa²³-nɔ¹
big-DIM-REINF / big-DIM-REINF
big little

gbɔ¹l-aa⁴-t-o²
big-PL-DIM-PL-INFL
rather big (PL)

gbɔ¹l-a¹⁴-waa-t²-nɔ¹
big-PL-DIM-PL-REINF
big little (PL)

## 4 The phrase

### 4.1 Nominal phrase

The nominal phrase functions at the sentence, the clause, and the phrase levels. At sentence level, the nominal phrase functions in the marginal vocative slot. At clause level, it functions in the subject, object, or complement slot. At phrase level, it functions in the head slot of all nominal phrases, except the simple, the modified, the definite, and the local possessive, and in the head slot of the standard circumstantial phrase (stCP) and the accessory phrase (AccP). The nominal phrase also functions in the referent slot of the genitival noun phrase (genNP), in the possessor slot of the possessive circumstantial phrase (possCP), and in the apposition slot of the coordinate possessor circumstantial phrase (copCP).

Ten basic kinds of nominal phrases and one nominal phrase extension have been noted: the SIMPLE noun phrase (sNP), the MODIFIED noun phrase (mNP), the DEFINITE noun phrase (defNP), the COORDINATED noun phrase (coNP), the GENITIVAL noun phrase (genNP), the APPOSITIONAL noun phrase (appNP), the REFERENTIAL noun phrase (refNP), the FOCAL noun phrase (focNP), the EMPHATIC noun phrase (emNP), the EMPHATIC POSSESSIVE noun phrase (epNP), and the noun phrase MARGIN ($NP_{mar}$).

**4.1.1 The simple noun phrase (sNP)** has the structure shown in (131).

(131)
$$\pm \text{ hd: rln n } \pm \text{ qlf:} \begin{Bmatrix} \text{aj} \\ \text{AjP} \\ \text{NmP} \end{Bmatrix}$$

The simple noun phrase has two tagmemes, at least one of which must be present:

— an optional HEAD slot, filled by a relational noun, and
— an optional QUALIFIER slot, filled by an adjective, an adjective phrase, or a number phrase.

This phrase type is set up especially to function in the head of the referential noun phrase (refNP) and the emphatic possessive noun phrase (epNP).

(132) refNP

sNP:AjP

nɔ² zaa¹ dɔɔm³¹-ɔ³
what other different-DEM
What other thing?

(133) refNP

sNP

rln n

kamɨ³ nɔ² zoos²-ɔ nɔ²
brought what prey-DEM REINF
What kind of game did he bring?

(134) S:epNP

| em pr | sNP | relCl |

gii¹ gɔn²wal²³ ɔ²nɛ³ bɔ¹ lug² pi²³ra²
he^EM inlaw^man his^SFOC REL planted^DEP (it)^sprouted
As for that planted by the father-in-law, it sprouted.

Some Major Structures of Doyayo Syntax            163

(135)                    IP$_{hd}$:epNP
                    ⎯⎯⎯⎯⎯⎯⎯⎯⎯⎯⎯⎯
                             sNP
                        ⎯⎯⎯⎯⎯⎯⎯⎯⎯
     bɔ²    gi¹   ɔks³  hi¹  dood²  rɔ¹bɛ³  yạ²nɛ³  wɔ¹
     INTDC  she   mix   with people true    theirs  PL^ART
     She must not mix it with those of the members of the chief's
     household.

**4.1.2 The modified noun phrase (mNP)** has the structure shown in (136).

(136) ± hd: $\begin{Bmatrix} \text{rln n} \\ \text{poss n} \end{Bmatrix}$ ± qlf$_1$: aj$_1$ ± indf: indf art ± qlf$_2$: aj$_2$

   ± qlf$_3$: aj$_3$  ± qnt: $\begin{Bmatrix} \text{NmP} \\ baa^4ri^1/nɔ^4ni^1 \end{Bmatrix}$ ± loc: CP

The modified noun phrase has seven tagmemes:

— an optional HEAD slot, filled by a noun in the shortened relational form or a possessed noun,
— an optional QUALIFIER$_1$ slot, filled by an adjective of first rank (This function can optionally occur immediately following the indefinite.),
— an optional INDEFINITE slot, filled by the indefinite article *zaa¹* (The indefinite functor may optionally be moved to a position immediately following the qualifier.),
— an optional QUALIFIER$_2$ slot, filled by an adjective of rank 2,
— an optional QUALIFIER$_3$ slot, filled by an adjective,
— an optional QUANTIFIER slot, filled by a number phrase, or by interrogative *baa⁴ri¹* or *nɔ⁴ni¹*, and
— an optional LOCATIVE slot, filled by a circumstantial phrase (CP) (The locative particle may occur after the indefinite slot.).

Any function of the mNP (except, of course, the bound possessive pronoun suffix, which requires a preceding noun) may represent the phrase in the absence of all others, as may also the NP margin which will be discussed later. Compare the phrases in (137).

(137) **luk¹   mi¹   nɔn⁴¹   bɔ¹**
      house  my    which    that
      which of my houses?

***luk¹   mi¹   nɔ⁴ni¹***
house my which
which house is mine/for me?

(138)         S:mNP

| n | NmP | loc | | | |
|---|---|---|---|---|---|

***doo²³   gbun¹   mɔɔt⁴¹   yɔ¹   yɔ¹   gbɛn²   gɛ²***
person one    only    LOC RES see    not
Not a single person here would see it.

(139)      S:mNP

| n | aj | qnt |
|---|---|---|

***dɛl²³   hjj¹sil³   baa⁴ri¹***
basket  full    how^many?
... how many baskets full?

(140)       S:focNP

| def | loc | sfoc | pr |
|---|---|---|---|

***bɔ¹   di¹   ɣ²nɛ³   bɛ²sum¹   gɛ²***
DEM LOC REINF good-for-me not
I don't like that one.

(141)              AccP_hd:mNP

| | n | indf | loc | aj |
|---|---|---|---|---|

***hi¹   doo²³   zaa¹   di¹   ɓat¹ta¹⁴waa²³***
with person other there ripe^DIM^child
with a little old man

## Some Major Structures of Doyayo Syntax

(142)    S:mNP

| n | indf | aj |
|---|---|---|
| rɔ⁴bɛ¹ | zaa¹dɛ³ | yɔl¹seen²ya¹ | hi³ gi² di¹ |
| alien^PL | other^PL | eye^see^DRV^FUNC | they were about |

There were foreign witnesses present.

(143)    O:mNP

| | poss n | |
|---|---|---|
| gɔ² be¹ | rek¹ | dɔy²hɛt¹be¹ | kpaak¹ ya³ |
| when I(CIT) | going | horse^grass^my | mowing INTS |

When I am on my way to mow the grass...

(144)    AccP_{hd}:mNP

| poss n | indf |
|---|---|
| hi¹ saam³¹mi¹ | zaa¹dɛ³ |
| with friend-my | other-PL |

and other friends of mine

When the noun phrase fills the subject slot of the stative clause, the number function is backshifted to a position preceding clause-final $gɛ^2$ 'not', $ro^2$ 'ATT MKR', $be^2$ 'CUM', etc. When the noun phrase fills the object slot, the backshifting is optional. In the absence of the number function, the reinforcer function may be backshifted.

(145)    O:mNP

| n | aj | indf | loc | qnt qnt | loc |
|---|---|---|---|---|---|
| mi³ gbɛn³ | wal²³ | sɛr¹ | zaa¹dɛ³ | di¹hɛ¹ | ee¹rɛ¹/ee¹rɛ¹ | di¹hɛ¹ |
| I saw | man | young | other^PL | here | two/two | here |

I saw two young men here.

(146)

```
            S:mNP
    ┌─────────────────────────┐
    n    aj    indf       loc    qnt
   ┌──┐ ┌──┐ ┌──────┐    ┌──┐  ┌──┐
```
wal²³ sɛr¹ zaa¹dɛ³ hi³ gi² di¹hɛ¹ ee¹rɛ¹
man  young other^PL they are here  two
Two young men are here.

(147)

```
         S:mNP
    ┌──────────────┐
    indf        qnt
   ┌────┐      ┌────┐
```
zaa¹ gi² du¹ gbu¹nu¹
other he^is in one
There is one among them ...

(148)

```
          S:mNP
    ┌──────────────────┐
    rln  n       CP
   ┌─────────┐ ┌─────────┐
```
dood² waal¹ nuŋ²³ sɛw³ hi³ baa⁴ gban³ya²³ se²go³
people country name all they sew clothing^their new
People all over the country sew new clothes for themselves.

(149)

```
                O:coNP
    ┌──────────────────────────────┐
       mNP      cj        mNP
      ┌─────────┐       ┌─────────────────┐
```
zaa¹ naa²³ na²sɔ³ hi¹ rɔɔs² dɛɛt¹ dum¹bi³li² na²sɔ³
other cow  four   and wealth small tens          four
Or four cows and forty shrouds.

**4.1.3 The definite noun phrase (defNP)** has the structure in (150).

(150) ± hd: $\begin{Bmatrix} \text{rln n} \\ \text{poss n} \end{Bmatrix}$ ± qlf₁: aj₁ ± indf: indf art ± qlf₂: aj₂

± qnt: NmP + def: $\begin{Bmatrix} \text{dem aj} \\ \text{relCl} \end{Bmatrix}$

The *definite* noun phrase has six tagmemes:

# Some Major Structures of Doyayo Syntax

— an optional HEAD slot, filled by either a relational noun or a possessed noun,
— an optional QUALIFIER$_1$ slot, filled by an adjective of first rank,
— an optional INDEFINITE slot, filled by the indefinite article *za* 'other',
— an optional QUALIFIER$_2$ slot, filled by an adjective of second rank,
— an optional QUANTIFIER slot, filled by a number phrase, and
— an obligatory DEFINER slot, filled by a demonstrative adjective or a rankshifted relative clause.

(151) S:defNP

```
        n       def
     wal²³     bɔ¹   zaa²³za¹
     man      DEM   came-RDP
```
The man has come.

(152) O:defNP

```
                              relCl
     el⁴     nuŋ²gɔ³    bɔ¹    dʒɔ²si¹ge¹
     he^calls name^her DEM   he^name^her^DEP
```
He calls out the name that he gave her.

(153) S:defNP

```
        indf         relCl
     zaa¹   bɔ¹   gin¹   hɛl²³   naan²   du¹   tal²³   gɔ¹   tees⁴¹
     other  DEM  he^has broom   hand    in   he^passes ANA  middle
     du¹
     in
```
The one holding the broom then goes to the middle.

(154) O:defNP

```
                                relCl
     bɔ²    mɔ¹fɔ⁴    gbɔ²nɔ¹   yɔ¹    fɔ²         naan²   yɛ³li¹
     INTDC  you^follow way      DEM   it^follow^DEP hand   left
```
Don't take the path that goes to the left.

(155)     O:emNP
          ┌─────────────────────────┐
              defNP:relCl
          ┌───────────────────┐
mɔ¹ɓ⁴    bɔ¹   rek²    a¹ tees⁴¹   du¹  ga¹
you^follow DEM it^go^DEP at middle in   it(SMEM)
Take the one that goes straight ahead.

(156) S:defNP:relCl
      ┌──────────────┐
wɛ¹    hi¹nɔɔ²      hi³  gbee¹zig¹ waal¹   tees⁴¹   be²
those they^ran^DEP  they crossing  country middle   CUM
Those who were running were cutting across the middle of the countryside.

(157)     S:defNP
          ┌──────────────┐
rln  n          relCl
┌────┐    ┌─────────────┐
zaan¹  bɔ¹   gɔ²   gi¹wɔɔ³be¹     mi¹da³        gɛ²
person DEM   HAB   he^will^seize^me he^be^found  not
The one who is going to marry me has yet to be seen.

(158)             O:defNP
          ┌──────────────────────────────┐
                    relCl
          ┌──────────────────────────┐
                subcj
          ┌──────┐
ji³    lɛl²³    bɔ¹  yɔ¹   zɛɛ²   nɛ    gi¹yaa⁴   zu¹lɔ³   du¹
he^bury place  DEM  REL   he^dig ANT   he^send   head^his  in
He filled up the place he had dug and stuck his head in.

(159)             O:defNP
          ┌──────────────────────────────┐
                    relCl
          ┌──────────────────────────┐
mɛɛ²    lɛl²³   yɔ¹   an¹   gɔ²   gi¹wɛɛ³   gi¹zɛm¹³   zoo²lɔ³   bɔ¹
he^know place   REL   that  POT   she^return she^find   skin^her  DEM
                                                                   gɛ²
                                                                   not
She didn't know where to go to find her skin.

# Some Major Structures of Doyayo Syntax

(160)      S:defNP:relCl

yɔ¹   mɔ¹gaa²zi¹be¹      bε¹zeb⁴  hε¹   ɓε¹   be²
REL  you^give^IMM^me  I^take  here  again  CUM
What about the other one you handed to me, which I took here?

(161)                          O:defNP

                                    relCl

mɔ¹  mid³si¹be³   lεl²-ɔ³    zaa¹   gum¹til³  gi²  du¹
you find^BEN^me  place^DEM  other   sick       is   in
If you find out for me where the other one, the sick one, is . . .

(162)           O:defNP:relCL

mi¹zεm²   bɔ¹   luk¹   du¹   gε²
I^find^DEP DEM  house  in    not
I couldn't find the one in the house.

(163)      fsO:defNP

                relCl

gɔɔ²³   bɔ¹   lel²³     mɔ³   biis⁴¹        ya⁴
peanut  DEM  yesterday  you   threw^away    Q
Did you throw away yesterday's peanuts?

(164)  S:defNP

laa¹   bɔ¹   bu¹da³
fire   that  it^conceived
The fire started.

(165)  fsO:defNP

       poss n   def

da³nε¹mi¹   bɔ¹   mi¹   taa¹²      zaa¹    loo¹ko³
hat^my      that  I     am^not    again    taking
I'm not going back to get my hat.

(166)      S:defNP

```
        ┌─────────────┐
        n    aj   def
        ┌────┐┌───┐┌──┐
```
gɔ̰ɔ̰²³   zaa¹   bɔ¹   hɛ̰ɛ̰¹mi¹kɔɔ¹³
peanut  other  DEM   they^are^so^delicious
Those peanuts are so delicious...!

(167)              O:defNP

```
        ┌─────────────────┐
        n      aj      def
        ┌────┐ ┌──────┐ ┌──┐
```
wa̰a̰z⁴     tam²³   dɔɔ¹ɓer¹kil³ya¹   bɔ¹   zaa²³   gaa⁴ge¹
he^caught sheep  leg^broken^her   that  he^came  he^gave^him
He caught the lame sheep and came and gave it to her.

(168)      S:defNP

```
        ┌─────────────┐
        aj   qnt   def
        ┌───┐┌───┐┌──┐
```
zaa¹   ee¹rɛ¹   wɛ¹rɛ¹   hi³   bud³     gɔ¹
other   two    these   they  conceived  ANA
The two others became pregnant.

(169)           S:defNP

```
        ┌──────────────────────────┐
        n    aj    aj    aj   qnt  def₁
        ┌──┐┌──┐ ┌──┐ ┌──┐ ┌──┐ ┌──┐
```
wa²lɛ³  sɛ¹rɛ³  rɔ⁴ɓe¹  gbɔ¹lɛ³  ee¹rɛ¹  wɔ¹rɔ¹  hi³  fṵṵz¹
men    young   foreign   big    two    those   they  come^from
ay¹²
where?
Where do those two big young aliens come from?

(170)      CP_{hd}:defNP

```
        ┌──────────┐
        n    def        NP_mar
        ┌──┐┌───┐       ┌────┐
```
a¹   nɔɔs²   wɔ¹   hi¹   zul¹   ha¹   sɛw³
at   bird   those  their  head   on   all
over all the birds

# Some Major Structures of Doyayo Syntax

**4.1.4 The coordinated noun phrase (coNP)** has the structure shown in (171).

(171)
$$+ \text{hd}_1: \begin{Bmatrix} \text{defNP} \\ \text{mNP} \\ \text{genNP} \\ \text{emNP} \\ \text{rln n} \\ \text{indp n} \\ \text{prop n} \end{Bmatrix} + \begin{bmatrix} \pm \text{ cj: } hi^1 + \text{hd}_2: \begin{Bmatrix} \text{defNP} \\ \text{mNP} \\ \text{genNP} \\ \text{emNP} \\ \text{appNP} \\ \text{rln n} \\ \text{prop n} \end{Bmatrix} \end{bmatrix}_{(n)}$$

The coordinated noun phrase has three tagmemes, two of which are obligatory:

— an obligatory HEAD$_1$ slot, filled by a definite noun phrase, modified noun phrase, a genitival noun phrase, an emphatic noun phrase, a relational noun, an independent noun, or a proper noun,

and an obligatory sequence of

— an optional conjunctor slot, filled by the conjunction *hi*, and
— an obligatory HEAD$_2$ slot, filled by a definite noun phrase, a modified noun phrase, a genitival noun phrase, an emphatic noun phrase, an appositional noun phrase, a relational noun, or a proper noun.

This sequence of two tagmemes can be repeated an indefinite number of times, as indicated by $(_n)$.

Normally, the heads are overtly connected, but in lists of three or more items the connector may be deleted, or retained only before the last function.

(172)      O:coNP
        ‾‾‾‾‾‾‾‾‾‾‾‾‾‾‾‾‾‾
        rln n    cj    rln n
                ‾‾‾‾‾‾‾‾‾‾‾
     gaam⁴  ko²ko³   hi¹   bi¹sɛ³
     give-me couscous and sauce
     Give me couscous and sauce.

(173)                          O:coNP
         ┌─────────────────────────────────────────┐
          rln n      rln n     cj   rln n    NP_mar
         ┌─────┐   ┌─────┐        ┌─────┐   ┌────┐
      mɔ³ gbɛn³  wa²le³   nɛɛ²dɛ³  hi¹  waat²   sɛw³
      you see    man^PL   woman^PL and  child^PL all
      You see men and women, and children, too.

(174) gɔ²   mɔ³ bɔɔ⁴  mo³ raas²³
      when you soak  you tell^to

                          IO:coNP
         ┌─────────────────────────────────────────┐
            emNP        cj      emNP       NP_mar
         ┌─────────┐          ┌─────────┐  ┌────┐
      waŋ²³tɔ¹   hii¹ya¹   hi¹  baa¹tɔ¹   hii¹   sɛw³
      brother^her they^EM  and  uncle^her they^EM all
      When you have brewed it (beer), you tell her brothers and her
      uncles, too.

(175)                          O:coNP
         ┌─────────────────────────────────────────┐
              mNP       cj              mNP
         ┌──────────┐         ┌──────────────────┐
      zaa¹  naa²³ na²sɔ³  hi¹  rɔɔs² dɛɛt¹ dum¹bi³li² na²sɔ³
      other cow   four    and  wealth small tens          four
      Or four cows and forty shrouds.

(176)                          O:coNP
         ┌─────────────────────────────────────────┐
               indp n       cj       genNP
            ┌────────────┐        ┌──────────────┐
      rek³   zɛm²³   su¹sug³¹yɔ¹  hi¹  doo²³   naa²nɛ³
      she^goes she^finds hair^INDP and  person  hand^RLN
      She went and found some hair and a human hand.

# Some Major Structures of Doyayo Syntax

(177)  S:coNP

| emNP | cj | prop | n |

wii¹ hi¹ al¹ka³li¹ wi³ raas²³ san³¹ bɔ¹ a¹ nɔk² gi²
we^EM and Alkali we told^IND Fulani DEM CIT war is
zaa¹ko¹
coming(INC)
Alkali and I told the Fulani that war was coming.

(178)  VocP:coNP

| emNP | | | mNP | | |

| em pr | relCl | cj | poss n | aj pl | cj |

rel

nɛɛ¹ yɔ¹ nɛ¹gi²ro³ hi¹ sa̧a̧m³¹mi¹ zaa¹dɛ³ hi¹
you who you^exist and friend^my other^PL and

| mNP |

| rln n | aj |

dɛn¹tɛ¹ zaa¹dɛ³
old^man^PL other^PL
You who are present and friends and gentlemen...

(179)

```
                                         coNP
        ┌─────────────────────────────────┴──────────────────────────────┐
                                                    appNP
                                         ┌───────────────┴──────────────────┐
           mNP           mNP                       mNP                    mNP
        ┌───┴──┐      ┌───┴──┐           ┌─┬───────┴─────┐           ┌─────┴──┐
        rln  n        rln  n             cj  poss       n            indf    rln  n
        an¹  dɛn¹tɛ¹  yaam³waa²to³       hi¹  na²bɛ¹                 za¹     wa²lɛ³
        like old^men  young^child^PL     and  companion^my           other   man^PL
```

```
                                                                              aj
                                                                          ┌───┴──┐
                                                                          sɛ¹rɛ³
                                                                          young^PL
```

like old men, children and my peers the young men

(180)

```
                                         emNP
        ┌────────────────────┴─────────────────────────────────────────┐
                         coNP
        ┌──────────────┴──────────────┐
             emNP              appNP
        ┌─────┴─────┐      ┌─────┴──────┐
        prop n  smem pr    cj   prop n       prop n                  smem pr
        pi³yɛr¹ gi¹ya¹     hi¹  ru¹bɛn³      baab²¹mi²rɔ³            hi¹
        Peter   he(SMEM)   and  Reuben       father^my^he^appeared   they
```

```
                                         qnt
                                      ┌───┴──┐
                                      ee¹rɛ¹
                                      two
```

It was both Peter and Reuben Baabmiro.

Some Major Structures of Doyayo Syntax         175

(181)

|  | O:coNP |  |  |  |  |
|---|---|---|---|---|---|
|  | emNP |  |  |  |  |
| defNP | NP$_{mar}$ | cj | rln | n | cj |

mɔ¹ gbaa⁴si⁴ge⁴   gbun¹ bɔ¹   gii¹   sew³   hi¹   taa²lɛ³   hi¹
you put^BEN^her^OPT   one   DEM   it^EM   all   and   shoe   and

| rln | n |
|---|---|

saa³bu¹la⁴
soap

You set aside for her the same thing(s) and shoes and soap.

(182)

|  |  | O:coNP |  |
|---|---|---|---|
|  | genNP | genNP |  |

zaa²³   bjj²³   naa⁴mi¹   nuŋ²gɔ³   baa²mi¹
he-came-IND he-wrote-IND mother^my name^her father^my

|  | genNP |  | mNP |  |
|---|---|---|---|---|
|  |  | cj |  | NP$_{mar}$ |

nuŋ²gɔ³   nis²mi¹   nuŋ²gɔ³   hi¹   raat¹mi¹   sɛw³
name^his wife^my name^her and family^my all

He came and wrote down the names of my mother, my father, my wife, and my whole family.

(183)

|  | coNP | | | | | |
|---|---|---|---|---|---|---|
| emNP cj | defNP | | | epNP | | |
| *mii¹ hi¹* | *nɛɛ²³* | *bɔ¹rɔ¹* | *mi³raa²³ nɛ¹* | *wɔrk²* | *miin¹* | |
| I^EM and | woman | that | I^say well | death | my^FOC^POSS | |

| AccP | |
|---|---|
| *hi¹* | *gi¹ya¹* |
| with | her^EM |

I'm dying of love for that woman.

(184)

|  |  | O:coNP | | | |
|---|---|---|---|---|---|
| | | defNP | | cj | mNP |
| *hi³* | *re³ka² hi³ zɛm²³* | *naad⁴¹* | *bɔ¹* | *hi¹* | *waaɔ²³* |
| they | went they found | old^woman | DEM | and | child^her |

They went and found the woman and her child.

When coNP occurs in the object function preceding CP, all but the first head is optionally backshifted to a position directly following CP.

(185)

|  | O:coNP | | |
|---|---|---|---|
| rln n | CP | cj | rln n |
| *gaa⁴mɔg⁴ tɛŋk¹* | *a¹ woo²sɔ³ ge¹ du¹* | *hi¹* | *ha¹to³* |
| give^him strength | at work^his it in | and | joy^RLN |

Give him strength and joy in his work. (from a prayer)

**4.1.5 The genitival noun phrase (genNP)** has the structure shown in (186).

(186)

$$+ \text{ref:} \begin{Bmatrix} \text{prop n} \\ \text{rln n} \\ \text{poss n} \\ \text{mNP} \\ \text{defNP} \\ \text{appNP} \\ \text{coNP} \end{Bmatrix} \pm \text{hd-ref:} \begin{Bmatrix} \text{rln n} \\ \text{poss n (3p)} \end{Bmatrix} + \text{hd:} \begin{Bmatrix} \text{rln n} \\ \text{indp n} \\ \text{poss n (3p)} \\ \text{coNPgh} \\ \text{sfoc poss aj} \\ \text{qnt aj} \end{Bmatrix}$$

The *genitive noun phrase* has three tagmemes:

— an obligatory REFERENT slot, filled by a proper noun, a relational noun, a possessed noun, a modified noun phrase, a definite noun phrase, an appositional noun phrase, or a coordinate noun phrase,[17] and
— an optional HEAD-REFERENT slot, filled by a relational noun, a third-person possessed noun or a genitive head coordinated noun phrase, and
— an obligatory HEAD slot, filled by a relational noun, a third-person possessed noun, a genitive head coordinated noun phrase, a semi-focal possessive adjective, or an adjective of quantity.

(187) genNP [ mNP indp n ]

*hi¹nɔ³   daŋt²   yaa¹yɔ¹*
thing^DEM game mouth
It's a game (literally 'question of a game').

(188) O:genNP [ defNP sfoc ]

*gaa⁴zin¹be³   hɔd²³ bɔ¹   be²nɛ³*
give^IMM^you^me^CIT bee DEM mine(SFOC POSS)
Give me my part of the honey.

(189) O:genNP [ defNP poss n cj poss n ]

*looz⁴   ma³ yaa²³ hob¹ bɔ¹   zu¹lɔ³   hi¹   zoo²lɔ³*
he^took^IMM DEIC monkey red DEM head^his and skin^his
He got the head and skin of of the red monkey.

---

[17]When a coNP fills the referent slot, all but the first head of the coNP is backshifted to a position following the genNP, and the head-referent function is omitted.

(190)  cmpd n:genNP
  ┌─────────────┐
  rln n  rln n  rln n
  ┌──┐   ┌──┐   ┌─┐

  **loo¹rɛ¹zul¹bum¹**         **bɔ¹   be²,  gi²   tuu¹ru¹ko¹**
  ancestorˆspiritˆheadˆbeer   DEM   CUM   itˆis   arriving
  Now, the beer festival of the the skulls was arriving.

(191)          genNP
       ┌─────────────────┐
        defNP      poss n
       ┌──────┐   ┌────┐

  **zaan¹raat¹ya¹    bɔ¹    ni²sɔ³    wɔɔ³¹rɔ¹**
  personˆCMPDˆer   DEM   wifeˆhis   sheˆdied
  The proprietor's wife died.

(192)                    genNP
                ┌─────────────────────────┐
                poss n       rln n  poss n
                ┌────┐       ┌──┐   ┌───┐

  **yɔ¹   be²  el⁴   yaa¹tɔ¹       luk¹   nuŋ²gɔ³   sɔm³**
  which  CUM  heˆcalls grandfatherˆhis  house  nameˆits  differently
  Each one calls the house of his grandfather by a different name.

(193)        emNP
       ┌─────────────────────┐
         genNP
        ┌──────────────┐
         defNP    poss n    em pr
        ┌────┐   ┌───┐     ┌──┐

  **waar¹  bɔ¹    nɔɔ¹tɔ¹   gii¹    wɔ²rɔ²**
  chief  DEM   motherˆhis  sheˆEM   dieˆDEP
  It was the chief's mother who died.

(194)                     genNP
                  ┌──────────────────────────┐
         fsO:defNP    defNP    rln n poss n
         ┌───────┐    ┌────┐   ┌──┐  ┌───┐

  **naa²waal²  bɔ¹   hi³   gis²¹   waar¹  bɔ¹   waal²  nis²tɔ¹   kaŋ¹ko³**
  cowˆmilk   DEM   they  areˆBEN   chief  DEM   heir   wifeˆhis  bringing
  The milk that's being taken to the wife of the chief's oldest son . . .

Some Major Structures of Doyayo Syntax

(195)
```
                      genNP
         ┌─────────────────────────────┐
                  appNP
         ┌──────────────────────┐
           defNP      prop n        poss n
         ┌──────┐   ┌──────────┐   ┌──────┐
          dɛnt¹  bɔ¹  kɔɔ³bil¹ba¹    baa¹tɔ¹
```
old^man DEM dry^couscous^male father^his
the father of old Koobilba

(196)
```
                 genNP
         ┌──────────────────┐
             defNP      qnt aj
         ┌──────────┐  ┌──────┐
  hi³ ɓeg³  zum¹ bɔ¹    kaa¹si¹
```
they scoop flour DEM a^little
You take a little bit of flour ...

(197)
```
                        genNPref:coNP
              ┌──────────────────────────────┐
                 rln n     rln n    cj   rln n
              ┌──────┐  ┌────────┐       ┌──────┐
  hi³  wɛɛn³   ma³  kɔ²baar²  yaa¹boo²nɛ³ hi¹  zu¹mɛ³
```
they return^CAUS DEIC egg    mouth^talk and flour
They started discussing about eggs and flour.

(198)
```
                                      O:genNP
                           ┌──────────────────────────────┐
                                   defNP
                           ┌──────────────────────┐
  hi³ zaa²³ hi³ gbɛɛ²³ hin¹ gbɔ¹lɛ³ wɔ¹rɔ¹ hi¹  wɔr²   ma³
```
they came they cut  thing big^PL those they died^DEP DEIC

```
    poss n
  ┌────────┐
   nam²ya²³
```
meat^their
They came and cut up the meat of those two big animals that died.

(199)

$$\underbrace{\underbrace{hi^1ni^2 \quad d\underset{\smile}{\varepsilon}\varepsilon r^2 \; ma^3}_{mNP} \quad \underbrace{baa^2mi \quad gaps^2}_{mNP}}_{O:genNP} \quad y\jmath^1 \quad ya^4$$

thing^DEM stop DEIC father^my violence DEM Q
Could anything put a stop to the violence of my ancestors?

**4.1.6 The appositional noun phrase (appNP)** has the structure shown in (200).

(200)

$$+ \text{hd}_1: \begin{Bmatrix} \text{defNP} \\ \text{mNP} \\ \text{rln n} \\ \text{em pr} \\ \text{prop n} \\ \text{pr} \end{Bmatrix} + \text{hd}_2: \begin{Bmatrix} \text{defNP} \\ \text{mNP} \\ \text{coNP} \\ \text{genNP} \\ \text{relCl} \\ \text{prop n} \end{Bmatrix} \quad \begin{array}{l}\text{(one repetition of} \\ \text{this function)}\end{array}$$

The appositional noun phrase basically has two tagmemes, but the second may be repeated once, thus making a maximum of three tagmemes:

— an obligatory HEAD$_1$ slot, filled by a definite noun phrase, a modified noun phrase, a relational noun, an emphatic pronoun, a proper noun, or a pronoun, and
— an obligatory HEAD$_2$ slot, filled by a definite noun phrase, a modified noun phrase, a coordinated noun phrase, a genitival noun phrase, a rankshifted relative clause, or a proper noun, and where applicable,
— a HEAD$_3$ slot, with the same potential fillers as the head$_2$ slot.

(201)

$$\underbrace{\underbrace{hi^3 \quad gaa^4hi^1}_{\text{rln n}} \quad \underbrace{lu^1ko^3 \quad luk^1 \quad r\jmath^1bo^3}_{\text{mNP}}}_{O:appNP}$$

they gave^them house house good^RLN
They gave them a house, a good house.

(202)  S:appNP

mNP | coNP

zaan¹ za¹ ma³ nɛɛ²³yɔ² hi waa²³siŋ²³ hi³ rɛk³ rɛnt²
person other DEIC woman and child^sister they went wood
ɓɛ¹li¹ko³
chopping
Somebody—a woman and her daughter—went to chop wood.

(203)  S:appNP

em pr | prop n

wii¹ doo²³waat² wi¹dɔɔ² du¹ gɛ²
we^EM man^children we^go^up in not
We Dowayos didn't go along.

(204)  S:appNP

em pr | genNP

gii¹ nis² bɔ¹ wa²lɔ³ bɛɛ² tuuk¹ bɛ²
he^EM woman DEM man^her have^just^DEP going^out CUM
As soon as he—the woman's husband—had gone out,...

(205)  S:appNP

prop n | prop n

buu²saml² gbaa⁴bɛ⁴du¹ naa³ hɛ¹di¹ haa¹
white^rough put^me^in he^chatted here a^long^time
Buusaml Gbaabedu visited here for a long time...

(206)

```
                                         emNP
        ┌──────────────────────────────────────────┐
                      coNP_hd2:appNP
                  ┌──────────────────────┐
coNP_hd1:emNP   cj   prop n      prop n
┌────────────┐
pi³yɛr¹ gi¹ya¹   hi¹   ru¹bɛn³  baab²¹mi¹rɔ³        hi¹
Peter  he(SMEM) and  Reuben  father^my^he^appeared they
```
```
┌──────┐
ee¹rɛ¹
two
```
It was both Peter and Reuben Baabmiro.

(207)
```
                 S:appNP
        ┌─────────────────────────────────────┐
hd₁:em pr           hd₂:depNP
┌──────┐    ┌────────────────────────────────┐
gii¹   wal²³ bɔ¹  rek²   maat¹ ɔɔn¹  zɛɛk¹  zaa²dir¹
he^EM  man  DEM   go^DEP yam   his^EM digging come^yet^DEP
       gɛ²  be²
       not  CUM
```
The other man, the one who went to dig up his yams, hadn't come yet.

(208)
```
                S:appNP
        ┌──────────────────────────────┐
hd₁:em pr  hd₂:mNP  hd₃:prop n
┌──────┐   ┌───────────────┐
gii¹    sąąm³¹mi¹  war³bɛ²to³  rek³        woo²sɛ³
he^EM   friend^my  Warbeto    he^went     work
```
As for my friend Warbeto, he went to work.

(209)
```
                S:appNP
        ┌──────────────────────────────────┐
hd₁:em pr   hd₂:genNP      hd₃:prop n
┌──────┐    ┌──────────────┐
gii¹    baa²mi¹   waa²³ bɔ¹   tɔ²kal³
he^EM   father^my child DEM   Tokal
```
Now my cousin Tokal ...

Some Major Structures of Doyayo Syntax 183

(210)

$\overbrace{\text{hd}_1\text{:em pr} \quad \text{hd}_2\text{:relCl}}^{\text{S:appNP}}$

$\overbrace{bee^1 \; y\mathfrak{o}^1}^{} \; \overbrace{be^1zoo^1sig^1 \quad l\varepsilon^3 \quad be^1led^{21} \quad h\varepsilon w^{31} \; g\varepsilon^2}^{}$
I^EM REL I^taking^honey thus I^eat^yet too not
Even I haven't eaten any, while I'm the one harvesting it.

(211)

$\overbrace{\text{cj} \quad \text{hd}_1\text{:mNP} \quad \text{hd}_2\text{:mNP}}^{\text{coNPhd}_2\text{:appNP}}$

$hi^1 \; \overbrace{na^2be^1 \quad za^1}^{} \; \overbrace{wa^2l\varepsilon^3 \quad s\varepsilon^1r\varepsilon^3}^{}$
and peer^my^CIT other man^PL young^PL
... and my peers, the young men

When the appositional phrase fills the object slot, the order of the heads is sometimes reversed, as in (212).

(212)

$\overbrace{\text{mNP:poss n} \quad \text{em pr}}^{\text{O:appNP}}$

$hi^3 \; w\varepsilon\varepsilon^3 \; hi^3 \; loo^4 \; \overbrace{wal^{23}t\mathfrak{o}^1}^{} \; \overbrace{m\mathfrak{o}^1ya^1}^{}$
they return they take husband^her you(SMEM)
Then they take you, her husband...

**4.1.7 The referential noun phrase (refNP)** has the structure shown in (213).

(213)

$+ \text{ref: intrr} \begin{Bmatrix} b\mathfrak{o}^2 \\ n\mathfrak{o}^2 \\ ri^1 \end{Bmatrix} \pm \left[ + \text{hd:} \begin{Bmatrix} \text{rln n} \\ \text{sNP} \end{Bmatrix} + \text{dem: dem sf(sg/pl)} \right]$

± reinf: $n\mathfrak{o}^2$

The referential noun phrase has four tagmemes:

— an obligatory REFERENT slot, filled by interrogative $b\mathfrak{o}^2$, $n\mathfrak{o}^2$, or $ri^1$,[18]

---

[18]When $ri^1$ fills the referent slot, the head function is obligatorily absent.

an optional sequence of

— a HEAD slot, filled by a relational noun or a simple noun phrase, and
— a DEMONSTRATIVE slot, filled by a singular or plural demonstrative suffix, and
— an optional clause-final REINFORCER slot, filled by *nɔ²*.

When a referential noun phrase fills the subject slot of a clause, the following verb is in the dependent mood.

The only overt distinction between the possessive and the demonstrative variants of this phrase type is that the demonstrative function is sometimes omitted in the possessive as shown in (214).

(214) *bɔ² zaa¹nɔ³*           'Who? (literally 'what person?')'
      *bɔ² waa²ɔ³ ~ bɔ² waa²³*  'Whose child?'
      *nɔ² waa²ɔ³*             'What child?'
      *nɔ² hin¹ɔ³*             'What?/What thing?'
      *nɔ² zu¹lɔ³*             'The head of what?'

(215) *an¹ be¹ gɔ²   ri¹   nɔ²*
      that I  do^OPT how REINF
      What am I supposed to do?

(216) *nɔ²  gɔ¹ni¹mɔ³           nɔ²*
      what did^with^you^DEP REINF
      What happened to you?

(217) *kamz³      nɔ²  zoo²sɔ³      nɔ²*
      he^brought what game^DEM INTRR^REINF
      What kind of game (animal) did he bring?

(218) *nɔ²  nɛ¹  yaa²ɔ³*
      what well monkey^DEM
      Oh, what kind of monkeys?

(219) *bɔ²  dood²-ya²³     zaa²*
      who people^DEM^PL came
      What people came?

## Some Major Structures of Doyayo Syntax

**4.1.8 The focal noun phrase (focNP)** has the structure shown in (220).

(220)   ± hd: $\begin{Bmatrix} \text{mNP} \\ \text{defNP} \\ \text{coNP} \\ \text{genNP} \\ \text{appNP} \\ \text{dem n} \\ \text{sfoc pr} \end{Bmatrix}$ + reinf: sfoc pr

The *focal* noun phrase has two tagmemes:

— an optional HEAD, filled by a modified, definite, coordinate, genitival or appositional noun phrase, a demonstratized noun or a semi-focal pronoun, and
— an obligatory REINFORCER, filled by a semi-focal pronoun.

(221)      S:focNP

$\overline{zaa^1nɔ^3 \qquad ɔ^2nɛ^3 \; gi^2 \; fuu^1zig^1 \qquad ay^{12}}$
person^DEM^SFOC PR    is   coming^from where
Where is that fellow going to come from?

(222)      IO:focNP

$\overline{bɛ^2nɛ^3 \qquad ɔ^2nɛ^3 \qquad haa^2bɛ^1 \qquad gɛ^{23}}$
I^CIT^SFOC  SFOC^SG  it^wants^me^DEP  not
As for me, I don't want it.

(223)                          coNP

$\overline{\phantom{xxxxxxxxxxxxxxxxxxxxxxxxxxxxxxxxxxxxxxxxxxxxxxxxxx}}$
                    focNP
$\overline{\phantom{xxxxxxxxxxxxxxxxxxxxxxxxxxx}}$
             appNP
$\overline{\phantom{xxxxxxxxxxxxxxx}}$
    defNP     prop n
$\overline{\phantom{xxxxxxx}}$ $\overline{\phantom{xxxxx}}$
*waa²³ bɔ¹  kpaar³baa¹  ɔ²nɛ³   hi¹  baa¹tɔ¹*
child  that  Kpaarba   SFOC^SG and father^his
As for the child Kpaarba and his father...

(224)      focNP
       ⎯⎯⎯⎯⎯⎯⎯⎯⎯⎯⎯⎯⎯⎯
         mNP        reinf
       ⎯⎯⎯⎯⎯⎯⎯    ⎯⎯⎯⎯⎯⎯
       *doo²waat²*   *wi²nɛ³*    *dɔgl²wi¹*   *taa¹²*   *du¹*
       man^children  SMEM^PR     word^our     is^not    in
       As for us Dowayos, we're not interested.

### 4.1.9 The emphatic noun phrase (emNP) has the structure shown in (225).

(225)  ± hd: $\begin{Bmatrix} \text{mNP} \\ \text{defNP} \\ \text{genNP} \\ \text{coNP} \\ \text{appNP} \\ \text{indp n} \\ \text{prop n} \end{Bmatrix}$ + em: $\begin{Bmatrix} \text{em pr} \\ \text{smem pr} \end{Bmatrix}$ ∓ spec: relCl

The emphatic noun phrase has three tagmemes:

— an optional HEAD, filled by a modified noun phrase, a definite noun phrase, a genitival noun phrase, a coordinate noun phrase, an appositional noun phrase, an independent noun,[19] a proper noun, or a proximal demonstrative noun,
— an obligatory EMPHASIZER, filled by an emphatic, or a semi-emphatic pronoun, and
— an optional SPECIFIER slot, filled by a relative clause. The latter functions in mutual exclusion with the head.

When the emphatic NP occupies the subject slot of the clause, it is followed in the predicate by the dependative or perfective mood.

---

[19] When the head slot is filled by an independent noun or a proximate demonstrative noun, this entails the obligatory absence of the emphasizer function.

Some Major Structures of Doyayo Syntax

(226)     S:emNP
          ⌜―――――――――――――――――⌝
             defNP
          ⌜―――――――――――⌝
   vaam²de³waa²³ yε¹rε¹ gii¹ haa²be¹
   donkey^child    this  it^EM it^want^me^DEP
   It's this donkey colt I want.

(227)        S:emNP
          ⌜―――――――――――――――⌝
             genNP
          ⌜―――――――――⌝
   tot²  bɔ¹  dɔg²lɔ³  gii¹  gε²
   sorghum that word^its it^EM not
   It's not about the sorghum.

(228) S:emNP
   ⌜――――⌝
   bee¹ gbɔŋ²ge¹
   I^EM kill^him^DEP
   *I* killed him.

(229)        S:emNP
          ⌜―――――――――――――――――⌝
              appNP
          ⌜―――――――――――⌝
   zaa¹  bɔ¹  see³lin¹ gii¹  dɔɔ²    bi¹sε³
   other DEM  Celine   she^EM she^cooked sauce^RLN
   It was Celine, the other one, who made some sauce.

(230) coNP_hd1:emNP    cj    coNP:h:dS:appNP
      ⌜――――――――――⌝          ⌜―――――――――――――――⌝
   pi³yεr¹³ gi¹ya¹   hi¹  ru¹bεn³  baab²¹mi²rɔ³
   Peter    he(SMEM) and  Reuben   father^my^he^appeared
            NP_mar
          ⌜―――――――⌝
   hi¹         ee¹rε¹
   they(SMEM)  two
   It was Peter and Reuben Baabmiro, the two of them.

(231)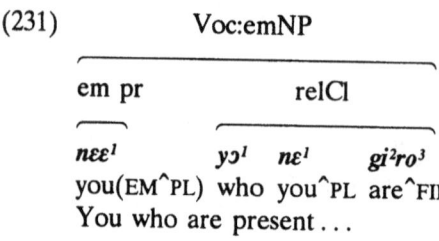

nɛɛ¹ yɔ¹ nɛ¹ gi²ro³
you(EM^PL) who you^PL are^FIN
You who are present...

(232)           O:emNP
                defNP:relCl

mɔ¹ ɓb⁴ bɔ¹ rek² a¹ tees⁴¹ du¹ ga¹
you follow DEM go^DEP LOC middle in SMEM^PR
Take the middle one.

One phenomenon is not accounted for in this analysis, as it seems not to function at phrase level at all, but rather at clause level, being not expandable into a phrase. That is the emphatic use of the independent noun form, which like the emNP, affects the mood of the ensuing predicate as shown in (233) and (234).

(233) hi¹ni² dɛɛr² ma³ baa²-mi¹ gaps² yɔ¹
thing^PROX^DEM cut^off^DEP DEIC father^my aggression this
ya⁴
Q
Could anything put a stop to the violence of my ancestors?

(234) buu²³² zaa² gi¹ dɛɛ⁴rɔ²
white^man^INDP he^came^DEP he cut^off
It's the white man who came and put a stop to it.

(235) mc³ kamz³ gɔɔ²³² ya⁴
you brought peanuts^INDP Q
Did you bring peanuts?

# Some Major Structures of Doyayo Syntax

**4.1.10 The emphatic possessive noun phrase (epNP)** has the structure shown in (236).

(236)
$$\pm \text{ em: em pr } \pm \text{ hd: } \begin{Bmatrix} \text{sNP} \\ \text{rln n} \\ \text{poss n} \end{Bmatrix} + \text{poss: } \begin{Bmatrix} \text{smem poss aj/pr} \\ \text{em poss aj/pr} \end{Bmatrix}$$

$$\pm \text{ def: } \begin{Bmatrix} \text{dem aj} \\ \text{relCl} \end{Bmatrix}$$

The emphatic possessive noun phrase (epNP) has four tagmemes:

— an optional EMPHASIZER slot, filled by an emphatic pronoun,
— an optional HEAD slot, filled by a simple noun phrase, a relational noun or a possessed noun (the presence of which incurs the obligatory absence of the possessor function),
— an obligatory POSSESSOR slot, filled by a semi-emphatic or emphatic possessive adjective or pronoun, and
— an optional DEFINER slot, filled by a demonstrative adjective or a relative clause.

(237)     epNP

| smem poss pr | relCl |

*ɟn²³   bɔ¹   hąą²ge¹        gi¹   kpoos²du¹   dɔg²su³mɔ³*
hers DEM it^wants^her^DEP her heart in
She tells you what she really wants.

(238)     S:epNP

| em pr | rln n | smem poss | pr relCl |

*gii¹   gɔn²wal²³   ɟ²nɛ³   bɔ¹   lug²        pi²³ra²*
he^EM inlaw^man his^SFOC DEM he^plant^DEP it^sprouted
As for that planted by the father-in-law, it sprouted.

(239)           O:epNP
    ┌─────────────────────────────────┐
    em pr   smem          relCl
            poss pr
    ┌──────────────┐ ┌──────────────────────────┐
    mɔɔ¹    mɔ²nɛ³  wɔ¹   raa¹    du¹  hi¹zaa¹³   hi¹loo⁴
    you^EM  your    DEM   compound in   they^come they^take
    Yours at home will be taken.

(240)          S:epNP
    ┌──────────────────────────────┐
    VocP     em pr     poss n
    ┌──────┐ ┌────────────────┐
    wal²³yɔ¹  mɔɔ¹   yaa¹mɔ¹   diig³¹  hɛw³¹
    man^DEM   you^EM  mouth^your hurries also
    As for you, fellow, you're rather quick with your tongue, as well.

(241)                        IP_hd:epNP
            ┌────────────────────────────────────┐
            mNP           smem poss pr    dem aj
    ┌────────────────┐ ┌────────────────┐ ┌────┐
    bɔ²  gi¹ ɔks³ hi¹  dood²  rɔ¹bɛ³  ya²nɛ³   wɔ¹
    INTDC she mix with people good^PL  their^FOC POSS those
    She must not mix it with those of the other members of the chief's household.

(242)          C:epNP
    ┌─────────────────────┐
        rln n    em poss aj
        ┌────┐   ┌────────┐
    yɛ¹rɛ¹  luk¹   mii¹nɛ¹
    this    house  my^EM
    This is *my* house.

**4.1.11 The noun phrase margin (NP_mar).** There is an extension which can further modify any noun phrase except genNP, appNP, refNP, and focNP, and which is here called the *NP margin*. It can follow directly after the core of the noun phrase or, optionally, be backshifted to a position within the adverbial slot. The noun phrase margin can represent the noun phrase in the absence of the core. It has the structure shown in (243).

# Some Major Structures of Doyayo Syntax

(243) ± foc: $\begin{Bmatrix} \text{smem pr} \\ \text{em pr} \end{Bmatrix}$ ± qnt: nm

± reinf: $\begin{Bmatrix} \text{'some' } (kaa^1si^1, kaa^1ka^1, feg^1, \text{ etc.}) \\ \text{'all' } \phantom{o}(sew^3, mib^1, pad^1, kp\varepsilon\varepsilon d^{31}, \text{ etc.}) \\ \text{'only' } (kpɔd^{41}, ta^1, \text{ etc.}) \\ \text{other ideophone} \end{Bmatrix}$

The noun phrase margin has three tagmemes:

— an optional FOCAL slot, filled by a semi-emphatic or emphatic pronoun,
— an optional QUANTIFIER slot, filled by a number word, and
— an optional REINFORCER slot, filled by a word, usually an ideophone, of quantity of limitation, such as 'some', 'all' and 'only'.

When modifying an emNP, the $NP_{mar}$ has obligatory absence of the focal function.

When the noun phrase is embedded within a circumstantial phrase, the margin is obligatorily backshifted to a position immediately following the circumstantial phrase. When modifying the NP subject, the $NP_{mar}$ can remain joined to the NP, but tends to be backshifted to a position between CP and AP. Though all the functions are optional, $NP_{mar}$ cannot be represented by only *quantity*.

(244)  S:defNP

$\overbrace{\phantom{nnnnnnnnnnnnnnnnnnnnnnnnnn}}$
  $\phantom{nnnnnnnnn}$ $NP_{mar}$
  $\phantom{nnnnnnnnn}\overbrace{\phantom{nnnnnnn}}$
*nɔɔs² wɔ¹   sεw³  hi³  rek³  hεt¹  du¹*
bird DEM^PL all they went grass in

  $\phantom{nn}$defNP $\phantom{nnnnnnnnnnnnnnnn}$ $NP_{mar}$
  $\overbrace{\phantom{nnnnnnn}}\phantom{nnnnnnnnnnnnnn}\overbrace{\phantom{nnnn}}$
*nɔɔs² wɔ¹   hi³  rek³  hεt¹  du¹  sεw³*
bird DEM^PL they went grass in  all
All the birds went out into the bush.

(245) 
                                                                     CP

                             $CP_{hd}$:defNP          $NP_{mar}$

$gii^1$   $w\varepsilon\varepsilon^2$         $waar^1$ $a^1$ $nɔɔs^2$ $wɔ^1$   $hi^1$   $zul^1$  $ha^1$  $s\varepsilon w^3$
he^EM he^become^DEP chief at bird those they head on all
*He* became the chief of all the birds.

(246)  S:$NP_{mar}$                     S:$NP_{mar}$

$s\varepsilon w^3$ $gi^2$ $an^1bɔ^1$  / $gi^2$ $an^1bɔ^1$ $s\varepsilon w^3$
all   it^is like^that
It's all like that.

(247)      S:defNP                                        $NP_{mar}$

$n\varepsilon\varepsilon d^2$     $s\varepsilon^1r\varepsilon^3$     $wɔ^1$     $hi^3$   $ɓaks^1$   $ma^3$  $gɔ^1$  $kp\varepsilon\varepsilon d^{31}$
woman^PL young^PL DEM^PL they lined^up DEIC ANA all
   $hi^1$   $wa^2l\varepsilon^3$   $s\varepsilon^1r\varepsilon^3$    $wɔɔ^{13}$
with man^PL young^PL DEM^PL
And now the young women all line up with the young men.

(248)                       O:emNP

                   emNP        $NP_{mar}$

$mɔ^3$ $gb\varepsilon ns^{31}$ $hɔd^{23}$ $wɔ^1$    $hii^1$    $kpɔd^{41}$
you see^INT bee  DEM^PL they^EM only
You see only the bees.

(249)                     O:em$NP_{mar}$

$mɔ^1loo^4si^4be^4$         $gii^1$    $kpɔd^{41}$
you^will^take^BEN^me her^EM only
Just get *her* for me.

(250) S:pr                 $NP_{mar}$

$mi^3$ $rek^3$ $luum^2$ $ha^1$ $mi^1$ $gbu^1nu^1$
I   went market on I   one
I went to the market alone (by myself).

Some Major Structures of Doyayo Syntax                                   193

(251)                coNP              NP$_{mar}$

pi$^3$yɛr$^{13}$ gi$^1$ya$^{13}$   hi$^1$  ru$^1$bɛn$^3$   hi$^1$   ee$^1$rɛ$^1$
Peter  he(SMEM) and Reuben  they two
It was Peter and Reuben, the two of them.

(252)                                          NP$_{mar}$

mɔ$^1$  ɓb$^4$   bɔ$^1$   rek$^2$   a$^1$   tees$^{41}$   du$^1$   ga$^1$
you follow DEM  goˆDEP  LOC  middle  in  SMEMˆPR
Take the middle one.

**4.1.12 Summary of nominal phrase types.**

(253)  sNP simple noun phrase

± hd: rln n   ± qlf: $\begin{Bmatrix} aj \\ AjP \\ NmP \end{Bmatrix}$

(254)  gɛrs$^2$   a   nɛɛ$^{23}$   za$^1$   hi$^1$   waa$^2$ɔ$^3$
miracle at woman INDF and childˆher
The strange experience of a woman and her son.

(255)  mNP modified noun phrase

± hd: $\begin{Bmatrix} \text{rln n} \\ \text{poss n} \end{Bmatrix}$   ± qlf$_1$: aj$_1$   ± indf: indf art   ± qlf$_2$: aj$_2$

± qlf$_3$: aj$_3$   ± qnt: $\begin{Bmatrix} \text{NmP} \\ baa^4ri^1/nɔ^4ni^1 \end{Bmatrix}$   ± loc: CP

(256)  rɔ$^4$bɛ$^1$   zaa$^1$dɛ$^3$   yɔl$^1$seen$^2$ya$^1$   hi$^3$   gi$^2$   di$^1$
foreignˆPL INDFˆPL eyeˆseeˆFUNC they were about
There were foreign witnesses present...

(257) defNP definite noun phrase

$$\pm \text{ hd:} \begin{Bmatrix} \text{rln n} \\ \text{poss n} \end{Bmatrix} \quad \pm \text{ qlf}_1\text{: aj}_1 \quad \pm \text{ indf: indf art} \quad \pm \text{ qlf}_2\text{: aj}_2$$

$$\pm \text{ qnt: NmP} \quad + \text{ def:} \begin{Bmatrix} \text{dem aj} \\ \text{rel cl} \end{Bmatrix}$$

(258) $wa^2l\varepsilon^3 \quad s\varepsilon^1r\varepsilon^3 \quad r\mathfrak{o}^4b\varepsilon^1 \quad gb\mathfrak{o}^1l\varepsilon^3 \quad ee^1r\varepsilon^1 \quad w\mathfrak{o}^1r\mathfrak{o}^1 \quad hi^3$
man^PL young^PL foreign^PL big^PL two those they
$f\underset{\sim}{u}\underset{\sim}{u}z^1 \quad ay^{12}$
come^IMM where
Where do those two big young aliens come from?

(259) coNP coordinated noun phrase

$$+ \text{ hd}_1: \begin{Bmatrix} \text{defNP} \\ \text{mNP} \\ \text{genNP} \\ \text{emNP} \\ \text{rln n} \\ \text{indp n} \\ \text{prop n} \end{Bmatrix} + \left[ \pm \text{ cj: } hi^1 + \text{ hd}_2: \begin{Bmatrix} \text{defNP} \\ \text{mNP} \\ \text{genNP} \\ \text{emNP} \\ \text{appNP} \\ \text{rln n} \\ \text{prop n} \end{Bmatrix} \right]_{(n)}$$

(260) $an^1 \quad d\varepsilon nt\varepsilon^1 \quad y\underset{\sim}{a}\underset{\sim}{a}m^3waa^2to^3 \quad hi^1 \quad na^2b\varepsilon^1 \quad za^1 \quad wa^2l\varepsilon^3$
like old^man^PL child^PL   and peer^my INDF man^PL
$s\varepsilon^1r\varepsilon^3$
young^PL
...like old men, children and my peers, the young men

(261) genNP genitival noun phrase

$$+ \text{ ref:} \begin{Bmatrix} \text{prop n} \\ \text{rln n} \\ \text{poss n} \\ \text{mNP} \\ \text{defNP} \\ \text{appNP} \\ \text{coNP} \end{Bmatrix} \pm \text{ hd-ref:} \begin{Bmatrix} \text{rln n} \\ \text{poss n (3p)} \end{Bmatrix} + \text{ hd:} \begin{Bmatrix} \text{rln n} \\ \text{indp n} \\ \text{poss n (3p)} \\ \text{coNPgh} \\ \text{sfoc poss aj} \\ \text{qnt aj} \end{Bmatrix}$$

Some Major Structures of Doyayo Syntax                                    195

(262)  dɛnt¹     bɔ¹    kɔɔ³bil¹ba¹         baa¹tɔ¹
       old^man  DEF   dry^eating^male    father^his
       The father of old Koobilba

(263) appNP appositional noun phrase

$$+ \text{hd}_1: \begin{Bmatrix} \text{defNP} \\ \text{mNP} \\ \text{rln n} \\ \text{em pr} \\ \text{prop n} \\ \text{pr} \end{Bmatrix} + \text{hd}_2: \begin{Bmatrix} \text{defNP} \\ \text{mNP} \\ \text{coNP} \\ \text{genNP} \\ \text{relCl} \\ \text{prop n} \end{Bmatrix} \quad \text{(one repetition of this function)}$$

(264)  gii¹    saam³¹mi¹    war³bɛ²tɔ³   rek³   woo²sɛ³
       he^EM  friend^my    ask^God      went   work
       My friend Warbeto, for his part, went to work.

(265) refNP referential noun phrase

$$+ \text{ref: intrr} \begin{Bmatrix} bɔ² \\ nɔ² \\ ri¹ \end{Bmatrix} \pm \left[ + \text{hd:} \begin{Bmatrix} \text{rln n} \\ \text{sNP} \end{Bmatrix} + \text{dem: dem sf(sg/pl)} \right]$$

$$\pm \text{reinf: } nɔ²$$

(266)  kamz³    nɔ²    zoo²sɔ³       nɔ²³
       brought  what   prey^DEM     REINF
       What sort of game did he bring?

(267) focNP focal noun phrase

$$\pm \text{hd:} \begin{Bmatrix} \text{mNP} \\ \text{defNP} \\ \text{coNP} \\ \text{genNP} \\ \text{appNP} \\ \text{dem n} \\ \text{sfoc pr} \end{Bmatrix} + \text{reinf: sfoc pr}$$

(268) **zaa¹nɔ³**   **ɔ²nɛ³**   **gi²**   **fųų¹zig¹**   **ay¹²**
person^DEM he^SFOC is coming^from where
Where is that fellow going to come from?

(269) emNP emphatic noun phrase

$$\pm \text{ hd:} \begin{Bmatrix} \text{mNP} \\ \text{defNP} \\ \text{genNP} \\ \text{coNP} \\ \text{appNP} \\ \text{indp n} \\ \text{prop n} \end{Bmatrix} + \text{em:} \begin{Bmatrix} \text{em pr} \\ \text{smem pr} \end{Bmatrix} \mp \text{spec: relCl}$$

(270) **vąąm²de³waa²³**   **yɛ¹rɛ¹**   **gii¹**   **hąą²be¹**
donkey^child this her^EM wants^me
It's this donkey colt I love.

(271) epNP emphatic possessive noun phrase

$$\pm \text{ em: em pr} \quad \pm \text{ hd:} \begin{Bmatrix} \text{sNP} \\ \text{rln n} \\ \text{poss n} \end{Bmatrix} + \text{poss:} \begin{Bmatrix} \text{smem poss aj/pr} \\ \text{em poss aj/pr} \end{Bmatrix}$$

$$\pm \text{ def:} \begin{Bmatrix} \text{dem aj} \\ \text{relCl} \end{Bmatrix}$$

(272) **gii¹**   **gɔn²wal²³**   **ɔ²nɛ³**   **bɔ¹**   **lug²**   **pi²³ra²**
he^EM father^in^law his^SFOC REL planted sprouted
As for that planted by the father-in-law, it sprouted.

# Some Major Structures of Doyayo Syntax

(273) NP$_{mar}$ noun phrase margin

$$\pm \text{ foc: } \begin{Bmatrix} \text{smem pr} \\ \text{em pr} \end{Bmatrix} \quad \pm \text{ qnt: nm}$$

$$\pm \text{ reinf: } \begin{Bmatrix} \text{'some' } (kaa^1si^1, kaa^1ka^1, feg^1, \text{ etc.}) \\ \text{'all' } (sew^3, mib^1, pad^1, kp\varepsilon\varepsilon d^{31}, \text{ etc.}) \\ \text{'only' } (kpɔd^{41}, ta^1, \text{ etc.}) \\ \text{other ideophone} \end{Bmatrix}$$

(274)                                                                                   NP$_{mar}$

nɛɛd$^1$   sɛ$^1$rɛ$^3$   wɔ$^1$   hi$^3$   ɓaks$^1$   ma$^3$   gɔ$^1$   kpɛɛd$^{31}$ hi$^1$
woman^PL young^PL DEF they lined^up DEIC ANA all(ID) with
wa$^3$lɛ$^3$   sɛ$^1$rɛ$^3$   wɔ$^1$
man^PL young^PL DEF

And then all the young ladies lined up together with the young men.

## 4.2 Circumstantial phrase

The circumstantial phrase functions at *clause level*, in the initial margin and the adverbial slot, and at *phrase level*, in the modified noun phrase.

Six kinds of circumstantial phrases have been examined: the *standard* (stCP), the *possessive* (posCP), the *coordinate* (coCP), the *coordinate possessor* (copCP), the *interrogative* (intrrCP), and the *relator* (relCP). All the above types have been found to be locative, but only the standard, coordinate, and interrogative types have been found to be temporal.

**4.2.1 The standard circumstantial phrase (stCP)** has the structure shown in (275).

(275)

$$\pm \text{ cmkr: } a^1 \quad \pm \text{ rem: } da^3 \quad + \left[ \pm \text{ hd:} \begin{Bmatrix} \text{rln n} \\ \text{mNP} \\ \text{defNP} \\ \text{genNP} \\ \text{loc/temp wd} \\ \text{em pr} \\ \text{intrr } nɔ^2/bɔ^2 \end{Bmatrix} \right.$$

$$\left. \pm \text{ cind}_{(4)}: \right] \begin{Bmatrix} \text{spec} \\ \text{loc part} \end{Bmatrix} \quad \pm \text{ reinf: NP}_{\text{mar}}$$

The standard circumstantial phrase has five tagmemes, all of which are optional, but either the head or the circumstantial indicator function must be present. There is, first,

— a CIRCUMSTANTIAL MARKER slot, filled by the particle $a^1$,
— a REMOTE slot, filled by the particle $da^3$,
— the HEAD slot, filled by a relational noun, modified noun phrase, a definite noun phrase, a genitival noun phrase, a locative or temporal word, an emphatic pronoun, or interrogative $nɔ^2$ or $bɔ^2$,
— a CIRCUMSTANTIAL slot, filled by specifier $ge^1$ (SG) / $hi^1$ (PL) or a locative particle, and
— a REINFORCER slot, filled by a noun phrase margin (NP$_{\text{mar}}$).

The circumstantial indicator function can be repeated up to four times.

(276)  stCP

rln n

$a^1$ $da^3$ $luum^2$ $ya^1$ $ha^1$ $hɛ^1$
at REM market beside on here
way up by the market

(277)

```
                      stCP
        ┌──────────────────────────┐
                   defNP
        ┌────────────────────┐
```
a¹ hɛ̰t¹dɔŋ²³  yɛ¹rɛ¹  ge¹  du¹  hɛ¹  di¹
at  grass^side  this  SPEC  in  here  upon
out here in this wilderness

(278)

```
                           stCP
            ┌──────────────────────────────────┐
                         genNP
            ┌──────────────────────────┐
```
zaa²³   maa³   hɛ̰t¹  bɔ¹  yɔ̰ɔ̰²lɔ³  di¹sɔ³  ge¹
he^comes he^glues grass DEM anus^its under^its SPEC
He glued it to the bottom of the grass.

(279)

```
                  stCP
        ┌──────────────────────┐
                 rln n
           ┌───────────┐
```
mɔ¹  kã²be¹    mɛm¹lɛl²³    gɛ²  be²
you take^me^DEP water^place not CUM
Besides, you didn't take me to a place where I could drink.

(280)

```
                  stCP
        ┌──────────────┐
```
yɔ¹  mɔ¹  gi²   di¹   gbɔɔl¹tɔ¹nɔ¹  gor³¹yɔ¹
as  you  be^DEP  upon  big^very      ID
as big as you are, standing there, ...

(281)

```
                stCP
        ┌──────────────┐
```
hi³  rek³  hi³  ɔɔ³  di¹  hɔ¹
they went they left upon over^there
They went off and left some there.

(282)                              stCP
                           ⌜─────────⌝
                           rln  n  spec
                           ⌜──⌝  ⌜──⌝
    zaan²³         waar¹  ge¹
    he^came^with  chief  SPEC
    He came to the chief with it.

(283)                                                  stCP
                                               ⌜─────────────⌝
                                               loc part  loc part
                                                ⌜────⌝  ⌜────⌝
    yɔ¹    wi¹   mɔks¹         lel⁴¹bɔ¹        di¹    hɛ¹     rɛ¹
    when   we    assemble^DEP  yesterday^DEM   upon   here    CJ
    When we met here the other day,...

(284)                              stCP
                           ⌜───────────────⌝
                           rln  n    loc part
                           ⌜──⌝    ⌜──────⌝
    mɔ¹zaa¹³         naa²³baan³  du¹
    you^come^OPT     cow^rope    in
    Come at three p.m.

(285)       stCP
       ⌜─────────────⌝
       cmkr rln n loc part
       ⌜─⌝ ⌜──⌝ ⌜──⌝
    a¹   riib¹   du¹   dood²   hi³   hii²¹sɔ¹
    at   pasture in    people  they  are^full
    The pasture is full of people.

(286)                      stCP
                      ⌜─────────────⌝
                      cmkr rln n loc part
                      ⌜─⌝ ⌜──⌝ ⌜──⌝
    yɔ¹   mɔ¹  gum²       a¹   woos²   du¹   zaa¹   sɛɛ²³   gbu¹nu¹
    when  you  hurt^DEP   at   work    in    other  month   one
    When you have sick leave from work, sometimes for a month,...

## Some Major Structures of Doyayo Syntax

(287)   stCP
   rln n loc part

gɔ² lɛɛ¹sig³ du¹
when afternoon in
When it is afternoon, . . .

(288)   stCP
  defNP

hi³ wɔ⁴ sil¹ bɔ¹ ge¹ du¹ hi³ re³kɔ²
they tied mat DEM SPEC in they went
They tied him up in the mat and left.

(289)   stCP
  mNP

hi³ kar⁴ tɛɛ¹ wɔ¹ ha¹ hi¹
they climb tree DEM on SPEC
They climbed up the trees.

(290)   stCP
  em pr

mi³ zaa²³ a¹ mɔɔ¹ ge¹
I came at you-EM SPEC
I have come to *you*.

(291)   stCP
    temp wd

mɔ¹ too⁴sib⁴ toos¹ nɛɛ²³kɔ²
you pay^BEN^me^OPT RDP today
You're going to pay me today, for sure.

(292)        stCP
         ⏞
     re³    bɔ²   ge¹
     sheˆwent who SPEC
     To whom did she go?

(293)           stCP
              ⏞
     mi¹ yaa⁴    a¹ nɔ²  du¹
     I   sendˆOPT at what in
     What should I put it in?

**4.2.2 The possessive circumstantial phrase (possCP)** has the structure shown in (294).

(294)

$$\pm \text{ cmkr: a} + \left[\pm \text{ ref:} \begin{Bmatrix} \text{mNP} \\ \text{intrr} \\ \text{defNP} \end{Bmatrix}\right] \pm \text{ poss ind: pr} \pm \text{ hd:} \begin{Bmatrix} \text{rln n} \\ \text{loc/temp wd} \end{Bmatrix}$$

$$\pm \text{ cind}_{(2)}\text{: loc part} \pm \text{ reinf:} \begin{Bmatrix} \text{id} \\ \text{NP}_{\text{mar}} \\ nɔ² \end{Bmatrix}$$

The *possessive circumstantial phrase* has six tagmemes:

— an optional CIRCUMSTANTIAL MARKER slot, filled by the circumstantial particle *a*,
— an optional POSSESSOR slot, filled by a modified noun phrase, an interrogative pronoun or a definite noun phrase,[20]
— an optional POSSESSIVE INDICATOR, filled by a nonfocal pronoun,
— an obligatory *head* slot, filled by a noun or a locative or temporal word,
— an optional CIRCUMSTANTIAL INDICATOR slot, with up to two occurrences, filled by a locative particle, and
— an optional REINFORCER slot, filled by an ideophone, a noun phrase margin or *nɔɔ*[23].

---

[20] When a defNP fills the referent slot, the possessive indicator function becomes obligatory.

# Some Major Structures of Doyayo Syntax

Though both the possessor and the possessive indicator functions are optional, one of these two functions must always be present.

(295)                               possCP

       $is^{31}$    $wɛɛ^3$        $a^1$ $gi^1$ $lɛ^2lɛ^3$
       goat    he^returned    at he place
       The goat went home.

(296)                               possCP

       $ka^4si^1be^3$          $mɔ^1$ $yɛl^{23}$ $du^1$
       rise^CAUS^me(IMP) you back in
       Lift me up on your back.

(297)                                           possCP

                                             $CP_{hd}$

       $hi^3$    $ɔ^3sig^3$       $ma^3$ $hɔd^{23}dak^1$     $yɔ^1$    $muu^1lɛ^3$
       they   left^BEN^him   DEIC   bee^calabash   this   body
       They left the honey calabashes on him.

(298)                                     possCP

                                mNP       hd

       $yɔ^1$ $gi^2$ $tuu^1zig^1$      $a^1$ $baa^1tɔ^1$   $tu^1tin^3$    $du^1$ $yɔ^1$
       as he^is go^out^IMM^INC   at father^his   entry^hut   in   here
       As he was coming out of his father's entry hut . . .

(299)                             possCP           stCP

              cmkr    ref     hd    loc           reinf

       $is^{31}$ $be^2$ $gi^2$ $gɔ^1$ $a^1$ $sąą^3mɔ^3$ $yɛl^{23}$ $duu^{13}$ $wɛɛ^2ha^1$ $lad^1$
       goat CUM he^is ANA at friend^his back in    toward^on ID
       As for the goat, there he was on his friend's back, way up high.

(300)  wɛɛn³         dɔɔ¹ɔ³  wɔ¹   hi¹  zu¹lɔ³
       he^returned-CAUS leg^his DEM-PL and head^his

```
                    possCP
              ┌───────────────────┐
              cmkr  poss  hd   loc
              ┌──┐ ┌──┐ ┌────┐ ┌──┐
       bɔ¹    a¹   gi¹  kɔ¹kil³ du¹  sɔɔd¹
       DEM    at   he   shell  in   ID
```
He quickly retracted his legs and his head into his shell.

(301)              possCP
         ┌───────────────────┐
         cmkr  ref   hd   loc
         ┌──┐ ┌────┐ ┌──┐ ┌──┐
   hạb²³  a¹  nam²nɔ¹ durk² du¹
   he^tied at  elephant neck in
   He tied it to the elephant's neck...

(302)                          possCP
              ┌──────────────────────────────────┐
              cmkr poss:defNP poss ind  hd   loc
              ┌──┐ ┌──────┐  ┌──┐ ┌──┐ ┌──┐
   gii¹  wɛɛ²  waar¹ a¹   nɔɔs² wɔ¹  hi¹  zul¹ ha¹
   he-EM he^returns-DEP chief at bird DEM^PL they head on

   NP_mar
   ┌────┐
   sɛw³
   all
It was he who became the chief over all the birds.

(303)            possCP
         ┌───────────────┐
         cmkr intrr  hd
         ┌──┐ ┌──┐ ┌──┐
   mɔ³  fụụz¹   a¹  bɔ²  lɛ²lɛ³
   You come^from at who place
   Whose place did you come from?

(304)
$$\overbrace{\text{wɛɛ}^3 \quad \text{waar}^1 \quad a^1 \quad bɔ^2 \quad \text{zul}^1 \quad ha^1 \quad nɔ^2}^{\text{possCP}}$$
became chief at who head on what
Over whom did he become chief?

(305)
$$\text{mɔ}^1 \quad \text{tɛ̰ɛ̰}^{13} \quad \text{zept}^2 \quad \overbrace{bɔ^1 \quad gi^1 \quad \text{muu}^1\text{lɛ}^3}^{\text{possCP}}$$
You will^trace magic^plant that its body
Trace on it with the plant ...

**4.2.3 The coordinate circumstantial phrase (coCP)** has the structure shown in (306).

(306)
$$+ \text{hd}_1: \begin{Bmatrix} \text{stCP} \\ \text{loc/temp wd} \\ \text{place name} \end{Bmatrix} + \left[ \pm \text{ cj } hi^1 + \text{hd}_2: \begin{Bmatrix} \text{stCP} \\ \text{loc/temp wd} \\ \text{place name} \end{Bmatrix} \right]_{(n)}$$

$\pm$ reinf: $\text{NP}_{\text{mar}}$

The sequence of conjunctor plus head$_2$ can be repeated n number of times. Before the last repetition, the conjunctor function is obligatory, except in a long enumeration.

The *coordinate circumstantial phrase* has four tagmemes:

— an obligatory HEAD$_1$ slot, filled by a standard circumstantial phrase,[21] a locative, or temporal word or a place name,

an obligatory sequence of:

— an optional CONJUNCTOR slot, filled by $hi^1$, and
— an obligatory HEAD$_2$ slot, filled by a standard circumstantial phrase, a locative or temporal word, or a place name, and
— an optional REINFORCER slot, filled by a noun phrase margin.

---

[21]There is obligatory absence of the circumstantial marker in the stCP within the head$_2$ slot.

(307)

```
                               coCP
                    ┌───────────────────────────┐
                      stCP              stCP       NP_mar
                    ┌──────────────┐  ┌─────────┐ ┌───┐
waa²³   bɔ¹   gi²   kaak¹   lurk¹  du¹   hi¹   yɛms¹  du¹   sɛw³
child   DEM   he^is crying   day   in   and   night   in    all
```
The baby cries day and night.

(308)

```
                                            coCP
                               ┌───────────────────────────────┐
                                   stCP              stCP
                               ┌──────────────┐  ┌──────────────┐
bee¹    gi²    gɛr²³   rɔ¹bo³  a¹   bɛt²   ha¹   hi¹   hɛbt²   di¹
I^CIT^EM be^DEP healer  good   at   sky    on    and   earth   upon
```
I am the real physician in heaven and on earth.

(309)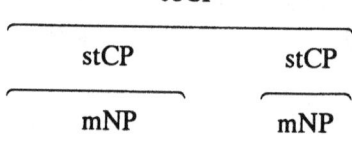

```
gɛrs²    a¹    nɛɛ²³    za¹    hi¹    waa²ɔ³
miracle  at   woman    other  and    child^her
```
A strange thing that happened to a woman and her child.

(310)

```
                        coCP
               ┌─────────────────────┐
                   loc          loc
               ┌────────┐   ┌────────┐
hi¹   nab⁴   nɛɛk²³²   hi¹   yoo¹su³gɔ³
they  will^dance  today   and   tomorrow
```
They will dance today and tomorrow.

(311)                              coCP
         ┌─────────────────────────────────────────────┐
              stCP                            stCP
         ┌──────────────────┐          ┌──────────────────┐
              genNP                         genNP
         ┌──────────────┐            ┌──────────────┐
hạb²³    a¹ nam²nɔ¹ durk² du¹ hi¹ ber¹        durk² du¹
he^attached at elephant neck in  and hippopotamus neck in
He tied it to the necks of the elephant and the hippopotamus.

(312)                              coCP
         ┌─────────────────────────────────────────────────────┐
dood²  goo²dɛ³  pɔ⁴li¹  fj³yɔɔ²lɛ³  waạ⁴tɛ¹  dzun⁴tɛ²  kur³tɛ¹sɛ³  ga¹rɛ³
people  Gode    Poli    Fignole    Wante    Djounte   Courtesse  Gare

dɛ¹ta⁴  bul¹ko³  kpɛ̣ɛ̣¹di¹  hi³  baa²³ba¹       dɔj²gɔ³  di¹
Detta  Boulko  all       they were^complete side^its upon
All the people from Gode, Poli, Fignole, Wante, Djounte, Courtesse,
Gare, Detta, Boulko, filled that place.

**4.2.4 The coordinate possessive circumstantial phrase (copCP)** has the structure shown in (313).

(313)
                         ⎧ rln n  ⎫                  ⎧ rln n    ⎫
  ± cmkr: a¹  ± ref:    ⎨ prop n ⎬  ± poss: pr + hd:⎨ defNP    ⎬
                         ⎪ defNP  ⎪                  ⎪ coNP     ⎪
                         ⎩ coNP   ⎭                  ⎩ loc/temp wd ⎭

  ± cind₍₂₎:  ⎧ spec     ⎫
              ⎩ loc part ⎭

The *coordinate possessive circumstantial phrase* has five tagmemes:

— an optional CIRCUMSTANTIAL MARKER slot, filled by the particle *a¹*,
— an optional REFERENT slot, filled by a relational noun, a proper noun, a definite noun phrase, or a coordinate noun phrase,
— an optional POSSESSOR slot, filled by a non-focal pronoun,
— an obligatory HEAD slot, filled by a relational noun, a definite noun phrase, a coordinate noun phrase or a locative or temporal word, and

— an optional CIRCUMSTANTIAL INDICATOR slot, with up to two occurrences, filled by a specifier or a locative particle.

The filler of either the referent or the head function must be a coordinate noun phrase. When a coordinate noun phrase fills the head slot, there is obligatory backshifting of all but the first head of the coordinated phrase to final position in the circumstantial phrase. When a coordinate noun phrase fills the referent slot, the referent function is backshifted.

When a coordinate noun phrase fills the referent slot, the pronoun in the possessor indicator slot must be plural, representing the sum of the persons mentioned in the coordinate noun phrase; when a coordinate noun phrase fills the head slot, the possessor indicator function is obligatorily absent.

(314)
$$\text{copCP}$$
$$\overbrace{\text{poss copCP}_{hd} \text{ loc} \quad \text{copCP}_{ref}\text{:coNP}}$$
ind

nɔ² gi² a¹ wɛ¹ tees⁴¹ du¹ bee¹ hi¹ mɔ¹ya¹
what it^be^DEP at our middle in I^EM and you^EM
What is there between me and you?

(315)
$$\text{copCP}$$
$$\overbrace{\text{copCP}_{ref}\text{:coNP}}$$
poss CP$_{hd}$ loc
ind

a¹ wal²³ bɔ¹ hi¹ zul¹ ha¹ hi¹ nis²ɔ³
at man that their head on and wife^his
about the man and his wife

**4.2.5 The interrogative circumstantial phrase (intrrCP)** has the structure shown in (316).

(316) + hd: loc/temp intrr ± reinf: nɔ²

The interrogative circumstantial phrase is discontinuous and has two tagmemes:

## Some Major Structures of Doyayo Syntax

— an obligatory HEAD slot, filled by a locative or temporal interrogative word and
— an optional clause-final REINFORCER slot, filled by the particle $nɔ^2$.

(317)  intrrCP

be¹ hol¹³   sii²³
I   rest(FUT) where
Where will I rest?

(318)  intrrCP

be¹ rek³   be¹ dɔg¹³   hi¹nɔ³   ay¹²
I   go(FUT) I   tell(FUT) thing^its where
Where shall I go and tell it?

(319)  intrrCP

mɔ³ wɛɛk¹   hi²   ma³   nɔ²
you returning where DEIC REINF
Where do you think you are going?

(320)  intrrCP

be³ waa̰⁴   tam²³   mɔ¹   bɔ¹   bi¹li¹
I   caught sheep your DEM when
When did I take you sheep?

(321)  intrrCP

mi¹ zaa¹³   lɛl²³li¹
I   come(FUT) place^how
What time shall I come?

**4.2.6 The relator circumstantial phrase (relCP)** has the structure shown in (322).

(322)   + hd: $lɛl^{23}$ + rel: relCl + spec: $ge^1$

There are three tagmemes, all of which are obligatory:

— a HEAD slot, filled by locative $lɛl^{23}$ 'place',
— a RELATOR slot, filled by a relative clause, and
— a SPECIFIER slot, filled by the locative particle *ge*.

There is obligatory frontshifting of the relative clause subject function to a position immediately preceding the head of the relator circumstantial phrase.

(323)
```
                         relCP
        ┌─────────────────────────────────────────┐
                   relCP_rel:relCl
        ┌─────────────────────────────┐
   relCl_hd   relCP_hd                           relCP_spec
   ┌──────┐  ┌──────┐                            ┌──────┐
   gi²    marˡta⁴   lɛl²³   bɔ¹    da²gi¹ge¹     nɛ¹   ge¹
   heˆis  Martha    place   DEM    heˆreceivesˆherˆDEP ANT LOC
```
He was at the place where Martha had met him.

(324)
```
                                  relCP
              ┌──────────────────────────────────────────┐
                         relCP_rel:relCl
              ┌───────────────────────────────┐
         relCl_hd  relCP_hd                            relCP_spec
         ┌──────┐ ┌──────┐                             ┌──────┐
   hi³   tuur⁴   gɔ¹   a¹  bɛt²   lɛl²³   bɔ¹   raag²³¹      ge¹
   they  arrived ANA   at  God    place   DEM   heˆsaysˆhimˆDEP LOC
```
Then they arrived at the place God had told him of.

(325)
```
                                  relCP
              ┌─────────────────────────────────────────────────┐
                         relCP_rel:relCl                   relCP_spec
              ┌───────────────────────────────┐            ┌──────┐
         relCl_hd:NP       relCP_hd
         ┌─────────┐       ┌──────┐
   wɛɛ³    a¹ tam²³  wɔ¹   lɛl²³   yɔ¹   hi¹   gi²   du¹   ge¹³
   heˆreturns at sheep DEMˆPL place   DEM   they  areˆDEP in   SPEC
```
He went back to where the sheep were.

### 4.2.7 Summary of circumstantial phrase types.

(326) stCP standard circumstantial phrase

$$\pm \text{ cmkr: } a^1 \quad \pm \text{ rem: } da^3 \quad + \left[ \pm \text{ hd:} \begin{cases} \text{rln n} \\ \text{mNP} \\ \text{defNP} \\ \text{genNP} \\ \text{loc/temp wd} \\ \text{em pr} \\ \text{intrr } n\mathfrak{I}^2/b\mathfrak{I}^2 \end{cases} \right.$$

$$\pm \text{ cind}_{(4)}: \left. \right] \begin{cases} \text{spec} \\ \text{loc part} \end{cases} \quad \pm \text{ reinf: } NP_{mar}$$

(327) $hi^3 \quad rek^3 \quad hi^3 \quad \mathfrak{I}\mathfrak{I}^3 \quad di^1 \quad h\mathfrak{I}^1$
they went they left around upon
They went off and left some there.

(328) possCP possessive circumstantial phrase

$$\pm \text{ cmkr: a} \quad + \left[ \pm \text{ ref:} \begin{cases} \text{mNP} \\ \text{intrr} \\ \text{defNP} \end{cases} \pm \text{ poss ind: pr} \right] \pm \text{ hd:} \begin{cases} \text{rln n} \\ \text{loc/temp wd} \end{cases}$$

$$\pm \text{ cind}_{(2)}: \text{loc part} \quad \pm \text{ reinf:} \begin{cases} \text{id} \\ NP_{mar} \\ n\mathfrak{I}^2 \end{cases}$$

(329) $gii^1 \quad w\varepsilon\varepsilon^2 \quad waar^1 \quad a^1 \quad n\mathfrak{I}\mathfrak{I}s^2 \quad w\mathfrak{I}^1 \quad hi^1 \quad zul^1 \quad ha^1 \quad s\varepsilon w^3$
he^EM became chief at bird DEF their head on all
It was he who became chief over all the birds.

(330) coCP coordinate circumstantial phrase

$$+ \ hd_1: \begin{Bmatrix} stCP \\ loc/temp\ wd \\ place\ name \end{Bmatrix} + \begin{bmatrix} \pm\ cj\ hi^1\ +\ hd_2: \begin{Bmatrix} stCP \\ loc/temp\ wd \\ place\ name \end{Bmatrix} \end{bmatrix}_{(n)}$$

$\pm$ reinf: $NP_{mar}$

(331) $hi^1$  $nab^4$  $nɛɛk^{232}$ $hi^1$  $yoo^1su^3go^3$
they dance today and tomorrow
They will dance today and tomorrow.

(332) copCP coordinate possessor circumstantial phrase

$$\pm\ cmkr:\ a^1\ \pm\ ref: \begin{Bmatrix} rln\ n \\ prop\ n \\ defNP \\ coNP_1 \end{Bmatrix} \pm\ poss:\ pr\ +\ hd: \begin{Bmatrix} rln\ n \\ defNP \\ coNP_1 \\ loc/temp\ wd \end{Bmatrix}$$

$\pm\ cind_{(2)}: \begin{Bmatrix} spec \\ loc\ part \end{Bmatrix}$

(333) $nɔ^2$  $gi^2$ $a^1$ $wɛ^1$ $tees^{41}$  $du^1$ $bee^1$ $hi^1$ $mɔɔ^1$   $nɔ^2$
what is at our middle in I^EM and you^EM REINF
What is there between me and you?

(334) intrrCP interrogative circumstantial phrase

+ hd: loc/temp intrr   $\pm$ reinf: $nɔ^2$

(335) $mɔ^3$  $wɛɛk^1$   $hi^2$   $ma^3$  $nɔ^2$
You returning where DEIC REINF
Where do you think you're going?

(336) relCP relator circumstantial phrase

+ hd: $lɛl^{23}$ + rel: relCl + spec: $ge^1$

# Some Major Structures of Doyayo Syntax

(337) wɛɛ³   a¹ tam²³ wɔ¹ lɛl²³ yɔ¹ hi¹ gi² du¹ ge¹
returned at sheep DEM place REL they are in SPEC
He returned to where the sheep were.

## 4.3 Accessory phrase

The *accessory phrase (AccP)* functions at clause level, in the adverbial slot. It has the structure shown in (338).

(338)

$$+ \text{ acc mkr:} \begin{Bmatrix} hi^1 \\ hi^1 \ zaa^1 \ hi^1 \end{Bmatrix} + \text{ hd:} \begin{Bmatrix} \text{mNP} \\ \text{genNP} \\ \text{emNP} \\ \text{epNP} \\ \text{rln n} \\ \text{indep n} \\ nɔ^2/bɔ^2 \end{Bmatrix} \pm \text{ cind:} \begin{Bmatrix} e^1lo^2/ \\ lɛl^{23}gbu^1nu^1 \\ \text{stCP} \\ \text{AP} \end{Bmatrix}$$

The accessory phrase has three tagmemes:

— an obligatory ACCESSORY MARKER slot, filled by the conjunction $hi^1$ or $hi^1\ zaa^1\ hi^1$ 'and, with',
— an obligatory HEAD slot, filled by a modified noun phrase, a genitival noun phrase, an emphatic noun phrase, an emphatic possessive noun phrase, a relational noun, an independent noun, or interrogative $nɔ^2/bɔ^2$ 'what?, who?', and
— an optional CIRCUMSTANTIAL INDICATOR slot, filled by $e^1lo^2/lɛl^{23}gbu^1nu^1$ 'together', standard circumstantial phrase, or an adverbial phrase.

(339)                    acc mkr              mNP

mi³ sok³     gɔ¹  hi¹  doo²³  za¹  di¹  ɓat¹ta¹³waa²³
I   went^along ANA with person other upon mature^DIM^child
So I went along with someone there a little older than me.

(340)                    acc mkr      defNP

wi³ oo³ni³ge³       hi¹  waa²tɔ³      wɔ¹   lɛl²³gbu¹nu¹
we waited^with^him  with child^PL^his DEM^PL place^one
I kept it for him and waited from him together with his children.

(341)                              acc mkr   epNP
ɔ³    be¹  kam¹si¹mɔ³     hi¹    zul¹   be²nɛ³
HRT  I    bring^BEN^you  with   head   my(SMEM)
Let me bring you some myself.

(342)                              acc mkr
yaa²³   hob¹   hi³   naak¹   hi¹   zaa¹   hi¹   rɔ²ma²³
monkey  red    they  chatting and  other  and   hare
The red monkey was visiting with the hare.

(343)                           acc mkr       genNP
hi¹   goo⁴          dɔn³¹  bɔ¹   hi¹   gɔɔ²³   bɔ¹   mɛ¹mɔ³
they  place^on^stove pot   DEM   with  peanut  DEM   water^its

     stCP
du¹  hɔ¹
in   there
The pot is set on the fire with the peanut water in it.

(344)                     acc mkr  emNP
hạạm²³¹       gabs²  hi¹   mii¹    ya⁴
it^wants^you  evil   with  me-EM   Q
Do you want a fight with me?

(345)            acc mkr
mi³   gi²   hi¹   doo²³²   ya⁴
I     am    with  person   Q
Do I have anyone?

Some Major Structures of Doyayo Syntax    215

(346) hi³ wɔb⁴ gɔ¹ a¹ durk² duu¹³ a¹ ruuk¹   bɔ¹ gi¹ durk² du¹
      they tie ANA at neck in     at water^jar DEM it neck in

      acc mkr  rln n
      ⏜     ⏜
      hi¹    sɛɛ²sɛ³
      with   sheep's^hair
      Then it is tied to the neck, the neck of the jar, with sheep's hair.

(347) nɛɛd²    sɛ¹rɛ³    wɔ¹    hi³ ɓaks¹  ma³ gɔ¹  kpɛɛd³
      woman^PL young^PL DEM PL they line^up DEIC ANA all

      acc mkr         defNP
      ⏜      ⏜
      hi¹  wa²lɛ³  sɛ¹rɛ³   wɔ¹
      with  man^PL young^PL those
      And now the young women all line up with the young men.

(348)                    AccP
                  ⎯⎯⎯⎯⎯⎯⎯⎯⎯⎯⎯⎯⎯
                  acc mkr intrr  stCP
                         ⏜    ⏜
      hi¹ goo⁴            hi¹ nɔ²  du¹ hɔ¹
      they will^set^on^stove with what in there
      What should be in there when I set it on the fire?

(349)           AccP
          ⎯⎯⎯⎯⎯⎯⎯⎯⎯⎯
          acc mkr intrr
                ⏜  ⏜
      mɔ³ zaa²³ hi¹ bɔ²
      you came with who
      With whom did you come?

(350)                    AccP
                  ⎯⎯⎯⎯⎯⎯⎯⎯⎯⎯⎯⎯⎯⎯⎯⎯
                  acc mkr  mNP    AP
                         ⏜   ⏜   ⏜
      wi³   re³tin¹    hi¹ wal²³ mi¹  ɔɔk² wi¹
      we(EXCL) went^reflex with man my apart our
      My husband and I went by ourselves.

## 4.4 The verbal phrase

The *verbal phrase* functions at clause level, filling the predicate slot. Dooyąąyɔ has two basic types of verb phrases that are simple and one basic type that is complex. However, within each type there are a number of subtypes, each having a variation of the basic formula. The three basic types are the modified verbal phrase (mVP), the incompletive verbal phrase (incVP), and the intentive verbal phrase (intvVP).

**4.4.1 The modified verbal phrase (mVP)** has the basic structure shown in (351).

(351)   $\pm$ hab: (infl) $gɔ^2$   $\pm$ (aux: infl aux)$_{(3)}$   $\pm$ rem: infl $\begin{Bmatrix} da^3 \\ za^1 \end{Bmatrix}$

hd: infl v   $\pm$ ant: $nɛ^1$   $\pm$ reinf: $\begin{Bmatrix} \text{rdp} \\ \text{id} \end{Bmatrix}$ vb

The phrase is in the completive aspect, and there is concord of person and tense.

The habitual function has a temporal meaning ('when') in a subordinated clause, and a habitual or purposive meaning (depending on the mood that accompanies it) in an independent clause. Though normally not inflected, it sometimes does have the subject pronoun prefixed to it, or can even take the subject pronoun of the following inflected auxiliary or head. Note the three forms in (352), all with identical meanings:

(352)   $gɔ^2$ $mɔ^3$ $re^3kɔ^2$         'when you go'
        $mɔ^3$ $gɔ^2$ $re^3kɔ^2$
        $mɔ^3$ $gɔ^2$ $mɔ^3$ $re^3kɔ^2$

The forms are in free fluctuation, but the first is the most common.[22]

The remoteness indicator has two basically different uses: $da^3$ indicating remoteness in time or space, with a sense of 'away from and back' and $za^1$ indicating an undesirable potential. Usually the presence of anterior $nɛ^1$ in the same phrase imposes on $da^3$ the meaning of temporal remoteness. $da^3$ and $za^1$ are normally inflected but can occasionally manifest the same

---

[22] See the auxiliary chart in the appendix for the ordering of the auxiliaries within the verbal phrase. The presence of the subject pronoun is obligatory in each auxiliary and in the head verb of the modified verbal phrase, and normally in the remote indicator function. While analyzed as a bound form (verbal prefix) the subject pronoun is written separately as a free form throughout this paper.

# Some Major Structures of Doyayo Syntax

irregularities of inflection as $gɔ^2$ above. The reinforcer, when present, is optionally backshifted to a position following the object of the clause.

The modified verbal phrase has six tagmemes, as shown above:

— an optional HABITUAL slot, filled by optionally inflected habitual/potential $gɔ^2$,
— an optional AUXILIARY slot, with up to three occurrences, each with a different auxiliary, inflected as to person and number,
— an optional REMOTENESS slot, filled by inflected remote/undesirable $da^3$ or $za^1$,
— the obligatory HEAD slot, filled by an inflected verb,
— an optional ANTERIOR slot, filled by the anterior particle $nɛ^1$ ($nɛ^1ko^1$ in pause-group final position), and
— an optional REINFORCER slot, filled by a reduplication of the uninflected stem of the head verb, or by an ideophone.

Normally there is concord of mood throughout the phrase. The dependative and imperative moods, however, constitute exceptions, because only the first auxiliary or, in the absence of auxiliaries, the head may be in the dependative or imperative. With a dependative, all remaining constituents must be in the perfective mood. (This includes the temporal function and the remote function, even if they precede the dependative form). With an imperative, all remaining constituents must be in the optative mood. There is another apparent exception to the rule of modal concord, which is in fact an instance of *tone change*. Resultative $yɔ^1$ causes an immediately following high tone to change to mid, yielding a form that resembles an indicative, while all the remaining constituents of the phrase are in the optative as shown in (353).

(353) $be^1$ $re^3$ $be^1$ $tɔ^4mɔ^1$     $gɔ^1$  $ya^4$
　　　 I　 go　I　devour^you　ANA　Q

　　　 $yɔ^1$ $be^3$ $re^3$ $be^1$ $tɔ^4mɔ^1$     $gɔ^1$  $ya^4$
　　　 RES　I　go　I　devour^you　ANA　Q
　　　 Would I then (be so mean as to) eat you up?

The fact that we are dealing with tone change becomes evident when resultative $yɔ^1$ precedes a negative phrase, for the tone change that occurs results in a tone pattern that is unique and does not correspond with any of the moods of the language so you get the differences shown in (354).

(354) *be¹ tɔ⁴mɔ¹   gɛ²*
      I   eat^you  not
      I will not eat you up.

   *be¹ tɔ²mɔ¹   gɛ²*
   I   eat^you  not
   I didn't/don't/am not eat(ing) you up.

   *yɔ¹ be³ tɔ²mɔ¹   gɛ²*
   RES I   eat^you  not
   I wouldn't eat you up.

The following neutralizations of mood occur regularly in the language: The distinction optative-perfective is neutralized in all but the ²³ verbs (i.e., verbs carrying the mid high-mid glide on the root). The three-fold distinction optative-perfective-dependative is neutralized in all high tone (¹) and mid-high tone (²) verbs.

(355)
| INDICATIVE-AORIST | OPTATIVE-FUTURE | PERFECTIVE | DEPENDATIVE MOOD | |
|---|---|---|---|---|
| *mi³ gaa⁴* | *mi¹ gaa⁴* | *mi¹ gaa⁴* | *mi¹ gaa²* | 'I give' |
| *mi³ baan³* | *mi¹ baan³* | *mi¹ baan³* | *mi¹ baan²* | 'I thank' |
| *mi³ aan³¹* | *mi¹ aan³¹* | *mi¹ aan³¹* | *mi¹ aan²¹* | 'I forbid' |
| *mi³ zaa²³* | *mi¹ zaa¹³* | *mi¹ zaa²³* | *mi¹ zaa²* | 'I come' |
| *mi³ le²* | *mi¹ le²* | *mi¹ le²* | *mi¹ le²* | 'I eat' |
| *mi³ zagl¹* | *mi¹ zagl¹* | *mi¹ zagl¹* | *mi¹ zagl¹* | 'I crawl' |

These moods are further characterized by the absence of the third-person singular pronoun prefix. Thus, the verb 'come' in the third-person singular would pattern *zaa²³, gi¹ zaa¹³, gi¹ zaa²³, zaa²*.

The modified verbal phrase is divided into eight subtypes based on mood and tense, as listed above: indicative-aorist, optative-future, perfective, dependative, imperative, hortatory, reiterative, and negative.

**The indicative-aorist modified verbal phrase (mVP$_{ia}$).** The indicative mood marks real, non-future actions, processes, or states in a main clause, or in a subordinate clause introduced by a conjunction like *an¹* or *gɔ²* 'when'.

The indicative-aorist modified verbal phrase (mVP$_{ia}$) has the structure shown in (356).

# Some Major Structures of Doyayo Syntax

(356) $\pm$ hab: (infl) $gɔ^2$ $\pm$ (aux: infl aux$_{ia}$)$_{(3)}$ $\pm$ rem: infl $da^3{}_{ia}$
+ hd: infl v$_{ia}$ $\pm$ ant: $nɛ^1$ $\pm$ reinf: $\begin{Bmatrix} \text{rdp v} \\ \text{id} \end{Bmatrix}$

Thus, there are, as in the basic formula, six tagmemes:

— an optional HABITUAL slot, filled by optionally inflected habitual $gɔ^2$,
— an optional AUXILIARY slot, with up to three occurrences, filled by an inflected auxiliary verb in the indicative mood (see chart in the appendix for ordering of auxiliaries),
— an optional REMOTENESS slot, filled by the inflected time/space remoteness particle $da^3$ in the indicative mood,
— the obligatory HEAD slot, filled by an inflected verb in the indicative mood,
— an optional ANTERIOR slot, filled by the anterior particle $nɛ^1$, and
— an optional REINFORCER slot, filled by a reduplication of the stem of the head verb or by an ideophone.

(357) aux₁ aux₂ hd stCP
$wɛɛ^3$ $tuu^4$ $rek^3$ $a^1$ $hɛt^1$ $du^1$
he^returns he^goes^out he^goes at grass in
He left again and went to the bush.

(358) aux hd
$yaa^{23}$ $hob^1$ $zaa^{23}$ $zɛŋ^{23}ge^1$
monkey red he^comes he^finds^him
The red monkey came and found him.

(359) VP$_{hd}$
$hi^3$ $da^3$ $hi^3$ $mɔɔ^2ni^3wi^3$ $nɛ^1$ $gban^3di^3li^2$ $ya^4$
they REM they bear^with^us ANT clothes Q
Were we born with clothes on?

(360) VP$_{hd}$
$yaa^{23}$ $hob^1$ $bib^4ti^4ge^4$
monkey red he^wraps^up^him
The red monkey wrapped him up.

(361)    VP_hd

an¹ wɛ³    mɛɛ³yɔ²
if  we^INCL know
If we had known...

(362)          rem VP_hd

mɔɔ¹   mɔ³  da³   fɛ⁴   bee¹  lab³¹ ya⁴
you^EM you REM blow me^EM thus Q
Did you blow like that for me?

(363) temp    rem     VP_hd

gɔ²   hi³  da³   hi³   e⁴li⁴mɔ⁴
when they REM they call^you
When they would call you...

(364)         mVP           mVP

            rem VP_hd   hd        rdp

yɔ¹   gɔ²   zaa²³   i²³ni¹ge¹   i¹nɔ¹
DEM HAB comes refuses^him RDP
She refused whoever came.

**The optative-future modified verbal phrase (mVP_of).** The optative-future mood marks actions, processes or states that are real and future or have varying degrees of probability or desirability, or constitute polite imperatives. It also follows certain conjunctions, such as *an¹* 'so that' and *gɔ²* 'when (+FUT)'.

The optative future modified verbal phrase (mVP_of) has the structure shown in (365).

(365)  ± hab: (infl) gɔ²   ± (aux: infl aux_of)(3)   ± rem: infl da³/za¹_of
       + hd: infl v_of   ± ant: nɛ¹   ± reinf: rdp v

Thus, the *optative-future verbal phrase (mVP_of)* has six tagmemes:

— an optional HABITUAL slot, filled by optionally inflected potential *gɔ²*,
— an optional AUXILIARY slot (with up to three occurrences), filled by an inflected verbal auxiliary in the optative mood,

# Some Major Structures of Doyayo Syntax

— an optional REMOTENESS slot, filled by inflected $da^3$ or $za^1$ (undesirable potential),
— the HEAD slot, filled by a verb inflected as to subject and object, in the optative mood,
— an optional ANTERIOR slot, filled by anterior particle $nɛ^1$, and
— an optional REINFORCER slot, filled by a reduplication of the stem of the head verb.

Note: Though analyzed as a free form, the reduplicated verb, when immediately following an unsuffixed verb head, is joined to it.

(366)   rem       aux              hd

$hi^1$  $za^1$  $hi^1$  $zaa^{13}$  $hi^1$  $lɔ^3mɔ^1$
they  pot  they  come  they  bite^you
They might come and bite you.

(367)             hd

$wɛ^1$       $fɔk^4$   $bid^{41}yɔ^1$
we(INCL)  tell      folk^tale
Let's tell a story.

(368)                        mVP$_{of}$                              mVP$_{of}$

$siŋ^{23}mɔ^1$   $gɔ^2$   $gi^1$   $gaa^{13}$   $bįį̇l^2$   $du^1$   $mɔ^1$   $yaa^1si^3ge^3$
sister^your  when  it  lights^up  morning  in  you  send^BEN^her
When it's morning, ... you pour some down for your sister.

(369)                hd

$be^2nɛ^3$   $mɔ^1$   $loo^4si^4be^4$   $gii^1$   $kpɔd^{41}$
me(SFOC)  you  take^BEN^me  her^EM  only
As for me, I just want you to get her for me.

(370)   aux       hd       rdp

$be^1$  $sil^{13}$   $be^1$   $waa̧^4wa̧^1$
I       descend    I       seize^RDP
I'm going to get down and catch her.

(371)   rem        hd
       ⎴          ⎴
       hi¹ da³ hi¹ taa³be¹
       they POT they shoot^me
       They might shoot me./I might get shot.

(372)           mVP_of
                ⎴
       gɔ² gi¹ ka¹za³    ma¹ta³
       PURP he climb^IMM he^falls
       When he tried to climb up, he fell.

(373)           mVP_of
                ⎴
       ┌─────────────┐
       pot     hd
       ⎴       ⎴
       gɔ² mɔ¹ mid³ nɛ¹ nɔ²
       PURP you find ANT what
       What could you have found?

(374)           mVP_of
                ⎴
       ┌──────────────────┐
       pot    hd     rdp
       ⎴      ⎴      ⎴
       gɔ² mɔ¹ tuu⁴tu¹    ya⁴
       PURP you go-out-RDP Q
       Are you thinking of going out?

(375)           mVP_of
                ⎴
       an¹ mi¹ goo⁴  hin¹ za¹ mi¹ goo² gɛ²
       that I answer thing other I answer not
       I didn't answer at all.

(376)                mVP_of
                     ⎴
              ┌─────────────────┐
              hd           reinf
              ⎴            ⎴
       nɛ    mi¹ fɔg⁴¹    fɔ¹bɔ¹
       well^then I follow^her RDP
       Well then. I'm going to go after her.

Some Major Structures of Doyayo Syntax

(377)   mVP_of   mVP_of        mVP_of

   mɔ¹ wɔ⁴ gi¹ ɓaa¹³   du¹³ hi¹ za¹ ta¹zɔ³   (3 optative VP's)
   you tie it be^hard INTS they POT pass^IMM
   Tie it tightly; they might come in.

(378)              mVP_of

        aux      hd           reinf

   ɓe¹ re³ ɓe¹ raas¹³  baa²ɓe¹  raa¹ sɔ¹
   I   go  I   say^BEN  father^my RDP V
   I'm going to go and tell my master.

(379)         mVP_of

         pot   hd

   nɛ¹ gɔ² nɛ¹ gɔ² nɔ² du¹
   well POT you do what LOC
   Well, what can you do about it?

(380)            mVP_of

         aux₁  aux₂  hd

   ɓee¹ ɓe¹ kam³ ɓe¹ re³ ɓe¹ gaa⁴ zoo²do³
   I-EM I  carry I  go I  give Zoodo
   I will go and give it to Zoodo...

(381)              mVP_of

              pot   hd

   hɔ⁴nɛ¹ yɔ¹  mii¹ gɔ² mi¹ tuu⁴  ɓe² hoob¹ hąąm²³¹ hąą¹
   but   SUBCJ I^EM pot I  go^out CUM fear wants^me RDP
   But, as for me, I was too scared to go out.

(382)          mVP$_{of}$
         ┌─────────────┐
          pot    hd
         ┌───┐  ┌───┐
yɔ¹   gɔ²   mi¹   wɛɛ³   hɛ¹   yɛbr⁴mi¹   bɔ¹   gu³mi¹   gu¹mɔ¹
SUBCJ POT  I    return  here  ribsˆmy    DEM   hurtˆme   RDP
Whenever I wanted to turn this way, my ribs hurt.

(383)          mVP$_{of}$
         ┌─────────────┐
                hd
               ┌───┐
yɔ¹   gɔ²   gi¹   wɛɛ³         lɛl²³   gaa²³   gaa¹
SUBCJ POT   he   returnˆIMM    place   shines   RDP
Before he could return day broke.

(384)             mVP$_{of}$
         ┌───────────────────────┐
          aux         hd      reinf
         ┌────┐      ┌────┐
bɛ¹   tuuz⁴¹        bɛ¹   da³gi¹gɛ¹   da¹gɔ¹
I     goˆoutˆIMM    I     meetˆhim    RDP
I'm going to go out and meet him.

(385)       mVP$_{of}$            mVP$_{of}$
        ┌──────────┐          ┌──────────┐
         aux    hd              aux    hd
        ┌───┐  ┌───┐            ┌───┐  ┌───┐
mɔ¹   wɛɛ³   mɔ¹   dɛ³mɔ³   gi¹   wɛɛ³   gi¹   hɔɔ³     (2 optative VP's)
you  return  you   clap      it   return   it   growˆtall
Then you clap again and it will grow tall again.

(386)              mVP$_{of}$
              ┌──────────┐
bɛl²³   gi²   naŋ¹ko¹   an¹   hi¹   lug³   hi¹nɛ³
rain     is    rainˆINC  that  they  plant  thing
It was time for planting because the rains had started.

The perfective modified verbal phrase (**mVP$_{perf}$**) has the structure shown in (387).

(387)   ± (aux: infl aux$_{prf}$)$_{(3)}$   + hd: infl v$_{prf}$

# Some Major Structures of Doyayo Syntax

Only two of the six basic tagmemes are present:

— an optional AUXILIARY slot—occurring up to three times—filled by a subject-prefixed auxiliary in the perfective mood, and
— the obligatory HEAD slot, filled by a subject-prefixed and optionally object-suffixed verb, also in the perfective mood.

The *perfective mood* subordinates *real, non-future* actions, processes or states in conditional clauses preceding the primary nucleus of the sentence, and in resultative clauses (not marked by $yɔ^1$) following the primary nucleus. It occurs in non-initial constituents of an indicative or dependative verbal phrase within a subordinate clause to show conjunction.

It also occurs following interrogatives that do not fill the subject slot of a clause, and following a non-contrastive emphatic subject.

(388)                  $mVP_{prf}$

$buu^{23}$ $za^1$   $be^2$   $gi^1$ $gaa^{23}$   $bįįl^2$    $du^1$
white   other   CUM   it shines   morning   in
Another white man, if it's morning ...

(389)     $mVP_{of}$      $mVP_{prf}$

$mɔ^1$ $gben^3$   $hi^1$   $raa^{23}$
you   see      they   say
If, for example, you have been told ...

(390)                 $mVP_{prf}$

$yɔ^1$   $wɛɛ^2$       $gi^1$ $raa^{23}$     $ma^3$   $an^1bɔ^1$   $la^3bɔ^1$
when return^DEP   he says^PRF   DEIC   like^that   thus
And when he had said this, ...

(391)           $mVP_{of}$     $mVP_{prf}$

$mɔɔ^1$    $mɔ^1$ $tuur^4$   $mɔ^1$ $raa^{23}$
you^EM   you arrive   you say
Then you come along and say ...

(392) mVP_prf

siŋ²³mɔ¹  gi¹  gaa²³  bįįl²    du¹ gi¹  gi²  lɛl²³   hɛ¹di¹go³
sister^you it  shines morning in  she is  place sweep^INC
My it's morning and your sister is sweeping, ...

(393) mVP_prf

bɛ³ gbɛr³¹za³     lɛnd¹   waa²³ zaa¹  a¹ hęt¹  du¹ bɛ¹ gu³ma²
I   slaughter^IMM cannibal child other at grass in  I   hurt
I'm sick because I killed the son of a cannibal in the bush.

(394) mVP_prf

mi³ gbɛn³ ɗoo³di¹  gi² zaa¹ko³   mi¹ kaa³
I   see   bogeyman is  come^into I   cry
I cried because I saw the bogeyman coming.

(395) mVP_prf

gi¹ lɛ³mɔ¹    ma³ ya⁴
he strike^you DEIC Q
And so he beat you up?

(396) mVP_prf

yąą¹³nɛ² mi¹ zaa²³ ɛr¹ko³
therefore I   come ask^INC
That's why I came to ask.

(397) mVP_prf

nɔ²  ɔ²nɛ³  gi¹ zaa²³ a¹ bɛt² ha¹  nɔ²
why REINF it come  at sky  on INTRR^REINF
But why does it come from the sky?

(398) mVP_prf

waa²³bɛ¹  ri¹  hi¹   rek³ hi¹  mɔɔ²³gɛ¹     a¹ dɛɛm³² nɔ²
child^my  how  they  go   they bear^him     at Deeme  REINF
Now how did it come about that my child was born in Deeme?

# Some Major Structures of Doyayo Syntax

(399)    mVP$_{ia}$    mVP$_{prf}$

yɔ¹ hi³ loo⁴ge¹ hi¹ rɛ³ hi¹ raa²si³gɛ³ maa¹kɔ³ a¹
result they take^him they go they say^BEN^him custom^his at
gi¹ lɛ²lɛ³
he place
They would take him and perform the rites for him in his hometown.

The **dependative modified verbal phrase** (mVP$_{dep}$) has the structure shown in (400).

(400)  ± (aux: infl aux$_{dep-prf}$)(3)  ± rem: infl da³  + hd: infl v$_{dep-prf}$
       ± ant: nɛ¹

This phrase has four of the basic tagmemes:

— an optional AUXILIARY slot, with up to three occurrences, filled by a subject-prefixed auxiliary, the first occurrence of which must be in the dependative mood and all others in the perfective mood,
— an optional REMOTENESS slot, filled by subject-prefixed da³,
— the HEAD slot, filled by a subject-prefixed and optionally object-prefixed verb, in the dependative mood when no auxiliary precedes, otherwise in the perfective mood, and
— an optional ANTERIOR slot, filled by the anterior particle nɛ¹.

The *dependative mood* subordinates actions, processes or states that are real, non-future, and unconditional (except when preceded by 'unreal condition' conjunction a⁴). In main clauses, the dependative mood occurs following a contrastive emphatic or focal noun phrase (cf. §4.1.8) or in conjunction with the negative particle gɛ² 'not'.

(401)  mVP$_{dep}$  mVP$_{dep}$

lug² rɛ¹ pir² gɛ²
plant INTS sprout not
When she planted it, it did not sprout.

(402)

$\overbrace{\phantom{mVPdep}}^{\text{mVPdep}}$

$\overbrace{\text{aux-dep}}\quad\overbrace{\text{hd-prf}}$

yɔ¹   hi¹   zaa²      hi¹   mur²³yɔ¹
when they come^DEP  they arrive^PRF
When they arrived...

(403)

$\overbrace{\phantom{mVP_{dep}}}$ mVP$_{dep}$

hi¹nii²¹         nɔɔ²hi¹
thing^DEM^when anger^them
When they got mad about something...

(404) mVP$_{dep}$

$\overbrace{\text{hd}\quad\text{ant}}$

a⁴  zaa²  nɛ¹  wi¹      tees⁴¹ du¹ ro²
if  come  ANT  we(EXCL) midst  in  INTS
Mind you, if he had come into our midst...

(405)

mVPdep

$\overbrace{\text{aux-dep}}\quad\overbrace{\text{hd-prf}}$

yɔ¹  hi¹  zaa²   hi¹  tuu⁴rɔ²
when they come  they arrive
When they arrived...

(406)

mVPdep

$\overbrace{\text{aux-dep}}\quad\overbrace{\text{hd-prf}}$

yɔ¹   wi¹  zaa²   wi¹  zɛŋ²³ge¹
when  we   come   we   find^him
When we came and found him...

Some Major Structures of Doyayo Syntax

(407)      mVP$_{dep}$      mVP$_{of}$

yɔ$^1$   bɛ$^1$ raa$^2$ ma$^3$   bɛ$^1$ loo$^4$si$^4$ge$^4$   doo$^{23}$yɔ$^2$
when I   say DEIC   I   take^BEN^him   person
When all the time I said I would get him a human wife!

(408)                mVP$_{dep}$

vaam$^2$de$^1$   ɔɔ$^2$ bɔ$^1$   gii$^1$    guŋ$^2$gɛ$^1$
donkey   his DEM   she^EM   she^hurt^him
It's his donkey he's got a crush on.

(409)                mVP$_{def}$

vaam$^2$de$^1$ bɔ$^1$   bi$^1$sɔ$^3$    ram$^2$zɔ$^2$
donkey DEM   sauce^its   it^is^done^IMM
When the donkey's sauce is done,...

(410)           mVP$_{dep}$

            rem      hd     ant

a$^4$ bɔ$^2$   bɛ$^1$ da$^3$   bɛ$^1$ loo$^2$   nɛ$^1$   zɛn$^{23}$mɔ$^1$   bɔ$^1$   gɛ$^2$ rɛ$^1$
if INTDC   I REM   I take   ANT   root^your   DEM   not INTS
If I hadn't taken your roots,...

(411)   mVP$_{dep}$

bɛ$^1$ mɛks$^2$ hi$^1$nɔ$^3$      gɛ$^2$
I   know thing^DEM   not
I don't know what it is.

**The imperative modified verbal phrase (mVP$_{imp}$).** The imperative mood marks direct commands. As previously noted, only the first inflected constituent is in the imperative mood; all others are in the optative mood. There is obligatory absence of the temporal function. This subtype of the modified verbal phrase occurs only in main clauses. As in all modified verbal phrases, there is obligatory concord of subject and of object.

The imperative modified verbal phrase (mVP$_{imp}$) has the structure shown in (412).

(412)   ± (aux: infl aux$_{imp-opt}$)(3)   ± infl rem: $da^3_{opt}$   + hd: infl V$_{imp/opt}$

Thus, the imperative modified verbal phrase has three tagmemes:

— an optional AUXILIARY slot, with up to three occurrences, filled by a prefixed auxiliary, of which only the first is in the imperative and all others are in the optative mood,
— an optional REMOTENESS slot, filled by spatial remoteness $da^3$, prefixed as to subject, and
— the obligatory HEAD slot, filled by a prefixed and optionally suffixed verb (in the imperative only when no auxiliary precedes, otherwise in the optative mood).

(413) mVP$_{imp}$

*tuu⁴zu¹mɔ³*
go^out^IMM^you(IMP)
Come out.

(414)                           mVP$_{of}$

| mVP$_{imp}$ | aux | hd |
|---|---|---|

*kɔb⁴si¹be³*       *be¹ zaa¹³*       *be¹ yɔ²*
draw^BEN^me^IMP   I come^OPT       I drink^OPT
Draw some for me, so I can come and drink it.

(415)            mVP$_{imp}$

| aux-imp | hd-opt |
|---|---|

*re³kum¹*    *mɔ¹ kams³    gɔn²³be¹*
take^you^IMP  you carry^BEN mother-in-law^my
Go and take it to my mother-in-law...

(416)                      mVP$_{imp}$

| aux$_1$-imp | aux$_2$-opt | aux$_3$-opt | hd-opt |
|---|---|---|---|

*loo⁴mɔ²*     *mɔ¹ kam³*     *mɔ¹ rek³*     *mɔ¹ gaa⁴*
take^you^IMP  you carry^OPT  you go^OPT     you give^OPT
    *baa²mɔ¹*
    father^your
Take this and go and give it to your father.

# Some Major Structures of Doyayo Syntax

(417)  $\overbrace{\text{mVP}_{\text{imp}}}$

*re³mɔ²     mɔ¹ zebz⁴     taab³¹yɔ¹*
go-you(IMP)  you buy-IMM  tobacco
Go buy some tobacco.

(418)  $\overbrace{\text{mVP}_{\text{imp}}}$

*gaa⁴ʑin¹be³           hɔd²³ bɔ¹  be²nɛ³*
give^IMM^you^PL^me    bee   DEM  mine
Give me my share of the honey.

(419)  $\overbrace{\text{mVP}_{\text{imp}}}$

| aux-imp | hd-opt |
|---|---|

*zaa²³mɔ²         mɔ¹  zɛɛ⁴      zɛŋ¹ko³*
come^you(IMP)    you  dig^OPT   hole
Come and dig a hole.

(420)  $\overbrace{\text{mVP}_{\text{imp}}}$

| aux₁-IMP | aux₂-opt | hd-opt |
|---|---|---|

*loo⁴mɔ²        mɔ¹ rek³     mɔ¹ zɛm¹³ naad⁴¹  bɔ¹  yɔ¹*
take^you^IMP   you go^OPT   you find  woman   DEM  LOC
Take it and go to that woman over there.

(421)  mVP_of                mVP_imp

*gi¹ ɛr³        to²to³    gaa⁴mɔ⁴ge⁴*
he ask^OPT    sorghum   give^you^her
If she asks for sorghum, give it to her.

The hortatory modified verbal phrase (mVP$_{\text{hrt}}$) has the structure shown in (422).

(422)  $+ \text{hrt}: \begin{Bmatrix} \text{hrt} \\ \text{intdc} \end{Bmatrix} \pm (\text{aux: infl aux}_{\text{opt}})_{(3)} \pm \text{rem: infl } da^3$
$+ \text{hd: infl cmpl } v_{\text{opt}} \pm \text{reinf}_1: nɛ^1 \pm \text{reinf}_2: \text{id}$

Four of the basic tagmemes are present, while the temporal slot of the basic formula is replaced by a hortatory slot. The extra reinforcer function (reinf₁) occurs only when the hortatory slot is filled by an interdictory particle, yielding a negative imperative. Thus, there are six tagmemes:

- an obligatory HORTATORY slot, filled by a hortatory or an interdictory particle,
- an optional AUXILIARY slot, with up to three occurrences, filled by a subject-prefixed auxiliary in the optative mood,
- an optional REMOTENESS slot, filled by subject-prefixed spatial remoteness $da^3$ in the optative mood,
- the obligatory HEAD slot, filled by a subject-prefixed and optionally object-suffixed completive verb, again in the optative mood,
- an optional REINFORCER₁ slot, filled by the emphatic particle $n\varepsilon^1$, and
- an optional REINFORCER₂ slot, filled by an ideophone.

(423) *bɔ²mɔ¹ kaa³*
not^you weep
Don't cry!

(424) *bɔ²gi¹ ɔks³ hi¹ dood² rɔ¹bɛ³ ya̱²nɛ³ wɔ¹*
not^she mix with people good^PL theirs those
She must not mix it with those of the members of the chief's household.

(425)          mVP_hrt

| hrt | aux-opt | hd-opt | reinf |
|---|---|---|---|
| ɔ³ | be¹ dɔɔ⁴ | be¹ sɔ̱ɔ̱⁴ hi¹nɔ³ | ta̱a̱¹ |
| let | I go^up | I see thing^DEM | ID |

Just let me go over and have a look.

(426) hrt hd-opt

| ɔ³ | be¹ fɔ⁴ | ge¹ du¹ | gɛ² |
|---|---|---|---|
| let | I follow | SPEC in | not |

Let me not go that way.

Some Major Structures of Doyayo Syntax                                    233

(427)  hrt  hd-opt

    $\overbrace{d\varepsilon\varepsilon^{41}\ dey^1}\ \overbrace{gban^3dil^3y\mathfrak{z}^2}$
    let's wear  clothing
    Let's wear clothes.

N.B. $d\varepsilon\varepsilon^{41}$ = elision of $d\varepsilon\varepsilon^4$ 'let' + $w\varepsilon^1$ 'we, us'.

(428)  hrt  hd-opt

    $\overbrace{d\varepsilon\varepsilon^4\ w\varepsilon^1}\ rek^3\ a^1\ b\varepsilon t^2\ d\mathfrak{z}gl^2\ du^1$
    let's  we  go  at  God  word  in
    Let's go to church.

(429)         mVP$_{hrt}$                    mVP$_{of}$

        hd-opt

    $y\varepsilon^4\ \overbrace{mi^1\ oo^3be^1}\ \ \ \ be^1\ \ \ \ ho^1t\mathfrak{z}^3$
    HRT  I   wait^me(QUOT)  I(QUOT)  bathe
    He asked me to wait for him while he had his bath.

(430)         mVP$_{hrt}$

    hrt    aux    hd

    $y\varepsilon^4\ \ w\varepsilon^1\ rek^3\ w\varepsilon^1\ hag^3\ a^1\ da^3\ h\varepsilon t^1\ du^1$
    let's  we  go  we  make  at  REM  grass  in
    Let's go make them out in the bush.

(431)    mVP$_{hrt}$

    hrt   hd

    $da^3\ m\mathfrak{z}^1\ rek^3\ h\mathfrak{z}^1$
    INJ  you  go   over^there
    You go over there.

(432)         mVP$_{hrt}$
              ┌─────────────────┐
              hrt        hd
              ┌─────────────────┐
  *da³   nɛ¹    tii³tin¹         a¹   bak²   yɔɔl¹di¹sɛ³*
  HRT   you^PL  descend^it^ACC  at   field   anus^under
  Go down to the end of the field, both of you.

(433)         mVP$_{hrt}$
              ┌─────────────────┐
                         hd
              ┌─────────────────┐
  *da³   mɔ¹   waa⁴si⁴bɛ⁴        ruu²³*
  HRT   you   catch^BEN^me     wife^thief
  Go catch the adulterer for me,...

The **reiterative modified verbal phrase** (**mVP$_{rit}$**) has the structure shown in (434).

(434) $\pm$ (aux: infl aux$_{cmpl}$)(3) + hd: $\begin{Bmatrix} \text{s-pref cmpl v st} \\ \text{s-s cmpl v st} \end{Bmatrix}_{(n)}$

There are two tagmemes the latter of which must be repeated at least once. The phrase consists of

— an optional *auxiliary* slot, with up to three occurrences, filled by an auxiliary verb in the completive aspect and
— an obligatory *head* slot, filled by either a subject-prefixed completive verb stem (the subject of which is optionally deleted in all but the first occurrence), or a subject-suffixed completive verb stem.

The repetition of the head signals duration or repetition of an action.

(435)         mVP$_{rit}$
              ┌─────────────────────────┐
                 hd              hd
              ┌──────────┐  ┌──────────┐
  *hi³   ɓɛ³ti¹nu³       hi³   ɓɛ³ti¹nu³*
  they  count^it^ACC    they  count^it^ACC
  They counted one another over and over...

Some Major Structures of Doyayo Syntax    235

(436)             mVP$_{rit}$

        hd$_1$    hd$_2$  hd$_3$

    hi$^3$  dɔ$^2$gɔ$^3$  dɔ$^2$gɔ$^3$  dɔ$^2$gɔ$^3$
    they  say     say     say
    They all said it.

(437)              mVP$_{rit}$

        hd$_1$    hd$_2$    hd$_3$

    baa$^4$  he$^{23}$ga$^2$  he$^{23}$ga$^2$  he$^{23}$ga$^3$
    sewed  put^on  put^on  put^on
    He sewed it, then wore it again and again.

(438)              mVP$_{rit}$

      aux$_1$   aux$_2$   hd$_1$    hd$_2$

    gii$^1$   wɛɛ$^2$  dɔɔt$^4$  kaa$^3$ge$^1$  kaa$^3$ge$^1$
    she^EM  returns  sits  cries^she  cries^she
    As for her, she sat down and cried.

(439)              mVP$_{rit}$

        hd$_1$    hd$_2$    hd$_3$    hd$_4$

    bɛl$^{23}$ bɔ$^1$  naŋ$^{23}$gi$^1$ge$^1$  naŋ$^{23}$gi$^1$ge$^1$  naŋ$^{23}$gi$^1$ge$^1$  naŋ$^{23}$gi$^1$ge$^1$
    rain DEM  rains^it  rains^it  rains^it  rains^it
    It rained and rained.

(440)              mVP$_{rit}$

    gɔn$^2$siŋ$^{23}$    re$^3$ka$^2$  re$^3$ka$^2$  re$^3$ka$^2$  re$^3$ka$^2$  re$^3$ka$^2$  re$^3$ka$^2$
    mother-in-law  went  went  went  went  went  went
    The mother-in-law walked for a long, long time.

(441)       mVP$_{ia}$              mVP$_{rit}$

laa¹ bɔ¹ bu¹da³   dʒʒ²³¹sa¹ dʒʒ²³¹sa¹ dʒʒ²³¹sa¹
fire DEM is^conceived burns^INTS burns^INTS burns^INTS

dʒʒ²³¹sa¹
burns^INTS

The fire started and just burned and burned.

**The negative modified verbal phrase (mVP$_{neg}$)** has the structure shown in (442).

(442)   ± hd: infl v $\begin{Bmatrix} ia \\ of \\ dep \end{Bmatrix}$   ± reinf$_1$: nɛ¹ + neg: gɛ² ± reinf$_2$: id

There are four tagmemes:

— an obligatory HEAD slot, filled by an inflected verb in the indicative-aorist, optative-future, or dependative mood,
— an optional REINFORCER$_1$ slot, filled by the emphatic particle nɛ¹,
— the obligatory NEGATIVE slot, filled by the negative particle gɛ², and
— an optional REINFORCER$_2$ slot, filled by an ideophone.

(443)  yɔ¹   be³   tɔ⁴mɔ¹      gɛ²
would I(CIT) devour^you not
I would not eat you up.

(444)  a¹  hi¹  tuu²   gɛ²
CIT they go^out not
He said, "They didn't get out."

(445)  gi¹     rek³ gɛ²
he^will  go   not
He will not go.

(446)  mi¹   loo⁴  nɛ¹ gɛ² zaŋ¹
I^will take EM not at^all
I will most certainly not take it!

## Some Major Structures of Doyayo Syntax

**4.4.2 The incompletive verbal phrase (incVP).** All the verbal phrases described above were in the completive aspect, i.e., they focussed on actions as completed, well-defined events happening at a certain point in time.

The incompletive aspect focusses on things in the process of happening and/or describes a state or condition as related to an event.

Like the completive verbal phrase, the incompletive verbal phrase has a basic structure but cannot be adequately described without also setting up a number of subtypes.

The incompletive verbal phrase (incVP) has the basic structure shown in (447).

(447)  $\pm$ hab: (infl) $gɔ^2$   $\pm$ aux: infl $aux_{cmpl}$   $\pm$ rem: infl $da^3$
       $\pm$ prog aux: infl $gi^2$   $\pm$ ant: $nɛ^1$   + prog hd: inc v
       $\pm$ reinf: rdp v hd

There are seven tagmemes in the basic formula:

— an optional HABITUAL slot, filled by habitual/potential $gɔ^2$,
— an optional AUXILIARY slot, filled by a subject-prefixed auxiliary verb in the completive aspect,
— an optional REMOTENESS slot, filled by subject-prefixed $da^3$,
— an optional PROGRESSIVE AUXILIARY slot, filled by subject-prefixed and optionally object-suffixed $gi^2$,
— an optional ANTERIOR slot, filled by the anterior particle $nɛ^1$,
— an optional PROGRESSIVE HEAD slot, filled by an incompletive verb, and
— an optional REINFORCER slot, filled by a reduplication of the stem of the progressive head verb.

The progressive auxiliary function can have a minimal realization, consisting of just the subject pronoun, which, in the indicative and dependative moods, is zero for the third-person singular. In the dependative mood, the absence of the third-person singular subject pronoun makes $gi^2$ obligatory. Thus, the *minimal* paradigm is as in (448) (with the optative-perfective distinction completely neutralized, and the distinction between the former and the dependative seen only in the third-person singular).

(448)  

| | INDICATIVE-AORIST | OPTATIVE/PERFECTIVE | DEPENDATIVE | |
|---|---|---|---|---|
| | $mi^3$ | $mi^1$ | $mi^1$ | 'I am' |
| | $be^3$ | $be^1$ | $be^1$ | 'I (QUOT) am' |
| | $mɔ^3$ | $mɔ^1$ | $mɔ^1$ | 'you (SG) are' |
| | $gi^2$ | $gi^1$ | $gi^2$ | 'he, she, it is' |
| | $wɛ^3$ | $wɔ^1$ | $wɔ^1$ | 'we (INCL) are' |
| | $wi^3$ | $wi^1$ | $wi^1$ | 'we (EXCL) are' |
| | $nɛ^3$ | $nɛ^1$ | $nɛ^1$ | 'you (PL) are' |
| | $hi^3$ | $hi^1$ | $hi^1$ | 'they are' |

$gi^2$ becomes obligatory whenever the anterior indicator $nɛ^1$ is present immediately following the progressive auxiliary function. It also becomes obligatory whenever pronominal suffixes are present in the phrase, because *all pronominal suffixation occurs on the progressive auxiliary*.

There is optional frontshifting of the object function of the clause to a position immediately preceding the phrase head, making the verbal phrase discontinuous as shown in (449).

(449) *$mi^3gi^2$ $woos^{32}$ $woo^1ko^3$*
I^am  work   work^INC^MID
I am working.

*$mi^3gi^2$ $wook^1$   $woo^3sɛ^2$*
I^am  work^INC work
I am working.

Both forms are equally acceptable and used interchangeably. The incompletive verb head has two realizations, which we call *incompletive-high* and *incompletive-mid*. The distinction between them is somewhat comparable to that between the independent noun and the relational. Basically, incompletive-high is the narrative form, while incompletive-mid is used in subordinated clauses, in a question-response situation, and when the preceding subject bears emphasis (emNP etc.).

(450) *$dood^2$    $hi^3$   $bum^1$  $yɔ^1ko^1$*
person^PL they beer   drink^INC^HI
The people are drinking beer. (unelicited remark)

*$dood^2$    $hi^3$   $bum^1$  $yɔ^1ko^3$*
person^PL they beer   drink^INC^MID
The people are drinking beer. (response to a question)

# Some Major Structures of Doyayo Syntax

$dood^2$    $hi^1$    $bum^1$    $yɔ^1ko^3$
person^PL they beer drink^INC^MID
While the people are drinking beer....

Due to loss of the final vowel, the distinction between the incompletive-high and incompletive-mid is neutralized in the absence of pause so you get an unelicited remark or a reponse to a question as in (451). There is obligatory concord of subject throughout the phrase.

(451) $dood^2$    $hi^3$    $bum^1$    $yɔk^1$    $kɛ^3nɛ^1$
person^PL they beer drink^INC first
The people are drinking beer just now.

**The indicative-aorist incompletive verb phrase (incVP$_{ia}$)** has the structure shown in (452).

(452) ± hab: infl $gɔ^2$    ± aux: infl aux$_{ia}$    ± rem: infl $da^3{}_{ia}$
      ± prog aux: $gi^2{}_{ia}$    ± ant: $nɛ^1$    + prog hd: inc v    ± reinf: rdp hd

All seven tagmemes of the basic formula are present, with the specification that the auxiliary, remoteness, and progressive auxiliary functions must be in the indicative mood. For the explanation of the formula, see the incompletive verbal phrase (incVP).

(453)                               incVP$_{ia}$

                              aux

$gɔn^2siŋ^{23}$    $rek^3$    $gi^2hi^1$    $boo^1ko^1$
parent^in^law^female she^goes he^is^them greeting(INC^HI)
The mother-in-law went to greet them.

(454)      incVP$_{ia}$

$rɔm^{23}$    $gi^2ge^1$    $raak^1$    $a^1$    $luk^1$    $du^1$    $hɔ^1$
rabbit he^is^him saying at house in over^there
The hare was telling him from over there in the house...

(455)　　mVP_ia　　　　　　incVP_ia
　　　　⌒⎯⎯⎯⏜　　　⌒⎯ ⎯ ⎯ ⎯⏜
　　　　zɛ²³hi¹　　　hi³　gi²　hin¹　na¹ko¹
　　　　he^finds^them　they are thing dancing(INC^HI)
　　　　He found them dancing.

(456)　　incVP_ia
　　　　⌒⎯⎯⏜
　　　　mi³　tąąk¹　　an¹bɔ¹　ro²
　　　　I　answering　like^that　INTS
　　　　That's how I'm answering!

(457)　　　　　　　　incVP_ia
　　　　　　　⌒⎯ ⎯ ⎯ ⎯ ⎯ ⎯ ⎯ ⎯⏜
　　　　mɔ³　gi²be¹　nɔ²　tɛ̨ɛɔ¹³　baa¹ti¹nu³　　mi²
　　　　you are^me why tree^DEM pierce^it^ACC^INC INTRR^REINF
　　　　I say, why are you pricking me with that stick?

(458)　　　　incVP_ia　　　　incVP_ia
　　　　⌒⎯ ⎯ ⎯⏜　　　⌒⎯ ⎯ ⎯⏜
　　　　hi³　bum¹　yɔ¹ko¹　hi³　gaps²　boo¹ko¹
　　　　they beer drinking they fight talking
　　　　They would be drinking beer and quarrelling.

(459)　　　　　　　incVP_ia
　　　　　　　⌒⎯ ⎯ ⎯ ⎯ ⎯ ⎯⏜
　　　　waa²³　bɔ¹　wɛɛ³　　gi²　dɔɔ¹tig¹　a¹　zoos²　bɔ¹　dɔŋ²gɔ³　di¹
　　　　child DEM he^returns is sitting at prey DEM side^its upon
　　　　ge¹
　　　　SPEC
　　　　The child was again sitting beside the prey.

(460)　temp　incVP_ia
　　　　⌒⏜　⌒⎯⏜
　　　　gɔ²　gi²　fɛ¹ko³
　　　　when is blowing(INC^MID)
　　　　While he is blowing, . . .

## Some Major Structures of Doyayo Syntax

(461)               incVP$_{ia}$

kɔ²³ba¹    gi²be¹ daa¹rik¹    daa¹rɔ¹
chicken^male is^me pass^INTS^INC RDP
The rooster is surpassing me.

(462)          incVP$_{ia}$

mɔ³ gi²si¹ge¹    nɔ²   gɔk¹   lab³¹ nɔ²
you are^BEN^her what doing thus INTRR^REINF
What's that you're doing to her?

(463)          incVP$_{ia}$

aux

zaa²³    gi² lɛl²³   hɛ¹di¹go¹
she^comes is place sweeping(INC^HI)
She came and was sweeping.

(464)             incVP$_{ia}$

gii¹   ma³   wɛɛ³     dɔɔ¹tig¹ aa¹kil³    du¹
he^EM DEIC he^returns sitting open^space in
Then here he was sitting in the open...

(465)    mVP$_{ia}$             incVP$_{ia}$

be³ zɛm²³ nis²    yɛ¹rɛ¹ ba²kɔ³    bal¹ko³
I   find   woman this   field^her cultivating(INC^MID)
I found this woman working in her garden.

(466)       mVP$_{ia}$        incVP$_{ia}$

mi³ zaa²³ mi³ zɛŋ²³ge¹   dɔɔ¹tig¹ a¹ va³ran¹da³ ha¹
I   come I   find^him sitting at veranda   on
I came and found him sitting on the porch.

(467) incVP$_{ia}$

    $\overbrace{\text{gɔ}^2 \quad \text{gi}^2 \quad \text{zɛɛ}^1\text{zig}^1}$     maat$^1$    luur$^2$
    HAB is dig^IMM^INC cocoyam theft
    He would steal cocoyams by digging them up...

(468)        mVP$_{ia}$            incVP$_{ia}$

    rɔm$^{23}$ $\overbrace{\text{zaa}^{23} \quad \text{zɛm}^{23}}$ naam$^{31}$ $\overbrace{\text{gi}^2 \quad \text{ku}^1\text{si}^1\text{go}^1}$
    rabbit came found panther is lie^down^INC^HI
    The hare came and found the panther lying down.

(469) incVP$_{ia}$

    $\overbrace{\text{be}^3 \quad \text{re}^1\text{ko}^1}$
    I     go^INC^HI
    I'm going.

(470)            incVP$_{ia}$

    $\overbrace{\text{mɔ}^3\text{gi}^2 \quad \text{waa}^{23}\text{be}^1 \quad \text{tɔms}^1 \quad \text{yaak}^1 \quad \text{faa}^1}$
    you^are child^my message send^INC always
    You are always sending my child on errands.

(471)               incVP$_{ia}$

    wal$^{23}$tɔ$^1$ $\overbrace{\text{gi}^2\text{ge}^1 \quad \text{kaal}^1 \quad \text{hąąk}^1}$ ma$^3$
    man^her is^him crying want^INC DEIC
    Now her husband felt like crying.

(472)        incVP$_{ia}$

    mɔ$^1$ gbɛn$^2$ $\overbrace{\text{rek}^1}$ hɛt$^1$ du$^1$ tee$^{13}$bre$^3$ gɛ$^2$
    you see go^INC grass in ID not
    You don't see him going out into the bush very much.

(473)        mVP$_{ia}$            incVP$_{ia}$

    gɔ$^2$ $\overbrace{\text{hi}^3 \quad \text{heg}^{23}}$ hin$^1$ gɔ$^2$ $\overbrace{\text{hi}^3 \quad \text{dɔɔ}^1\text{nik}^1}$ a$^1$ di$^1$hɛ$^1$
    when they put^on thing when they go^up^ACC^INC at here
    When they put on something and come up here like that, ...

(474)     incVP_ia

doo²³ hi³ nɔɔk¹ nɔɔ¹
person they run^INC RDP
... people run away.

(475)     incVP_ia
           - - -
           aux

nɛɛk²³² ma³ wɛɛ³ gi² dood² mɔg¹lik¹ gɔ¹
today DEIC returns is people assemble^INC ANA
And now, today, he is calling the people together.

(476)     incVP_ia

hi³ gi²bɛ¹ nin¹zig¹ nin¹zɔ¹
they are^me chase^IMM^INC RDP
I'm being pursued.

(477)     incVP_ia           mVP_neg

bɛ³ gim²¹ nɛ¹ tɛk¹     bɛ¹ gbɛ²num¹ gɛ²
I am^you ANT look^for^INC  I see^you not
I was looking for you and couldn't find you.

(478)     incVP_ia

da³ gi²gɛ¹ zaa¹sig¹ zaas¹ ya⁴
REM is^him get^well^CAUS^INC RDP Q
Is it going to save him over yonder?

**The optative-future incompletive verbal phrase (incVP_of)** has the structure shown in (479).

(479)  ± hab: (infl) gɔ²   ± infl aux: aux_opt   ± prog aux: infl $gi^2_{opt}$
       + prog hd: inc v    ± reinf: rdp hd

Five of the seven tagmemes of the basic formula are seen in the optative-future incompletive phrase:

— an optional HABITUAL slot, filled by optionally inflected habitual/potential $gɔ^2$,
— an optional AUXILIARY slot, filled by a subject-prefixed auxiliary verb in the optative mood,
— an optional PROGRESSIVE AUXILIARY slot, filled by subject-prefixed and optionally object-suffixed $gi^2$, in the optative mood,
— an obligatory PROGRESSIVE HEAD slot, filled by an incompletive verb, and
— an optional REINFORCER slot, filled by a reduplication of the stem of the progressive head verb.

(480)      incVP$_{of}$
$gɔ^2$  $be^1$  $rek^1$   $dɔy^2hɛt^1be^1$  $kpaak^1$  $ya^3$
when  I  go^INC  horse^grass  mow^INC  INTS
When I am on my way to mow the grass...

(481)      incVP$_{of}$
$gɔ^2$  $mɔ^1$  $gi^2$  $dork^1$     $ya^3$
when  you are  precede^INC  INTS
As you are going on ahead (future)...

(482)    incVP$_{of}$
$gɔ^2$  $mɔ^1$  $rek^3$  $rɔps^{41}$  $ya^4$
POT   you   go    abroads   Q
Might you be going on a journey?

(483)       incVP$_{of}$
$gɔ^2$  $mɔ^1$  $gi^2be^1$   $bib^1ti^1go^3$
when  you are^me  wrap^INC^MID
When you are wrapping me up (future)...

(484)       incVP$_{of}$
$waa^{23}$  $bɔ^1$  $gi^1$  $gi^2$  $kaak^1$   $kaa^1$  $ma^3$
child  DEM  he is  cry^INC  RDP  DEIC
The baby must be crying.

(485)        incVP$_{of}$

      *hi¹*    *zaa¹ni¹ko³*
      if^they come^ACC^INC^MID
      If they are bringing it.

(486)        incVP$_{of}$

      *wi¹*   *gi²*  *rɛnt²*  *gbo¹ko³*
      if^we are wood chop^INC^MID
      If we are chopping wood...

(487)        incVP$_{of}$

      *mɔ¹*  *wɛɛ¹zig¹*     *du¹*  *hɛ¹*  *i³si¹*  *kpɔd⁴¹*
      if^you return^IMM^INC in   here goat only
      If you're coming back in here, it's only with a goat.

(488)        incVP$_{of}$

      *mɔ¹*  *mɔ¹kig¹*  *bee¹*  *ge¹*  *bɛɛ³¹rɔ¹*
      if^you think^INC me^EM SPEC is^good
      If you are thinking about me, that's good.

(489)    mVP$_{ia}$         incVP$_{of}$

      *hi³*  *dɛk³*  *an¹*  *hi¹*   *hɔn¹tig¹*   *bay³yi²*
      they sift   like they toast^INC cassave
      You sift it as if you were going to toast cassave.

(490)    mVP$_{of}$             incVP$_{of}$

      *gɔ²*  *gi¹*  *gaa¹³*  *bįįl²*   *du¹*  *gi¹*  *gi²*  *lɛl²³*  *hɛ¹du¹go³*
      when it shines morning in   she is place sweep^INC^MID
      When it's morning and she is sweeping...

(491)           incVP_of
        ⎧―――――――――――⎫
         aux        hd
        ⎧――――⎫ ⎧―――――⎫
        be¹ gi² rek¹  ɛm¹bi¹ko³
        I am go^INC   walk^INC^MID
        ... so I'm going for a walk.

(492)   mVP_ia                                incVP_of
        ⎧――――⎫                                ⎧――――⎫
        ɔ³si³mi³    hor¹si¹ma⁴ bɔ¹  gi¹ gbu¹nu¹  mi¹ gi²
        leave^BEN^me last^DIM   DEM  he  one      I   am

                ⎧――――――⎫
                nɛɛ¹ki¹go⁴
                watch^INC^MID
        That leaves me with just the youngest one and I'm taking care of
        him.

(493)           incVP_of
                ⎧――――――――――⎫
        nɛ¹  wɛɛ³  nɛ¹ gɔ¹tig¹   wuu¹³wur¹ a¹ nɔ² dɔŋ²go³
        you^PL return you make^it^INC well   at what cause
        ... and why are you making wells all over the place?

(494)   mVP_perf                  incVP_of
        ⎧――――――――⎫                ⎧―――――⎫
        gi¹ sąąs³ ka³fe¹   ʔʔ²³ gi¹ yʒ¹ko³
        if^he heats coffee^his  he  drink^INC^MID
        ... if he has heated his coffee and is drinking it ...

The dependative incompletive verbal phrase (incVP_dep) has the structure shown in (495).

(495)  ± aux: infl aux_dep   ± rem: infl da³_prf   ± prog aux: infl gi²_dep-prf
       ± ant: nɛ¹   + prog hd: inc v_mid

Five of the seven tagmemes of the basic formula are present:

— an optional AUXILIARY slot, filled by a subject-prefixed auxiliary verb,
  in the dependative mood,

# Some Major Structures of Doyayo Syntax

— an optional REMOTENESS slot, filled by subject-prefixed $da^3$, non-indicative in the perfective mood,
— an optional PROGRESSIVE AUXILIARY slot, filled by subject-prefixed and optionally object-suffixed $gi^2$, in the dependative or, if auxiliary function is present, in the perfective mood,
— an optional ANTERIOR slot, filled by anterior $n\varepsilon^1$, and
— an obligatory PROGRESSIVE HEAD slot, filled by a verb in the incompletive-mid aspect.

(496)  incVP$_{dep}$

$kaal^1wi^1$ $y\mathrm{o}^1$ $wi^1$ $kaa^1ko^3$
crying^our rel we cry^INC^MID
How we are crying!

(497)  incVP$_{dep}$

    rem    prog hd

$y\mathrm{o}^1$ $hi^1$ $da^3$ $hi^1$ $d\mathrm{o}\mathrm{o}^1ti^1go^3$
when they REM they sit^INC^MID
When they were living...

(498)  incVP$_{dep}$

    prog aux    hd

$hin^1$ $y\mathrm{o}^1$ $m\mathrm{o}^1$ $gi^2si^1be^3$ $g\mathrm{o}^1tig^1$ $y\mathrm{o}^1$
thing REL you are^BEN^me do^it^INC here
What you keep doing to me here...

(499)  incVP$_{dep}$    mVP$_{of}$

    prog aux  hd

$n\varepsilon\varepsilon^{23}$ $b\mathrm{o}^1$ $baa^2m\mathrm{o}^1$ $gi^2si^1m\mathrm{o}^1$ $loo^1ko^3$ $m\mathrm{o}^1$ $\mathrm{oo}^3$
woman DEM father^your is^BEN^you take^INC^MID you leave

$\mathrm{oo}^1$
RDP
Don't take the wife your father is getting for you.

(500)   incVP_dep

ɔmt² bɔ¹  da³  gi²  nɛ¹  le¹ko³
fig   REL  REM  is   ANT  eat^INC^MID
The wild fig he had been eating...

(501)                              incVP_dep

              prog aux

naa²waal²  bɔ¹  hi¹  gis²¹   waar¹  bɔ¹   waal²  nis²tɔ¹
cow^milk   REL  they are^BEN chief  DEM   heir   wife^his

           prog hd

           kaŋ¹ko³
           bring^INC^MID
... the milk that's being taken to the wife of the chief's oldest son?

(502)                         incVP_dep

yɔ¹   buu²³  yɔ¹   da³  gii²wɛ¹    nɛ¹   gbaa¹ko³
when  white  when  REM  be^EM^us   ANT   keep^INC^MID
Before, when the white man really was taking care of us...

(503)                              incVP_dep

              prog aux      prog hd

yaar¹   yɔ¹  hi¹   gi²wi¹   ma³   haa¹nik¹          yɔ¹
suffering REL they are^us  DEIC  want^CAUS^INC     LOC
The way they are making us suffer...

(504)   incVP_dep

           prog hd

yɔ¹  mi¹  rek¹    buu¹  pu¹pu¹pul¹  yɔ¹
as   I    go^INC  belly ID          LOC
Since I'm going (i.e., dying) with an empty stomach...

# Some Major Structures of Doyayo Syntax

(505) incVP_dep

prog hd

yɔ¹ wi¹ **tuu¹ko³**     a¹ gar¹ba⁴ gar¹ba⁴
as  we  go^out^INC^MID  CIT Garba   Garba
As we were going out, we heard someone cry, Garba! Garba!

(506)            incVP_dep

        prog aux      prog hd

nɛ¹ bɔ² nɛ¹ gi²mɔ¹ nɛ¹ **nin¹zi¹go³**
well who then is^you INTS chase^IMM^INC^MID
Well now, and who is chasing you?

(507)         incVP_dep

       prog aux  prog hd

ʔt³¹ bɔ¹ yɔ¹ gi² **le¹ko³**
sun DEM when is  get^stuck^INC^MID
When the sun was going down, ...

(508)         incVP_dep

         prog hd

bee¹ yɔ¹ be¹ zoo¹sig¹   lɛ³ be¹ led²¹       hɛw³¹ gɛ²
I^EM REL I  harvest^INC thus I   eat^PREPC  also  not
Even I haven't eaten any yet, although I'm harvesting it.

(509)           incVP_dep

       prog aux             prog hd

yɔ¹ mɔ¹ gi² nɛ¹ zɛn²³mɔ¹ bɔ¹ **yaa¹nik¹** be²
as  you are ANT root^your DEM forbid^INC  CUM
Anyway, since you were forbidding (me to eat) your roots, ...

(510)                    incVP$_{dep}$
         ┌─────────────────────────┐
            rem    prog aux   prog hd
         ┌─────┐ ┌──────────┐ ┌──────────┐
    yɔ$^1$   wɛ$^1$ daa$^{31}$   gi$^2$ taa$^1$ko$^3$      (elision of wɛ$^1$da$^3$ wɛ$^1$gi$^2$)
    when   we REM^we are   shoot^INC^MID
    When we were going out and shooting, ...

(511)                    incVP$_{dep}$
                  ┌──────────────────┐
                    prog aux   prog hd
                  ┌──────────┐ ┌──────────┐
    wal$^{23}$ yɛ$^1$rɛ$^1$ gii$^1$   gi$^2$be$^1$ loo$^1$ko$^3$
    man   this    he^EM    is^me take^INC^MID
    This man is the one who is marrying me.

**The negative incompletive verbal phrase (incVP$_{neg}$)** has the structure shown in (512).

(512)   + prog aux: infl *taa$^{12}$*   ± ints: *nɛ$^1$*   ± dlm: *zaa$^1$*
        + prog hd: inc v$_{mid}$   ± reinf: id

Five of the seven basic tagmemes are present:

— an obligatory PROGRESSIVE AUXILIARY slot, filled by subject-prefixed and optionally object-suffixed *taa$^{12}$* 'not be',
— an optional INTENSIVE slot, filled by the anterior particle *nɛ$^1$*,
— an optional DELIMITING slot, filled by *zaa$^1$* 'other, again, any more',
— an obligatory PROGRESSIVE HEAD slot, filled by a verb in the incompletive-mid aspect, and
— an optional REINFORCER slot, filled by an ideophone.

Although it might be expected that the regular auxiliary and the remoteness functions would be present in the negative phrase, no examples were found in the data to confirm this.

(513) incVP_neg

prog aux    prog hd

bɛ¹ taa¹² wɛɛ¹zi¹go³
I  am^not return^IMM^INC^MID
I'm not coming back.

(514) incVP_neg

prog aux

wal²³ taa¹²bɛ¹ el¹ko³
man is^not^me call^INC^MID
I'm not having an affair with anyone.

(515) incVP_neg

bɛn²³ bɛ¹ taa¹² nɛ¹ rek¹ zaŋ¹
I^SFOC I am^not INTS go^INC at^all
I most certainly am not going!

(516) incVP_neg

prog aux

taa¹²si¹bɛ¹ bɛr¹ko³
is^not^me be^good^INC^MID
...I sure don't like it.

(517) incVP_neg

prog aux

wɛɛ³ hi¹ taa¹² yaa¹ boo¹ti¹nu³
CJ they are^not mouth speak^it^ACC^INC
But they weren't speaking together.

(518)         incVP$_{neg}$

nɛɛ²³   bɔ¹   taa¹²si¹gɛ¹      bis¹   ɓaa¹ko³
woman DEM is^not^BEN^him sauce serve^INC^MID
The woman is not going to serve him any sauce.

(519)   incVP$_{neg}$

taa¹²gɛ¹      guŋ¹ko³
is^not^him hurt^INC^MID
It doesn't hurt him.

(520)         incVP$_{neg}$

da³nɛ¹mi¹ bɔ¹   mi¹  taa¹²   zaa¹   loo¹ko³
hat^my   DEM I   am^not other take^INC^MID
I'm not going back to get my hat.

(521)         incVP$_{neg}$

hi¹   taa¹²wɛ¹         seek¹        an¹   doo²³   rɔ¹ɓo³
they are^not^us(INCL) look^at^INC like person true
They don't consider us respectable people.

(522)        incVP$_{neg}$

hi¹   taa¹²   nɛ¹   re¹nik¹      luum²   ha¹   gɛɛ²³
they are^not ANT go^ACC^INC market on   not
If they hadn't been taking it to the market...

**The reiterative incompletive verbal phrase (incVP$_{rit}$)** has the structure shown in (523).

(523)  ± prog aux: infl $gi^2$  +  (progr hd: inc $v_{mid}$)(3)

Only two of the seven tagmemes occur in this phrase:

— the optional PROGRESSIVE AUXILIARY slot, filled by subject- prefixed and optionally object-suffixed $gi^2$ 'be', and
— the obligatory PROGRESSIVE HEAD, filled by a verb in the incompletive-mid aspect, which is repeated to a total of three times.

# Some Major Structures of Doyayo Syntax

The term REITERATIVE here refers to continuation or repetition of an action or process or plurality of agent. This subtype of incompletive phrase is infrequent.

(524)    prog aux         prog hd(3)

hin¹ yɔ¹ doo²³¹ hi¹ gi² dɔ¹ko³    dɔ¹ko³
thing REL person they are say^INC^MID  say^INC^MID

dɔ¹ko³
say^INC^MID

What people everywhere are saying...

(525) gi² le¹ko³       le¹ko³        le¹ko³
is eat^INC^MID eat^INC^MID eat^INC^MID
All the while, he kept on eating.

**4.4.3 The intentive verbal phrase (intvVP).** The third major type of verbal phrase is that involving what we have chosen to call an *intentive auxiliary*. A number of common verbs like *rek³* 'go', *zaa²³* 'come', *yɛɛl⁴/baar⁴* 'start', *ɔɔ³* 'leave, stop', *haą²³* 'want', and *waa³* 'live' can function as intentive auxiliaries but there are also a few verbs which seem to have only that function, such as in these phrases: *bɛɛ³* 'have just...', *gbor³* 'go ahead and...', and *mɛɛ²³* 'start...'.

The *intentive verbal phrase (intvVP)* has the structure shown in (526).

(526)
$$+ \text{ intv aux: } \begin{Bmatrix} \text{mVP} \\ \text{incVP} \end{Bmatrix} + \text{ intv hd}_{(3)}: \begin{Bmatrix} \text{inc v} \\ \text{inf} \\ \text{verbal dem} \end{Bmatrix} \pm \text{reinf: rdp v}$$

The intentive verbal phrase has three tagmemes of which the first two are obligatory:

— an INTENTIVE AUXILIARY slot, filled by a modified verbal phrase or an incompletive verbal phrase,
— an INTENTIVE HEAD, with up to three repetitions, filled by an incompletive verb, an infinitive, or a verbal demonstrative. Each repetition must be with the same type of verb (i.e., all incompletives, all infinitives, or all verbal demonstratives), and

— an optional REINFORCER slot, filled by a reduplication of the preceding incompletive verb, as neither infinitive nor verbal demonstrative can be reduplicated. In transitive clauses, the intentive verbal phrase is normally discontinuous, the object of the clause being frontshifted to a position immediately preceding the phrase head.

Three subtypes are set up, based on restrictions concerning the occurrence of the fillers of the auxiliary and head slots.

**Subtype 1** includes those phrases where the head of the embedded modified or incompletive verbal phrase is $bɛɛ^3$ 'have just', $rek^3$ 'go', $zaa^{23}$ 'come', or $ɔɔ^3$ 'then do'. These require an incompletive verb in the intentive head slot.

**The incompletive intentive verbal phrase (intvVP$_{inc}$)** has the structure shown in (527).

(527)

$$+ \text{intv aux: mVP/incVP:} \begin{Bmatrix} bɛɛ^3 \\ rek^3 \\ zaa^{23} \\ ɔɔ^3 \end{Bmatrix} + \text{intv hd}_{(3)}: \text{inc v} \pm \text{reinf: rdp v}$$

(528) $hin^1$   $za^1$   $gɔ^2$   $bɛɛ^3$   $nam^1zig^1$   $hug^{41}$   $du^1$
thing other when hasˆjust moveˆIMMˆINC deathˆhut in
As soon as something moves in death-hut,...

(529) $yɔ^1$   $bɛɛ^2$   $mɔɔ^1$   $hark^1$   $be^2$
as hasˆjust youˆEM pleaseˆINC CUM
In the same way that you like her...

(530) $yɔ^1$   $bɛɛ^2ge^1$   $nɔɔ^1ko^3$
as hasˆjustˆhim angerˆINCˆMID
The minute he gets angry,...

(531) $bud^1$   $bɛɛ^2$   $mɛɛk^1$   $ha^1$   $bud^1$   $bɔ^1$   $wɔɔ^{31}rɔ^1$
fly hasˆjust fallˆINC on fly DEM dies
Just as soon as a fly lights on it, it dies.

(532) $mi^3$   $rek^3$   $dam^3ti^1$   $ɓɛɛ^1ko^3$
I go hedgehog seekˆINCˆMID
I went hunting for hedgehogs.

# Some Major Structures of Doyayo Syntax

(533) $wa^2la^4$ $bɔ^1$ $gi^2$ $rek^1$ $ɛm^1bi^1ko^1$
man^DIM DEM is go^INC walk^INC^HI
The boy was going for a walk.

(534) $baa^2mɔ^1$ $gi^2mɔ^1$ $rek^1$ $gbɔŋk^1$ $gbɔ^1mɔ^1$
father^your is^you go^INC kill^INC RDP
Your father is going to kill you.

(535)     mNP$_o$    intvVP$_{inc}$

$wal^{23}$ $za^1$ $zaa^{23}$ $ta^2mɔ^3$ $tɛ^1ko^3$
man other came sheep^his look^for^INC^MID
A man came looking for his sheep.

(536)     mNP$_o$

$be^3$ $zaa^{23}$ $bak^2$ $been^1$ $bal^1ko^3$
I came field my^EM cultivate^INC^MID
I came to work in my field.

(537) $mɔ^3$ $zaa^{23}$ $nɔ^2$ $gɔk^1$ $du^1$ $hɛ^1$ $be^2$
you came what do^INC in here CUM
What did you come to do here anyway?

(538) $mi^3$ $zaak^1$ $look^1$ $lee^1so^3yɔ^2$
I come^INC take^INC bed
I'm coming to get a bed.

(539) $ɓor^3$ $tot^2$ $bɔ^1$ $gi^1$ $ɔɔ^3$ $pir^1ko^3$
then sorghum DEM it then sprout^INC^MID
After that, the sorghum will sprout.

(540)     NP$_o$

$be^1$ $ɔ^3si^3mɔ^3$ $mɔn^{23}$ $bɔ^1$ $dɔ^1ko^3$
I then^BEN^you your DEM say^INC^MID
After that, I'll tell you yours.

(541) lɛl²³   yɔ¹   gaa²   ro²   gid¹   ɔɔ³   tuuk¹   nɔɔk¹
place when shine INTS if(real) he^then go^out^INC run^INC
re¹ko³
go^INC^MID
Only after daybreak will he get out and run away.

**Subtype 2** includes those intentive phrases where the head of the embedded modified or incompletive verbal phrase is *gbor³* 'just, go ahead, keep on', which requires an infinitive in the intentive head slot; or *ɔɔ³* 'stop', which requires a demonstrative in the intentive head slot.

**The infinitive intentive verbal phrase (intVP$_{inf}$)** has the structure shown in (542).

(542)  ± intv aux: infl aux$_{cmpl}$   + intv aux: mVP/incVP: *gbor³*
       + intv hd$_{(3)}$: inf   ± reinf: rdp v

(543) gɔ²   gi²   gbork¹        le¹ki¹
      HAB is keep^on^INC eat^INF
      He would keep on eating(it).

(544) gbor³    kɔm¹bi¹ki¹
      he^just stay^INF
      He didn't do anything.

(545) mɔ¹ raa²³    a¹   zaa²³mɔ²   gi¹   gbor³    re¹ki¹
      you say^PERF CIT come^IMP if^he keep^PRF go^INF
      If you say, "Come," and he keeps going.

(546) we³ gbo¹sig¹        hin¹   haal²   mɔ¹ki¹gi¹
      we keep^INTS^INC thing evil think^INF
      We're always having bad thoughts.

(547) hi³    gi²mi¹    gbork¹         kpɛɛ¹li¹ki¹
      they are^me keep^on^INC laugh^DIST^INF
      They keep making fun of me.

(548) mɔ¹ dund³    mɔ¹ gbor³ gbɔ²nɔ¹ bɔ¹   kpɛɛ¹ri¹ki¹
      you rise^OPT you just   door   DEM close^INTS^INF
      You quickly get up and open the door.

Some Major Structures of Doyayo Syntax 257

(549) *mi¹ ɔɔ³   le¹kɔ¹³   gɛ² be²*
I   leave^OPT eat^DEM not CUM
Anyway, I'm not going to stop eating it.

**Subtype 3** groups all remaining verbs that can function as head of the intentive auxiliary slot. These impose no restriction on the filler of the intentive head slot.

**The general intentive verbal phrase (intVP$_{gnrl}$)** has the structure shown in (550).

(550)

$$+ \text{ intv aux: mVP/incVP:} \begin{Bmatrix} \text{any verb except} \\ \text{types a) and b)} \end{Bmatrix} + \begin{bmatrix} \text{intv hd}_{(3)}: \begin{Bmatrix} \text{inc v} \\ \text{inf} \\ \text{v dem} \end{Bmatrix} \end{bmatrix}$$

± reinf: rdp v

(551) *yaa¹la¹   mɛɛ²³ hin¹   ɛɛk¹yɔ¹*
suddenly starts thing sing^INF
Suddenly he started singing.

(552) *hi³   mɛɛ²³ hin¹   na¹ko³*
they start thing dance^INC^MID
They started dancing.

(553) *vạạm⁴de³waa²³ bɔ¹   ma³   mɛɛ²³   kɛɛ¹kɔ¹³   gɔ¹   ma³*
donkey^child   DEM DEIC started reproduce^DEM ANA DEIC
*du¹*
upon
And now the little donkey started reproducing.

(554) *be¹ dɛɛ² ɛɛk¹   gɛ²*
I   can sing^INC not
I can't sing.

(555) *mɔ³   dɛɛ²³dɛ¹   zaŋ¹gi¹gi¹*
you can^RDP read^INF
You really can read.

(556) sąąm³¹mi¹ dɛɛ² is³¹ bɔ¹ wąą¹kɔ¹³  gɛ²
friend^my can goat DEM catch^DEM not
My friend doesn't know how to catch goats.
(polite for: You don't know...)

(557) pir²wol³ bɔ¹ gi² yɛɛ¹lik¹  zaa¹ko³
airplane DEM is start^INC come^INC
Airplanes were beginning to come.

(558) yɛɛl⁴  hin¹ ɛɛ¹ko³/ɛɛ¹ki¹
he^starts thing sing^INC^INF
He started singing.

(559) hi³ wɛɛ³ hi³ yɛɛl⁴ ma³ hin¹ bɔ¹ gii¹  na¹kɔɔ¹³
they return they start DEIC thing DEM it^EM dance^DEM
So they started the dance at last.

(560) mɔ³ waa³ loo¹rɛ¹ nuŋ²³ naak¹  a¹ yąą¹ du¹
you live spirit name converse^INC at mouth in
You keep on talking about the spirits. (impers)

(561) hi³ waa³si³gɛ³  ma³ nɔk² bɔ¹ wɔ¹ki¹
they live^BEN^him DEIC wound DEM bind^INF
They (impers) keep bandaging the wound for him.

(562) hi³ yaa⁴mi¹ bi¹yɛr¹³ zeb¹zi¹go³
they send^me beer buy^IMM^INC^MID
They sent me to buy beer.

(563) hąąg²³¹  bee¹  gbɔŋ¹ko³.
wants^him me^EM kill^INC^MID
He wants to kill me.

(564) gid¹ gi²mɔ¹ hąąk¹  tɔk¹yɔ¹
if(real) is^you want^INC eat^INF
If you are wanting to eat it,...

(565) hi³ zaa²³ hi³baar⁴ ma³ hin¹-yą²³ bɔ¹ na¹kɔ¹³
they came they^started DEIC thing-their DEM dance^DEM
   lɛ²lɔ³
   place^DEM
They came and started their dance right there.

(566) yɛ²ru³mɔ²         dor¹ko³
      supercede^you^(IMP) precede^INC^MID
      Take a turn being first.

(567) mɔ³ zɛn²³zig¹    zɛnz¹ kam¹zig¹  ya⁴
      you forget^IMM^it RDP   bring^IMM Q
      Did you forget to bring it?

### 4.4.4 Summary of verbal phrase types

**(mVP) modified verbal phrase**

(568) (mVP$_{ia}$) indicative-aorist

$$\pm \text{ hab: (infl) } gɔ² \quad \pm \text{ (aux: infl aux}_{ia})_{(3)} \quad \pm \text{ rem: infl } da³_{ia}$$
$$+ \text{ hd: infl } v_{ia} \quad \pm \text{ ant: } nɛ¹ \quad \pm \text{ reinf: } \begin{Bmatrix} \text{rdp v} \\ \text{id} \end{Bmatrix}$$

(569) wɛɛ³      tuu⁴       rek³    a¹ hęt¹ du¹
      he^returns he^goes^out he^goes at grass in
      He left again and went to the bush.

(570) (mVP$_{of}$) optative-future

$$\pm \text{ hab: (infl) } gɔ² \quad \pm \text{ (aux: infl aux}_{of})_{(3)} \quad \pm \text{ rem: infl } da³/za¹_{of}$$
$$+ \text{ hd: infl } v_{of} \quad \pm \text{ ant: } nɛ¹ \quad \pm \text{ reinf: rdp v}$$

(571) hi¹ za¹ hi¹ zaa¹³ hi¹ lɔ³mɔ¹
      they pot they come they bite^you
      They might come and bite you.

(572) (mVP$_{prf}$) perfective

$$\pm \text{ (aux: infl aux}_{prf})_{(3)} \quad + \text{ hd: infl } v_{prf}$$

(573) mɔ¹ gben³ hi¹   raa²³
      you  see   they say
      If, for example, you have been told...

(574) (mVP$_{dep}$) dependative

± (aux: infl aux$_{dep-prf}$)(3)   ± rem: infl $da^3$   + hd: infl v$_{dep-prf}$
± ant: $nɛ^1$

(575) $a^4$ $bɔ^2$   $be^1$ $da^3$   $be^1$ $loo^2$ $nɛ^1$   $zęn^{23}mɔ^1$ $bɔ^1$   $gɛ^2$ $rɛ^1$
   if  INTDC I   REM  I   take   ANT   root^your   DEM  not   INTS
   If I hadn't taken your roots...

(576) (mVP$_{imp}$) imperative

± (aux: infl aux$_{imp-opt}$)(3)   ± infl rem: $da^3_{opt}$   + hd: infl v$_{imp/opt}$

(577) $loo^4mɔ^2$      $mɔ^1$ $kam^3$      $mɔ^1$ $rek^3$      $mɔ^1$ $gaa^4$
   take^you^IMP   you carry^OPT   you go^OPT   you give^OPT
   $baa^2mɔ^1$
   father^your
   Take this and go and give it to your father.

(578) (mVP$_{hrt}$) hortatory

+ hrt: $\begin{Bmatrix} \text{hrt} \\ \text{intdc} \end{Bmatrix}$ ± (aux: infl aux$_{opt}$)(3)   ± rem: infl $da^3$
+ hd: infl cmpl v$_{opt}$   ± reinf$_1$: $nɛ^1$   ± reinf$_2$: id

(579) $ɔ^3$   $be^1$ $dɔɔ^4$   $be^1$ $sęę^4$   $hi^1nɔ^3$      $tęę^1$
   let   I   go^up   I   see   thing^DEM   ID
   Just let me go over and have a look.

(580) (mVP$_{rit}$) reiterative

± (aux: infl aux$_{cmpl}$)(3)   + hd: $\begin{Bmatrix} \text{s-pref cmpl v st} \\ \text{s-sf cmpl v st} \end{Bmatrix}$(n)

(581) $hi^3$   $dɔ^2gɔ^3$   $dɔ^2gɔ^3$   $dɔ^2gɔ^3$
   they say   say   say
   They all said it.

# Some Major Structures of Doyayo Syntax

(582) (mVP$_{neg}$) negative

$$\pm \text{ hd: infl v} \begin{Bmatrix} \text{ia} \\ \text{of} \\ \text{dep} \end{Bmatrix} \pm \text{reinf}_1: n\varepsilon^1 + \text{neg: } g\varepsilon^2 \pm \text{reinf}_2: \text{id}$$

(583) $a^1$   $hi^1$   $tuu^2$   $g\varepsilon^2$
CIT they go^out not
He said, "They didn't get out."

**(incVP) incompletive verbal phrase**

(584) (incVP$_{ia}$) indicative-aorist

$\pm$ hab: infl $gɔ^2$   $\pm$ aux: infl aux$_{ia}$   $\pm$ rem: infl $da^3{}_{ia}$
$\pm$ prog aux: $gi^2{}_{ia}$   $\pm$ ant: $n\varepsilon^1$   + prog hd: inc v   $\pm$ reinf: rdp hd

(585) $hi^3$   $bum^1$   $yɔ^1ko^1$   $hi^3$   $gaps^2$   $boo^1ko^1$
they beer drinking they fight talking
They would be drinking beer and quarrelling.

(586) (incVP$_{of}$) optative-future

$\pm$ hab: (infl) $gɔ^2$   $\pm$ infl aux: aux$_{opt}$   $\pm$ prog aux: infl $gi^2{}_{opt}$
+ prog hd: inc v   $\pm$ reinf: rdp hd

(587) $gɔ^2$   $mɔ^1$   $gi^2be^1$   $bib^1ti^1go^3$
when you are^me wrap^INC^MID
When you are wrapping me up (future)...

(588) (incVP$_{dep}$) dependative

$\pm$ aux: infl aux$_{dep}$   $\pm$ rem: infl $da^3{}_{perf}$   $\pm$ prog aux: infl $gi^2{}_{dep\text{-}prf}$
$\pm$ ant: $n\varepsilon^1$   + prog hd: inc v$_{mid}$

(589) $lɔmt^2$   $bɔ^1$   $da^3$   $gi^2$   $n\varepsilon^1$   $le^1ko^3$
fig REL REM is ANT eat^INC^MID
The wild fig he had been eating...

(590) (incVP$_{neg}$) negative

   + prog aux: infl *taa*$^{12}$   ± ints: *nɛ*$^1$   ± dlm: *zaa*$^1$
   + prog hd: inc v$_{mid}$   ± reinf: id

(591) *ben*$^{23}$   *be*$^1$   *taa*$^{12}$   *nɛ*$^1$   *rek*$^1$   *zaŋ*$^1$
   I^SFOC   I   am^not   INTS   go^INC   at^all
   I most certainly am not going!

(592) (incVP$_{rit}$) reiterative

   ± prog aux: infl *gi*$^2$   + (progr hd: inc v$_{mid}$)$_{(3)}$

(593) *hin*$^1$   *yɔ*$^1$   *doo*$^{231}$   *hi*$^1$   *gi*$^2$   *dɔ*$^1$*ko*$^3$   *dɔ*$^1$*ko*$^3$
   thing REL person they are say^INC^MID say^INC^MID
   *dɔ*$^1$*ko*$^3$
   say^INC^MID
   What people everywhere are saying...

## (intvVP) intentive verbal phrase

(594) (intvVP$_{inc}$) incompletive

   + intv aux: mVP/incVP: $\begin{Bmatrix} bɛɛ^3 \\ rek^3 \\ zaa^{23} \\ ɔɔ^3 \end{Bmatrix}$ + intv hd$_{(3)}$: inc v ± reinf: rdp v

(595) *baa*$^2$*mɔ*$^1$   *gi*$^2$*mɔ*$^1$   *rek*$^1$   *gbɔŋk*$^1$   *gbɔ*$^1$*mɔ*$^1$
   father^your is^you go^IC kill^INC RDP
   Your father is going to kill you.

(596) (intvVP$_{inf}$) infinitive

   ± intv aux: infl aux$_{compl}$   + intv aux: mVP/incVP: *gbor*$^3$
   + intv hd$_{(3)}$: inf   ± reinf: rdp v

(597) *mɔ*$^1$ *dund*$^3$   *mɔ*$^1$ *gbor*$^3$ *gbɔ*$^2$*nɔ*$^1$ *bɔ*$^1$   *kpɛɛ*$^1$*ri*$^1$*ki*$^1$
   you rise^OPT you just door DEM close^INTS^INF
   You quickly get up and open the door.

# Some Major Structures of Doyayo Syntax

(598) (intvVP$_{gnrl}$) general

+ intv aux: mVP/incVP: $\left\{\begin{array}{l}\text{any verb except}\\\text{types a) and b)}\end{array}\right\}$ + $\left[\text{intv hd}_{(3)}: \left\{\begin{array}{l}\text{inc v}\\\text{inf}\\\text{v dem}\end{array}\right\}\right]$

± reinf: rdp v

(599) sąam³¹mi¹ dɛɛ² is³¹ bɔ¹ wąą¹kɔ¹³ gɛ²
friend^my can goat DEM catch^DEM not
My friend doesn't know how to catch goats.

## Appendix

### Chart of Internal Ordering of the Verbal Phrase in the Completive Aspect

| | Auxiliary 1 | 2 | 3 | 4 | 5 | 6 | Verb Head | Verb phrase | Translation |
|---|---|---|---|---|---|---|---|---|---|
| | wɛɛ³ | tuu⁴ | tal²³ | zaa²³ | da³ | gi²/taa¹² | | | |
| | ɔɔ³ | wir²³ | dük³ | rek³ | dɛɛ⁴ | | | | |
| | ɔ³† | loo⁴ | nɔɔ⁴ | | | | | | |
| | yɛ⁴† | | dɔɔ⁴ | | | | | | |
| | | | loo⁴ | | | | | | |
| | | | sɔɔ²³ | | | | | | |
| | | | kam³ | | | | | | |
| (1) | | | | | mi¹ da³ | | mi¹ ɛ'ri¹ge¹ | mi¹ da³ mi¹ ɛ'ri¹ge¹ | 'I'll go ask him.' |
| (2) | | loo⁴ | | | da³ | | ba¹lɔ³ | loo⁴ da³ ba¹lɔ³ | 'He took and planted.' |
| (3) | | | | | da³ | | gbɛn³ | da³ gbɛn³ | 'there he saw' |
| (4) | | | | zaa²³ | | | gaa⁴ | zaa²³ gaa⁴ | 'he came and gave' |
| (5) | | loo⁴mɔ² | mɔ¹ kam³ | mɔ¹ rek³ | | | mɔ¹ gaa⁴ | loo⁴mɔ² mɔ¹ kam³ mɔ¹ rek³ mɔ¹ gaa⁴ | 'Take it along and go give it...' |
| (6) | | | bel kam³ | bel re³ | | | bel gaa⁴ | bel kam³ bel re³ bel gaa⁴ | 'I will take it and go give it...' |
| (7) | | | mi³ dük³ | | | | mi³ zaa²³za¹ | mi³ dük³ mi³ zaa²³za¹ | 'I rose and came' |
| (8) | | | dugz³¹ | zaa²³ | | | ɛɛ³ | dugz³¹ zaa²³ ɛɛ³ | 'she got up and came and sang' |
| (9) | mi³ wɛɛ³ | | | mi³ zaa²³ | | | mi³ gbaa⁴jɔ² | mi³ wɛɛ³ mi³ zaa²³ mi³ gbaa⁴jɔ² | 'I came again and laid it down' |
| (10) | hi³ wɛɛ³ | | | hi³ zaa²³ | | | hi³ kpelk⁴ | hi³ wɛɛ³ hi³ zaa²³ hi³ kpelk⁴ | 'they came again and poured' |
| (11) | | | | rek³ | | | tuu⁴ra-r | ek³ tuu⁴ra² | 'he went and arrived' |
| (12) | hi³ wɛɛ³ | | hi³sɔɔ²³ | | | | hi³ tuur⁴ | hi³ wɛɛ³ hi³sɔɔ²³ hi³ tuur⁴ | 'they moved again and arrived...' |
| (13) | | | nɔɔ⁴ | rek³ | | | ɛ'hi¹ | nɔɔ⁴ rek³ ɛ'hi¹ | 'he ran and followed them.' |
| (14) | gi¹ ɔɔ³ | tuuk¹ | nɔɔk¹ | | | | re¹ko³ | gi¹ ɔɔ³ tuuk¹ nɔɔk¹ re¹ko³ | 'then he will go out and run away.' |
| (15) | wɛɛ³ | tuu⁴ | | | | | rek³ | wɛɛ³ tuu⁴ rek³ | 'he left and went' |
| (16) | hi³ wɛɛ³ | | | | hi³ da³ | | hi³ rek³ | hi³ wɛɛ³ hi³ da³ hi³ rek³ | 'they went off again...' |
| (17) | | | | hi³ zaa²³ | | hi³ gi² | ...baa¹ko³ | hi³ zaa²³ hi³ gi²...baa¹ko³ | 'they came and are dancing' |
| (18) | wɛɛ³ | | | | | | wɛɛ²zɔ³ | wɛɛ³ wɛɛ²zɔ³ | 'he came back again' |

# Some Major Structures of Doyayo Syntax 265

(19) wir²³ nɔɔ⁴hɔ¹ 'he escaped and ran away'
(20) bel¹ tal¹³ bel¹ tuu⁴ 'I went out and left'
(21) hi³ wɛɛ³ hi³ da³ hi³ rek³ 'then they went off'
(22) mɔ¹ dɔɔ⁴ mɔ¹ rek³ rek³ mɔ¹ dɔɔ⁴ mɔ¹ rek³ mɔ¹ loo¹sɛ¹ 'you go up and get for us...'
(23) da³ gi² le¹ko³ 'he was eating'
(24) (yɔ¹) hi³ loo⁴ge¹ hi¹rek³ (yɔ¹) hi³ loo⁴ge¹ hi¹-rek³ hi¹ raa²si²ge³ 'they would take her and go tell her...'
(25) dɛɛ⁴ wɛ¹ rek³ 'let's go!'
(26) da³ mɔ¹ rek³ 'go'
(27) yɛ⁴ wɛ¹ rek³ yɛ⁴ wɛ¹ rek³ wɛ¹ hag³ 'let's go and make'
(28) ɔ³ be¹dɔɔ⁴ ɔ³ be¹dɔɔ⁴ bel¹ sɔɔ⁴ 'let me go up and have a look'
(29) rek³ gi²(hi¹) boo¹ko³ 'she has gone to visit (greet) them'

†All auxiliaries except these can also function as verb heads.

## Meaning of the auxiliaries:

| | | |
|---|---|---|
| wɛɛ³ | 'become, return, (do) again' | |
| ɔɔ³ | 'leave, then (do)' | |
| ɔ³ | 'HORTATORY 1 SG' | |
| da³ | 'HORTATORY 2' | |
| yɛ⁴/dɛɛ⁴ | 'HORTATORY 1 PL' | |

| tuu⁴ | 'go out' | nɔɔ⁴ | 'run (away)' | rek³ | 'go' |
| wir²³ | 'escape' | loo⁴ | 'take' | da³ | 'go and…' /ANT |
| dɔɔ⁴ | 'go up' | sɔɔ²³ | 'move away' | gi² | 'be' |
| tal²³ | 'pass' | kam³ | 'bring' | taa¹² | 'not be' |
| duk³ | 'get up' | zaa²³ | 'come' | | |

## Ordering of the suxiliaries:

Aux 1: wɛɛ³, ɔɔ³, ɔ³, yɛ⁴
Aux 2: tuu⁴, wir²³, loo⁴
Aux 3: tal²³, duk³, nɔɔ⁴, (loo⁴), sɔɔ²³, kam³
Aux 4: zaa²³, rek³
Aux 5: da³, dɛɛ⁴
Aux 6: gi²/taa¹²

# Features of Doyayo Folk Tales

### Elisabeth Wiering

The purpose of this article is to examine the special characteristics of the short story in *Dooyaayɔ*. Here is an inventory of the stories, for the reader's convenience. Where the *Dooyaayɔ* title (in the form of the beginning sentence) differs from the one we have given, it is included in parentheses.

    BA  'The Corpse' ('A man and his wife')
    BB  'Miracle of a Woman and Her Son'
    BC  'The Hyena and the Red Monkey' ('The hyena fell into a hole.')
    BD  'The Song of the Bird' ('A certain woman found seed pods...')
    BE  'The Boy and the Monkeys' ('A certain person cultivated his field.')
    BF  'The Hare and His Mother-in-Law' ('The hare got married.')
    BG  'Nana Rescues the Cannibal's Wife' ('A certain person...')
    BH  'The Hare and the Red Monkey' ('The red monkey was conversing with the hare.')
    BI  'The Cock and the Hare'
    BJ  'Three Deaf People'
    BK  'The Hunter and the Cannibal' ('A certain young man who was a hunter...')
    BL  'A Cannibal's Wife is Rescued by Her Brother' ('Someone had a daughter.')
    BM  'The Donkey Wife' ('A chief had three wives.')

From the booklet *Bidyɔ*:

B1   'The Camel and the Goat'
B4   'The Hyena and the Tortoise'
B7   'The Hare, the Elephant, and the Hippopotamus'
B8   'The Chieftainship of the Owl over Other Birds'
B9   'The Hunter and the Crocodile'

## 1 Internal structure of the narrative

The short story has the basic structure of an introduction, a corpus, an optional coda, and a conclusion.

The corpus consists of from one to seven major episodes. The episode has the basic structure of a setting, the development, a climax, a complication, and a solution.

The non-initial, non-final episodes often omit setting, complication, and/or solution. The grand climax usually occurs in the last episode.

Of the eighteen stories examined, eleven contain one major episode. BJ, BL, B1, and B9 each have two main episodes, BA and BH have three episodes, and BM has seven.

Three short stories (BM, BI, and BA) have been selected by way of illustration to examine their internal structure.

### The Donkey Wife (BM)

The story of 'The Donkey Wife', told by Lapɔrti, a man renowned for his gift of storytelling among the Dowayos, is extraordinary not only for its literary style and versatility, but also for the graceful and intricate development of its plot.

### Episode 1 (BM 1–25)

**Setting (doubles as introduction).** 'A certain chief had three wives. Those two became pregnant and had children; this other one was childless.'

**Development.** The ignominy and grief of the childless woman is set forth, culminating in the cry that it doesn't matter to her what she bears—a mouse, a frog, a snail, a slug, a horse, or a donkey—as long as she can give birth to something. That same month, she becomes pregnant.

# Features of Doyayo Folk Tales

She bears a donkey child. She cares for it very lovingly and it grows up. Then it happens....

**Climax.** The chief's servant catches sight of the donkey girl bathing in the river. She has taken off her donkey skin and is a beautiful woman.

## Episode 2 (BM 26–54)

**Setting.** The servant tells the chief's son the secret about the donkey.

**Development.** The chief's son doesn't believe the servant, but finally he agrees to go and see. From their vantage point, they see the donkey arrive, and the storyteller prepares the audience for the impending climax by elaborating on the mounting indignation of the chief's son, who sees but a mere donkey.

**Climax.** Suddenly the donkey removes her skin, and the chief's son is speechless. The servant just barely succeeds in preventing him from rushing down and grabbing the girl.

## Episode 3 (BM 55–110)

**Setting.** The chief's son tells his father he wants to marry the donkey girl. The chief is perplexed.

**Development.** With great difficulty, the chief's son finally succeeds in persuading his father and the donkey girl's family that his heart is set on no other, and they agree.

**Climax.** At last, there is a great celebration in honor of the wedding of the chief's son with the donkey girl.

**Complication.** To his utter consternation, the chief's son discovers after the wedding that he cannot get his wife to remove her donkey skin.

## Episode 4 (BM 111–137)

**Setting.** The chief's son consults an old woman.

**Development.** Following her instructions, he prepares a washing place for his wife. While she is washing herself, a bird suddenly swoops down and carries away her skin. Greatly distressed but having no choice, she puts on the clothes her husband put there for her and then prepares his dinner.

**Climax.** The husband arrives home. The narrator vividly describes how, with increasing excitement, the man looks over the washing place and approaches the house, and how enraptured he is on entering to find his wife without her donkey skin.

### Episode 5 (BM 138–182)

**Setting.** The chief's son invites his father and his whole family to a feast, so as to show them his beautiful wife.

**Problem/Development.** The chief becomes jealous of his son and devises a plan to kill him. The donkey wife hears of it and warns him. She gives him a seed and a ring to take along. Together with ten slaves, the father and son go to a certain well. He tells his son to climb down and fetch water for him. The slaves all offer to do it instead, but the chief will not hear of it. Again, the storyteller makes use of numerous devices to create an atmosphere of mounting tension.

**Climax.** The son climbs down into the well and the father traps him inside and departs, together with his slaves.

### Episode 6 (BM 183–227)

**Setting.** The chief's son is in the well.

**Development.** The seed planted in the well by the chief's son sprouts and grows into a tree. He subsists on the fruit of the tree.

**Climax.** Contrary to the general rule mentioned above, this next to the last episode harbors the grand climax of the story. In its style, it is a literary gem of extraordinary quality, and intensely dramatic. The peak of excitement is maintained over a very long stretch, from BM 187, that is, the moment the tree pushes the stone off the well, to BM 209 (22 sentences later), the end of the prince's enigmatic message for his wife. Later, we will refer to some of the exceptional literary features that make this passage so remarkable. The climax continues, with a sort of gradual decrescendo, up through BM 227, as the wife receives the cryptic message with the ring, finds her husband, brings him home secretly, and nurtures him.

# Features of Doyayo Folk Tales

**Episode 7 (BM 228–254)**

**Setting.** The young man is back home with his wife. The chief is in his entrance hut.

**Development.** The son decides to take vengeance on his father. The chief's wives see him approaching on horseback and tell the chief. He doesn't believe them.

**Climax.** Suddenly, the chief sees his son and goes out to meet him. The son cuts off his head, then makes a great funeral celebration for him.

## Coda

The chief's son marries all his father's widows, and now his own wife begins to bear. They get so many children that they can supply husbands and wives for all the slaves in their household.

## Ending:

"There, it's finished. I am Lapɔrti of Bakdɔŋko."

## The Cock and the Hare

In contrast with the very intricate and elaborate story of 'The Donkey Wife', we will now look at the structure of a very simple short story with just one episode.

**Opening:** 'The Cock and the Hare' (title)

**Setting.** The hare suggests to the cock that they go out to the bush together to make drums.

**Development.** The hare makes his drum very quickly and goes to the chief to demonstrate it, but it is a complete flop. Meanwhile, the cock makes his with great care.

**Climax.** The cock's drum has a very beautiful sound. (The narrator sings the song of the cock.) As soon as the chief hears it, he declares the cock the winner and gives him all the prizes (various kinds of food), while chasing the hare away.

**Complication.** The hare becomes very angry and starts picking a fight with the cock.

**Solution.** The chief wisely directs them to the end of the field, where they find Panther. They push him into a hole.

**Ending:** The panther stays in the hole forever.

### 'The Corpse' (BA)

We conclude with a story containing three main episodes.

**Opening** 'A man and his wife, the two of them ... '

### Episode 1 (BA 2–27)

**Setting** The man suspects his wife of being unfaithful.

**Development** The husband discovers that his wife has hidden some beer for her lover. He secretly puts poison in it and then announces that he is going away on a long journey. The same night, the wife calls her lover to come and starts serving him the beer. Dramatic reference is made to the husband, who has returned and is listening outside.

**Clima** . The woman offers to fill the calabash a third time. "Wait a minute," says her lover. Suddenly he succumbs to the poison. The woman cries out in despair, and her husband quickly rushes to the scene.

**Complication** The problem of the wife's unfaithfulness is resolved, but now what to do with the dead body?

**Resolution** The husband devises a good plan for getting rid of the corpse which is detailed in the next episode.

### Episode 2 (BA 28–53)

**Setting** The next-door-neighbor has the habit of stealing yams from other people's gardens by night, passing them to his wife over the top of the hedge that surrounds his compound.

# Features of Doyayo Folk Tales

**Development** The man wraps up the body and takes it along to the neighbor's hedge, where he calls the wife of the thief to get it. She takes it innocently and puts it in the hut. When her husband arrives a few minutes later with his load of stolen yams, she expresses her surprise that there are two packages this time instead of just one. At this point, direct speech and cryptic utterances alert the audience to the impending climax.

**Climax** The thief enters the hut and uncovers the dead body.

**Complication** Now the thief, in turn, must find a way to get rid of the awful package.

**Resolution** He is not at a loss, but immediately devises an excellent plan.

## Episode 3 (BA 54–78)

**Setting** Not far from the thief's compound, two men are up in a tree smoking out bees to harvest their honey.

**Development** The thief comes up and quietly places the dead body at the base of the tree. Then he says to the men, "Give me some honey." They respond that he cannot expect them to give him honey, while they haven't even tasted it themselves. "Well, if you won't give me any honey, I'll die on you right here," exclaims the thief. Then he quietly departs.

**Grand Climax** Having finished harvesting the honey, the two men start climbing down. To their horror, they discover a dead body. This climax is drawn out and highly dramatized, with the help of minimally-marked report and the particles *ma* and demonstrative *yɔ*. More will be said about this in §4 on special dramatic devices.

**Complication** The men with the honey are now stuck with the dead body which they, in turn, must get rid of.

**Resolution** They have a brilliant idea. Dragging the corpse to the roadside, they dump the honey on top of it to give the impression that the man had been stung to death while trying to harvest honey.

**Ending:** The story ends with the two men running home.

## 2 Opening and closing formulas

A common opening formula for a short story is some variation of '(Let's tell) a(nother) story.' However, this is not obligatory, nor is a title. When neither is present, the story is recognized by its opening sentence which introduces the main or beginning participants. Occasionally, the title is saved for the end so as not to make the tale too predictable (cf. 'The Three Deaf People'). This is the only story with both an opening formula and a title, and that may also be the reason why the title was saved for the end.

Of the eighteen stories, eight used some variation of the opening formula (1), seven opened with the title (2), and three began by introducing the initial or main participants (3).

(1)     BC, BL    *Wɛ ɓk bidyɔ.*
                     'Let's tell a story.'
        BD, BK    *Bidyɔ.*
                     '(This is) a short story.'
        BE         *Wɛ ɓk bid bɔ za ɓɛ.*
                     'Let's tell another story.'
        BF         *Wɛ ɓk bid za ɓɛ.*
                     'Let's tell another story.'
        BJ         *Laginɛ bid za gɔ ɓɛ.*
                     'Listen to another story.'
        BH         *Ɔwɛ ɓk bid kaasi.*
                     'Let's tell stories for a while.'

(2)     BB        *Gɛrs a nɛɛ za hi waaɔ*
                     'Miracle of a Woman and Her Son'
        BI          *Kɔba hi rɔma*
                     'The Cock and the Hare'
        B1          *Gɛloba hi isi*
                     'The Camel and the Goat' (title)
        B4          *Kpaatir hi kundiri*
                     'The Hyena and the Tortoise' (title)
        B7          *Rɔma, namnɔ hi beri*
                     'The Hare, the Elephant, and the Hippopotamus' (title)
        B8          *Gum waarumsɔ hi nɔɔs zaadɛ*
                     'The Owl's Chieftainship over Other Birds' (title)
        B9          *Taarumba hi zaabo*
                     'The Hunter and the Crocodile' (title)

Features of Doyayo Folk Tales 275

(3)   BA     *Wal za bɔ ma hi nisɔ, hi eerɛ ...*
             'A certain man and his wife, the two of them ...'
    BG     *Zaạn za ma, nɛɛyɔ hi waasiŋ ...*
             'A certain person, a woman and her daughter ...'
    BM     *Waaryɔ, gin nɛɛd taarɛ.*
             'A chief (once) had three wives.'

The most common closing formula for any kind of discourse is *anbɔ/anbɔ labɔ* 'That's how it is'. Also quite common is *dạạdạ* 'it's finished'. There are a number of variations and combinations of these two alternatives. Often the closing formula in (4) is replaced by some expression of cessation or permanence related to the closing events of the story as in (5).

(4)   BB     *Bidɔ ma anbɔ.*
             'That's how the story goes.'
    BC     *Anbɔ labɔ.*
             'That's how it is (literally: like-that thus).'
    BE     *Dạạdạ.*
             'It's finished.'
    BF     *Dɔglɔ dạạ anbɔ.*
             'The matter finishes that way.'
    BG     *Dạạdạ anbɔ.*
             'It's finished like that.'
  BH, BL   *Dạạ labɔ.*
             'It finishes thus.'
    BJ     *Bidɔ hi wɛɛ hi el ma a dood lagɛ taarɛ.*
             'So the story is called "Three deaf people."'
    BM     *Gɔ, dạạ gɔ. Mii ...*
             'There, it's finished. I'm ... (see above)'
    B1     *Hinɔ anbɔ labɔ.*
             'That's how the thing goes.' (literally: its-thing like-that thus)
  B7, B8   *Hinɔ ma anbɔ labɔ.*
             'That's how the thing goes.'

(5)   BA     *Hi nɔɔ hi zaa ma raa du.*
             'Then they ran home.'
    BD     *A gɔrɔ, dạạsimɔ ma, riiri.*
             'She said, "All right, you can stop now, that's enough!"'
    BI     *Naam bɔ dɔɔts ma gaati a sạạl du hɔ.*
             'And the panther stayed in that hole forever.'
    BK     *Wala bɔ be, baatɔ loo wɛɛnig gi lɛl be.*
             'As for the boy, his father brought him home again.'

B4  *Kar rek be.*
    'He climbed up (from the river's edge) and left.'
B9  *Taarumba bɔ kaŋg gɔ.*
    'So the hunter carried him off.'

As can be clearly seen in the above data, the Dowayo storyteller has a wide range of choices for opening and closing his stories, because even the standard opening/closing formulas allow for considerable variation.

## 3 Linkage

The main types of linkage found in the stories are sentence markers/conjunctors in (6), paragraph markers (initial, interjectory) in (7), discourse-level markers in (8), temporal words, phrases, or clauses, and overlap.

(6) wɛɛ    'then, and then'
    gɔ     'then, so then' (non-initial; also functions at higher levels)
    be     contrastive/cumulative particle

(7) gɔ     'Well then, so there, all right'
    hɔnɛ   'Now'
    tɔɔ    'Well now, all right'

(8) yaala  'suddenly'
    ma     deictic particle, often used for setting and climax

The type of linkage used can reflect the relative ability of the narrator. The most inexperienced storyteller was a woman, who resorted almost exclusively to the simple *wɛɛ* 'and then'. Half of all the sentences of her story (BD) use *wɛɛ*, while the sentence introducing the climax uses overlap. One other story makes abundant use of *wɛɛ* (BC), but then, as if by premeditated choice, only in the nine sentences marking the development of the plot. In the rest of this story, a minimum of overt linkage occurs, except in the climax, which uses temporal clauses and non-initial *gɔ*, and in the final resolution which again uses a temporal clause.

The particle *ma* is often used discourse-initial and/or final and at certain stages in the plot, where it has a dramatic function (to be discussed below). It can be used at the end of the story in conjunction with *gɔ* to express finality. *ma* is often used with the introduction of new characters in the story. When the element of contrast, as opposed to vividness, is being emphasized, the characters can be introduced with *be*.

# Features of Doyayo Folk Tales

The story of 'The Three Deaf People' makes use of a large number of the linkage devices mentioned above. The first two main participants are introduced with *ma* (BJ 2,5); the third major participant, the chief, a rather passive, weak personality, enters the story as an object of the action of characters 1 and 2, and is introduced with *gɔ* 'so then'. Contrastive *be* occurs frequently in the story, marking interjected information. The development alternates the use of *wɛɛ, gɔ,* and *be,* with major points of progression marked by *tɔɔ*. The climax is marked by *tɔɔ* and *yaala.* The amused reaction of the chief's assistants to his decision is marked by *tɔɔ,* and by contrastive *be.* In the closing formula and ensuing title, we find *hɔnɛ* and *wɛɛ,* while *ma* is used to provide emphasis and permanence.

Noticeably absent in the story of 'The Three Deaf People' are temporal phrases and clauses. A story which makes abundant use of temporal linkage is 'The Miracle of a Woman and Her Son'. Here a series of temporal phrases mark the development of the plot and the start of the climax. The latter is also signalled by *tɔɔ, hɔnɛ* (a temporal clause), and *yaala.* The culmination of the climax is marked by a temporal clause with *bɛɛ* ('just as soon as') and *ma ... gɔ,* which indicates finality. The resolution section makes use of *wɛɛ,* contrastive *be,* overlap, and a temporal clause. It culminates with two *ma ... gɔ* sentences, the last expressing a thought comparable to our 'and they lived happily ever after'.

The story of 'The Cock and the Hare' uses overt linkage in the climax (twice *gɔ*), in the resolution (*ma* and temporal clause with intensifying *rɛ*), and in the coda (*ma ... gɔ*). In the introduction and development sections, it makes use of what might be called semantic linkage: the repetition of certain verbs, a value judgment drawing together the previous statements, and a following remark that contrasts with the preceding remark.

Another story that makes use of semantic linkage is that of 'The Boy and the Monkeys'. In the entire story there are only four initial dependent clauses to indicate overlap. *wɛɛ* is used unconventionally to mark the progression of the climax in each episode, and *ma ... gɔ* occurs only once, just before the closing formula. The rest of the story holds together using various degrees of semantic overlap or repetition. This element of repetition, the sobriety with regard to overt linkage, a large amount of dialogue, and the almost exclusive use of simple sentences, give this narrator a very unique and vivid style.

The standard type of overlap most typical of procedural discourse is relatively infrequent in the short stories, but it is used in at least two of the tales (BC and BG) to mark the progression in the climax (where BE uses *wɛɛ*).

The master storyteller has such a grasp of his language that he can draw from a wide range of overt and non-overt linkage devices, adeptly choosing those most appropriate at any particular point in the plot.

## 4 Special dramatizing devices

The Dowayo storyteller has a number of devices at his disposal to vivify his style or create an atmosphere of mounting tension. Some of these devices are use of linkage, emphasis and contrast, chants and refrains, repetition, and unmarked report.

### 4.1 Use of linkage to heighten drama

This has already been touched upon with the use of overlap or of *wɛɛ* to mark the climax of a story.

If there is one word most naturally associated with the climax, it is *yaala* 'suddenly'. It often marks the turning point (i.e., onset of the climax) or the climactic peak. However, extremely vital to the build-up of the climax are certain particles. Of these, the favorite is *ma*. *ma* functions in discourse-initial position, in the setting or the introduction of characters, and discourse-finally (often in conjunction with *gɔ*) to indicate completeness or finality. It also functions discourse-medially to heighten the suspense leading up to the climax (see (9)) or to make the climax and sometimes the resolution more vivid.

In the first episode of the story of 'The Corpse', just before the climax, there is a dramatic appearance of the husband, who has returned home prematurely and is secretly waiting and listening outside as his wife unwittingly serves poisoned beer to her lover.

(9)     BA 15 (freely translated)

'Meanwhile *ma*, the husband had come back *ma* from his journey, he had indeed *ma*, and he was *ma* right up by the hedge.'

In the last episode of the same story, nearly all the sentences of the climax and the resolution contain *ma*, thus sustaining the feeling of suspense until the very end of the story, when the two terrified men run home.

The 'Red Monkey and the Hare' uses *ma* to intensify the peak of the grand climax in (10).

(10)    BH 122

'Then he climbed *ma* into the granary, got *ma* the head and skin of the red monkey, put them *ma* on his head and came down *ma*.'

The story of 'The Three Deaf People' uses *gɔ* instead of *ma* to mark the climax and major progression in the plot. The feeling associated with *gɔ* is

# Features of Doyayo Folk Tales

more that of culmination than that of suspense. It is often best translated with 'and so'. gɔ is action- and goal-oriented. ma, on the other hand, is static, vivid, exciting, gripping, captivating, and, in a position of finality, permanent.

## 4.2 Dramatic use of emphasis and contrast

The Dowayo storyteller has at his disposal a whole gamut of emphatic pronouns, intensifying particles, and suffixes to provide emphasis and contrast and thus heighten suspense. Here are lists of the emphatic pronouns in (11), some of the most common particles in (12), and suffixes in (13). Other emphasizing/contrasting devices are reduplication of the verb stem, inversion, ideophones, and ejaculation. Reduplication is normal in sentence-final position, and provides emphasis when used sentence- or clause-medially. Inversion is obtained by suffixing the subject pronoun (in a form identical with that of the object pronoun) to the intensified verb stem as in (14).

(11) SG 1 *mii; miinɛ* 'I, mine'
            *bee; beenɛ* 'I, mine (CIT)'
         2 *mɔɔ; mɔɔnɛ* 'you, yours'
         3 *gii; ɡɔnɛ* 'he, his'
     PL 1 *wii; wiinɛ* 'we, ours (EXCL)'
            *wɛɛ; wɛɛnɛ* 'we, ours (INCL)'
         2 *nɛɛ; nɛɛnɛ* 'you, yours'
         3 *hii; yaanɛ* 'they, theirs'

(12) *ro, dey*[1]   'focal particle, attention marker'
     *rɛ*           'subordinating conjunction of abnormal or intensified condition'
     *wɛ*           'emphasizer'
     *mi*           'isn't it so?'
     *be*           'contrastive particle'
     *yɔ, bɔ*       'demonstrative'
     *di, hɛ, gɛ, ha, hɔ, yɛ, a*  'locative particles'
     *lɛ*           'thus'

(13) *-s*           'verbal intensive suffix'
     *re(k)*        'he went'
     *res*          'he went (EM)'
     *-z*           'verbal suffix of proximity'

---

[1]Fulani loanword.

|   |   |
|---|---|
| *-kɔ* | 'stative verbal intensive suffix' |
| *-ɔ, -i, -ii* | 'nominal demonstrative suffix' |

(14)  res + -i- + -g(e) → *resig(e)*
            EP      3SG
    'he kept going on and on'

As the Dowayos have a great predilection for emphasis and contrast, there is sufficient material in the stories at hand for an extensive study on the subject. However, since that would considerably exceed the scope of this paper, we will concentrate on 'The Corpse' and then touch on some salient features from other tales.

In the story, suspense begins to build up right away as attention is focused on the husband, who is convinced of his wife's unfaithfulness. She secretly hides some beer for her lover, but...

(15)  BA  9   'The husband saw the beer *be* (CONTR), but he remained -*s* (INTS) *sɔsɔg* (ID meaning 'tacit, not saying a word').'
        10  'The husband knew (EM by RDP) *be* (CONTR) that beer *yɔ* ('this here') she set aside for her lover.'
        11A 'He took some poison and poured it into beer -*i* ('this').'
        12A (onset of climax)
            'Just as soon as he (EM), the woman's husband, had left...'

        23  (climactic peak)
            'Suddenly, her husband entered *huud* (ID 'suddenly and unexpectedly')...'

        28  (setting of episode 2)
            'There was another man *be* (CONTR), the edge of their hedge was *di* (LOC) *lɛ* (DEM) *bed* (ID 'very close by').'

        33  (build-up episode 2)
            'It was the man-with-the-dead-body *ma dey* (ATT MKR); as for the husband, *gii* (he EM) went to dig up his yams and hadn't come yet *be* (CONTR).'

        59  (build-up episode 3)
            'The man put-*z* (PROX) the corpse by the trunk of the tree *dud* (ID 'plop').'

# Features of Doyayo Folk Tales

    60    'He propped it up against the tree like yɔ ('this') *gberke* (ID 'something leaning limply') and came (home).'

    61B   (climactic peak of episode 3)
'As one of them yɔ ('this one here') started to descend -z (PROX) with his foot yɔ ('this') lɛ ('that way'), he stepped on the dead body yɔ ('this') *gii* ('it' EM) its head yɔ+*gli* (ID 'something soft and yielding'). The dead body yɔ ('this here') it was soft.'

    69    (continuation of climax, episode 3)
'*Gii* ('he' EM) *ma* ('now') wɛɛ ('so then') was sitting a little distance away like yɔ ('this') lɛ ('thus').'

    74    (resolution)
'His companion took *ma* the honey yɔ ('this') and broke the honey calabash yɔ ('this here') gɛ ('here-it-is') on him.' (This is followed by three more sentences using the same particles.)

(16) Intensive -*s*
    BB 16   (end of climax)
'She departed-*s* for good.'
    BI 21   (close of 'The Cock and the Hare')
'The panther stayed-*s ma* forever in that hole hɔ.'

(17) Intensive -*kɔɔ*
    BL 132  (coda)
'They went and they found his sister, she-was-beautiful-*kɔɔ*, like a white woman.'

(18) Inversion
    BM 7  'And she sat down and cried and cried (*kaage kaage*).'

The story of 'The Donkey Wife' makes especially good use of ideophones for vividness of style and dramatic effect. As this story is extremely long, we will look at just a brief excerpt in (19), taken from the climax of episode 1.

(19)  BM 21  'The donkey child *kilkil* (ID 'clumsy and ugly') came gɔ ('so then') to the riverbank.'

22 'She looked *lɛ* ('this way'), she looked *lɛ* ('that way'), she saw no one and went back.'
23 'She took off *gɔ* ('so then') her skin *pod* (ID 'sudden, quick action').'
24 '[Her] breasts [were] *anbɔ* ('like that') *gi-i* (ID 'full and beautifully formed') *di* (LOC), her hair reached her shoulders *anbɔ* ('like that') *tɛsrɛ* (ID 'long and full') like a white woman.'
25 'The slave, seeing *anbɔ* ('that') *a* (CIT) *kpii* (EJAC 'Wow!') I'm going to tell (RDP) my master, I'm going to tell (RDP) the chief's son.'

## 4.3 Chants and refrains

Many of the folk tales examined contained one or more chants or refrains as a prominent feature in the plot. The terms CHANT and SONG are here used interchangeably, as opposed to REFRAIN, the latter being used to designate an utterance that is repeated but not sung. Among the chants and refrains noted were those in (20)–(27).

(20) Song of the bird in BD 6–7

> *Bee bal zɛn be karkili.*
> *Zaanɔ loo ma bootngi bootngi.*
>
> 'I cultivated my tubercles;
> that one took them;
> (he) didn't consult me
> (he) didn't consult me.'

(21) Song of the bird in B3[2]

> (first time:)
> *Be zɛm ma zɛn be karkili*
> *zaanɔ loo ma boongi, boongi.*

---

[2]B3, though the same story as BD, is told by a different narrator, and the song of the bird is considerably longer and fuller.

# Features of Doyayo Folk Tales

'I found my tubercles;
that one took them;
(he) didn't consult me
(he) didn't consult me.'

(second time:)

*Be zɛm ma zɛn be karkili,*
*ząąnɔ loo ma boongi, boongi*     (2 times)
*duudndu, duudndu!*
*Be zɛm ma zɛn be karkili,*
*ząąnɔ loo ma boongi, boongi.*
*Duudndu, duudndu,*
*ząąnɔ loo ma boongi, boongi.*

'I found my tubercles;
that one took them;
(he) didn't consult me,
(he) didn't consult me.     (2 times)
Chirp, chirp!
I found my tubercles...'

(22) Chant of the boy in BE

*Biitiŋ, baami qaami*
*a mi tuusibe yaayɔ.* (3 times)
*Biitiŋ, biitiŋ, baami dɛmi*
*a mi tuusibe yaayɔ.*
*Biitiŋ, biitiŋ, baami ninimi*
*a mi tuusibe yaayɔ.*

'Bang! My father beat me,
saying I let the monkeys escape.     (3 times)
Bang, bang! My father slapped me,
saying I let the monkeys escape.
Bang, bang! My father chased me away,
saying I let the monkeys escape.'

(23) First and third chant of the cannibal in BG

*Mi gbɔŋ gɔnmi siŋgo,*
*mi tɔbzig du lagrum,*
*mi zaa wɔrkɔ du, haay, haay!*     (2 times)

'I killed my mother-in-law and ate
her right up, and I've come
to her funeral, oh dear, oh dear!'

(24)  Second chant of the cannibal:

*Hi gbɔm gɔnmi siŋgo,*
*hi raa mii gbɔŋge,*
*mi zaa wɔrkɔ du, haay, haay!*   (2 times)

'They killed my mother-in-law.
They say I (EM) killed her.
I've come for her funeral,
oh dear, oh dear!'   (2 times)

(25)  Refrain of the cannibal in BG

*Luk za yɔ rɔbtɔnɔ sosor be,*
*nɔɔnɔ totorɔ fṳṳ wɛ hij,*
*gi giwɛ lɔmtig yɔ?*   (2 times)

'With such an excellent house,
wherever do those ants come from
that are biting us?'   (2 times)

(26)  Refrain of the girl in BG

*Gisɛwɛ wɔko,*
*be gisɛwɛ gbaage lɔlko.*   (3 times)

'(You) will be tying up (firewood);
I will be watching my lover.'   (3 times)

(27)  Song of the drum in BI and B5

*Zɛlɛŋ, zɛlɛŋ, zɛlɛŋ,*
*mi tii taryɔ, zɛlɛŋ, zɛlɛŋ;*
*zɛlɛŋ, zɛlɛŋ, zɛlɛŋ, zɛlɛŋ,*
*mi tii taryɔ, zɛlɛŋ.*

'Bong, bong, bong!
I'll go down to the Fulani's,
Bong, bong!
Bong, bong, bong, bong!
I'll go down to the Fulani's.
Bong!'

## 4.4 Repetition

This section overlaps some with the previous one. The occurrence of chants and refrains is not surprising in a story in which the repetition of entire utterances, with the regular addition of one new element to allow for progression in the plot, plays a prominent role. Repetition has the function of making the story more vivid, more pleasing to the ear, and easier to retain. The stories that use repetition of entire utterances are 'The Hyena and the Red Monkey', 'The Hare and the Red Monkey', and 'The Boy and the Monkeys'. The excerpts from these stories are back-translated into English. The parentheses enclose information that is implicit but not overtly stated in the text.

(28)    BC 5–24

The red monkey refused. He said, "Uncle, if I put down my tail (for) you (to) climb up on it, you would not let me go. You would eat me up. That's why I don't want to do it."

"No, uncle," said the hyena, "I wouldn't eat you up. How many years I (have been) in this hole! I have neither seen (the) outside (world) nor drunk (any) water. If you got me up (and out of here), would I then eat you up?"

The red monkey said, "You would eat me up."

The hyena said, "No, uncle, I wouldn't eat you up."

(The red monkey) put down his tail. (The hyena) climbed up on it.

When he had climbed up, the red monkey said, "Uncle, now let me go."

(The hyena) said, "Well, take me into (the) shade." He took him into (the) shade.

Then the red monkey said to him, "Uncle, I've brought you into the shade; now let go of me, so I can go."

(The hyena) said, "But I haven't rested at all, because you haven't brought me to a water place." Then he brought him to a water place. He drank some water.

(The red monkey) said, "Well, uncle, you've drunk some water. Now let go of me so I can go."

(The hyena) said, "But you haven't brought me into the shade. I haven't had a rest at all."

(The red monkey) brought him back into the shade (and) put him down.

Then the red monkey said to him, "Uncle, let me go!"

The hyena said, "No, uncle! How many years I've been in that hole! If I let you go, what will I have to move my tongue on?"

Note the rhythmic quality and very gradual progression in the plot obtained by repetition in the two excerpts from 'The Hare and the Red Monkey' in (29) and (30).

(29) BH 14–21

The hare said to the red monkey, "Wrap me (up) in here." The red monkey wrapped him (up).

(The hare) said, "When you are wrapping me up, don't wrap me up tight; tie me just a little." The red monkey wrapped him up.

(The hare) said, "When you are wrapping me up, don't wrap me up tight; tie me just a little." The monkey tied him like that.

(30) BH 42–55

The hare said, "Hey, child, why are you pricking me with that stick?"

# Features of Doyayo Folk Tales

Then the child called to its mother, "Mommy, the game talked." "Oh, come on!" she said. "You're lying. How can the game talk?"

"Come and see", said (the child).

"I'm busy; let me do my work. If you're wanting to eat it, go and cut some wood."

The child sat down again, and again he pricked him with the stick.

(The hare) said, "Hey, child, why are you pricking me with that stick?"

(The child) said, "Mommy, the game talked."

"Come on!" she said. "You're lying. How can the game talk? Go (and) cut some wood." (He/she) went and cut the wood.

In the excerpt from 'The Boy and the Monkeys' in (31), the pattern created by the repetition is reminiscent of the movement of the waves in the upcoming tide.

(31) BE 16-43

They left it open. The monkeys came running like this; they came (and) jumped in. Each one (that) came running jumped in (the) hole; each one (that) came running jumped in (the) hole. All the monkeys passed in there.

His father came (and) closed (it). (He) said to the boy, "I'm going to cut some thornbushes. Don't let the monkeys out."

The boy said, "OK." He sat down by the mouth of the hole.

(One of the monkeys) said, "Friend, open the hole a wee bit for me (so) I (can) look in my eye, won't you?"

The boy said to him, "If I opened (it) for you, you would go out."

(He) said, "I wouldn't go out. I'm hot. Something fell in my eye here."

(The boy) said, "If I opened (it) for (you), you would go out."

(The monkey) said, "No, I wouldn't go out. Something fell in my eye. Open (up) for me (so) I can look (and) see." The boy removed the stone a little.

(The monkey) said, "Move (it) away some more." He removed it some more.

(The monkey) said, "Move (it) away some more." Then he opened (it) wide. They came out, quick as a wink; they ran away.

Six monkeys were left. His father came. (He) said, "Maybe you let my monkeys out." The boy was afraid.

(The father) said, "They got out." (The boy) said, "They didn't get out." Then he said nothing more.

His father opened (the hole and) looked. He found six monkeys. (He) said, "You let them get out (RDP). Well, cut some wood."

They came (and) put (it) on the hole. They burned the monkeys. (The monkeys) burned up.

Then he seized his son (and) beat him (and) tied him up (and) then chased him away, saying, "You let my monkeys get away."

Near the beginning of the first episode of 'The Donkey Wife', is the desperate cry of the childless woman in (32).

(32)  BM 9–14

> *An be mɔɔ zeebo, yɔ bɛsibe.*
> *An be mɔɔ pulyɔ, yɔ bɛsibe.*
> *An kurkyɔ, yɔ bɛsibe.*
> *An lɔɔdyɔ, yɔ bɛsibe.*
> *An dɔyyɔ, yɔ bɛsibe.*
> *An vaamdewaayɔ,³ yɔ bɛsibe.*

---

[3] Fulani loanword. The normal term for young donkey in Doyayo is *pɛɛ⁴zum¹waa²³yɔ²*, literally: 'carries-flour-child-INFL'.

# Features of Doyayo Folk Tales

'If I gave birth to a mouse, I'd be pleased.
If I gave birth to a frog, I'd be pleased.
If to a snail, I'd be pleased.
If to a slug, I'd be pleased.
If to a horse, I'd be pleased.
If to a donkey child, I'd be pleased.'

(33) BM 127–129

*Loo waltɔ gbandilɔ bɔ hegɔ;*
*loo taalɔ bɔ hegɔ;*
*loo salabi ɣɔ duu zul ha.*

'She took her husband's clothes (and) put (them) on;
she took his shoes (and) put (them) on;
she took his scarf (and) tied (it) on her head.'

Note how certain utterances are repeated verbatim and others are restated in other words in (34)–(36). Note also how the alternation or intertwining of the repeated elements makes these passages highly poetic.

(34) BM 21–23

*Vaamdewaa bɔ kilkil...*
*Yaa lɔl lɛ, yaa lɔl lɛ,*
*gbɛn doo gɛ, wɛɛ rekɔ,*
*hod zoolɔ gɔ pod.*

'The donkey child came along clumsily...
(She) looked this way, (she) looked that way,
(she) saw no one, then (she) went (and)
took off her skin, rip!'

(35) BM 39–45

*Bɛnɛ yɔ be lɛmɔ lɛbɔ...*
*Nɛ erimɔ ket ro.*
*Bɛnɛ yɔ be ɓaamɔ ɓa...*
*Baa, erimɔ kete.*
*Zaa gɔ, sɔɔ lɔl lɛ,*
*gbɛn doo gɛ,*
*hod zoolɔ bɔ gɔ pod.*

' "As for me, I feel like hitting you ... "
"Hey, wait a minute!"
"As for me, I feel like beating you (up) ... "
"Sir, wait a minute!"
Then (she) came; (she) looked (around) thus;
(she) didn't see anyone, so (she) took off her skin, rip!'

(36) BM 119–123

*Loo mɛm bɔ hotin gɔ.*
*Wɛɛ gbaa zoolɔ bɔ gɔ an yɛrɛ lɛ.*
*Bąąr za gi imz bɛt ha anbɔ vęęd.*
*Gi daŋk gɔ hi mɛm bɔ be.*
*Bąąr bɔ zaa pɛɛ zoolɔ bɔ gɔ lad.*

'(She) took the water (and) bathed with (it),
And (she) put her skin (down) like this.
A bird of prey dived down from the sky, swoop!
Meanwhile, (she) was playing with the water.
The bird of prey came and carried off her skin, swish!'

The height of the grand climax in the sixth episode boasts a superb example of poetic literature quite reminiscent in its style of the Psalms. Note in (37) how each line is restated, with the second line being either synonymous or containing one new element; and how the thoughts of the first stanza are interlaced, yielding the pattern a b a b.

(37) BM 183–192

*Gii tęę bɔ hɔɔ gɔ, ram gɔ;*
*gi leko, leko, leko.*
*Tęę bɔ dɔɔz ɓęę ɓęę.*
*Gɔ gi gbork leki.*

*Yaala tęę bɔ dɔɔz anyɔ*
*mibr bɛt bɔ gbal hębt di.*
*Gii wɛɛ tuuz gɔ gandran.*
*Zaa dɔɔt gɔ a bɔrig du,*
*hɔɔ, a gbɔnɔ hɛksim du.*
*Gbɛn bororo nɛɛd hi zaak gɔ;*
*Nɛɛd sɛrɛ hi zaasig di.*

# Features of Doyayo Folk Tales

'But then the tree grew tall (and) bore fruit.
(He) was eating (and) eating (and) eating.
The tree rose up very tall.
He just kept on eating.

Suddenly, having risen up like this,
the tree opened the stone (lid) (and) pushed it to the ground.
So then he came climbing out.
He came (and) sat down on the roadside,
yes, at the crossing of the road.
Then he saw cowherd women coming;
Young women were coming along.'

Another way repetition is used is to intensify an action. Near the beginning of the first episode of 'The Boy and the Monkeys', the repetition of the verbal expression *hi daazɔ* 'they came passing this way' emphasizes that there were very many monkeys and adds color and rapidity to their movement. The listener is caught up in a sort of crescendo that reaches its peak after the sixth repetition and then ends very abruptly with *hi tuurɔ* 'they arrived' at which point the audience visualizes the monkeys all on the verge of falling into the trap.

(38) BE 14

*Hi daazɔ, hi daazɔ, hi daazɔ,
hi daazɔ, hi daazɔ, hi daazɔ, hi tuurɔ.*

The same story uses this kind of repetition a second time, quite fittingly near the end of the last episode, at the peak of the grand climax.

(39) BE 80

*Laa bɔ buda,
dɔɔʒa, dɔɔʒa, dɔɔʒa, dɔɔʒa, dɔɔʒa.
Nam wɔ sɛw, dɔɔhi sɛw.*

'The fire ignited, (and)
(it) burned (and) burned (and) burned (and) burned (and) burned.
It burned up all the animals.'

It should be noted that here the action of burning is further intensified by the use of intensive *-s*. The repetition emphasizes not only the extent and the duration of the burning, but also the large number of animals that were burned.

In 'A Cannibal's Wife is Rescued by Her Brother', the repetition of the verb with the modificational suffix -z, indicating direction toward the speaker, emphasizes the speed and duration of the action, and the extreme effort exerted by the brother and sister to avoid being caught by the pursuing cannibal.

(40)  BL 107–108

    *Hi reka.*
    *Hi nɔɔza, hi nɔɔza, hi nɔɔza, hi nɔɔza, hi nɔɔza, hi nɔɔza, hi nɔɔza.*

    'They departed.
    They ran (and) ran (and) ran (and) ran (and) ran (and) ran (and) ran.'

Just prior to the climax of the first episode in 'Nana Rescues the Cannibal's Wife', the repetition of the verb emphasizes the distance and the time involved in the action.

(41)  BG 17

    *Gɔnsiŋ reka, reka, reka, reka, reka, reka.*
    *Rek zɛm keeyɔ.*

    'The mother-in-law went (on and on and on ...
    until she) went (and) found a big rock.'

## 4.5 Unmarked report

The normal way report is marked in Dooyaayɔ is with a verb of speech plus the citational particle *a*. However, when it is clear who the speaker is, the verb *say* can be optionally omitted. When there is much speech being reported, many narrators omit the speech verb quite regularly, to obtain both succinctness and greater vividness of style. For an even more dramatic effect, the narrator will sometimes omit even the citational particle. This is a clear instance of poetic license, because when one reviews such a text sentence by sentence with a Dowayo, he will involuntarily supply the missing *a* and, when questioned about it, explain that the omission was a mistake.

# Features of Doyayo Folk Tales

Laporti makes far more use of unmarked report than any of the other narrators. In fact, there is probably more unmarked than marked report in his story. This definitely contributes to the high degree of dramatic tension maintained throughout the tale. By way of illustration, in (42) and (43) we will look at a back-translation of a couple of passages from 'The Donkey Wife'. To the left, we have noted the speech verb and citational particle, where these are present.

(42)   BM 158–168 (from the development of episode 5)

| | |
|---|---|
| raa | Then he came and said to the oldest son, |
| a | "Tomorrow we will go on a journey." |
| a | The oldest son said, "Yes." The woman was smart. |
| raa a | The woman said, "My husband, your father is going to kill you. As for me, I can't (let that happen), so I'm telling you ahead of time." |
| — | "Well, what's the use? If he wants to kill me, let him kill me."... His wife made some couscous and took some meat and cut it in three pieces and gave it to him. He ate it. |
| raa | She said, "All right then..." |

(43)   BM 192–205 (from the grand climax in episode 6)

| | |
|---|---|
| | Some young women were coming along. |
| a | "Pour me (some of) the milk." |
| — | "The milk that's being brought to the wife of the oldest son of the chief, are they going to turn around and give this milk to a tramp like you?" |
| | Now there was one woman... |
| — | "Ma'am!" |
| — | "Yes?" |
| — | "Hand me (some of) your milk." |
| — | "Who (are you) there?" |
| — | "It's me." |
| | So she took down (the milk from her head). She scooped (some out for him). |
| | He drank. |
| | She scooped. |
| | He drank. |
| — | "Ma'am, here is my ring..." |

The passage leading up to the climax of episode 1 in 'The Hare and the Red Monkey' is shown in (44). Note that the rising tension is made even more dramatic by the omission of all speech indicators as the climax is reached.

(44)  BH 22–38

| | |
|---|---|
| raa | He said to the red monkey |
| a | "Friend, take (this) (and) go (and) find that woman over there. |
| say | Say, 'Ma'am, here is (some) game. I'm hungry; give me the peanuts in its place.' " |
| | They went (and) found the woman and her child. |
| | Her child called (to) her. |
| raa a | He said, "Mommy, here is (some) game." |
| war a | She asked him, "Who brought (it)?" |
| a | "It was this person." |
| a | "What (kind of) game did he bring?" |
| a | 'He brought this game here. I don't know what (kind of) game it is." |
| a | "What does he say about it?" |
| a | "I(CIT)'m hungry." |
| a | "I(CIT)'m hungry?" |
| — | "Yes." |
| — | "For me to do what?" |
| — | "For you to give me(CIT) the peanuts in place of it…" |
| | The woman took the peanuts and gave (them) to them. |
| | They left the game. |

In episode 2 of the same story, the narrator makes use of unmarked report again to mark the beginning of the climax as shown in (45).

(45)  BH 82–87

| | |
|---|---|
| raa | He said (to the) red monkey, |
| a | "Fan me (and) put (in) lots of grass." |
| | The red monkey got (some) grass, closed (the hole) and made the fire. |
| | While he was fanning (him), |
| raa | the hare was saying to him (from) in the hut there, |
| a | "Peanuts are delicious with smoke! Peanuts are delicious with smoke!" |

|   | — | Then the red monkey (cried), |
|---|---|---|
|   | — | "Friend, come out (and let) me have a turn, too!..." |
|   | a | The hare (said), "Really?" |

## 5 Stories with a moral

A number of the short stories were observed to have a moral, which is a message conveyed by the outcome of the story and sometimes expressed in a proverb, but often not made explicit.

The morals in (46) were noted.

(46) B1 'The Camel and the Goat'
'A friend in need is worth more than a debtor.'

B4 'The Hyena and the Tortoise'
Dooyąąyɔ proverb: 'Tie up a chicken and you have a pigeon.'
Meaning: 'A bird in the hand is worth two in the bush.'
The moral could also be:
'By his lack of wisdom, a fool loses even the little he manages to acquire.'

B7 'The Hare, the Hippopotamus, and the Elephant'
1. 'The battle is not to the strong.'
2. 'Presumption leads to self-destruction.'

B8 'The Owl's Chieftainship over Other Birds'
'Wisdom is discerning what people do in the dark, i.e., in secret.'
This story also underscores the fact that a rich or important person in African culture travels as little as possible, because others are expected to come to him.

BA 'The Corpse'
'The perfect solution to bloodguilt (which requires life-for-life retaliation only when discovered) is finding a non-human perpetrator.'

BB  'Miracle of a Woman and Her Son'
1. 'A coward may speak big words, but time will tell.'
2. 'A gift resolves guilt and restores friendship.'

BC  'The Hyena and the Red Monkey'
1. 'Intelligence is better than strength', i.e., 'The battle is not to the strong.'
2. 'Don't take revenge on a brother (friend), but vent your anger appropriately on a common enemy.' (See §6.)

BI  'The Cock and the Hare'
1. 'A job worth doing is worth doing well.'
2. 'Don't take revenge on a brother (friend), but vent your anger on a common enemy (enemy of society).' (See §6.)

BD  'The Woman and the Bird'
'By sharing with others we ourselves are enriched.'

BH  'The Hare and the Red Monkey'
The moral of this story goes a step further than that of BD, namely:
'If you won't share, you yourself will be shared, i.e., it may cost you your life.'

BJ  'The Three Deaf People'
'The good intentions and actions of upright men are often misunderstood.'
In this connection, it is interesting to note that Doyayo has a special verb, *hɛb,* meaning 'to be misunderstood for one's good actions'.

## 6 Personality, role, and significance of animal and non-animal characters

Each of the animals in the short stories portrays a certain personality type. Our failure to realize this made some of the stories (at least, their conclusion) incomprehensible to us for a long time. Especially the role of the Panther eluded us. For example, whatever did the Panther have to do with the quarrel between the Hare and the Cock, and why did the chief send them after him? The answer, as we see it, is that the Panther

# Features of Doyayo Folk Tales

symbolizes someone who preys on society and naturally attracts to himself the fury that cannot be acceptably vented on a friend or brother. This interpretation may be challenged by those who prefer to treat Panther simply as a CODA character.[4]

The Hyena, the Panther, and the Crocodile always play the VILLAIN and, as such, never occur simultaneously in any one short story. The villain in non-animal stories is Cannibal.

**Hyena.** Hyena is cunning, predatory and untrustworthy (a liar), but not smart enough to be able to keep his prey after he has caught it. He is always outwitted, either by his prey or by the hare, who happens along at the crucial moment.

**Panther.** Though clearly an evil and dangerous character, Panther is cowardly and stupid, making him a perfect scapegoat for venting one's anger and frustration.

**Crocodile.** Crocodile is a brute, picking a fight for nothing and taking advantage of others' kindnesses to him. Fortunately, he is as dumb as he is blunt, so that his prey invariably escapes.

**Cannibal.** Cannibal is selfish, antisocial, crafty, cruel, and perverted. He is forever seducing beautiful, innocent girls to marry him and killing or trying to kill their mothers or other family members who come to visit. Fortunately, they are always eventually rescued, and quite often the cannibal is killed.

Three animal characters occur in the role of VICTIM. They are Red Monkey, Elephant, and Hippopotamus.

**Red Monkey.** Red Monkey is not especially good or bad, but his negative traits tend to be more predominant. He is curious, selfish, greedy, and gullible, and becomes a victim by his own fault. In this role, he is sometimes a laughing-stock and at other times an object of pity.

**Elephant and Hippopotamus.** Elephant and Hippopotamus occur in just one of the stories, where together they become victims of their own presumptuousness. In their dogged determination to prove their (physical) superiority, they destroy themselves.

---

[4]Cf. Jürgen H. Ennulat. 1971. Participant categories in Fali stories. In Joseph Grimes (ed.), Papers on discourse.

Two of the animal characters do not clearly fall into any of the three major roles. They are Goat and Cock.

**Goat.** Goat is rude, naggy, impatient, and unsympathetic, but sensitive enough to be able to learn a lesson and even humble himself and show gratitude. Initially, he functions as a semi-villain by the way he harrasses Camel about his debts. (N.B. The audience automatically sides with the debtor.) When Hyena appears on the scene, Goat realizes that if he does not stop victimizing Camel, he himself will become a victim, and that his life is worth more to him than retrieving his money.

**Cock.** Cock is a somewhat passive character, needing someone else to spur him to action, but once he has started, he turns out to be intelligent, adroit, meticulous, enterprising, and disarming. His role is that of a competitor and near-victim of Hare, who considers himself as the sole hero and will not tolerate any competition.

Two of the animal characters fulfill the role of VICTIM-TURNED-HERO.

**Tortoise.** Tortoise, caught by Hyena, is fearless, self-confident, and has a good sense of humor, as well. He succeeds in tricking Hyena into letting him go, making a fool of him in the process.

**Camel.** Camel is friendly, soft-spoken, and meek but firm, with a propensity for expressing righteous indignation suitably by word and deed (cf. the demonstrative way he shakes off Goat the moment Hyena stops howling). He is scrupulous and perspicacious, making doubly sure he has a solemn promise from Goat as to the cancelling of his debt before agreeing to let him take refuge on his back again. Thus, he ends up as the hero of the story, who, instead of the initial sympathy, now commands profound respect.

Two animal characters fulfill the role of HERO.

**Owl.** Owl occurs only in the story of the birds, which is atypical in the sense that it does not contain a villain or a victim. So owl is not a hero in the traditional sense, but he is elected as the hero, or chief, of the birds because of his superior wisdom and insight.

**Hare.** Although he definitely has his faults (sloppiness, fits of rage, and, occasionally, down-right cruelty) hare always functions as hero in the

## Features of Doyayo Folk Tales

stories in which he occurs. He is quick, clever (outwitting Hyena, Panther, Elephant, and Hippopotamus), and self-confident. He has a knack for appearing at just the right moment to rescue the victim out of the claws of the villain.

In conclusion, it seems quite apparent that the animal characters have a didactic function, imbedding in the young Dowayo soul an appreciation for those traits that are considered admirable and warning him against aberrations. Thus, they have a unifying effect, both educationally and culturally.

www.ingramcontent.com/pod-product-compliance
Lightning Source LLC
Chambersburg PA
CBHW052152300426
44115CB00011B/1627